...lows i...

Politics, Science, and the Environment
Peter M. Haas, Sheila Jasanoff, and Gene Rochlin, editors

Shadows in the Forest: Japan and the Politics of Timber in Southeast Asia, Peter Dauvergne

Shadows in the Forest

Japan and the Politics of Timber in Southeast Asia

Peter Dauvergne

The MIT Press
Cambridge, Massachusetts
London, England

This book was set in Palatino on the Miles 33 typesetting system by Graphic Composition, Inc.

Printed and bound in the United States of America.

Library of Congress Cataloging-in Publication Data

Dauvergne, Peter.
Shadows in the forest: Japan and the politics of timber in Southeast Asia / Peter Dauvergne.
p. cm. — (Politics, science, and the environment)
Includes bibliographical references and index, ISBN 0–262–04160–X (alk. paper). —ISBN 0–262–54087–8 (pbk. alk. paper)
1. Forest management—Environmental aspects—Asia, Southeastern. 2. Forest products industry—Environmental aspects—Japan. 3. Forest products industry—Environmental aspects—Asia, Southeastern. 4. Forest policy—Environmental aspects—Asia, Southeastern. 5. Deforestation—Political aspects—Asia, Southeastern. 6. Logging—Political aspects—Asia, Southeasten. 7. Timber—Political aspects—Asia, Southeastern. 8. Asia, Southeastern—Politics and government.
I. Title. II. Series.
SD387.E58D38 1997
333.75′137′0959—dc21 96-50982
CIP

The paper used in this publication is both acid and totally chlorine free (TCF). It meets the minimum requirements of American Standard for Information Sciences-Permanence of Paper for Printed Library Materials, ANSI Z39.48–1984. ♾

Contents

Contents

Series Foreword

As our understanding of environmental threats deepens and broadens, it is increasingly clear that many environmental issues cannot be simply understood, analyzed, or acted upon. The multifaceted relationships between human beings, social and political institutions, and the physical environment in which they are situated extend across disciplinary as well as geopolitical confines, and cannot be analyzed or resolved in isolation.

The purpose of this series is to address the increasingly complex questions of how societies come to understand, confront, and cope with both the sources and the manifestations of present and potential environmental threats. Works in the series may focus on matters political, scientific, technical, social, or economic. What they share is attention to the intertwined roles of politics, science, and technology in the recognition, framing, analysis, and management of environmentally related contemporary issues, and a manifest relevance to the increasingly difficult problems of identifying and forging environmentally sound public policy.

Peter M. Haas
Sheila Jasanoff
Gene Rochlin

Acknowledgments

This project was supported by generous funds from an Alcan Fellowship in Japanese Studies (1991–92) and an Eco-Research Fellowship (1992–95), a cross-disciplinary award from the Social Sciences and Humanities Research Council of Canada, the Natural Sciences and Engineering Research Council of Canada, and the Medical Research Council of Canada. A 1994 Canada-ASEAN Center travel grant supplied financial assistance for research in Southeast Asia, and the Institute of Social Science (*Shaken*), University of Tokyo, provided an apartment, office, and support for research in Tokyo. I extend thanks to former Director Yamazaki Hiroaki, former Director Banno Junji, Shibagaki Kazuo, and Kase Kazutoshi at the Institute of Social Science for their assistance, and to Lonny Carlile for his help arranging my affiliation.

I am deeply indebted to Ivan Head. His interdisciplinary knowledge of environmental issues, careful edits, and thoughtful suggestions were invaluable. I am grateful to Diane Mauzy for her expert guidance through the diverse Southeast Asian political systems and dense literature on patron-client theory, and to Brian Job for his strong support and perceptive advice on international relations. Arthur Hanson, Ilan Vertinsky, John Wood, and the three anonymous reviewers for the MIT Press provided detailed and constructive comments. As well, I greatly appreciate the unwavering support and encouragement of Madeline Sunley at the MIT Press. The book has also profited from vigorous discussions with my colleagues at the Research School of Pacific and Asian Studies, Australian National University. I extend special thanks to Robin Ward for her untiring editorial and research help, David Sullivan for his editorial advice, Lynne Payne for her assistance with figure 6.1, and the Cartography Unit at the Research School of Pacific and Asian Studies for the map of the Southeast Asian region. Finally, I am indebted to numerous people throughout Southeast Asia and Japan whose ideas and data are the backbone of this book.

This book would have been impossible without the intellectual and emotional support of my entire family. My wife, Cayte, was indefatigably patient and loving, even on the days I wanted to quit. Throughout she was my toughest critic and my best friend. My son Duncan—although he strenuously denies responsibility for any errors—had perhaps the greatest influence on my work. Before he could even walk, he volunteered to be my research assistant in Tokyo. After he learned to walk, his help became indispensable as he strategically shuffled and hid key documents and studiously shredded any irrelevant or misleading information. My daughter Nina arrived near the end of this project. But she has also been remarkably helpful, taking me on long walks in the middle of the night, where we fine-tuned my analysis. My children, however, have been far more than able researchers; every day they have demonstrated that life is about much more than books. Without this perspective, I would still be at my computer, mesmerized by the vision that I would write a great work, instead of mired in the humbling world of diapers and messy drafts.

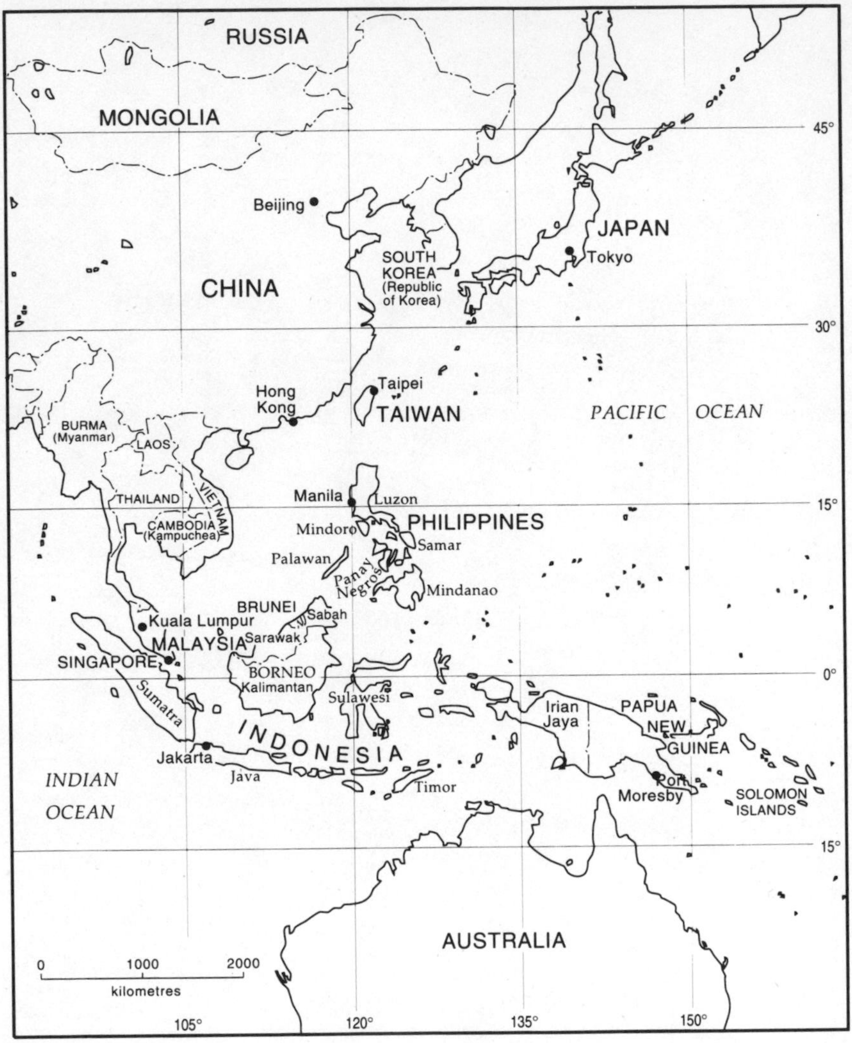

Southeast and Northeast Asia

Introduction: Ecological Shadows

Illegal and legal loggers have degraded much of Southeast Asia's old-growth forests, triggering widespread deforestation. Only 20 percent of the Philippines, once blanketed in tropical forests, now has significant forest cover. About 800 thousand hectares are primary dipterocarp forests, accounting for less than 3 percent of total land area.[1] From 1963 to 1985, loggers in the East Malaysian state of Sarawak harvested about 30 percent of the total forest area.[2] By the end of the 1980s, only 4–5 million hectares of Sarawak's primary forests were left.[3] At the current rate of illegal and legal logging, the primary forests of the Philippines and Sarawak will disappear in the next decade. The situation in the East Malaysian state of Sabah is equally ominous. As logging boomed in the 1970s and early 1980s, Sabah's primary forest cover fell sharply, from 55 percent of total land area in 1973 to only 25 percent in 1983.[4] By the early 1990s, loggers had cut more than 80 percent of dipterocarp forests officially set aside for commercial harvests. With log production averaging 9.6 million cubic meters from 1992 to 1994, even more of these forests are now degraded.[5] Indonesia contains around half of Asia's remaining forests. With log production far above sustainable limits, without drastic changes these vast primary forests will vanish in the next three decades.[6] Southeast Asian governments target the year 2000 for sustainable forest management. There is no chance of reaching this goal.

Southeast Asian loggers irreparably decrease the economic, biological, and environmental value of old-growth forests. They also ignite the process of deforestation—defined as the complete loss of forest cover.[7] They build roads that provide access for slash-and-burn farmers. They leave debris and create open spaces that make forests susceptible to devastating fires. And they decrease the financial value of primary forests, providing incentives to convert logged areas (secondary forests) to commercial crops or large development projects.[8] As a result, logging is the most important agent driving deforestation in Southeast Asia. Both direct factors and underlying forces contribute to rapid, careless, shortsighted logging. While Southeast Asian state managers and timber operators play direct roles, international corporations, markets, money, consumption, technology, and trade practices cast an oppressive shadow that constrains Southeast Asian decisions, provides incentives for quick and destructive logging, and accelerates deforestation.

Japan has had the greatest indirect impact on Southeast Asia's commercial forests. Japan has been the world's largest tropical timber importer since the 1960s.[9] Over the last four decades, over 90 percent of Japan's tropical timber imports have come from Indonesia, East Malaysia (Sabah and Sarawak), and the Philippines, which have been, by far, Southeast Asia's largest tropical timber exporters.[10] Until the 1980s, Japanese companies imported mainly unprocessed logs. During the height of the Philippine log export boom (1964–73), the Sabah boom (1972–87), and the Indonesian boom (1970–80), Japan imported over half of total log production for these areas.[11] Sarawak is now Japan's main source of tropical logs. From 1993 to 1995, Japan accounted for more than half of Sarawak's log exports.[12] Japan also imports huge amounts of tropical plywood. From 1990–95, Japan imported over 20 million cubic meters of tropical plywood, nearly three times more than mainland China, the world's second largest importer.[13] Most of this plywood has come from Indonesia.

This book examines the residual and immediate environmental impact of Japanese bilateral relations on commercial timber management in Indonesia, East Malaysia, and the Philippines. Japan's role is analyzed in the context of Southeast Asian domestic political economies of timber. This is essential because Japan's impact is indirect—an underlying cause that is comprehensible only in the context of the more proximate causes and agents of unsustainable logging. As a result, this book is not merely about Japan—and by extension other tropical timber importers, investors, and lenders. Instead, en route to discerning Japan's role, it provides a comprehensive picture of the international and domestic political and economic forces that drive Southeast Asian timber mismanagement, which in turn triggers the process of deforestation.

I develop two theoretical tools to analyze these forces. First, in the latter half of the introduction, I refine the concept of "shadow ecology" to evaluate the environmental impact of *one* country's economy on resource management in another country or area. A country's shadow ecology is the aggregate environmental impact on resources outside its territory of government practices, especially official development assistance (ODA); corporate conduct, investment and technology transfers; and trade, including consumption, export and consumer prices, and import tariffs. A country's "ecological shadow of tropical timber" is the combined environmental effect of these factors on tropical timber management in other countries. Second, in chapter 2, I construct an analytical lens to uncover salient domestic political factors behind timber mismanagement. This spotlights modern patron-client links between Southeast Asian officials and private operators that debilitate state capacity to implement resource policies.

Together, Japan's ecological shadow and Southeast Asian patron-client politics create a context that supports and accelerates destructive and illegal logging, contributes to ineffective reforestation and conservation policies, and undermines sustainable timber management. These forces are interlocked. Japanese trade has been distorted by corporate structures and purchasing practices, corporate investments and technology transfers, Japanese government policies, wasteful consumption, plywood tariffs, international market prices, and conventional economic calculations that ignore environmental and social costs. This trade has generated formidable financial incentives for unsustainable loggers and their state patrons. The residual and cumulative effects have left deep environmental scars that impede current efforts to improve timber management. Meanwhile, Japanese ODA has done little to offset past and current effects of Japanese practices; in some cases, aid projects have even expedited destructive logging and unsustainable trade in tropical timber.

Southeast Asian politics and policies have generally reinforced and aggravated ecological shadows, including Japan's. "Modern" patron-client ties are a central feature of Southeast Asia's political economies of resource management. Like traditional patron-client exchange relations, these ties are vertical, asymmetrical, reciprocal, personal, material-based, and noncontractual. But modern links are generally more opportunistic, volatile, materialistic, and have weaker loyalty bonds. In a continual struggle to retain power in societies with fragmented social control, Southeast Asian state leaders—such as Indonesia's President Suharto and Sarawak's Chief Minister Datuk Patinggi Tan Sri Haji Abdul Taib Mahmud—have built powerful patron-client networks, with family, friends, and close associates at the center. With leverage over state resources, top political patrons provide security, funds, licenses, and concessions to other elites in exchange for political support, financial backing, and stability. Many of these political, bureaucratic, and military clients then create their own networks, contributing to patron-client ties flourishing at all levels of the state and society. In this setting, state bureaus and agencies are often unable, or at least unwilling, to enforce resource management rules. In exchange for gifts, money, or security, implementors often ignore or assist destructive and illegal resource producers, smugglers, and tax evaders. Minimal supervision of implementors also contributes to straightforward "corruption," where a state enforcement officer accepts a bribe without becoming integrated into a patron-client network.

Patron-client links certainly do not explain all political, bureaucratic, or social interaction in Southeast Asia. But these ties are central to the allocation and management of timber concessions. Top state patrons have dispensed timber concessions to reward and placate key political, bureaucratic, and military leaders. With little logging experience or equipment, many of these elites have subcontracted the management of these concessions, often to ethnic-Chinese logging companies. Some of these companies have then made further subcontracting agreements with local leaders. Particularly in the Philippines and East Malaysia, where concessions have been redistributed as patrons rise and fall, these arrangements contribute to unpredictable management conditions. Not surprisingly, murky layers of subcontractors and an unpredictable backdrop encourage and facilitate quick and destructive logging. As well, patron-client ties distort state timber management guidelines, weaken state supervision, channel profits to a small elite, encourage logging companies to hide profits overseas, and undermine implementation of logging rules. Given this context, Southeast Asian legal loggers routinely mine concessions. Illegal loggers—protected by patrons at all levels of the state—are an equally great problem. They log outside legal concessions, and in parks, watersheds, and wildlife sanctuaries. Some illegal logs are smuggled overseas, although perhaps more important, these logs feed inefficient local mills that then export "legal" products.

Patron-client ties also contribute to unsuitable tax and royalty rates, processing incentives, and conservation and reforestation policies. Inadequate forest fees have left Southeast Asian governments with only a small portion of timber rents. Processors, concessionaires, and loggers have made windfall legal profits. Moreover, despite these low timber fees and considerable legal profits, logging and processing companies have methodically forged export records and transportation documents, misrepresented harvest totals, and evaded reforestation fees and duties. Low fees and tax evasion subsidize inefficient processors and allow destructive loggers to export logs and plywood at remarkably low prices. In addition, this encourages companies to log concessions as fast as possible, in case the government suddenly increases forest fees or improves revenue collection. Logging companies have also faced little pressure to regenerate logged areas or conserve primary forests. Finally, pervasive patron-client links have undermined attempts to improve commercial timber management in Southeast Asia.

The inability and unwillingness of Southeast Asian states to charge and collect sufficient forest fees, rampant illegal logging, quick and destructive logging techniques, disregard for conservation and natural forest regeneration, inadequate and inappropriate reforestation, international market prices, and conventional economic calculations have magnified ecological shadows of tropical timber. In this context, Japan, and to a lesser extent other importers, have consumed huge volumes of logs, and more recently plywood, paying prices that ignore environmental and social costs. As well, this setting has distorted foreign direct investments, technology transfers, and foreign aid projects. Southeast Asian politics and policies (especially log export bans)—coupled with international market shifts, declining log stocks, changes to corporate priorities, and to a lesser extent, new Northern government and corporate overseas environmental policies—have also altered the characteristics of ecological shadows over time and across states. Yet even when these changes greatly decrease trade—as in the Philippines and Sabah—they have not alleviated the cumulative impact of past practices. In some cases, they have even exacerbated environmental problems. As a result, ecological shadows continue to undermine sustainable management throughout Southeast Asia.

All countries cast ecological shadows. But Japan's is perhaps the world's largest. This is in part because of limited Japanese natural resources and rapid economic growth since World War II. It is, however, also a result of the tactics and economic function of Japan's sixteen general trading companies (*sogo shosha*). These companies, including Mitsubishi Corporation, Mitsui & Company Ltd., Itochu & Company Ltd., Sumitomo Corporation, Marubeni Corporation, and Nissho Iwai Corporation, are at the core of Japan's corporate groups.[14] According to *Fortune*'s 1995 Global 500 list, in terms of sales, Mitsubishi is the world's largest corporation, then Mitsui, Itochu, and Sumitomo. Marubeni ranks sixth and Nissho Iwai is ninth.[15] These dynamic companies have propelled Japanese economic growth. But they have also triggered and accelerated widespread environmental degradation in resource-rich countries. This is not an insidious conspiracy to deplete the world's natural resources. Rather, it is a natural outcome of the logic of sogo shosha.

They are primarily trade intermediaries that thrive on resources extracted from unsustainable sources and sold at prices that ignore environmental and social costs. Unlike most multinational corporations, they do not try to maximize profits. Instead, for small fees, they supply a range of services to facilitate and coordinate trade. To function as intermediaries, they work at remarkably low profit margins. To remain viable at such low profit margins, they import huge volumes of natural resources. Through their control of trade chains, and by aggressively seeking out cheap resource stocks, they stimulate and maintain demand for these immense volumes.

Sogo shosha have imported the bulk of Southeast Asian tropical logs into Japan. But even more important, these companies have dominated tropical log trade chains and Japanese plywood processors. Through financial and structural arrangements with affiliated firms involved in the tropical log trade, they have facilitated transfer pricing and indirectly supported illegal loggers, smugglers, and schemes to evade taxes and royalties. They have also provided credit and equipment to Southeast Asian loggers, often in exchange for logs or guaranteed purchasing agreements. Not surprisingly, they have exerted strong pressure on supply and demand, generally pushing up production and pushing down prices. Southeast Asian policies and practices, along with international markets and economic indicators that ignore environmental and social costs, have further depressed log prices. These low prices—coupled with illegal logging, transfer pricing, smuggling, inadequate forest charges, and tax evasion—have decreased state revenues. This has left Southeast Asian states struggling to find the funds to cope with a plethora of environmental and economic problems. Low prices have also spurred "wasteful" consumption of tropical timber in Japan—that is, consumption that ignores recycling and is intrinsically far above potential sustainable production.

Japanese log traders have not been concerned with sustainable management. After log stocks disappear, or after Southeast Asian states cut supply lines, they have simply moved to new sources. This pattern has been remarkably consistent. In the 1950s and 1960s, the Philippines was the main source of logs. In the 1970s, as Japanese demand for tropical logs soared, and as valuable and accessible logs became increasingly scarce in the Philippines, Japanese traders turned to Sabah and Indonesia. As Indonesia implemented a ban on log exports from 1980 to 1985, Japanese companies moved to Sarawak while maintaining steady log imports from Sabah. In 1993, Sabah banned log exports. Sarawak now accounts for about 60 percent of Japanese tropical log imports,[16] although as logs stocks deplete, and as the government gradually restricts log exports, Japanese traders are increasingly heading to Papua New Guinea (PNG) and the Solomon Islands. Even with adroit maneuvers by Japanese traders to maximize cheap log purchases, over the last four decades, Japanese log imports from Southeast Asia have dropped as log stocks erode, as Japanese domestic plywood processors fold, and as more and more governments restrict log exports. In 1995, Japan imported less than 6 million cubic meters of Southeast Asian logs (including PNG and the Solomon Islands), almost 21 million cubic meters lower than the 1973 peak.[17] Despite this overall decrease, however, Japanese traders still have a critical impact on production and export prices in Sarawak, Papua New Guinea, and the Solomon Islands.

Japan also continues to have a critical impact on Indonesian forest management. After the log export ban in the mid-1980s, Indonesia built huge domestic sawnwood and plywood industries. This altered Japan's ecological shadow in key ways. Compared to the 1970s, there is now relatively little Japanese investment in Indonesia's timber industry. Indonesian loggers no longer need Japanese equipment. Only a small amount of Japanese aid is currently linked to commercial logging. And Japanese traders and investors now have little impact on log production or export prices. But Japanese consumers and import tariffs still undermine sustainable timber management as Apkindo (Indonesian Wood Panel Association), which now controls almost two-thirds of world trade in tropical plywood, bombards Japan with cheap plywood.[18]

Under Bob Hasan, a key client of President Suharto, Apkindo controls Indonesian plywood processors. Apkindo has flooded the world market with cheap plywood made from logs extracted from unsustainable sources. Despite Japan's 10–15 percent import tariffs on plywood, Apkindo has aimed about one-third of exports at Japan, often selling high-grade plywood below world market prices to break open the Japanese market and to undercut Japanese domestic plywood processors. As a result, Japan now imports more Indonesian plywood than tropical logs (in roundwood equivalent).[19] Apkindo's tactics have had serious economic and environmental costs. Indonesian plywood production has exploded over the last fifteen years, averaging around 10 million cubic meters per year in the first half of the 1990s.[20] To feed large numbers of inefficient mills, illegal and destructive loggers have pushed annual harvests to between 35 and 44 million cubic meters, far higher than a recent World Bank estimate of sustainable production (22 million cubic meters).[21]

Compared to Indonesia and Sarawak, Japanese trade no longer has a major impact on timber management in Sabah and the Philippines. But the cumulative and residual effects of Japan's past practices still hamper efforts to implement sustainable timber management. Managers do not have sufficient funds to tackle widespread forest degradation or concomitant environmental and social problems. Japanese aid and corporate environmental investments are logical sources of funds. So far, however, this aid has done little to offset the effects of past practices. In the Philippines, recent Japanese environmental loans for reforestation may even create greater problems as the state searches for ways to repay its debt.

Since the beginning of the 1990s, the Japanese government and major corporations have announced new policies to alleviate the environmental effects of overseas activities. The Japanese government has developed a new environmental aid program and has attempted to reform general ODA initiatives. Serious problems, however, remain. Meanwhile, the largest sogo shosha have established environmental departments and overseas environmental guidelines. In turn, these actions have strengthened environmental rhetoric and have contributed to support for token forest conservation projects. But business practices have not changed much. Japanese business groups and major corporations—with national and municipal government support—have also announced nonbinding targets to reduce tropical timber consumption, especially tropical plywood to mold concrete (*kon-pane*), which is generally discarded after being used two or three times. Yet despite impressive rhetoric and a substantial drop in tropical log imports, in roundwood equivalent, Japanese tropical hardwood imports were roughly the same in 1991 and 1994, as was Japanese tropical plywood consumption.[22] Seen in light of both the consequences of Japan's historical practices and contemporary problems, Japanese government and corporate efforts are essentially cosmetic. More disturbing, they create a smoke screen that obscures the more important consequences of sogo shosha trade structures and purchasing practices, timber imports from unsustainable sources, low export and consumer prices that ignore environmental and social costs, wasteful consumption, import tariffs on plywood that siphon Southeast Asian state revenues, and the cumulative environmental effects of past practices. As the rest of this book demonstrates, these forces have had a critical impact on forest management in Southeast Asia. It is important to stress, however, that, like poverty, foreign debt, and population growth, Japan's ecological shadow of tropical timber is an underlying cause of deforestation—a shadow that is part of a complex process of interlocked indirect and proximate causes that drive unsustainable production and provide incentives and opportunities for illegal and destructive loggers.

Research Parameters

The boggling array of factors that influence Southeast Asian deforestation and the potential for endless diversions have forced me to focus my research. I concentrate on commercial logging in primary and secondary forests. Reaching sustainable timber production, reducing destructive logging, and protecting primary forests are my main environmental concerns; my central economic concern is maximizing the amount of money invested in sustainable timber management.[23] Reluctantly, I do not address Japanese contributions to multilateral institutions. Although these are undoubtedly important—Japan is the biggest contributor to the Asian Development Bank (ADB), the second largest to the International Monetary Fund and the World Bank, and strongly backs organizations like the International Tropical Timber Organization (ITTO)—it is exceedingly difficult to determine the extent to which Japanese money shapes the policies and practices of these organizations.[24] To avoid diluting an understanding of Japan's bilateral impact on timber management, I also do not delve into the role of related pressures created by Southern debt, although this hovers in the background. Even though foreign debts undeniably create incentives to export resources to meet payments,[25] it is quite difficult to isolate and analyze Japan's contribution to these debts. It is equally difficult to determine the role this then has on the management of *one* resource.

Also lingering in the background, but not directly analyzed, is the importance of population growth, poverty, land tenure, indigenous rights, swidden farming, social and community forestry, nonforestry policies (e.g., resettlement and exchange rate policies), low status of environmental concerns in the bureaucratic hierarchy, as well as the impact of other industrialized countries, international financial organizations, and world pressure to "develop."[26] These factors are certainly important. But directly tackling them would push my work toward ground already well covered by other writers and divert attention from the largely unexplored terrain of the environmental impact of bilateral state relations on the commercial management of one natural resource.

To maintain focus throughout this project, I concentrate mainly on political factors. Academics concerned with natural resource management increasingly see political relations as a key force driving environmental degradation. But few political studies of environmental management have focused on the peaceful interaction between states.[27] One reason is the difficulty of isolating and clarifying important factors that shape resource management. There is a danger of exaggerating or oversimplifying the impact of a single state as variables are removed from the context of the world capitalist system and from domestic political settings. There is also a risk of including too many aspects, thus diluting or diverting attention from more important factors. To spotlight how one state influences resource management in another state, I develop the concept of a shadow ecology.

Shadow Ecology

The genesis of the term "shadow ecology" is from the book *Beyond Interdependence*. Jim MacNeill, Pieter Winsemius, and Taizo Yakushiji argue that economically powerful industrialized countries

> . . . draw upon the ecological capital of all other nations to provide food for their populations, energy and materials for their economies, and even land, air, and water to assimilate their waste by-products. This ecological capital, which may be found thousands of miles from the regions in which it is used, forms the "shadow ecology" of an economy . . . . In essence, the ecological shadow of a country is the environmental resources it draws from other countries and the global commons.[28]

Although all countries cast ecological shadows, those in the North tend to draw far more environmental resources than those in the South. According to the United Nations Development Program, Northern (developed) countries, "with just 25% of the world's population, consume 70% of its energy, 75% of its metals, 85% of its wood and 60% of its food."[29] Highly industrialized states with few natural resources—like Japan—often have the largest ecological shadows. Unfortunately, the authors of *Beyond Interdependence* do not examine the idea of a shadow ecology in detail. The goal in the following section is simple: to delineate clear definitional boundaries to boost its heuristic power.[30]

Environmental resources include water, trees, minerals, soil, and air. Yet ecological shadows are more than the number of trees and minerals consumed, the amount of soil removed, and the extent of water and air polluted. To fully understand the impact of a shadow ecology, it is imperative to go beyond merely counting the amount consumed or destroyed, and examine the price paid and the effect on resource management. Given enough time, money, and knowledge, many environmental resources—certainly commercial timber—can be managed as a sustainable economic asset. Accepting this assumption, a country that consumes enormous quantities without paying and without restoring degraded areas draws far more environmental resources than another country consuming the same amount, yet paying high prices for resources from sustainable sources, and providing technical and financial support to facilitate better management. For this reason, the term shadow ecology embraces the amount consumed, the price paid, the source of the resource, and the effect of government actions and corporate practices on resource management. In other words, the ecological shadow of a national economy is the aggregate environmental impact on resources outside a country's territory of three sets of factors: government policies and practices, especially ODA and loans; corporate conduct, investments, technology transfers, and purchasing and distribution patterns; and trade, including export and consumer prices, amount and "type" of consumption, and import barriers. Specific ecological shadows include "ecological shadows of timber," "ecological shadows of mining," "ecological shadows of energy," "ecological shadows of agriculture," "ecological shadows of fishing," and, with some extension of the concept, "ecological shadows of tourism."

Some caveats and boundaries further refine this definition. First, shadow ecologies change intensity and composition. The relative importance of various components depends on the states involved, the resource sector, and the historical period. As well, actions of resource producers and international financial pressures can aggravate or alleviate shadow ecologies. To create a balanced perspective, it is imperative both to view ecological shadows in the context of overseas political economies and to keep in mind the role of the world capitalist system in shaping attitudes and practices. Second, an ecological shadow is a result of both intended and unintended consequences of government, corporate, and bank actions. It is not a result of a guided or conscious plan. This is especially relevant for Japan, where the decision-making process is fragmented. It is still possible, however, to control the consequences. Public and private policies in both developed and developing countries can significantly alter the impact of a shadow ecology.

Third, the term implies a two-way dependence between the North and South. A country like Japan relies on Southern raw materials, while the South relies on Northern markets, technology, aid, and investment. This moves "beyond interdependence" in its limited economic sense, and suggests a "meshing of the world's economy and the earth's ecology."[31] The relationship, however, is asymmetrical because environmental change more immediately affects the South. Economic and ecological interdependence suggests an inevitable impact of economic activity in the North on the environment of the South, and furthermore, an inevitable impact of environmental change in the South on the economies of the North.[32] Accepting this assumption, it makes sense to conceive of shadow ecologies on a continuum where sustainable activity falls on one end and environmental destruction falls on the other end. The logical task for policymakers, then, is not to eliminate these shadows but to minimize and counteract any negative consequences. Ideally, sustainable activity would involve South-North interaction that encourages mutual and equitable development, while environmental change is sustainable.

Finally, shadow ecologies tend to transfer to the South environmental costs of economic growth in the North. Nevertheless, it is important not to oversimplify and exaggerate the impact of shadow ecologies. Aid, investment, technology, and trade are certainly important factors shaping environmental management in the South. But these are only part of the explanation, their importance varies depending on the context, and they can simultaneously have both negative and positive implications for management. Although South-North interaction has had many destructive consequences in the past, a complete break would not ensure sustainable practices. Northern money, information, technology, and training—modified to fit Southern knowledge, experience, and conditions—provide the only practical route to sustainable management.[33] For background and further clarity, the next section examines some of the theoretical debates regarding the environmental impact of ODA, Northern technology, corporate investment, and trade on resource management in the South.

ODA, Government Loans, Technology, and the Environment

The environmental impact of ODA (grants, technical assistance, and concessional loans), as well as government loans not qualifying as ODA, has been examined extensively in recent years.[34] The media, nongovernmental organizations (NGOs), and environmentalists have scrutinized mega-development projects financed by multilateral and bilateral aid which create sensational environmental change. Popular interest in such schemes is further aroused by stories of corruption, connections to multinational corporations, and destruction of aboriginal cultures. Academic work has also looked closely at the links between environmental destruction and poorly conceived aid and loan priorities and projects, badly designed and managed Northern aid agencies, and strategic use of aid and loans to promote Northern business.[35] Some scholars, however, are wary about the connections made between ODA and environmental change. According to William Adams, although clearly a factor, "it remains an open question . . . as to how much influence aid agencies actually have on the nature and course of development projects. The power of aid donors is often exaggerated, and of course varies a great deal."[36] Moreover, it is important not to discount ongoing changes to aid policies as environmental awareness grows and aid is "greened."[37]

Assessing the environmental impact of ODA and nonconcessional lending is clearly difficult, and its importance debatable. There is a tendency—especially in government publications—to assume *all* reforestation or environmental technologies are beneficial. There is an equally dubious tendency among NGOs and environmentalists to label *all* aid as a capitalist ploy to exploit the natural resources of the South. Given that aid has the potential for both negative impacts—as when funding ill-conceived dams, roads, and equipment purchases—and positive impacts—as when funding conservation and environmental education—it is necessary to weigh each situation carefully, avoid simplistic condemnations, and consider its importance relative to overall environmental problems.

Technological transfers—by Northern governments through ODA or loans, or by multinational corporations (MNCs) as part of investment—can potentially alleviate environmental problems, for example, by replacing inefficient processing facilities and reducing pressure on a resource.[38] But technology can also create havoc by accelerating extraction and production before effective plans and policies are in place.[39] Martin Khor Kok Peng, director of the Third World Network, argues that "the importation of inappropriate Northern technologies has progressively destroyed the more ecological indigenous production systems in the south, besides simply destroying natural resources."[40] As with aid and loans, technology is a double-edged sword, and the environmental consequences must be weighed carefully.

Multinational Corporations and the Environment

According to Nazli Choucri, *all* theories of multinational corporations, including international relations studies in political science, "ignore the impacts of corporate activities on the natural environment and on ecological balances." These theories seem to assume "private investments and actions crossing borders are neutral relative to environmental, ecological, or atmospheric impacts."[41] Of course, many less-"theoretical" studies have examined the links between MNCs and environmental change.[42] Yet this gap in the MNC literature is indicative of a superficial understanding of the connections between environmental change and corporate investors and traders.

Multinational investors often create incentives and the means for rapid exploitation of Southern resources. These firms also tend to invest little in environmental projects such as reforestation, which have low profit margins, long-term returns, and high risks. As well, multinational traders—especially from Japan—purchase enormous quantities of cheap natural resources from unsustainable sources. Driven by these investment and purchasing practices, Southern partners ignore long-term management principles and quickly deplete resource stocks. In the 1980s, MNCs became more conscious of environmental issues. Little evidence exists, however, of concrete changes to multinational behavior in the South.[43]

Trade and the Environment

World trade swamps the financial flows of debt and aid. In the early 1990s, annual world trade in goods was about U.S.$3.5 trillion; including commercial services, it reached U.S.$4.3 trillion. In comparison, total annual ODA was around only U.S.$55 billion, while Southern debt service stood at about U.S.$130 billion.[44] After an initial spurt in the 1970s, then a lull in the 1980s, an explosion of writing has occurred in the 1990s on the links between trade and environmental management.[45] Hal Kane argues that trade is essentially "taking products made by using the environment, or taking the environment itself, and sending it off to other countries."[46] Understood in this way, trade inevitably creates environmental change. Yet change itself is not a problem; even sustainable development requires change. What is crucial is the impact of trade on resource management—whether it contributes to sustainability or irreparable change. This discussion must be approached cautiously: the arguments linking trade to the environment are complex and "there are few absolutes."[47] Four key trade issues that shape Southern resource management—consumption, price, import barriers, and export restrictions—are particularly contentious.

Consumption

For classical economists, rising consumption is a key element for economic growth. This assumes consumption is good: more food, more televisions, more luxurious homes and cars, all lead to greater prosperity. This ingrained view is being increasingly challenged, especially as the disparity continues to grow between rich Northern consumers and destitute Southern survivors. Cities are now polluted by swarms of vehicles; dumps are full of old appliances; rivers, lakes, and oceans are saturated with waste and chemicals; deserts are expanding and forests disappearing. As environmental problems spread, "environmental economists" have begun to question conventional economic indicators and analysis. They argue that economic growth and resources are finite; it is therefore essential to differentiate between quality consumption and the quantity consumed. Wasteful consumption such as excessive packaging, three-car families, or disposable tropical wood products contributes to mounds of garbage, pollution, and loss of biodiversity. "Conscientious" consumption can "save" resources that can be transferred to food, housing, medical facilities, education, and improved resource management in the South. In this view, shifting the pattern of world consumption from one of "blind" consumption to "conscientious" consumption is necessary for equitable and sustainable development.[48]

Price

Consumption and price are inseparable: lower prices encourage higher consumption and higher prices tend to lower consumption. Conventional economists argue that free markets create a natural equilibrium between supply and demand that generates a "fair" price. According to environmental economists, however, free markets fail "to properly value the services that the environment provides."[49] Markets have particular difficulty accounting for environmental integrity, such as biodiversity. Markets also tend to ignore external environmental damage, such as the costs of global warming. In addition, markets tend to shift environmental costs to future generations. These market failures are often reinforced or enhanced by Southern and Northern policies. As a result, consumer prices generally do not reflect environmental or social costs. Multinational and domestic corporations often drive down the prices of natural resources even further. Primary rain forest timber is particularly underpriced.[50] By treating the commons as a free good, the market "'externalizes', or transfers to the broader community, the costs of resource depletion . . . in the form of damages to ecosystems." As a result, "today's trade patterns contain a massive transfer of the environmental costs of world GNP to the resource-based economies of developing countries."[51]

Low and often volatile resource prices, along with poor rent capture and subsidies by Southern governments, encourage even greater extraction to earn foreign exchange, and preclude investment in sustainable production.[52] Furthermore, "underpricing . . . natural resources encourages wasteful and environmentally destructive patterns of consumption throughout the world."[53] For a realistic chance of sustainable management, it is necessary to maintain stable world commodity prices that internalize environmental and social costs[54]—that is, generate a price, perhaps through trade measures, that internalizes the added expense of careful, long-term management and that accounts for losses connected to inevitable ecological changes.[55] It is of course not possible, nor even desirable, to calculate the price of irreplaceable environmental costs, such as species extinction. In these cases, it is necessary to simply conserve environmental resources for future generations.

To combat ideological blinkers behind policies of ever-higher production and economic growth, there is a "world-wide effort . . . to explore the possibility of modifying the conventional economic accounts in order that they may better reflect environmental and natural resource degradation."[56] Robert Repetto argues that "failing to allow for depreciation of natural resource stocks when they are depleted or degraded disguises the sacrifice of future consumption, overstates income and capital formation, and justifies policies that waste natural resources in the name of economic growth."[57] By expressing environmental losses in monetary terms, economic statistics—touted by many governments as proof of their competence—can be corrected to reflect environmental degradation. Presumably, this will provide strong incentives to improve management as governments strive to raise these new economic indicators. Although technically difficult, the most innovative attempts to revise economic accounting include "the costs of environmental degradation and resource depletion occurring outside the country but related to consumption within the country"—for example, when resources are imported "at a price below the costs of their sustainable exploitation."[58] Ignoring these overseas environmental costs inflates the estimate of annual increases in gross domestic product (GDP).

Northern Tariffs and Import Restrictions

Tariffs can reduce resource consumption and raise consumer prices. In theory, if governments transferred tariff revenues to exporters, or if special tariffs were imposed on resources from unsustainable areas, then import charges could promote sustainable management. But this has never occurred in practice. Instead, import tariffs—which often escalate with the degree of finishing—have siphoned revenues from exporters, undermined local processors, and prevented economies from diversifying. Rather than protecting environments, tariffs have contributed to overexploitation and mismanagement.

Some environmental groups advocate import restrictions to promote sustainable management. But import barriers are crude instruments that easily misfire. Without compensation, import restrictions can create economic hardship for producers. These can lower prices and decrease the economic value of resource stocks. As well, import restrictions may reduce consumption only temporarily as new markets absorb the slack. In the case of tropical timber, a study for the ITTO concludes that a need exists to "improve rather than restrict access to import markets for tropical timber products." The report argues that "by adding value to forestry operations, the trade in tropical timber products could act as an incentive to sustainable production forest management—provided that the appropriate domestic forest management policies and regulations are also implemented by producer countries."[59]

Export Restrictions and Subsidies

In theory, if resource prices reflect environmental and social costs, if trade is limited to products from sustainable sources, if consumption falls to sustainable levels, and if import tariffs are dismantled, then exports of unprocessed, semiprocessed, and processed products should *all* promote sustainable management. Given that these conditions do not exist, many resource producers, as well as some environmentalists, argue that it is essential to ban natural resource exports and subsidize local processors. Advocates of export bans and subsidies maintain that, although temporary economic losses may occur, processing generates jobs, adds value, diversifies the economy, reduces the influence of MNCs, decreases the dependency on foreign markets, and creates long-term incentives to sustain the resource.[60] But in practice, export bans and subsidies have depressed prices and contributed to large numbers of inefficient and wasteful local processors, many of whom are protected by powerful political leaders.

Recognizing the economic and environmental drawbacks of export bans, some analysts argue that partial restrictions on unprocessed exports are more effective. They maintain that partial restrictions foster local processing, but still allow foreign demand and competition to increase prices and promote greater efficiency.[61] Although partial restrictions do provide higher short-term state revenues than export bans, in practice there has been little difference in terms of environmental management. Resource prices still ignore environmental and social costs, resource extraction is still well above sustainable levels, and processors are still wasteful and inefficient. As a World Bank researcher notes in the case of tropical timber, "the economic consequences of imposing log-export restrictions have been negative, both from the perspective of the forestry sector and the country as a whole. No analysis exists that demonstrates any positive impacts."[62]

At some point, governments must eliminate export restrictions and processing subsidies to raise efficiency and internalize environmental and social costs. Yet it is not accurate to assume—as is common among free trade advocates—that removing bans and subsidies will immediately improve resource management. In the current political and economic context, liberalizing trade could even aggravate resource mismanagement as new corporations pursue profits and as processors struggle to survive.[63] Before eliminating resource export bans and state subsidies, it is first necessary to internalize environmental and social costs into export and consumer prices, eliminate markets for unsustainable and illegal exports, place constraints on multinational investment and purchases, dismantle import tariffs, enforce state regulations, and ensure that revenues are channeled to sustainable resource managers.[64]

Having outlined the concept of shadow ecology and having sketched the broad theoretical debate over the environmental implications of bilateral state interaction, the next chapter examines recent changes to Japanese corporate and government policies that shape Japan's shadow ecology, especially regarding tropical forests. Chapter 2 then builds a comparative framework—the patron-client model modified to give more focus on the state and policy implementation—to analyze the domestic political economies of resource management in Southeast Asia. Using these analytical tools, and drawing on extensive primary sources and more than one hundred in-depth interviews, chapters 3 to 5 outline the political economies of timber in Indonesia, East Malaysia, and the Philippines, with particular attention to Japan. Even though Japanese timber traders and investors first entered the Philippines, this case is examined last because the residual effect of Japan's ecological shadow is now far more important than the immediate impact. The Philippines also illustrates the failure of Japanese ODA to offset the cumulative environmental repercussions of these past practices. Building on these empirical studies, the final chapter compares and assesses the impact of Japan's ecological shadow of tropical timber in the context of Southeast Asian clientelist states.

1 Japan's Shadow Ecology

To provide a foundation for understanding the impact of Japan's shadow ecology on timber management in Southeast Asia, this chapter outlines the major features and criticisms of Japanese government economic assistance, corporate structures and practices, and trade. Given that shadow ecologies can be moulded by policy, the chapter highlights recent moves by the government and sogo shosha to integrate overseas environmental concerns, particularly for tropical forests. I argue that the 1993 Basic Environment Law, the new environmental guidelines at the aid agencies, and the "environmental aid" program—while contributing to incremental increases in funding, research, and technical assistance for environmental and tropical forest projects—have conspicuous problems. The 1993 environment law and ODA guidelines are vague, the procedures for environmental reviews are unclear and convoluted, and no enforcement mechanisms or penalties are available. Environmental aid is partially a reclassification of traditional aid projects, such as water and sewage systems, and does not increase environmental funding as much as it appears to at first glance. Moreover, this aid is primarily in the form of loans. Bureaucratic turf battles have also undermined the effectiveness of environmental aid. Japan's Ministry of International Trade and Industry (MITI) has partially hijacked this aid program to justify and support corporate environmental technology exports. Meanwhile, the Environment Agency has minimal input into the management and distribution of this aid, and the Forestry Agency has shown little interest. In this setting, only a small amount of environmental aid supports forest conservation, reforestation, and improving tropical logging techniques.

Although government policies to improve the environmental management of overseas projects have clear defects, and although there is a tendency to exaggerate accomplishments, the discrepancy between public bluster and policy substance is even greater in the business world. Intense criticism of overseas environmental practices ignited a public relations counterattack by Japanese corporations in the 1990s. This has translated into a few showcase conservation and reforestation projects and a flood of grandiose claims of a new environmental awareness. Yet a wide gap exists between these claims and concrete procedures, mechanisms, and flow of money.

More perturbing, government and corporate efforts to improve overseas environmental policies focus on peripheral effects of Japan's shadow ecology. Although scattered statements are made that trade and corporations have environmental consequences, no comprehensive policies, or even consistent positions have been outlined. Corporate environmental departments and brochures appear designed to appease world and domestic critics of overseas environmental practices. In private, most Japanese government and business leaders downplay the impact of corporate practices and trade, invariably diverting conversations to the efforts to improve ODA or to the showcase projects of the major sogo shosha.

Environmental Impact of Japanese ODA and Government Loans

Japan's aid program began in the 1950s as reparation payments to Southeast Asia. During the 1960s, it was designed to promote Japanese exports; in the 1970s, particularly after the 1973 oil shock, aid became part of efforts to secure natural resources; in the 1980s, in addition to its economic role, aid emerged more as a tool of foreign policy, as part of "comprehensive security."[1] Today, in terms of quantity, Japan is an aid superpower, particularly in Asia. Japanese ODA in 1994 was US$13.47 billion, the largest in the world.[2] In 1994, 57.3 percent of bilateral aid went to Asia, and 19.5 percent to the countries of the Association of Southeast Asian Nations (ASEAN).[3] Japan is by far the most important bilateral aid donor for the Philippines and Indonesia.[4] In 1993, the government announced a five-year ODA target of U.S.$70–75 billion, 50 percent higher than the previous five years.[5]

The administration of Japanese ODA is confusing. Few clear lines of responsibility are evident. Four main government bodies have jurisdiction: MITI, the Ministry of Foreign Affairs, the Ministry of Finance, and the Economic Planning Agency (EPA). As well, more than a dozen ministries and agencies have limited input. The two main implementing organizations are the Overseas Economic Cooperation Fund (OECF), formed in 1961 to provide concessional loans, and the Japan International Cooperation Agency (JICA), which started in 1962 as the Overseas Technical Cooperation Agency to administer grants and technical assistance.[6] The OECF is officially attached to the EPA, although it is strongly influenced by the Finance Ministry. In fiscal year (FY) 1992, OECF loans comprised around half of total Japanese ODA (around 10 percent of world ODA); approximately 51.5 percent of this sum went to Southeast Asian countries.[7] Annual OECF development financing is equivalent to "the lending of the Asian Development Bank, the Inter-American Development Bank, and the African Development Bank combined."[8] These loans have relatively high interest rates and tend to fund large infrastructure projects.[9] JICA is controlled mainly by the Ministry of Foreign Affairs. However, MITI, or any ministry channeling aid funds through JICA, including the Ministry of Agriculture, Forestry, and Fisheries has influence over JICA projects.[10]

The Export-Import (EXIM) Bank of Japan provides project loans, and export, import, and investment credits to foreign governments and corporations and to Japanese companies that do not qualify for ODA loans.[11] It is officially under the control of the Finance Ministry, although MITI has significant input. In FY1992, the bank made U.S.$16.5 billion worth of commitments; at the end of the fiscal year, outstanding loans reached U.S.$71.4 billion, the highest in the history of the bank.[12] The EXIM Bank is designed to "facilitate Japan's economic interchange with foreign countries through the provision of a wide range of financial services to supplement and encourage financing by commercial banks and other financial institutions in Japan." A central priority is the "development and import into Japan of natural resources."[13]

Like other donors, Japan's lending policies and decision-making process have general problems that contribute to difficulties in evaluating and incorporating environmental concerns.[14] The greatest obstacles to improving ODA are administrative fragmentation and an emphasis on increasing quantity over clear goals and policies.[15] Battles among MITI (fighting for business interests), the Finance Ministry (stressing fiscal responsibility), and the Foreign Affairs Ministry (promoting foreign policy objectives) create administrative paralysis, dilute policies, and foster ad hoc solutions.[16] There is also little coordination between JICA and the OECF.[17] One OECF official claimed: "We get better cooperation with USAID [United States Agency for International Development] than we do with JICA."[18] Efforts to tackle environmental concerns are further weakened by already overworked staff responsible for increasingly large aid budgets.[19] Also, few staff have environmental expertise or overseas field experience. Senior JICA officials rotate frequently and often have little experience in Southern countries. As well, JICA staff tend to be generalists; experts are seconded from ministries or agencies and usually stay for a short period.[20] A mere 5 percent of JICA staff live overseas, compared to about 50 percent of USAID staff.[21]

Besides direct project funding, the OECF and JICA provide loans to Japanese companies to promote direct investment in the South, usually at very low interest rates.[22] This is generally part of combined packages of overseas economic assistance and private capital. These deals reduce environmental monitoring and accountability. Richard Forrest argues that "even if the ODA portion is covered by environmental or other restrictions, the auxiliary funding and secondary projects that often follow are outside the scope of environmental assessments, and have no policies to guide or regulate them."[23] Japanese ODA has other serious problems. Concessional loans comprise almost half of all ODA, more than any other country.[24] With the rapid appreciation of the yen over the last twenty years, these loans have often been costly, and have contributed to pressures on Southern governments, especially in Asia, to exploit natural resources to service their debts. In addition to the stress on lending, critics have pointed to poor pre- and post-project evaluations,[25] corruption and incompetence, inappropriate technology transfers,[26] the drawbacks of a "request-based" system,[27] aid tied to corporate interests,[28] an emphasis on large-scale development schemes over community projects, and a lack of cooperation with NGOs.[29] Analysts have been especially critical of the impact of aid on tropical forests.

General JICA projects and OECF loans—especially for agricultural development and infrastructure such as roads, dams, and ports—have contributed to forest destruction. Dams have flooded large areas of tropical forest, roads have opened up remote areas to slash-and-burn farming, and agricultural projects have cleared areas for cash-crop exports.[30] Aid channeled specifically to the forestry sector has also helped Japanese corporations exploit Southeast Asia's forests, especially in Indonesia where Japanese direct investment was an important force behind the logging boom in the late 1960s and 1970s. As Richard Forrest and Yuta Harago note, forestry aid has funded "inventories of forest resources for later logging," and transferred "knowledge and technology related to unsustainable logging techniques."[31] In the 1960s and 1970s, Indonesia received around 70 percent of OECF forestry loans—the bulk from 1969 to 1974, as logging peaked. During these two decades, JICA conducted logging surveys and feasibility studies; intergovernmental OECF loans funded infrastructural projects essential for logging and massive log exports; and OECF loans to Japanese companies offset risky timber investments.

In recent years, as attitudes change and world and domestic scrutiny intensifies, the Japanese government has tried to tackle some of the problems with its ODA. Although serious weaknesses remain, incremental changes are occurring. According to Alan Rix, although "reform and innovation in policy have not moved as fast as changes to public presentation of policy" there are microlevel adjustments "in the management and operation of aid flows."[32] In addition, there has been some movement toward greater transparency, more involvement of NGOs,[33] larger grants, more attention to basic human needs, and less overtly tied aid.[34] JICA now accepts the need for "institution building," "participatory development," and more careful allocation of grants to avoid past problems of building facilities that remain empty or sending equipment that is never used.[35] The Japanese government has also developed an environmental aid program and environmental guidelines and departments at JICA, the OECF, and the EXIM Bank.

Environmental Aid

Among ODA donors, no consistent definition of environmental assistance exists. The Japanese Foreign Ministry defines it as "assistance conducive to the resolution of environmental problems" including "the improvement of the living environment, forestry conservation and afforestation, disaster reduction, pollution control, the conservation of the natural environment (including the conservation of biological diversity) and the protection of the ozone layer."[36] In 1989, Japan announced an environmental aid target of ¥300 billion over the next three years. To encourage requests for this aid, teams from JICA, the OECF, the Ministry of Foreign Affairs, MITI, the Forestry Agency, and the Environment Agency went on environmental missions, including one to Southeast Asia.[37] This environmental aid target was exceeded by more than ¥100 billion. For FY1992, 16.9 percent of total ODA was defined as environmental aid.[38] Not all of this total represents "new" funds for environmental protection. Environmental aid has been partially derived by reclassifying projects such as "infrastructure development" or "irrigation and flood control" to "environmental projects."[39] So far around half of environmental aid has funded improvements to urban water and sewage systems.[40] As a result, about 70 percent of this aid has been in the form of loans.[41]

Environmental concerns gained momentum in Japan during 1992. The economic council advisory subcommittee to the prime minister called for better ODA guidelines to promote environmental conservation.[42] In June, the Cabinet approved an ODA charter; the first principle declares that "environmental conservation and development should be pursued in tandem."[43] At the United Nations Conference on Environment and Development (UNCED), Japan promised ¥900–1,000 billion of environmental aid over the next five years, the largest by any country.[44] In early 1993, the Japanese government announced it would expand environmental aid to the ASEAN countries.[45] In November 1993, the Japanese Diet passed the Basic Environment Law. The law explicitly addresses environmental links to ODA. Article 35, part 1 reads:

> The State, in implementing international cooperation, shall make efforts to consider global environmental conservation etc in the areas where its international cooperation is implemented.[46]

The Japanese government has been criticized for ignoring, or even encouraging, destructive corporate environmental practices. The new environment law addresses the role of the government in monitoring the impact on the environment of overseas corporations. Article 35, part 2 states:

> The State shall make efforts to take necessary measures e.g., providing information to corporations, so that the corporations can properly consider global environmental conservation etc. in the areas outside Japan where these corporations conduct their businesses.[47]

The impact of this article is not yet clear. The environment law has no enforcement clause, and the example of "providing information to corporations" is weak. At a minimum, it sends a signal to corporations to pay attention to environmental factors. At a maximum, it could provide a future means to require corporations to follow stricter overseas environmental regulations.[48] But this seems unlikely.

Battles over Environmental Aid

Typical of Japan's ODA administration, as funding and interest have risen, '"green' aid has become the subject of intense competition among various ministries involved in foreign assistance."[49] In a struggle over environmental turf, the Ministry of Foreign Affairs and MITI have become strong supporters of environmental aid. The Foreign Ministry allocated ¥4 billion in FY1992 to finance international organizations involved in environmental programs. As noted earlier, however, the bulk of the ministry's influence is through JICA.

MITI has aggressively staked out an environmental mandate. Its Environmental Policy Division emphasizes technological solutions and corporate technology exports to tackle global warming and promote energy conservation and alternative energy sources.[50] "New Earth 21," a MITI-backed proposal to the international community, calls for the development and "world-wide diffusion of environmentally sound technologies."[51] Specific MITI projects all aim at a technological fix for global environmental problems. The International Center for Environmental Technology Transfer (ICETT)—a nonprofit organization under MITI jurisdiction and with local government, academic, and industry participation—was established in 1991 to transfer Japanese pollution technology to developing countries.[52] In the same year, MITI announced its Green Aid Plan. In FY1992, Green Aid provided around ¥2.7 billion to support technological efforts to reduce water and air pollution and to improve waste treatment, recycling, and energy conservation in the South.[53] The Research Institute of Innovative Technology for the Earth (RITE)—a foundation administered by MITI—supports a joint industry, academic, and government research facility completed in 1993 to study environmental technologies, particularly for energy conservation and global warming.[54] In 1993, MITI and the Agency of Industrial Science and Technology amalgamated three existing projects, forming the New Sunshine Program "to develop innovative technology to create sustainable growth while solving energy and environmental issues."[55]

The Environment Agency—historically a weak player in ongoing bureaucratic struggles, especially over ODA—has had little input into overseas issues. Some signs, however, suggest that this may be changing.[56] Despite having no official mandate to impose overseas environmental guidelines or control environmental aid, the Environment Agency established a global environment division in 1990. This division tries to *encourage* overseas Japanese companies to consider environmental factors; it is also directly involved in some JICA projects.[57] In addition, as part of global efforts to reevaluate economic accounting, Environment Agency researchers are trying to measure in monetary terms the effects of "economic activities on foreign countries and the global environment, and . . . the impacts of global environmental change on domestic economic activity."[58] Another possible sign of growing influence is the 36 percent increase in the Environment Agency's aid budget in FY1991,[59] although it is still one of the smallest. Perhaps more significant, Environment Agency officials claim that, despite being quite critical of ODA environmental reviews, informal influence is beginning to develop. A possibility also exists that the Basic Environment Law will reinforce, perhaps even promote, Environment Agency input.[60] Not all trends, however, solidify the growing influence of the Environment Agency. As the environmental spark ignited by the 1992 UNCED conference fades, momentum has been lost in the Japanese Diet to make the Environment Agency a full ministry. More important, funding and personnel are still too limited for consistent influence.[61]

The Forestry Agency is quite conservative and has been less eager to dive into the fray for environmental aid.[62] In 1990, the agency published a position paper on tropical forests calling for large-scale tree plantations, more cooperation with NGOs, and timber purchases from sustainable sources.[63] Strangely, considering these kinds of reports tend to be full of fluff, the paper does not emphasize protecting biodiversity and primary forests or seriously consider the implications of tropical timber consumption. Instead, it advocates exporting Japanese forestry expertise, stimulating consumption, and expanding trade in timber.[64]

The OECF, the EXIM Bank, JICA, and the Environment

The OECF, JICA, and the EXIM Bank have all developed environmental departments and guidelines since the late 1980s. The OECF now has "an environment adviser, an Environment Committee and a senior manager in charge of environmental problems."[65] In 1989, the OECF established environmental guidelines to encourage environmentally sound Southern loan requests and provide the OECF with criteria to evaluate applications.[66] Generally, before an official request is made, a Japanese fact-finding mission is sent to evaluate the feasibility of Southern proposals. At this stage, based on a checklist, OECF officials apparently encourage prospective borrowers to consider environmental factors. According to an OECF official, as a result of this process, actual loan applications are rarely rejected for environmental reasons.[67]

OECF environmental guidelines could certainly be strengthened. Forrest and Harago argue that these guidelines "seem to be no more than a vague menu of items which should be considered, rather than conditions required to ensure environmental damage will not result before OECF provides funding."[68] Rix notes that the "environment is just one aspect of OECF appraisal of projects, and no strict impact statement is required."[69] Indicative of the weak environmental review process is one of the six main items for assessing applications, the lame question: "Is there sufficient environmental consideration in the project?"[70] Also indicative is the lack of any revision to the original guidelines, despite the mollifying, and now somewhat embarrassing note in the preface of the 1989 OECF environmental guidelines: "This is a first version, and we plan to make such improvements as prove necessary, with a view to making them more comprehensive and effective."[71]

The EXIM Bank first developed environmental guidelines in 1989; these were updated and made more stringent in late 1991. Little is known about these guidelines. They are confidential; even the Ministry of Finance has not seen a copy.[72] In theory, the bank as a whole reviews environmental guidelines. In each loan department, a senior official is responsible for assessing environmental aspects. Yet for many applications—such as importing aircraft technology—no environmental assessment is conducted because the proposal is not deemed to have any environmental implications. Although rare, if an application has obvious environmental problems, it is rejected.[73] When an application has unclear environmental implications, it is referred to the Environmental Affairs Section.

From April 1993 to April 1994, the Environmental Affairs Section reviewed about a dozen applications, one relating to logging in Sarawak. None of these was rejected. Instead, conditions were set. According to a bank official in the environment section, if these conditions are violated, then the bank can force early repayment of the loan. In addition, there is an informal understanding that it would be difficult to receive future loans.[74] Besides these apparent environmental checks, the bank claims that it now lends more money to improve environmental management. But without access to confidential bank records, it is impossible to assess comprehensively the environmental guidelines, the review process, or the environmental loans. Secret rules, weak penalties, vague lines of accountability, and few, if any, examples of applications rejected for environmental reasons all suggest that the bank's environmental record has serious shortcomings. An intuitive, precursory assessment is that the bank is more concerned with avoiding environmental scandals and public embarrassment than with genuine reviews of loan applications.[75]

While OECF and EXIM Bank environmental guidelines appear largely cosmetic, more concrete, although incremental changes have occurred at JICA. In 1989, JICA established the Environment Section of the Planning Department. Based on recommendations by the Development Assistance Committee of the Organization for Economic Cooperation and Development (OECD), in 1990 JICA introduced environmental guidelines for development initiatives including dams, agricultural estates, and forestry projects. Since then, JICA has tried to incorporate more environmental factors into grants and technical assistance. Conserving primary tropical forests and rehabilitating secondary forests have apparently been a major focus of these efforts.[76] In FY1992, ¥17.4 billion, or 13.5 percent of total JICA expenditures, went to the environmental sector, up from ¥8.1 billion in 1988. These funds trained 722 people in Japan, sent 129 experts overseas, and supported 67 development studies and 47 technical cooperation projects. In the same year, environmental specialists reviewed 108 projects.[77]

Despite more support for environmental projects, and plausible attempts to incorporate environmental factors into decision making, serious problems remain with implementing environmental guidelines. The environment section, along with a regional division of the Planning Department, determine whether a project requires an environmental impact assessment (EIA). If necessary, one of JICA's sector-based departments—such as forestry—then identifies the scope of the assessment. The actual EIA is handled by a team of private consultants and JICA officials who often have little experience with environmental or tropical forest management. The environmental guidelines are nonbinding reference materials, and are optional at all stages of the process. Details on specific projects are confidential and there is no post-project evaluation of environmental changes. Furthermore, environmental reviews do not consider alternatives to the proposed project and give little consideration to indirect social and environmental implications.[78] Specific problems with JICA's environmental guidelines and procedures are exacerbated by the fragmented ODA administration. The OECF and JICA have not consolidated environmental guidelines and do not coordinate environmental reviews. As a result, standards may change as a project progresses.[79] This problem is unlikely to be resolved soon. Environmental guidelines and aid plans vary across ministries, and despite the new environment law, little chance exists of developing a unified environmental aid policy.

Problems with environmental planning at JICA and superficial changes at the OECF and EXIM Bank lead Hiroshi Kanda to pan environmental aid. He argues that "there is no remarkable difference between 'Environment ODA' and 'regular ODA.' They both tend to support Japanese industry and Japanese economic aims."[80] This seems too harsh. It would be naive to assume the new rhetoric equals improved practices; but it is equally facile to assume these new policies have no practical effects. Environmental aid, policy changes at MITI and the Ministry of Foreign Affairs, and decisions by JICA, the OECF, and the EXIM Bank to create environmental committees and sections and to revise guidelines, indicate, at a minimum, a recognition of a need to be more sensitive to environmental concerns, at least in public statements. Evaluating the extent of concrete changes—rather than paper ones—is far from easy. Marginal improvements, however, have been made to Japanese forestry aid, especially JICA projects.

Since the early 1990s, fewer JICA intergovernmental forestry cooperation projects have been linked to commercial loggers or securing wood imports. More projects now stress regenerating degraded forests, conserving rain forests, and developing social and community forestry.[81] JICA has also changed the emphasis of forestry loans to Japanese corporations. From 1974 to the beginning of 1994, JICA provided 144 soft loans to Japanese companies investing in the South. Of these, fifty-one were forestry projects: fifteen in Indonesia; one in Limbang, Sarawak; and six in the Philippines.[82] In the past, many of these loans funded fast-growing monoculture tree plantations. NGOs and environmentalists criticized these projects for ignoring indigenous people's rights, clearing natural forests, and providing minimal environmental benefits. According to a senior JICA official, in an effort to appease these critics, JICA now ensures that concessional loans fund only plantations in degraded areas. JICA also encourages companies to plant a variety of endemic species to foster biodiversity.[83] In addition, to facilitate corporate participation in forestry conservation, JICA recently established an environmental protection credit line. Loans will supposedly reforest degraded areas, protect watersheds and primary forests, and support social and community forestry projects.[84]

Despite these apparent improvements, JICA's forestry and environmental projects still have significant problems. JICA's guidelines and procedures for pre- and post-project environmental reviews are vague and inconsistent. Projects still fund technology transfers with little institutional support—in some cases, the equipment never leaves the box.[85] As Forrest notes, instead of promoting conservation, Japan "transfers high-technology equipment, ensuring lucrative profits for Japanese companies."[86] As well, JICA still supports dubious reforestation techniques in Southeast Asia, particularly fast-growing eucalyptus and acacia mangium plantations.[87] Despite the new policies, as the studies of Japanese forest aid in chapters 3, 4, and 5 document, only a negligible portion of JICA technical cooperation actually supports social and community forestry projects, natural forest regeneration, and primary rainforest conservation. The changes at JICA are certainly far behind policy rhetoric. But the gap between glossy policy declarations and substantive procedural changes is even greater for Japanese corporations.

Environmental Impact of Sogo Shosha on Overseas Resources

Together Japanese government and corporate financial flows to the South are the largest in the world. In 1994, the flow of public and private funds to developing countries reached a record U.S.$28.5 billion.[88] The distinction between the environmental impact of government and private economic activity is rather artificial, especially in Japan where bureaucratic, political, and business elites have close personal links. Like other Northern donors, Japanese aid is tied closely to corporate investment and trade.[89] One structural reason for this is the custom of senior aid officials retiring "to lead aid consulting associations and companies working to gain ODA contracts."[90] In the cases of the Philippines, Indonesia, and Malaysia, ODA has "lowered the cost" of Japanese corporate investment "by providing essential infrastructure for host economies."[91] Strategically allocated ODA has contributed to Southeast Asia being a crucial zone of trade and investment, led by sogo shosha.

The English label "general trading company" for sogo shosha is somewhat misleading. The "big six"—Mitsubishi Corporation, Mitsui & Company Ltd., Itochu & Company Ltd., Sumitomo Corporation, Marubeni Corporation, and Nissho Iwai Corporation—are far more than traders.[92] These are complex conglomerates and all meet "the criteria set by international specialist literature for multinational or transnational concerns."[93] Yet sogo shosha are quite different from most multinational corporations. According to Michael Yoshino and Thomas Lifson, there are "really no comparable firms."[94] The largest sogo shosha form the "core" or the "command center" of powerful and complex industrial groups.[95] Itochu Group, for example, contains around eight hundred subsidiaries and affiliates. This network of firms is expanded further by close ties with suppliers, producers, and consumers.[96] They purchase and distribute almost every imaginable good,[97] provide fast and accurate market information, act as "quasi banks," invest in joint ventures, organize trade between countries other than Japan, link sellers and buyers, research and develop new technologies, and transport and market raw materials.[98]

Despite this wide range of activities, the central function of sogo shosha is to facilitate and coordinate trade, including trade in wood products, iron and steel, cotton, fuel, minerals, food, and chemicals.[99] These "spiders at the centre of Japan's global economic web" account for about 30 percent of Japan's total exports and 44 percent of imports.[100] Their joint turnover is roughly equal to one-quarter of Japan's GDP.[101] They often import large quantities of natural resources to support domestic processors. If necessary, sogo shosha will hold partial, and occasionally majority, shares in overseas companies that extract resources. But they prefer to act as trade intermediaries, providing funds and equipment to resource producers in exchange for favorable purchasing agreements.

Sogo shosha generally do not try to maximize profits. Instead, for small commissions, they provide services to promote and maintain trade, including supplying a constant flow of cheap raw materials, providing quick and accurate market information, and coordinating firms in the trade chain. Using money borrowed at low rates from affiliated banks, sogo shosha also provide promissory notes, credit, and loans to firms throughout the trade chain. To facilitate the tropical log trade, they finance loggers, shippers, exporters, plywood manufacturers, wholesalers, retailers, and final consumers (often construction companies).[102] They often extend loans—sometimes without interest—to small resource producers and manufacturers who would otherwise have difficulty receiving a bank loan.[103] Moreover, repayment is often delayed until after the firm sells its product, or sometimes firms simply barter. Yoshino and Lifson claim that "typically as much as 60 to 70 percent of a sogo shosha's assets is committed to financing suppliers and customers."[104] Sogo shosha funds have been critical for developing and maintaining Japan's tropical log trade. As a study for the World Bank notes, "money availability, the length of credit terms and the rates of interest would not be as favorable if money had to be supplied from the banks directly without going through the trading companies."[105]

Sogo shosha have been essential for the growth and survival of many Japanese natural resource processors. They provide processors with steady resource supplies, credit and low-interest loans, current market information, and reliable links to buyers (in some cases they buy the product back). As well, sogo shosha sometimes take short-term losses to help absorb fluctuations in currency exchange rates and resource supplies. This does not, however, translate into stable Southern prices, given that sogo shosha "themselves provoke speculative moves in international commodity markets, which they later smooth down in Japan."[106] According to Lawrence B. Krause and Sueo Sekiguchi, sogo shosha "follow-the-leader": "If one company, thinking a product is in short supply, makes anticipatory purchases, the others will follow suit, causing an excess of quantity requirements, rapid escalation in prices, and market instability; ultimately, the excess must be sold back into the market, causing a collapse in price."[107]

Sogo shosha have provided critical support for domestic plywood processors, enabling many to survive escalating costs and increasing competition from cheap Indonesian plywood. According to a study for the World Bank, sogo shosha provide "the plywood manufacturer a secure customer base, which reduces . . . risk[s] and make[s] production and distribution run without any major . . . fluctuations in demand." But financial and structural arrangements—coupled with access to the latest market information—enable sogo shosha to manipulate trade chains and control domestic processors. The same study for the World Bank notes: "the manufacturer has little influence on the market, prices and profits."[108]

Sogo shosha drive unsustainable resource extraction. This is not a result of some devious plan to exploit the South. It is, instead, a natural outgrowth of their economic raison d'être. To function as trade intermediaries, sogo shosha must work at low profit margins.[109] If the cost of their services outweighs the benefits, affiliated firms will do the service themselves, do without the service, or turn to another sogo shosha (although a strong sense of obligation exists between sogo shosha and their associated companies). To remain viable at low profit margins, they must import large volumes of cheap natural resources. The stress on huge volumes is reinforced by intense competition among sogo shosha to generate the greatest amount of sales.[110] As a result, unlike most multinational corporations that strive to maximize profits, sogo shosha—through their financial and structural arrangements with firms in the trade chain, coupled with control over distribution and market information—keep resource prices low and artificially stimulate demand to maintain large trade volumes.[111] Quite naturally, they thrive on resources—including tropical logs—sold at prices that ignore environmental and social costs.[112] These cheap resource imports trigger wasteful consumption. Viewed this way, it is apparent that sogo shosha need wasteful consumption to survive.[113]

Greening Corporate Japan

Besides a few showcase projects, multinational corporations around the world have shown little practical interest in supporting or funding environmental conservation.[114] Sogo shosha are no exception, focusing instead on exporting environmental technology developed to tackle pervasive pollution in the early 1970s. MITI predicts overseas environmental protection will become a lucrative business and vigorously backs these corporate efforts. Although the government strongly supports environmental technology exports, it applies little, if any, pressure on sogo shosha to monitor the environmental effects of general technology transfers.

MITI, Keidanren (Federation of Economic Organizations), and the most powerful companies have become increasingly worried about Japan's corporate image as environmentalists and NGOs depict Japanese companies as "eco-outlaws." To counter mounting criticism of corporate environmental practices, the Japanese government, Keidanren, and the sogo shosha have launched a campaign to "green" corporate Japan.

As environmental criticism increased in the 1980s and early 1990s, Keidanren and the largest sogo shosha counterattacked, creating new environmental sections, guidelines, conservation projects, and public relations brochures. In late 1990, Keidanren organized a "1% Club," and requested member firms and individuals to donate "one percent of their annual income to support socially beneficial activities."[115] In 1991, Keidanren proclaimed a Global Environment Charter. A year later, a Keidanren poll claimed that 70 percent of companies "had already used the charter to strengthen their ability to tackle environmental issues."[116] However, even if this optimistic claim is accepted, the charter has clear weaknesses, making its ability to "strengthen" anything debatable. Although it contains commendable principles, the wording is often vague and irresolute.[117] More important, no specific enforcement mechanism is in place. According to a Keidanren official, the guidelines are designed to encourage companies to consider overseas environmental factors; and although compliance is "expected," it is not mandatory, and leeway is provided.[118] In 1994, Keidanren reiterated its environmental stance, calling on Japanese companies "to work to protect the global environment" as part of "corporate responsibility."[119] However, despite these lofty principles, without any means to monitor and enforce regulations, many Japanese observers see the charter as little more than a public relations ploy.[120]

Since the early 1990s, the six largest sogo shosha have established environmental sections. These are remarkably similar and cooperate closely, perhaps to increase communication and maximize resources, perhaps, more cynically, to minimize competition and avoid a costly race to be the most "environmentally friendly." Mitsubishi's Environmental Affairs Department is typical. According to a spokesman, it has three aims: to raise the environmental consciousness of employees; to contribute to environmental projects in developing countries; and to share Japanese knowledge and experience of environmental protection while being careful to sell appropriate technology.[121] All of the environmental departments have developed environmental guidelines, although like the Keidanren charter they contain far more flowery language than concrete procedures.[122] Besides these guidelines, the largest sogo shosha have increased modestly funding for environmental projects in the South and for research in Japanese universities. Some sogo shosha have also instituted environmental reviews. For example, at Itochu the Global Environment Department evaluates a proposal when there is concern it may harm the environment. The process and criteria, however, are vague and no reliable evidence exists to suggest that proposals are ever rejected on environmental grounds.[123] Starting in FY1993, Marubeni plans to conduct an annual review of the environmental impact of its business activities, although like Itochu, the criteria and process are opaque.[124]

A vital function of the new environment departments is to improve corporate images. According to corporate representatives, Japan's wealth, powerful public relations sections of Western multinational corporations, the tendency in the international community to avoid criticizing developing states, and a Japanese cultural proclivity to accept criticism have all contributed to an unbalanced, simplistic, even inaccurate picture of the environmental record of Japanese corporations.[125] One example is a 1993 *New York Times* advertisement by the Rainforest Action Network that claimed Mitsubishi was destroying tropical forests and called for a boycott of their products.[126] Through a worldwide publicity campaign, meetings with NGOs, distributing information packages, and responding to letters, sogo shosha are trying to counteract what they consider unjustified and outrageous allegations.[127]

Japanese Corporate Environmental Policies and Tropical Forests

Japanese companies have generally avoided investment or research in reforestation given that primary forests have provided immediate and abundant high-quality tropical logs, whereas reforestation is expensive, involves long-term commitments and planning, and profits are unpredictable. Nevertheless, the effort to improve Japan's corporate environmental image—coupled with government financial and technical support—has produced a few small reforestation projects.[128] Some support also exists for research in tropical reforestation.[129] In 1991, nine private enterprises, in conjunction with the Ministry of Agriculture, Forestry, and Fisheries, established the Research Association for Reforestation of Tropical Forest (RETROF) with a five-year mandate. RETROF receives half its funding from private companies and half from the government. It coordinates, reviews, and advises specific corporate projects.[130] It is designed to transfer Japanese knowledge and technology to tropical reforestation projects, especially for developing mixed-species plantations.[131] Despite token corporate conservation projects and research on tropical reforestation, as we will see in later chapters, the impact of Japanese corporate research and investment in reforestation—driven more by a desire to generate favorable publicity than by a desire to support sustainable commercial timber operations—is limited.

Japanese Environmental Guidelines and Timber Consumption

There are scattered corporate calls to reduce wasteful tropical timber consumption and buy timber from sustainable sources. Marubeni claims that it "will only purchase timber from such logging companies who strictly follow laws and regulations on logging and adhere to environmentally sound management."[132] The Japan Building Contractors' Society—comprising eighty-one key companies—announced in 1992 a nonbinding target to reduce tropical kon-pane consumption by 35 percent over the next five years, "in order to help protect the world's tropical rain forests."[133] On a voluntary basis, in the early 1990s the Japan Lumber Importers' Association (JLIA)—comprising 131 companies, including the sogo shosha—developed import guidelines to improve forest management. Companies agreed to import in "an orderly manner," follow ITTO "Guidelines for Continued Management of Tropical Natural Forest," and urge "timber suppliers of long-term contract to abide by the ITTO guidelines." These companies also agreed to buy and use scrap wood, provide information to local loggers to encourage better cutting practices, and promote value-added processing in the South.[134] Meanwhile, the Japan Plywood Manufacturers' Association (JPMA)—with technological support from the Japanese government—also plans to lower tropical wood consumption and use softwood logs for 30 percent of plywood production by 1996.[135]

The Japanese government has also made sporadic calls to lower tropical timber imports, improve corporate purchasing practices, and internalize environmental costs into timber prices. The Construction Ministry's new industry guidelines call for builders to reduce practices that waste tropical timber. Building codes were also modified to encourage builders to substitute new materials for tropical timber.[136] The Forestry Agency has also announced plans to encourage companies to limit timber purchases to sustainable sources and decrease tropical timber imports.[137] Although the information has not been released to the public, since 1991 the Forestry Agency has required tropical timber traders to provide annual import data and submit five-year import plans. At a 1991 International Tropical Timber Council (ITTC) session, Japan declared that it "intends to make active contributions to a series of ITTO meetings which will estimate and examine the costs of sustainable management, aiming that prices of tropical timber cover the costs of sustainable management."[138] At the same meeting, the Japanese government announced a program for "rational utilization" to reduce tropical timber consumption. Japan agreed to support measures to use less and reuse more kon-pane, substitute nontropical logs to make plywood, and educate the Japanese public on the inherent value of tropical rain forests. Japan also agreed to promote research, training, and technology for value-added Southern processing, and to "study the utilization of nonwood forest products and the commercially less-accepted species."[139] Since then, several local Japanese governments—including Tokyo, Osaka, Kanegawa, Kyoto, Nagoya, and Sapporo—have also announced plans to reduce the amount of tropical kon-pane used in public projects.[140] More recently, the central government reiterated its support for the ITTO objective to limit trade to timber produced from sustainable sources by the year 2000, and agreed to "contribute to discussions to establish rules of timber trade, with a view to conserving the world's forests."[141]

These policies have had few concrete results. Over the last few years, tropical log imports, especially from Southeast Asia, have decreased. But this trend is a result of less abundant tropical log stocks, Southeast Asian log export bans, a shrinking Japanese plywood industry, and Japan's recession, not of greater concern for tropical forests. Moreover, although tropical timber imports fell substantially from the mid-1970s to the late 1980s, the average amount imported from 1991 to 1995 was only about 7.8 percent lower than the amount imported in 1990 (in roundwood equivalent).[142] The drop in tropical log imports has been offset by a sharp increase in Indonesian plywood imports. Moreover, in spite of the numerous government and corporate plans, total tropical plywood consumption has remained fairly stable (8.95 million cubic meters in 1990 and 8.70 million cubic meters in 1994).[143]

Conclusion

In sum, the new environment law, the creation of environmental guidelines and departments for loan and aid agencies, and environmental aid demonstrate that the Japanese government recognizes the need to address overseas environmental problems. JICA has made marginal improvements to its tropical forest projects. Yet there is far more rhetoric than substance. The new law and OECF, EXIM Bank, and JICA guidelines are vague and nonbinding. Environmental reviews are poorly coordinated, and there are no enforcement mechanisms, transparent procedures, or concrete penalties. As well, environmental aid is not clearly defined. A portion is merely a reclassification of conventional projects rather than a substantial reallocation of funds. As a result, so far the bulk of assistance has been in yen loans and has primarily funded water and sewage systems. Overseas environmental assistance is further undermined by a fractured administration dominated by economic interests. Despite marginal increases in input, the Environment Agency, although an earnest supporter of better overseas environmental guidelines, still has relatively little influence. The Forestry Agency has not aggressively tackled environmental issues, and instead cautiously promotes tree plantations, a transfer of silvicultural expertise, and expanded trade and consumption. Meanwhile, MITI has staked out environmental turf to promote technology transfers and business initiatives. Given this context, it is not surprising that even though Japan relies heavily on natural resource imports, conservation, reforestation, and resource management are peripheral to government overseas environmental policies.

Beginning in the early 1990s, the private sector, led by Keidanren and the major sogo shosha, counterattacked domestic and world environmental critics, producing a deluge of flowery policy statements, corporate brochures, and public advertisements. Although a tiny amount of money has shifted to environmental research and showcase conservation and reforestation projects, these cosmetic policies contain few concrete mechanisms or sanctions to control overseas environmental impacts. Not surprisingly, corporate and government plans to reduce tropical timber consumption have had little impact. Finally, while new government and corporate environmental policies provide only minor benefits for Southern resource management, they serve an inauspicious function, obscuring the far more important consequences of sogo shosha trade chains, wasteful consumption, low prices for raw materials, unsustainable purchasing practices, import barriers, and the residual effects of past practices. During 1994 discussions, government and business leaders pushed conversations away from these crucial factors and toward the content of the new environment law, the "comprehensive" environmental guidelines, the "extensive" investments in environmental and forest conservation projects, the "influential" environmental departments, and perhaps most consistently, Japan's "impressive" environmental aid. In short, the rhetoric enveloping Japanese overseas activities undeniably shifted in the early 1990s; but the accompanying policies are too diluted, inconsistent, and marginal to alter the nucleus of Japan's shadow ecology, and only minor, peripheral changes have occurred. Before turning to a specific analysis of the impact of Japan's shadow ecology on timber management in the Philippines, Indonesia, and East Malaysia, the next chapter outlines a framework to understand the domestic political economies of resource management in Southeast Asia.

2 A Model of Resource Management in Clientelist States

The allocation and management of natural resources in developing countries has gained increased attention in the last decade as worldwide scarcity and environmental catastrophe loom. Forestry management and the causes of tropical deforestation have received particular attention as loss of these trees has been linked to siltation, erosion, flooding, and most ominously, global warming. Most explanations of forestry problems have focused on technical or economic factors, the content of specific policies, the role of international organizations and finance,[1] and the impact of poverty and population growth. Surprisingly little attention has been given to the role of domestic political forces in the South, even though in many situations this appears to be a key factor.[2]

By paying more attention to the nature of the state and to policy implementation, this chapter builds on the patron-client model to understand links between Southern politics and resource management. I argue that "modern" patron-client networks interact with political executives, bureaucracies, courts, and militaries to lower Southeast Asian state capacity and willingness to enforce resource regulations. The first part of this chapter sketches the main features and analytical advantages of a patron-client framework. Then, after outlining the evolution of patron-client ties in Southeast Asia, I borrow ideas from Joel Migdal's work on state-society relations to explain how modern patron-client links undermine state capacity. This creates a model to analyze the political economies of resource management in clientelist states.

Patron-Client Model of Association

The patron-client model was initially developed by anthropologists to explain traditional village-level, dyadic power relations. The anthropological patron-client model is a personal exchange relationship between two persons with unequal status, power, or resources. The higher-ranked person provides protection and benefits (often material) to a lower-ranked person in exchange for loyalty and assistance, including personal services. Although the client usually benefits less than the patron, this reciprocity distinguishes patron-client relations from relations of pure coercion or formal authority which also link individuals of different status.[3] The personal and reciprocal qualities of patron-client relations contribute to feelings of trust, affection, and obligation, often creating a durable bond between the two people. In this way, patron-client relations create traditional legitimacy. The glue that binds the dyadic relationship is the agreement to "exchange favors and to come to each other's aid in time of need."[4] If either side neglects to reciprocate, the relationship generally ends. The essential defining characteristics of traditional dyadic patron-client relations, then, are asymmetry, informality, personal contact, and reciprocity.

Many patron-client theorists argue that clients enter into dyadic patron-client relationships to safeguard their subsistence and increase security.[5] This generalization apparently has numerous exceptions, including Sabah and Sarawak.[6] A more useful way of understanding client action is to view their strategies as "interest-maximizing rather than risk-minimizing."[7] In other words, clients enter into patron-client relationships because it is the most efficient and effective means to improve their socioeconomic position.

Building dyadic alliances is relatively easy because "it involves the simple trading of favors and not the more difficult task of furthering collective goals."[8] With clients eager to improve their lifestyle, patrons eager to increase their power, and alliances fairly easy to form, large groups develop based on dyadic patron-client exchange (sometimes called clientelism). Political scientists in the 1960s and 1970s extrapolated the anthropological model to understand these groups. A patron-client cluster is a patron's immediate following, perhaps twenty to thirty people. A patron-client pyramid comprises not only a patron's direct clients but also the immediate following of these clients. (It is assumed that one person can be both a client and a patron.) A patron-client network is a web of patron-client pyramids linked by a common patron. Alliances of patron-client clusters, pyramids, or networks can create factions.[9]

Extrapolating dyadic patron-client relations to these larger concepts has been criticized for overstretching a microlevel model to understand macrolevel phenomena.[10] It is in fact quite difficult, if not impossible, to "find" and accurately describe the dyadic components of patron-client political structures. To overcome this problem, rather than taking on the laborious task of determining the specific composition of patron-client clusters, pyramids, and networks, it is more useful to focus on informal, personal, reciprocal, and asymmetrical "patterns of interaction and exchange."[11] Emphasizing a specific type of exchange relationship rather than structure accepts that these ties can vary in their intensity, duration, and type of resources involved. Although expanding a microlevel model has unavoidable risks, there are a number of advantages, especially for understanding political forces that shape natural resource management in the South.

Advantages of Patron-Client Analysis

The patron-client model is not a grand theory capable of explaining everything; rather, as a middle-range perspective, it is confined to one particular set of political relationships.[12] This allows greater detail and nuance for analyzing how domestic politics shape natural resource use than is possible, for example, with world system theory or dependency frameworks. According to Christopher Clapham, it is "one of a number of middle-range concepts through which the possibility of a comparative social science may—however dimly and elusively—be glimpsed."[13]

The patron-client model enables the analyst to move beyond formal institutions, groups, and policies and toward informal power relations, fluid associations, and personal exchange. This helps account for dynamic and sudden change and for political systems characterized "by a lack of clear dividing lines between political groups and a great deal of shifting and switching among peripheral group members."[14] It also overcomes problems of many economic studies of natural resource management in the South that stress impersonal market-based exchange. As well, it helps explain why a bureaucrat's power can be based more on personal connections than on a formal position or why a political party may resemble an uncoordinated gathering of powerful leaders and their loyal followers.[15] Many political models are constrained by their focus on formal, institutional arrangements, and are unable to explain processes that occur outside this framework.[16] This can be a serious limitation because, as James Scott notes, "bureaucratic political parties in Southeast Asia are often thoroughly penetrated by informal patron-client networks that underlie the formal structure of authority."[17] By focusing on informal rather than formal relations, important insights can be gained into distribution patterns, including appointments to bureaucratic positions, awarding of government contracts, and allocation of state revenues. Formal structures, however, cannot be ignored when examining patron-client relations. At the very least, "formal structures are relevant to patron-client systems, if only because they provide the critical resources necessary to build and sustain such a system."[18]

Patron-client analysis accounts for the importance of traditional relations of power and concepts of legitimacy and authority. It provides continuity with the past and considers indigenous values and beliefs as well as contemporary variations. René Lemarchand argues that because the patron-client model "cuts across both 'traditional' and 'modern' referents," it has a "heuristic value generally missing from the conceptual arsenal of either 'modern' or 'traditional' polities, [and] it directs attention to processes of adjustment between traditional and modern patterns of behavior, expectations, and normative orientations to politics which might otherwise go unnoticed."[19] Traditional power arrangements and concepts of authority provide "modern" patron-client links, which would in many countries be viewed as simple corruption, with a certain degree of legitimacy. Corruption entails a legal violation that is perceived as illegitimate by the community and thus contributes to a loss of authority. Patron-client exchange may sometimes violate formal law, but its roots in tradition mean that even when it is labeled "corruption," there is not necessarily any loss of authority. In fact, ignoring patronage duties may even contribute to a greater loss of legitimacy and authority than violating formal laws.

Patron-client analysis accounts for vertical links from urban to rural areas that cut across class, ethnicity, language, and religious differences. Membership is based on ties to the leader and is specific to each link; it is not based on shared horizontal ties among followers. Models that isolate ethnic, religious, or class groups have difficulty explaining intragroup politics and cooperation among segments of different groups. For natural resource issues such as timber, patron-client analysis points to the important crosscutting ties between central financing, ownership, and control, and local contractors, managers, and workers. As well, in countries with competitive elections, a focus on patron-client politics directs attention to a partial vertical redistribution of natural resource profits as central party members "buy" rural votes.[20] Of course, not all patterns of political behavior are reducible to patron-client relations.[21] Ethnicity, class, religion, language, nationalism, party ideology, and central-regional relations are just some of the other factors that exist alongside patron-client links. Depending on the timing, situation, and specific context, the impact of patron-client relations will vary. Focusing on patron-client ties, however, is particularly useful for understanding logging in Southeast Asia, given that these have historically been, and continue to be, the dominant force shaping timber allocation and management.

Finally, the patron-client model is especially useful for understanding cooperation among individuals and groups in times of peace and stability. (In contrast, class or ethnic-based models have generally been limited to analyzing conflict.) It effectively explains the emergence, transformation, and continuance of groups whose membership is not based on shared horizontal characteristics but where people are linked vertically, sharing few common characteristics, often of different status, and perhaps not even knowing each other given that the common link is personal ties to the leader. The emphasis on cooperation, however, does not preclude an understanding of conflict. Robert Kaufman notes that while "patron-client exchange is premised on hierarchical distributions of power and resources, the concept simultaneously allows for (and at times suggests) the possibility of intense conflict between narrowly based, shifting patron-client clusters and pyramids."[22] The concept of factions is particularly valuable for analyzing conflict between patron-client units,[23] or conflict within, for example, an ethnic group.

Despite these advantages, for much of the 1980s and the first half of the 1990s, relatively little has been written on patron-client relations.[24] As patron-client ties evolve—and some argue dissipate—many comparative politics specialists have turned to other analytic tools. Yet, these relations are still a key feature of many Southern states. Luis Roniger writes: "While it would be absurd to predict that certain types of relationships—friendship, for instance—would disappear following development, this has been the main argument regarding clientelism (in both cases, it would seem more reasonable to expect changes in structure rather than their natural demise)."[25] In Southeast Asia, patron-client ties remain extensive, although most of these are "modern" rather than "traditional" relations.

Modern Patron-Client Relations in Southeast Asia

Relatively few traditional patron-client ties still exist in Southeast Asia. Traditional relations are characterized by highly affective ties based on kinship, village, or neighborhood bonds. A patron typically relies on personal skills, wealth (largely through private control of local resources), and sometimes connections to more powerful patrons. Loyalty, obligation, honor, and nonmaterial rewards supplement material exchanges. These ties involve face-to-face contact and multiple kinds of exchange.

Colonialism, the shift from colonialism to independence, the spread of market capitalism in the twentieth century, urbanization, evolving social and political circumstances, and the growth of the state over the last fifty years or so have contributed to important changes to most traditional patron-client relations. Exploiting political power to accumulate wealth has a long tradition in insular Southeast Asia. Monarchs taxed peasants and controlled commerce, using these funds to reward loyal followers. Colonialism and global economic links greatly increased the economic power and scope of the state, making it a key source of patronage.[26] After independence, states continued to expand. In countries like the Philippines, as the size of the state increased, "access to the state machinery became more important than ever for the creation of wealth."[27] As a result, the state became a key source of material incentives to bind modern patron-client ties, including funds, licenses, and career opportunities. State officials have also been absorbed by patron-client networks, ignoring state rules in exchange for presents, bribes, or some other particularistic concession. This extensive state patronage has fostered larger and larger patron-client networks in Southeast Asia. As Gordon Means notes, the state "provides the institutional framework for the extension of patron-client networks beyond the immediate circle of individual loyalties and friendships."[28]

Patron-client exchange is now generally more specific and less personal. Patrons are less likely to maintain regular contact with a client and more likely to exchange tangible goods, such as a license for a "political contribution." As a result, modern patron-client relations are also based less on loyalty, obligation, and honor.[29] Instead, patronage is a crucial means of building "loyal" followers (at least temporarily). This is reinforced by immigration and domestic migration to large cities and towns which has produced large numbers of people who are most efficiently turned into "loyal" followers using material incentives. For this reason, political patrons often need to provide money, gifts, and government jobs to build power and maintain prestige and legitimacy. In areas with competitive elections, this has been encouraged further as patron-client relations have become "closely linked to the national [or state] level with jobs, cash, and petty favors flowing down the network, and votes or support flowing upward."[30] These trends contributed by the 1970s to "a comparatively large 'fairweather' periphery, a comparatively small core following, and a less 'constant' patron as well."[31]

Patron-client connections have become increasingly unstable as the size of patron-client networks has grown, as personal contact has decreased, as clients have lost their sense of obligation, and as the number of "fairweather" followers has increased. This instability is natural because "those on the periphery of the patron-client network become alienated and are cross-pressured between their pursuit of immediate but meagre benefits (in relation to other more favoured clients) and their aspirations for improved opportunities with a new winning coalition."[32] Despite these changes, the personal and asymmetrical nature of exchange, the lack of formal-legal contracts or institutional ties, and the reciprocal expectations make modern patron-client exchange significantly different from market exchange.[33] These exchange relations are a dominant characteristic of the societies of Southeast Asia. As patron-client structures evolve, and with the increase in the size and power of Southern states over the last fifty years or so, it is essential to understand the consequences of these clientelist societies on the state. Neopatrimonial studies are one attempt to give more attention to the links between the state and patron-client networks.

Neopatrimonial Studies

Neopatrimonial studies are rooted in Max Weber's analysis of traditional authority where the distinction between public and private is obscured: there is neither one objective law for all nor a principle of bureaucratic impartiality. Instead, decisions are based on "personal connections, favors, promises, and privileges."[34] Jean-François Medard bluntly declares, in a patrimonial state, "politics becomes a kind of business with two modes of exchange: connections and money. The state is a pie that every one wants to eat."[35] Although focusing more on a single ruler, neopatrimonialism points to many of the same features as patron-clientelism—including informal relations, particularism, and instrumental exchange.[36] For example, Paul Hutchcroft's neopatrimonial analysis of natural resource exploitation in the Philippines focuses on changes to patron-client relations as access to the state has become increasingly important for collecting and distributing patronage. In the

Philippines, this has created a state where key bureaucratic officials and political leaders (especially Ferdinand Marcos and family) have plundered the natural resources for personal gain.[37] Neopatrimonial analysis is particularly valuable in pointing to the dominance of intrastate factional competition over substantive policy debates in determining the distribution of natural resources. The difference between the patron-client model and the neopatrimonial model is largely a matter of emphasis,[38] and patron-client analysis can be strengthened by the empirical findings and conceptual conclusions of neopatrimonial studies.

Yet despite the similarity to patron-clientelism, a neopatrimonial framework has certain drawbacks for analyzing resource management in Southeast Asia. The model tends to overestimate the dominance of the state and neglect significant societal constraints to state management.[39] Neopatrimonial studies emphasize central elites, and often point to a "superpatron" as a key source of mismanagement. Actors further down the causal chain—such as contractors, subcontractors, and middle-level administrators—are often neglected. On the other hand, the patron-client model spotlights multiple levels of interaction yet still places primary responsibility with the most powerful elites.[40] Neopatrimonial studies also downplay the role of urban-rural links, instrumental exchange that occurs outside of the state, and the impact of societal structure and social resistance on state directives, policies, and goals. As a result, a neopatrimonial framework has difficulty explaining the resilience of pervasive patronage in absence of, or after the fall of, a superpatron.[41] Neopatrimonial studies, however, do have the analytical advantage of focusing close attention to the state as a source of patronage. To shift the focus of the patron-client model more to the role of state patronage, and to gain a better understanding of the consequences of pervasive patron-clientelism on the nature of the state itself,[42] I now turn to the theoretical work of Migdal.

Strong Societies and Weak States

Borrowing some of Migdal's concepts sharpens the analytical power of the patron-client model.[43] In the tradition of Weber, he defines a state as an organization composed of institutions (military, bureaucracy, courts, police) coordinated by state leaders (executive), that has the authority or ability to make and enforce "rules of the game" in a given territory, at least partially through a monopoly on violence.[44] For Migdal, a society is the arena in which states and nonstate organizations interact.[45] He argues that to understand Southern politics it is crucial to examine "how the organization of society, even in remote areas, may dictate the character and capabilities of politics at the center, as well as how the state (often in unintended ways) changes society."[46] Migdal's dependent variable is "state capabilities." These include state capacity to affect societal structures and relations even in remote areas, "regulate social relationships, extract resources, and appropriate and use resources in determined ways." Strong states have high capabilities, weak states have low capabilities. State capacity is determined by the structure of society and the reciprocal consequences of the interplay between the state and other social organizations. The key question to determine the extent of state capacity is simple: Are states able to "get people in society to do what they want them to do?"[47] To answer this question, it is essential to examine societal forces that resist or cooperate with state directives, actions, and policies. It is also necessary to look at legislation, national plans, and management regulations, because these represent state goals and priorities. In strong states like Israel, nonstate organizations "not only comply with state rules to an impressive degree, but they also accept the rightness of the state's making the rules of the game."[48] In weak states like Sierra Leone, faced with the cumulative resistance of nonstate organizations, the state is often unable or unwilling to enforce laws or collect taxes.

Migdal develops a model of a society in which the state battles other organizations for social control—"a mélange in which the state is one organization among many."[49] This model points to both formal and informal political and social forces within society that resist state rules and authority. It emphasizes "multiple sets of rules of the game in society" and conflict and competition between these sets of rules. For Migdal, "the central political and social drama of recent history has been the battle pitting the state and organizations allied with it (often from a particular social class) against other social organizations dotting society's landscape." Low state capacity is directly related to the structure of society. State power is corroded by "the resistance posed by chiefs, landlords, bosses, rich peasants, clan leaders," and "their various social organizations." These organizations "make rules against the wishes and goals of state leaders."[50] In the case of Sierra Leone, British colonization—in the context of rapid changes to the world economy and technology—laid the basis for a weak state. This created "a society of fragments—each fragment with its own forms of social control, its own array of rules, rewards, sanctions, and symbols." The resulting conflict between state and nonstate organizations determines "which strategies are to be adopted, who will make the rules, and who will determine the property rights that define the use of assets and resources in society."[51]

In most of the South, societies are surprisingly resilient, like "an intricate spider's web; one could snip a corner of the web away and the rest of the web would swing majestically between the branches, just as one could snip center strands and have the web continue to exist." Fragmented social control is the key reason for this resilience. Even though the state is the most powerful organization in these "weblike" societies, the combined influence and resistance of other social organizations is considerable. For example, in Sierra Leone, "no single chief can stand up to the strength of the state's leaders, but the sum total of all the chiefs' quiet control in remote parts of the country can have a crippling effect on state leaders' attempts to increase state capabilities." It is also important not to equate state capacity with the ability to remove one "strongman." According to Migdal, "individual strongmen may go, but the overall distribution of social control may remain remarkably constant."[52]

Migdal builds from his model and develops a theory to explain why most Southern states are weak and a few are strong. For parsimony, his model portrays the state as "a more or less monolithic organization, a single actor, without significant differentiation of parts." As he develops his theory, however, he refines this view of the state by pointing to "situations of accommodation between parts of the state and social organizations with opposing rules of the game."[53] Differentiating the state makes it clear that executive decisions are distinct from state output. Internal divisions and interaction with other social organizations alter the impact of a state so it is often different than the intent of the leaders. As we will see later, this has a critical impact on state capacity to implement policies.

To facilitate melding Migdal's work with patron-client analysis, it is useful to narrow some of his core ideas.[54] He argues that most states fall on the weak end of a strong-weak continuum. My study does not attempt to place the states of Southeast Asia on this continuum. Although factors like poor tax and royalty collection, minimal reforestation, general disregard for regulations, widespread illegal logging, and smuggling all indicate "weak" states, they only point to low capacity in *one* policy sector. The same states could have much greater control over, for example, manufacturing. Migdal's weak-strong continuum can be refined by developing continuums of individual state capacity depending on different policy sectors.[55] Logically, a weak state will have the majority of its policy initiatives fall on the weak end of the continuum. Even here, however, cases of high state capacity may be evident. This makes sense because, depending on the policy area and the stakes, societal resistance to state initiatives and state determination to enforce its rules will vary. For example, environmental issues are generally a low priority for states, whereas environmental regulations are often quite threatening to nonstate organizations, particularly powerful businesses. As a result, state capacity to enforce environmental regulations is frequently low. On the other hand, state resolution to tackle foreign control over natural resources may be strong, whereas resistance from nonstate organizations may be minimal; or in some instances, these organizations may even support the state. Therefore, a state may appear weak when tackling environmental problems yet seem strong when tackling foreign control.

A second useful modification to Migdal's model is to highlight different societal organizations depending on the specific issue, problem, or state policy. This is logical because nonstate organizations can pick areas of resistance, whereas states have diverse, often contradictory goals, and must tackle a plethora of issues and crises. Undeniably, even in the face of strong resistance from organizations in society, state actions have critical consequences, although often these are unintended. This is hardly surprising. Compared to other social organizations, states have huge budgets, complex bureaucracies, and powerful coercive tools. Yet societal organizations, while having far fewer financial and human resources than a state, can concentrate their opposition or seek alliances, sometimes even dominating sections of the state. For example, for a policy like affirmative action, the business community may be the decisive societal group opposing the state. For timber in Southeast Asia, patron-client networks are the most important obstacle to state initiatives and the major alternative set of "rules of the game" for management and allocation. Other organizations, like tribes (Penan in Sarawak) and insurgency movements (communists in the Philippines), contribute to resistance but have minor consequences compared to patron-client ties. For this reason, when examining state initiatives to manage timber in Southeast Asia, it is most efficient to concentrate on patron-client networks because they are the central societal force undermining state control.[56]

A state confronting and penetrated by ubiquitous patron-client relations can be seen as one kind of weak state—what some authors have labeled a clientelist state.[57] In clientelist states, goals and priorities are modified by particularistic, rent-seeking behavior of patrons and clients as they interact with the state. For resource management, Southeast Asian states can be broadly conceived as clientelist states.[58]

Clientelist States and Policy

When discussing state control over resource policies, it is important to distinguish clearly between policy formation and policy implementation. In terms of policy development, a state may dominate—that is, there is little or minimal societal input. Yet this same state may be "weak" in the sense of facing formidable obstacles to implementing state rules. For example, the Indonesian state dominates policy formation but in some cases has great difficulty enforcing policy regulations and maintaining societal compliance.[59] The sharp contrast between state power to develop policies and the power to enforce policies has contributed to sharp differences between scholars who see Southern states as irrevocably weak and those who see these states as strong.[60] It is also important to distinguish between the content and effects of policies. Many comparative studies of Southern policies make direct links between policy substance and the mismanagement of natural resources. These studies show that many Southern policies have serious technical flaws that contribute to environmental degradation. They also demonstrate that the ability of the bureaucracy to develop policies is weakened by organizational difficulties and elite attitudes.[61] But even though the content of resource policies is undeniably important, a more *immediate* factor driving mismanagement is often the willingness and ability of the state to implement policies.

Northern states also have poor records for environmental protection and resource management, partially resulting from corporate lobbying and partially from the tendency for economic interests to dominate bureaucracies. Yet, unlike in the South, in most cases, key battles to improve resource management occur *within* the state—battles over legislation, interpretation of policy, and budget allocations. While Northern policies are certainly watered down during implementation, societal compliance to state regulations is much higher than it is in the South. For this reason, it is logical to dissect, analyze, and debate the nuances of Northern policies. But to do the same for Southern policies may simply divert attention from the more immediate problem: enforcement and compliance. This *does not* mean that resource management will be better in the North than in the South. But the core of the problem is likely to be different: in the North, policies dominated by economic concerns with weak environmental regulations; in the South, policies that are widely ignored.

The next section sketches a model to explain why clientelist states of Southeast Asia are generally unable to enforce natural resource management rules. There are three interrelated reasons: the structure and norms of society support institutionalized "corruption"; in order to survive, state leaders, facing a web of patron-client relations, sacrifice state capacity to enforce resource regulations; and finally, with minimal supervision, many middle- and lower-level bureaucrats become involved in patron-client exchange, ignoring state rules in order to make money, advance their careers, or create small patron-client units.

Patron-Client Relations and Systemic "Corruption"

Like the patron-client model, Migdal provides a nuanced understanding of corruption. He points to societal structure and state reactions as keys to understanding flagrant violations of state laws. He argues that "much of what is commonly called corruption is . . . behavior according to dissenting rules, established by organizations other than the state."[62] Furthermore, "nepotism, cronyism, corruption, and arrogance" of state leaders is partially a response to surviving in a setting of fragmented social control. Seen in this light, "corruption and arrogance are mere symptoms of a complex relationship between state leaders and local strongmen."[63] In societies dominated by clientelism, patron-client ties permeate the state and nonstate organizations. Although modern patron-client relations differ from older forms in terms of stability and the nature of exchange, they are nevertheless a legitimate, accepted, even expected, part of the political process. While allegations of corruption and pejorative labels such as "crony" are part of formal debate and are used to justify investigations, these prevalent practices flow from societal structures and alternative rules of the game. There are of course instances where state officials accept straightforward bribes. But many material exchanges cannot be dismissed as simple "corruption." Focusing on specific cases of "corruption" highlights a symptom rather than the cause of poor implementation. For this reason, campaigns in the Philippines, Malaysia, and Indonesia that have tried to stamp out "corruption" with token firings, fines, and jail sentences have had little impact. Of course, not all state officials in clientelist states are "corrupt."

Some bureaucrats, military officers, and politicians work diligently to enforce laws, improve regulations, and raise revenue, even without strict supervision.[64] For management of a resource like timber, however, these officials tend to be either outside patron-client networks or belong to networks based on material incentives other than timber, although in some cases they are simply "loyal" to the state.

Leaders and Low State Capacity

In the clientelist states of Southeast Asia, political structures concentrate power among a small elite who are often motivated by personal gain. Top state leaders, including presidents, prime ministers, and chief ministers, are often powerful patrons. But at the same time, leaders must maneuver in a societal web of patron-client relations. Confronted by strong resistance from nonstate organizations, and faced with potential threats from institutions within the state (often the military), state leaders, in order to survive and maintain societal stability, follow strategies that undermine state capabilities—what Migdal calls the "politics of survival."[65] To weaken challenges from sections of the state, top leaders remove and shuffle state-agency elites. To maintain or increase power, they appoint loyal followers, friends, and family. As well, to preserve stability, they make nonmerit appointments to coopt powerful patrons and ethnic, regional, and business leaders outside the state. They also use nonmerit appointments to hinder independent power centers from developing within the state. These coopted elites are often allowed to get rich through "corruption." This provides a means of control for state leaders. If these "corrupt" officials step out of line, they can be charged and legally dismissed or jailed.

These survival strategies by leaders undermine state capacity. Shuffling administrative heads and making nonmerit appointments lower morale and loyalty to the state (as opposed to the leader) and weaken the ability and willingness to oppose local strongmen.[66] Surviving as leader involves maintaining an intricate balance between "restraining agencies sufficiently so they pose no threat to rulers while allowing sufficient organization so the agencies can perform the tasks necessary for state and leader survival."[67] This is often a difficult balance. As state capacity declines and the state is unable to provide basic services, leaders lose legitimacy. To maintain control, leaders distribute even more patronage. This dynamic—state leaders using patronage to maintain loyalty and patronage undermining state capacity to keep citizens loyal—

can eventually spiral into a regime dominated by "politics of plunder," as in the Philippines under Marcos. While the survival strategies of leaders weaken state agencies at the top, these actions also debilitate state implementation.

Patron-Client Ties and State Implementors

Effective state implementors—middle- and lower-level bureaucrats responsible for collecting taxes, monitoring projects, and enforcing rules—are crucial for "determining whose authority and rules will take hold in region after region, the state's or the strongmen's." Migdal postulates that "the politics of survival lessens backing and threats of sanctions from supervisors, thus making the implementor more attentive to possible career costs involving strongmen and peer officials. The result is a further weakening of the state's ability to make the rules governing people's behavior."[68] In the weakest states, there is almost no control of implementors; they will follow rules vastly different from those outlined in laws and policies. With poor supervision of middle- and lower-level bureaucrats, implementation is largely shaped by bargaining and deals between implementors, other state and party officials, and strongmen outside the state.[69] In clientelist states, bureaucrats who actually attempt to impose state rules must confront patron-client ties among state officials, local strongmen, and party officials, usually putting their career at great risk. These patron-client ties contribute to severe perversions in the use and distribution of state resources, and to state resources being used in ways that thwart state laws and regulations.[70]

As a result of poor supervision and close ties between state implementors and patron-client networks, patrons sometimes capture segments of clientelist states. These patrons place followers, friends, and family "in critical state posts to ensure allocation of resources according to their own rules, rather than the rules propounded in the official rhetoric, policy statements, and legislation generated in the capital city or those put forth by a strong implementor."[71] These patron-client ties, operating in the middle and lower levels of the military, bureaucracy, police, and courts, contribute to widespread violations of state laws and regulations. State implementors, such as customs officials, enforcement officers, concession monitors, and permit issuers, "look the other way" in exchange for cash, gifts, or career maintenance or advancement. Combating illegal or lucrative timber "mining" is particularly difficult because timber licenses, concessions, and profits have been a key, and in some cases, the main glue for modern patron-client ties in Southeast Asia. Weak enforcement is reinforced by attitudes held by the elite that place little value on natural resources. As a result, state rhetoric is generally misleading. Bureaucratic policies and political statements often oppose groups who overexploit resources. Yet in reality, some state agencies accommodate, assist, or even strengthen the practices that destroy natural resources.

Conclusion

In sum, I posit a model of a state that is battling patron-client networks for control over the rules of the game for the management and allocation of natural resources. In the clientelist states of Southeast Asia, state leaders are confronted with pervasive, unstable, informal, material-based patron-client ties throughout society. To survive in this fragmented society, leaders use patronage to construct large patron-client followings and coopt other powerful patrons. These vertical links contribute to stability by extending the influence of state leaders to outlying areas, and by cutting across classes and ideologies. Paradoxically, even though distributing patronage is a legitimate, even expected, part of building and maintaining power in Southeast Asia, it has disastrous consequences for state capacity. Extensive nonmerit appointments undermine state morale, lower state efficiency, contribute to a cynical view of state laws, and perhaps most important, weaken supervision of state implementors. Implementors become integrated into patron-client units, receiving money or career advancements in exchange for ignoring management, tax, or customs regulations. Poorly supervised and underpaid implementors are also more likely to accept straightforward bribes. In some cases, societal patrons manage to capture parts of the state, placing family, friends, and followers in strategic positions. This contributes to state assets being used in ways inimical to state goals. It also makes it relatively easy for these patrons to skirt, resist, and even ignore state policies. As a result, state resource management is dismal. Little chance exists of quickly improving resource management in clientelist states. Pervasive patron-client ties throughout society lead state leaders to undermine state capacity and supervision in order to survive and maintain stability. The alliances and agreements made between implementors and regional patrons and politicians then reinforce these patron-client networks. This creates a circle that leaves little hope of ever breaking the pattern of poor implementation.[72]

This modified patron-client model of resource management, by paying close attention to the nature of the state, the power of patrons at the state helm, and policy implementation, gains heuristic strength while maintaining the advantages of focusing on informal and personal exchange relations, traditional concepts of power and legitimacy, cooperation between vertically linked individuals at all levels of society, and fluid ad hoc groups. Looking through this lens in subsequent chapters reveals salient features of the timber industries in Indonesia, East Malaysia, and the Philippines including: a distribution of timber profits that mainly benefits the state political and business elite; unsustainable logging and ineffective forest management; formal policies and institutions weakened by informal practices and unstable "rules of the game"; feeble state enforcement of timber regulations; and logging concessions, licenses, and profits that link state leaders and implementors to timber-based patron-client networks.

3 Japan, Patron-Client Politics, and Timber Mismanagement in the Outer Islands of Indonesia

Indonesia has around half of the remaining tropical forests of Asia. These remarkable forests contain "more species of plants and birds than the entire African continent."[1] The bulk of Indonesia's valuable timber is on the outer islands of Kalimantan, Sumatra, Sulawesi, and New Guinea (Irian Jaya).[2] This resource is rapidly disappearing. Commercial logging is the most important factor driving deforestation,[3] estimated at over 1 million hectares per year.[4] Modern patron-client links among top politicians, military officers, bureaucrats, and timber operators drive destructive logging and undermine state capacity and willingness to manage the forests.[5] Ties at the pinnacle of the state distort policies and weaken supervision of middle- and lower-level state implementors. Many implementors join or form timber-based patron-client networks, ignoring timber regulations in exchange for money, gifts, or career advancement. Timber companies are able to ignore selective logging rules and reforestation duties, extract enormous amounts of illegal logs, evade corporate taxes and royalties, and secure generous state subsidies to process logs. Meanwhile, over the last thirty years, Japan has provided crucial financial support and incentives for destructive and illegal loggers and unsustainable timber exporters, first as the dominant log buyer (backed by strategic investments and aid), and now as the largest consumer of Indonesian plywood. Before proceeding to examine the impact of modern patron-client ties and Japan's ecological shadow on forest management, the next section outlines traditional Indonesian patron-client relations, explaining how these have evolved in the twentieth century, and now shape the New Order government under President Suharto.

Traditional and Modern Patron-Client Relations in Indonesia

Traditional Javanese patron-client relations are dyadic, vertical, personal, unequal, and reciprocal. Patrons tend to inherit clients rather than building these ties based on personal achievements. These ties involve more than simply "exchanging rewards for services" and do not "involve calculation of immediate personal interests by the follower."[6] Patrons are "expected to serve as provider, protector, educator, and source of values. . . . In turn, the follower is expected to reciprocate by volunteering his labor, his vote, and in some cases even his life although these obligations are seldom explicit either when incurred or called due."[7] Clients feel a strong sense of loyalty that transcends monetary debts and specific requests, and that can be passed down through generations. Patrons also feel a strong moral obligation to protect and support their clients. Finally, an "aura of absolutism" surrounds a traditional patron, which contributes to reflexive obedience and makes these relations fairly predictable and stable.[8]

Traditional patron-client ties still exist in Indonesia, particularly in rural areas. However, colonialism, the gradual dominance of market exchange, the growth of the state and its increasing control over economic development, internal upheavals (such as the fight for independence and the 1965 coup attempt), and migration from rural villages to large cities have shattered many traditional ties. In most instances, these have reconfigured to form modern patron-client links. Although both traditional and modern patron-client relations are known as *bapak-anak buah*, there are important distinctions. Karl Jackson documents the difference in patron-client ties among villagers, urbanites born in a village, and urbanites born in a city. He shows that as people migrate from villages, traditional patron-client relations dissolve. After relocating, new relations develop as people struggle to improve their living standard. These modern ties are rooted in traditional relations but are "more limited, instrumental, opportunistic, specialized, achievement-based, and focused on the recent present rather than the distant past."[9]

Compared to traditional relations, modern ties tend to have weaker feelings of loyalty and obligation, although there is still a "debt of moral obligation," or *hutang budi*, "extending beyond the purely monetary aspect of the debt." In modern relations, however, "the lengths to which the individual will go to pay back *hutang budi* are much more limited." For modern links, a patron's power is closely related to "his own resources, official position, or his hold over specialized knowledge," while "noble birth" or "good family," although still useful, are less important.[10]

As well, modern patron-client ties are far more likely to revolve around material exchanges. Clients tend to calculate the costs and benefits of their participation. If better opportunities arise, clients may well abandon their patron and join another patronage network. In some cases, clients attach themselves to more than one patron, making it easier to change allegiances as political tides shift. Patrons are also more willing to dispose of individual clients, particularly if the behavior of a client is undermining the power or prestige of the leader or the group as a whole. For this reason, modern ties last for shorter periods than traditional ties and are unlikely to transfer across generations. Unlike in traditional villages, shifting patron-client networks create an uncertain and unpredictable atmosphere. Patrons can never be assured of a loyal following and clients can never be confident of their patron's protection. This uncertainty is aggravated by the unwieldy size of many modern patron-client networks, by networks that extend beyond organizational or geographic boundaries, and by people who migrated to cities as adults and are not well integrated into patron-client units.[11]

Despite these contrasts, modern and traditional patron-client relations have important similarities. In both, links are vertical and asymmetrical. A patron fuses together a heterogeneous group of individuals with complementary abilities, divergent ideological beliefs, and different ethnic and social backgrounds. As Jackson notes, a "truly powerful patron is one who has the capacity to concentrate within his circle clients of varying intellectual, social, official, and financial resources, thus making this person the vital connecting link in the exchange pattern animating the circle."[12] A patron is clearly more powerful than any individual client, although successful patrons must conscientiously maintain their client base. Modern patron-client ties also remain essentially personal, informal, and noncontractual. Patrons supply clients with licenses, jobs, and political protection, or allow clients to ignore laws and regulations, in exchange for immediate or future gifts, money, loyalty, or support. Modern patrons are also expected to perform some traditional duties, including giving advice "on ideological, personal, religious, and mystical matters."[13]

Patron-Client Ties and the Indonesian State

The use of public office to reward clients has strong cultural and historical roots in Indonesia. State patronage was pervasive in the precolonial and colonial eras.[14] After independence in 1945 patronage expanded with the growth of the state—especially under Sukarno's Guided

Democracy (1959–1965). As G. McGuire and Bob Hering note, "all ruling groups in Indonesia's history" have dispensed patronage. "Indeed the ability to do so is considered an example of one's status and personal skill."[15] Traditional village values and roles in Java, where leaders function as community patrons, have had important implications for the behavior of state administrators. It has meant that "for the villager who rises to the level of district or subdistrict officer today, traditionally accepted behaviour and values suddenly become legally corrupt behaviour and values."[16] As a result, the legal definition and cultural understanding of "corruption" differ.[17]

Of course, not all political action and inaction in Indonesia can be explained by the impact of patron-client relations. Religion can be an important factor. Although 87 percent of the population is officially Muslim, the deep cleavage between orthodox (*santri*) and syncretistic (*abangan*) Muslims can have explosive implications. Sharp differences also exist within the orthodox Muslim community. The ethnic and regional composition of Indonesia is another significant factor that shapes political interaction.[18] In a population of around 200 million, there are more than 300 different ethnic groups and 250 languages spread across a plethora of islands. Sixty percent of the population lives on Java, which represents only 7 percent of the land. Yet the Javanese dominate top political, military, and bureaucratic positions,[19] while Indonesian Chinese, who comprise only 3 percent of the population, control much of the business world.[20] Certain cultural norms also shape political decisions. A respect for age and seniority, an emphasis on deference and self-control, and a desire for consensual decision making contribute to policies that reflect elite preferences. Elite attitudes also have important ramifications. Western-educated bureaucrats often have a decisive impact on the content of current policies, and are instrumental in developing the five-year plans (Repelita). These technocrats tend to support rapid economic growth at all costs. As a result, policies like conservation, reforestation, and environmental management are low priorities.[21]

Despite the obvious relevance of religion, ethnicity, language, regional diversity, culture, and attitudes for understanding Indonesian politics, focusing on patron-client relations reveals key features of the current Indonesian state. Patron-client relations permeate and tie together the political executive, the legislature, the military, the bureaucracy, the courts, and the business community. At the apex of politics, the battle for power is largely between "circles of high-ranking bureaucrats and military officers . . . held together by an elaborate system of personal ties and mutual obligations." To some extent these "circles" are reinforced by family connections, friendships, ethnic backgrounds, religious views, and ideological positions. But the crucial glue is "patron-client bonds."[22]

The New Order, established after Sukarno was ousted from power in the mid-1960s, is dominated by President Suharto (a former general), underpinned by the army, and steered by the bureaucracy.[23] The New Order government, which arose partially as a reaction to the turmoil of the 1950s and 1960s, has emphasized stability and national integration. President Suharto has gradually consolidated and centralized control, by eliminating Communist Party members, eradicating troublesome factions in the military, purging and streamlining the bureaucracy, placing strict controls on political parties, and sponsoring corporatist structures to organize social and economic groups. Suharto's control is reinforced by his authority to appoint cabinet members and regional governors, to proclaim laws, and to control the armed services. The People's Consultative Assembly (MPR), which under the 1945 constitution is the highest authority and elects the president and vice-president, and the legislative House of Representatives (DPR) provide some legitimacy but no substantive checks on executive and bureaucratic decisions.[24] The ruling Golkar party, under the firm grip of Suharto and the military, controls the national and regional assemblies.[25] The two main opposition political parties, the Partai Persatuan Pembangunan and the Partai Demokrasi Indonesia, do not pose serious challenges. The power of regional governments is limited by lack of revenues and close supervision from Jakarta.[26] In the early 1980s, many provinces received up to 90 percent of their revenue from central grants. Interest groups, the media, students, NGOs, and the general public also have little input or influence on policy formulation.[27] With firm control, in 1993, Suharto was easily elected for a sixth five-year presidential term.[28]

Despite Suharto's undeniable power, Indonesia is not a one-man state. Suharto needs the support of influential military generals and top bureaucrats. As Dwight King notes, "most observers would agree that Suharto's leadership style has been deliberate, predictable and, above all, consultative. Key policy decisions seem far more the product of a military-technocrat oligarchy than the discretion of a military dictator."[29] Although coercion has been indisputably important, Suharto has maintained loyalty in part through judicious distribution of patronage. He has built a powerful group of followers, including key political, military, business, bureaucratic, and regional leaders. This patron-client network is the nucleus of power and the bastion for elite stability.

Suharto's family is at the center of this network. His relatives—first his wife and half brother and now his six children and their affiliated companies—have received key government licenses, monopolistic contracts, and crucial access to the corridors of power, enabling them to build substantial fortunes.[30] Even state bank loans are often underpinned by personal connections, not by collateral or persuasive investment proposals.[31] Although President Suharto avoids any direct role in business, according to one foreign businessman: "You cannot get involved in an important deal any more if you don't bring in at least one of the children."[32] An academic claims: "At least 80 percent of major government projects go in some form to the President's children or friends."[33] Suharto has also used patronage to placate and integrate potential rivals. As Harold Crouch notes, after gaining control in the mid-1960s, "Suharto rewarded his key supporters handsomely; but he was careful not to antagonize unnecessarily those who had lost in the intergroup struggles: many losers were also compensated with appointments and opportunities."[34] As well, he has allowed key military and bureaucratic leaders to establish their own clientele, and has permitted pervasive patron-client exchange at the middle and lower levels of the state. By partially redistributing the benefits of rapid economic development and oil exports, these extensive patron-client networks have enhanced stability, created a powerful group with a vested interest in the status quo, and bolstered Suharto's legitimacy.[35]

To some extent, the legitimacy of Indonesian state leaders is not connected to obeying laws and procedures but to using their position to reward followers. As Jackson points out, "social injustice and corruption are felt only if a patron fails to redistribute his bounty among his clients or if the patron in adapting to market pressures abandons [his] diffuse responsibilities."[36] For this reason, Suharto's overt use of political power to enhance the fortunes of his clients, family, and friends has strengthened his grip rather than undermined his legitimacy.[37] This helps explain why Suharto is "undefensive about his position and the activities of his children" and why he "will easily move from a conversation about macroeconomic policy to one about a contract or a regulation affecting" one of his followers.[38] This also helps explain why Suharto has not become directly involved in business operations and has avoided lavish displays of personal wealth. As was evident with Sukarno, this kind of behavior is seen as irresponsible and "corrupt" and contributes to a loss of legitimacy in the eyes of the ruling elite.

Chinese Business Clients

Links between powerful state patrons (mainly Javanese) and Indonesian Chinese business clients (*cukongs*) are a dominant feature of the New Order.[39] Compared to ties between Javanese, these connections are less likely to have strong bonds of loyalty and honor and more likely to be held together by mutual need and a mutual desire to make money. Political and military patrons supply credit, contracts, licenses, access, and protection while Chinese clients provide vital expertise and capital to operate a business.[40] Chinese clients also provide crucial access to markets and funds through Chinese contacts in Singapore and Hong Kong. Even though both sides clearly benefit, this relationship is not equal. Indonesian Chinese are in a subordinate position and are vulnerable to political shifts and societal backlash. As Ernst Utrecht explains, "the *cukong* is a so-called back-door broker, because often strong anti-Chinese sentiments within society have prevented even Jakarta generals receiving Chinese business associates through the front-door of office or home."[41] Although most Indonesian Chinese have been in Indonesia for generations, speak *bahasa* Indonesia, and even have Indonesian sounding names, strong prejudice persists against this group. Despite the stability of the New Order, signs of hostility and racism are clear, especially against the increasingly visible and prosperous Chinese middle class.[42] As a result of pervasive racism, according to Go Gien Tjwan, "today's Indonesian society is not attractive enough for many *Peranakan* Chinese [people of Chinese ancestry born in Indonesia] to wholeheartedly [participate] in it."[43] The subordinate status and vulnerability of Indonesian Chinese business leaders is manifested in most wealthy Chinese channeling profits outside the country, not only to avoid royalties and taxes but also for personal security.

Since Suharto consolidated and centralized control, patron-client networks at the top of the state have been fairly stable. But a sense of uncertainty remains. Chinese business clients are wary of sudden racial backlashes. The fall of Sukarno and the purge of many of his followers is also an important reminder of the tenuous nature of these ties. After Suharto steps down or dies in office, patron-client networks connected to his reign may well be pushed aside or eliminated. For members of patron-client groups grazing on state coffers, especially Chinese clients, this creates a continual sense of unease despite the stability of the New Order.

Military

The military is the cornerstone of the New Order. The military establishment maintains that it should have a central political role, and military officers have held key political, bureaucratic, and corporate posts.[44] Yet the military has not dominated political decisions. Suharto has been careful to appease and coopt powerful military generals. As well, to hinder alternative power centers from coalescing in the military, he has reorganized the armed services, rotated regional commanders, and encouraged early retirement. As Donald Emmerson notes, "the price of outspoken independence, several generals have discovered, is an ambassadorship."[45] Suharto has also prevented the emergence of powerful military successors. Crouch argues that in the 1980s, "like the traditional Javanese sultans who kept rival groups of courtiers in balance, Suharto made sure that no single group of officers gained a position from which they could challenge his rule and that no single, clear-cut candidate for the succession emerged."[46] As a result of this prudent management of the military, the New Order government "has become the master rather than the servant of the military establishment."[47]

Military links to local business grew in the early 1950s as civilian cabinets reduced the military budget. According to Ruth McVey, as the army's income fell, "regional commanders began to make deals with local business interests which enabled them to support their troops and preserve the loyalties of their subordinates. This gave them a financial base independent of the center."[48] Army interference and participation in business continued to increase during the chaotic years of Sukarno's Guided Democracy (1959–65). By the time Suharto and the army secured power in the mid-1960s, the weak economy and fragmented administration convinced the new government that "it had little prospect of raising adequate funds for the armed forces through taxation."[49] To maintain a stable and loyal military, and to compensate for budget and personnel cutbacks, the New Order government has allowed, even encouraged, the old practices of military officers raising revenue through business connections and patron-client exchange.[50] Patron-client relations within the military also have important consequences. The army hierarchy is split between managers who occupy key administrative posts or operate trading companies and field officers who are responsible for security. These managers often supply money to field officers for protection, contributing to a need for managers to become involved in "illegal" activities.[51]

Bureaucracy

Suharto has purged and pared down the bureaucracy, increased salaries, and made administrators more active. To increase loyalty and control, he has placed military officers in strategic positions.[52] By the mid-1980s, about 60 percent of senior bureaucrats in Jakarta had military backgrounds.[53] To undermine competing political allegiances, Suharto used to require bureaucrats to join Golkar. Despite Suharto's moves to "backbone" the bureaucracy with loyal military officers and curtail political activities, civilian bureaucrats have still had significant influence. Jackson claims that "the ideas of the civilian technocrats have probably had more impact on policy in Indonesia than in almost any other country in the Third World."[54]

At all levels, the bureaucracy is perforated by patron-client ties.[55] At the top, informal networks connect senior bureaucrats to powerful military officers, prominent politicians, and wealthy business leaders. At the middle and lower levels, patron-client networks also operate within departments, between different departments, and between departmental officials and powerful political, military, and business leaders. As a result, a bureaucrat's power and status are often not related to his or her position, but to connections. According to McVey, "a powerful patron will have clients in several ministries or armed units; his true strength as an official will depend on his personal connections and the access his position provides to wealth." For this reason, successful officials use "the economic possibilities of [their] position to the full."[56]

Although the principal goal of intrabureaucratic patron-client clusters and networks is to preserve or enhance power and wealth, these groups also have organizational and policy aims. Prevalent patron-client ties do not always prevent organizational effectiveness. However, particularly when resources are scarce, personal interests tend to override organizational objectives—the financial collapse of the national oil company Pertamina and the failure of the agency responsible for rice stabilization (Badan Urusan Logistik, Bulog) are two well-known cases from the 1970s. In both instances, "the directors of the agencies and the long chains of clients extending downward from the directors' closest confidants . . . prospered while the organizational objectives . . . faltered."[57] The dominance of particularistic, rent-seeking aims of patron-client groups over organizational objectives also contributed to the fall of Sukarno. According to Jackson, "in almost all organizations at the close of Guided Democracy there were no slack resources whatever, and the satisfaction of personal or group objectives precluded the accomplishment of almost all organizational ends."[58] Although Pertamina and Bulog's management of rice in the 1970s are exceptions, since the late 1960s, foreign investment and loans, massive exports of raw materials (especially oil), and manageable rates of inflation have provided the "slack that has allowed less than optimally efficient organizations to perform effectively."[59] Yet the New Order bureaucracy is clearly more effective in some areas than in others. As we will see later, in the case of timber management, the bureaucracy does not adequately monitor and enforce regulations.

Japan and Patron-Client Relations

Although Japanese corporate executives sometimes bribe state officials, this is not in the context of long-term patron-client exchange relations.[60] According to Utrecht, Japanese investors prefer to use Chinese brokers in Hong Kong and Singapore to avoid incredibly "corrupt" Indonesian (especially non-Chinese) businessmen.[61] Nevertheless, Japanese money has had a significant impact on patron-client ties. Since the late 1960s, aid, investment, and resource purchases have supplied key funds to fuel ubiquitous patron-client exchanges. According to a 1980 study, "Japanese capital promotes bribery and corruption in Indonesia and encourages the formation of a comprador bourgeoisie that is in collusion with high government officials, the military and overseas Chinese."[62]

Societal Structure and Policy Implementation

Modern and traditional patron-client ties in Indonesia disperse power; society is not a pyramid where all power flows to a peak. Instead of a single pyramid, separate hierarchies are present in regions, provinces, and villages. Even at the "bottom" there are "complex pecking orders" and "a little power goes a long way."[63] Society can be conceived in Migdal's terms as a web of patron-client links or in Jackson's terms as "an extremely complex molecule in which the different atoms have their separate nuclei and their circling electrons, but the bonds between the atoms can often be very weak and, indeed, many atoms have no bonds between them at all."[64] This societal structure has important implications for policy implementation. Whereas policy development is dominated by a small elite, subsequent rules must be filtered through multiple layers of patron-client clusters and networks. As policies are implemented, and work their way from the insulated departments in Jakarta to the remote outer islands, state patrons make particularistic concessions to their clients. If these modifications were isolated, they would have little overall impact. But taken as a whole they debilitate state capacity, and the actual effect of policies often bears little resemblance to the original content outlined in Jakarta.[65]

In sum, decisions and policies in the New Order are dominated by the state—in particular, President Suharto, the military, and the bureaucracy. Parliament, political parties, interest groups, the media, students, and academics are peripheral. Business has more influence, although this is constrained by pervasive anti-Chinese sentiments.[66] Yet, even though the state excludes societal input into policy formulation, extensive patron-client ties among politicians, military officers, bureaucrats, business executives, regional officials, and community leaders have a profound impact on the implementation of policies. For the management of timber, these ties drive destructive practices and undermine state capacity and willingness to implement policies.

Patron-Client Politics and Timber Management in Indonesia

Background

Under the 1945 constitution, all primary forests in Indonesia are owned by the state. The 1967 Basic Forestry Law is the foundation for forestry regulations. The total land area of Indonesia is about 190 million hectares. Officially, Indonesia has 143 million hectares of forests, mainly on the outer islands.[67] Conservation areas, such as national parks and wildlife reserves, cover 19 million hectares. Another 30 million hectares are set aside as protection forest, mostly for soil and water conservation. A further 30 million hectares are conversion forest, areas designated for conversion to agriculture, settlements, and plantations, often after logging. The remaining 64 million hectares are production forest, accounting for about 60 percent of legal commercial timber in Southeast Asia.[68] Production areas are supposed to be managed sustainably, mostly by selective cutting in primary and secondary forests. Numerous observers claim that official forestry statistics are inaccurate or dispute the definition of "forest cover." A 1990 fine-resolution mapping project estimated total forest cover at 108 million hectares. A 1990 World Bank study estimated total forest area at 100 million hectares.[69] The radical Indonesian NGO group SKEPHI (Network for Forest Conservation) is even more pessimistic, claiming that only 90 million hectares of forest remain.[70] Even a government economist at the National Planning Agency estimated that Indonesia's actual production forest area is only 32 million hectares, half the official figure.[71]

Numerous bureaucratic departments shape the environmental management of timber concessions. The Ministry of Forestry—with a staff of fifty thousand—is responsible for collecting taxes and royalties, setting annual allowable harvests, enforcing cutting and silvicultural guidelines, and monitoring timber regulations.[72] The Ministry of Industry promotes the economic development of forest resources. This ministry has been a key force behind the development of wood processing. In 1978, the government formed the State Ministry for Development Supervision and Environment, later renamed the State Ministry for Population and the Environment, and now called the State Ministry for the Environment. This ministry coordinates environmental management across departments, advises departments on environmental issues, evaluates the environmental impact of logging proposals, and monitors reforestation sites. Other departments and ministries also influence forest management, including Finance, Trade, Agriculture, Transmigration, Public Works, and Energy and Mines.[73]

Politicians, Patronage, and Chinese Timber Clients

Approximately 500 concessionaires, under the control of about fifty conglomerates, have licences to log more than 60 million hectares of production forest. Concession holders log around 800 thousand hectares a year, more than the rest of Southeast Asia combined.[74] Already by mid-1990, 25 million hectares had been logged.[75] About two-thirds of logging conglomerates are controlled by Chinese Indonesians. Non-Chinese timber businesses are limited mainly to local companies. Chinese companies, however, must rely on politicians for concessions and licenses, on military officers for protection, and on bureaucrats for "flexible" interpretation of management rules. Among Indonesian-Chinese timber leaders, Bob Hasan is the most powerful figure.[76] He is the head of four associations connected to forest management, including Apkindo, the Wood Panel Association that controls the plywood industry. One forestry official aptly declared: "The forestry department cooperates with Apkindo, but Apkindo really makes policy."[77] Hasan's power stems from his direct link to Suharto.[78] Hasan and President Suharto have had close ties since the late 1950s. According to one insider, Hasan, who has the rights to log

2 million hectares, is the de facto Minister of Forestry: the formal Minister of Forestry or the State Minister for the Environment can challenge him only to a limited degree.[79]

Asia's largest timber operator is Prajogo Pangestu, a second-generation Indonesian Chinese from Kalimantan. His main company is P. T. Barito Pacific Timber.[80] Like Hasan, Prajogo has close, personal ties to Suharto.[81] Prajogo's timber concessions cover 5.5 million hectares—the size of Switzerland—and he employs more than 50 thousand people. Prajogo is the world's largest exporter of tropical plywood, with annual sales around U.S.$600 million. The total value of Prajogo's forest land, logging infrastructure, and plywood mills is U.S.$5–6 billion. His Barito Pacific Group of companies is also the largest borrower of state funds, with more than U.S.$1 billion in loans. In 1992, he received "an unusually attractive . . . debt rescheduling that stretched repayment periods on about U.S.$460 million in timber industry borrowings into the next century."[82] He has recently established huge state-subsidized softwood plantations to supply a U.S.$1 billion pulp and paper mill in Sumatra. His partner is Suharto's eldest child, Siti Hardijanti Rukmana (known as Tutut). Not surprisingly, Prajogo has made substantial "donations" to charities and social programs connected to Suharto's family. Prajogo has also reportedly helped rescue poor investments linked to Suharto and the military.[83] Prajogo and his wife also conscientiously "nurture the relationship [with Suharto] with small gestures, such as gifts of home-cooked treats from Mrs. Prajogo's home province of North Sulawesi."[84]

Military Leaders and Timber

In 1967, Suharto distributed timber concessions to reward loyal generals, appease potential military dissidents, and supplement the military budget. In 1978, the Department of Defense (Hankam) business group P. T. Tri Usaha Bhakti, along with regional military commands, controlled at least fourteen timber companies.[85] Today the military is still heavily involved in logging. For example, in East Kalimantan, the International Timber Corporation of Indonesia (ITCI) operates a 600 thousand hectare concession, the largest in Indonesia. As well, by the year 2000, ITCI plans to develop 140 thousand hectares of timber plantations. Fifty-one percent of this company is controlled by the armed forces.[86] Of the remaining shares, P. T. Bimantara Citra—a conglomerate chaired by Suharto's second son, Bambang Trihatmodjo—holds 34 percent while Hasan owns 15 percent. According to Hasan, the military uses its profits to augment its official budget and build houses for soldiers.[87] P. T. Yamaker, which logs concessions in East Kalimantan near the border with East Malaysia, is another timber company linked to the army. This is deemed necessary for security. Not surprisingly, with strong military protection, little bureaucratic supervision of logging occurs in these remote areas. According to one insider, convoys of trucks smuggle illegal logs to Sabah.[88]

Patron-client ties between state leaders and timber operators weaken state supervision of bureaucratic implementors and distort state management policies. In the last few years, state leaders have declared a crackdown on illegal loggers and tax evaders. Despite the rhetoric, however, the state has had minimal impact on corporate practices.[89] Instead, top state patrons and powerful business clients continue to reap huge profits while middle-level state implementors continue to ignore state rules in exchange for bribes, gifts, and career stability. As we will see in the next section, the result is rampant illegal logging, timber smuggling, tax and royalty evasion, flagrant violations of logging rules, and avoidance of reforestation duties. As well, these patron-client ties have contributed to inappropriate and ineffective policies for plywood processing, foreign investment, conservation, and pulp and paper plantations.

Forestry Policies and Patron-Client Politics

Logging Rules and Concession Distribution

Until the late 1980s, Indonesian logging was regulated by the selective cutting system (TPI). This system divided concessions into thirty-five areas which were then logged annually on a thirty-five-year cycle. Loggers were only allowed to cut trees with a diameter of fifty centimeters or more at breast height. As well, if less than twenty-five trees with a diameter between twenty-five and forty-nine centimeters remained in a logged hectare, companies had to do enrichment planting.[90] In 1989, the government established a new cutting policy called the Indonesian selective cutting and replanting system (TPTI). Logging guidelines are essentially the same, although loggers are now required to replant commercial species. After several amendments, concessionaires are also required to submit annual harvest plans, and five-year and thirty-five-year management plans.[91] This new policy, however, has made little difference. According to the NGO WALHI (Forum for the Environment) and the Indonesian Legal Aid Foundation, "it wasn't application of a faulty management system, but rather the failure to apply any management system which resulted in so much degradation. Although improving management policies is useful, in reality the key to better forest management is better implementation and tighter enforcement."[92] There are certainly problems with timber management rules. For example, although companies are allowed to log areas on a thirty-five-year cycle, licenses are only granted for twenty years, with no guarantee of renewal. This obviously makes little sense.[93] But in the context of Indonesian politics this discrepancy is not critical. Even if concession licenses were granted for one hundred years, it would make little difference because it is clear to loggers—especially ethnic Chinese—that a shift in political or military power could change the rules overnight.

Historical allocation of timber concessions contributes to current management problems. In 1970, to quash provincial claims to timber areas that Suharto had awarded as "presents" to loyal military and political clients, the authority to distribute concessions was centralized under the Directorate-General of Forestry. As a result, small-scale loggers without Jakartan ties lost their concessions; many resorted to illegal logging. Jakarta-based concessionaires often had little forestry knowledge or capital, and turned to multinational corporations and Indonesian Chinese companies to handle logging operations.[94] This split between control of concessions and management of timber operations continues today, reducing accountability and transparency. According to Mariko Urano, "the increase in these absentee concessionaires has accelerated the rate of forest degradation."[95]

In July 1994, Forestry Minister Djamaludin Suryohadikusumo announced that annual timber harvests would be reduced to 22.5 million cubic meters by the year 1999.[96] But the state is unlikely to reach this target as informal connections between state implementors and corporate elite debilitate state enforcement and supervision of logging rules. As one observer notes, "in Indonesia, forestry law and management has been predicated on the efficacy of a strong State. The Indonesian government, however, has not been able to police its vast forest estate nor has it been capable of adequately enforcing its decrees."[97] Many forestry officers are reported to ignore logging violations in exchange for material rewards.[98] There are strong monetary incentives for enforcement staff to ignore logging violations. Forestry guards receive a meager salary to monitor an average area of 20 thousand hectares; it is easy for timber operators to supplement their wages.[99] Poor state enforcement is further hampered by technocratic attitudes that undervalue the forests, limited institutional resources, and poor training. Vast concessions—an average one is around 100 thousand hectares, although some are as large as 600 thousand hectares—in isolated regions with poor roads further impede monitors. As a result, there is little supervision of the few forestry officials in these areas; selective logging guidelines are flagrantly violated and operations are incredibly destructive.[100] Even the Ministry of Forestry estimates that in the 1970s and 1980s only 3.8 percent of loggers followed selective cutting guidelines.[101] A representative at SKEPHI is even more critical: "None of Indonesia's logging companies obey the rules."[102] A Western forestry adviser describes vividly timber management techniques in East Kalimantan: "I've seen people using a bulldozer to get a pack of cigarettes."[103]

As a result of these brazen violations of management rules, studies of East Kalimantan show that as many as half of the remaining trees in logged areas have been destroyed.[104] One report estimates that around 23 million hectares of Indonesia's forests have been severely degraded by loggers.[105] A 1991 World Bank study estimated that poor logging practices destroy 200 thousand hectares of productive forest every year in Indonesia. Other experts claim logging eliminates 300 thousand hectares of primary forests a year.[106] Besides direct links to forest degradation, loggers also contribute indirectly to deforestation. Logging roads and poor protection of concession areas after harvesting allow slash-and-burn farmers easy access. As well, heavily logged areas are susceptible to devastating forest fires. In 1983, around 3 million hectares of tropical forest burned in Kalimantan, an area as large as Holland.[107] In late 1994, raging fires in Sumatra and on the island of Borneo disrupted airline flights and polluted the air for thousands of square kilometers.[108]

With almost no state control over timber operators, illegal logging is rampant.[109] Illegal logging is connected to high-ranking political and military leaders, police, regional administrators, customs agents, and forestry staff.[110] The ITTO estimates that average log production from 1990 to 1995 was just over 36 million cubic meters.[111] Yet according to NGO experts, extensive illegal logging has pushed annual log production to around 44 million cubic meters, well above sustainable yields.[112] Companies use various techniques to evade log production quotas. Loggers overharvest their concessions and cut trees in national parks and conservation areas.

Smuggling rings involving top military, political, and business leaders, as well as local forestry officials, security officers, and foreign business executives (particularly Malaysians), transport many of these logs outside the country.[113] There are strong signs that Japanese companies are purchasing illegal logs from Kalimantan and moving them through East Malaysia.[114] In 1992, timber smuggling reportedly cost Indonesia Rp (rupiah) 135 billion.[115] Domestic processors, who face a chronic shortage of supply, are also deeply involved in illegal logging.[116] This is hardly surprising given that annual capacity of plywood plants and sawmills is about 60 million cubic meters, about twice as high as the Forestry Department's estimate of sustainable production from Indonesia's 64 million hectares of production forest.[117] As a result, processors are constantly scrambling for more logs. The *Jakarta Post* reported in late 1995 that "dozens of plywood companies were . . . on the brink of bankruptcy due to difficulties in obtaining raw materials."[118] According to a concession director, one way concessionaires increase supply is by hiring local people to cut logs illegally. These logs are reported "stolen" and then bought back to feed the company's processing mill.[119] This situation is likely to worsen. In April 1994, the government announced that over the next five years (five-year development plan for 1 April 1994–1 April 1999), Indonesia would reduce annual log production from natural forests to 22.5 million cubic meters.[120]

License Fees, Royalty Policies, and Timber Taxes

Plywood exports are not taxed.[121] Instead, concession holders must pay uniform ad valorem royalties on the volume of logs extracted. This aggravates logging mismanagement because loggers face few penalties for damaging timber stocks and have no incentives to cut defective or low-grade timber. Instead, loggers concentrate on removing the largest and most valuable species, often creating irreparable ecological harm.[122]

Poorly designed and insufficient license fees, royalties, and export taxes have contributed to Indonesia capturing a low percentage of timber rents. According to Repetto, from 1979 to 1982, "only $1.6 billion of a potential aggregate rent of $4.4 billion" was collected by the government—the remainder became private profit.[123] In 1992, the World Bank estimated that the Indonesian government collected only 30 percent of the economic rent from logging, compared with 85 percent for petroleum.[124] Even more alarming, a study by WALHI found that the government captured a mere 8 percent of timber rents in 1989. In 1990, after an increase in reforestation fees and timber taxes, WALHI calculated that the government still captured only 17 percent of timber rents. According to a WALHI representative, in 1993, the government likely captured around 15 percent of timber rents.[125]

Low government rent collection has important implications. To maximize profits before rules suddenly change, loggers quickly and recklessly extract logs while ignoring silvicultural treatments, reforestation, and sustainable management. According to one study, "when rent capture is low, it allows windfall profits to the concessionaires and/or their logging contractors. Inevitably, windfalls are perceived as short-term gains, and the beneficiaries will maximize them, as long as they last."[126] Low rent capture also creates a de facto subsidy that supports inefficient wood processors. As well, it allows exporters to sell high-grade timber at exceptionally low prices. The state needs to collect economic rents because private companies cannot be relied on to plow profits back into forest regeneration. Because reforestation and sustainable management involve long-term returns and high financial risks, and require political stability, corporations have a strong inclination to invest timber profits into other ventures, especially real estate which does not involve production, reinvestment, government licenses, or concessions.[127]

Even though low Indonesian forest charges allow companies to make substantial legal profits, loggers routinely forge export documents, falsify harvest yields, illegally log inside and outside concessions, and ignore reforestation fees. According to one corporation, nineteen out of twenty-one timber companies in South Sumatra manipulate their export documents to evade taxes.[128] Companies also elude royalties and distort figures on volume extracted by reusing timber transportation documents, sometimes as many as five times.[129]

Foreign Investment Policies

Prior to the mid-1960s, only limited logging took place on the outer islands. After 1967, government incentives under the new Foreign Capital Investment Law opened a door to large Northern and smaller Southern MNCs, triggering a logging boom in the primary forests.[130] In the 1970s, major foreign investors in the Indonesian timber sector were from the Philippines, Hong Kong, Malaysia, the United States, South Korea, and Japan. Before 1980, Southern firms accounted for two-thirds of foreign investment in the Indonesian timber sector, although many of these companies used equipment and techniques absorbed from earlier contact with Northern companies. From 1978 to 1981 Japanese investment expanded. But even in 1981 Southern firms still comprised over half of foreign timber investment.[131] During the 1970s, foreign timber technology and management advice accelerated the rate of extraction.[132] By 1979, 89 percent of production forest was divided into concessions. In 1980, the volume of logs extracted was five times greater than in 1968.[133] Multinational corporations made enormous profits by paying little for timber rights, "mining" concessions of the most valuable trees, ignoring reforestation, refusing to invest profits in processing or rehabilitation, and avoiding taxes and royalties through transfer pricing.[134] Many of these giant logging operations were in Kalimantan. By 1971, 65 percent of timber produced came from Kalimantan; 75 percent was exported. By 1974, around 11 million hectares of Kalimantan had been carved into timber concessions.[135]

During the 1960s and 1970s, multinational timber profits and log exports were lightly taxed. From 1967 until major tax reforms in 1983, foreign timber investors received income tax holidays for four to six years—which in practice sometimes exempted firms from paying any income tax.[136] As well, until 1978 log export taxes were only 10 percent of export value, compared to around 20 percent in Sabah.[137] As a result, companies made huge profits, nearly doubling after-tax investment returns. Despite increases in foreign exchange earnings from timber, in the early 1970s, the Indonesian government began to restrict foreign investment. The government was angry over low rates of reforestation, "unfair" and uncooperative foreign firms, evasion of timber taxes, and, most important, the reluctance of MNCs to invest in processing. In 1975, the government forbade further foreign ownership or joint ventures in logging, and allowed only equity shares in timber processing.[138]

Processing Policies

The first five-year plan, Repelita I (1969/70–1973/74), emphasized log exports and increasing foreign exchange earnings. During Repelita II (1974/75–1978/79), the central government pushed concessionaires to build processing plants. Beginning in 1977, the government collected a mandatory deposit on log exports to finance construction of processing plants. To encourage more processing, the Indonesian government doubled log export taxes in 1978.[139] Foreign firms that refused to participate in processing had the size of their concessions reduced. At the end of the 1970s, MNCs began to withdraw in anticipation of even greater government regulations and restrictions. Before leaving, however, many companies mined their concessions. Partially as a result, in 1978 log exports peaked at 19.2 million cubic meters.[140]

From 1980 to 1985, the government implemented a ban on log exports.[141] The World Bank and all major industrialized countries—including Japan and the United States—opposed this decision, based primarily on free-market arguments. Indonesia ignored this pressure, concluding it was essential to control the market and develop a timber processing industry. Three key reasons were given for this decision: first, to add value and diversify the economy away from a heavy emphasis on oil exports (Indonesian planners believed this would not occur in a free market); second, to create jobs; and third, to provide incentives for long-term forestry investments.[142] Even though the government had "rational" reasons for imposing a ban, state capacity to implement this policy was greatly increased by close cooperation and support from powerful domestic business leaders who wanted to concentrate and consolidate control. Hasan has played a crucial role in forming the state-business alliance that has strictly imposed this ban. Part of the reason the government has been able to enforce a ban on log exports is that it has increased, rather than undermined, financial opportunities for the most powerful timber companies. On the other hand, the Indonesian state has been unwilling and unable to control overexploitation and environmental mismanagement. Environmental concerns, as a low-profile, low-priority issue aligned against strong patron-client networks and business interests do not create the internal support necessary to generate strong state action.

Indonesia's plywood processors draw all their logs from natural forests.[143] With government support, Indonesia's plywood industry grew quickly—from 29 plywood mills in 1980 to 111 mills in 1988, with a tenfold rise in production from 1979 to 1988.[144] By the early 1990s, there were over 130 plywood mills and Indonesia controlled about 80 percent of world trade in tropical plywood, although this dropped to below 65 percent in 1995, mostly as a result of greater Malaysian plywood exports.[145] From 1991 to 1995, Indonesia exported on average more than 9 million cubic meters of plywood.[146] Indonesia's plywood export strategy has been simple: flood the market with cheap plywood and destroy competitors; once this is accomplished, gradually raise prices and government taxes. In some ways, this strategy has been successful.[147] Although the ban led to a temporary loss in foreign exchange earnings, by 1988, using equipment supplied by Taiwan, South Korea, and Japan,

Indonesia had regained its foreign exchange earnings. With control over the world market in tropical plywood, Indonesia can potentially be a "price leader."[148] But despite these apparent achievements, there have been major economic and environmental drawbacks to building a processing industry.

Dated technology, protective state policies, and the log export ban have contributed to large numbers of inefficient processing mills.[149] Even though many operate far below capacity—some as low as 30 percent—these mills waste valuable wood, putting even more pressure on forest resources.[150] The log export ban and powerful domestic processors have also contributed to low domestic log prices. For example, while the price of Sabah's Meranti log exports averaged about U.S.$160 per cubic meter from 1986 to 1993, and exceeded U.S.$300 per cubic meter in 1993, "equivalent logs in Indonesia averaged about U.S.$90 per cubic meter in 1993—maybe less, since most plywood operations are affiliated with concessions, and thus obtain logs at costs."[151] Besides fostering inefficiency and overcapacity, the ban on log exports and state subsidies for processing—including labor, electricity, and log costs—have contributed to enormous state revenue losses. One study calculated that as a result of the phased log export ban, between 1981 and 1986 the government lost U.S.$1.9–$3.1 billion in export revenues.[152] A World Bank study estimates that by eliminating export restrictions and improving rent collection, the Indonesian government could collect another U.S.$2 billion in forestry fees every year. According to this report, the export ban has depressed Indonesian log prices to around half the world level. This has contributed to "over-cutting and over-investment in processing capacity."[153]

Besides financial losses, generous processing incentives have added to environmental problems. In 1961, log production was only 3.9 million cubic meters. Pushed by foreign investment and technology, this climbed dramatically in the late 1960s and 1970s, reaching 26.6 million cubic meters in 1978. Between 1981 and 1985 as the log export ban was gradually imposed, log production dropped, averaging 24.3 million cubic meters.[154] Indonesian government and business leaders sometimes point to this decrease in logging rates as proof of the environmental benefits of the ban. But this was a temporary respite. By 1987, log production was even higher, estimated at 31.2 million cubic meters. By 1989, it had climbed to 36.7 million cubic meters. Today, driven by strong demand from the plywood industry, producers are putting even more pressure on the forests than at the height of log exports in the 1970s.[155] From 1991 to 1995, Indonesia produced on average more than 10 million cubic meters of plywood per year.[156] From 1996 to 1998, Indonesia plans to export about 10 million cubic meters of plywood per year, pushing production even higher.[157] The government estimates that annual log production is now around 30 million cubic meters.[158] The ITTO calculates that log production was about 35 million cubic meters in 1994. A World Bank report recently estimated that log production was over 40 million cubic meters.[159] According to NGO experts, Indonesian log production is more likely around 44 million cubic meters.[160] All of these figures are well above estimates of annual sustainable production by the Food and Agriculture Organization (FAO) (25 million cubic meters) and a study by the World Bank (22 million cubic meters).[161] According to economist Rizal Ramli, at the current rate of logging, Indonesia will deplete its natural forests in about thirty years.[162]

Many wood processors operate logging concessions. This is supposed to provide strong incentives for sustainable management because processors need steady future supplies. According to Hasan, "when you log, you don't care if there are any trees left at the end. But if you invested in a factory, then you must be sure of a supply of raw material."[163] In theory, Hasan may be right. But in practice, to maximize immediate profits processors mine their concessions and use illegal logs to feed their mills. Furthermore, allowing processors to own concessions distorts free-market signals which would raise the price of logs as plywood prices increase. Partially as a result, log prices are far too low to support sustainable management.[164]

Conservation, Reforestation, and Timber Plantations

An important distinction—often blurred by government policies and statistics—should be made between reforestation that regenerates natural rain forests or replants vital watersheds, and reforestation that builds huge, fast-growing, single-species timber plantations. Most reforestation in Indonesia—and throughout Southeast Asia—focuses on single-species plantations. Although these plantations can create employment, squeeze profits from degraded land, provide valuable timber stocks for pulp and paper producers, and perhaps even alleviate pressure to extract logs from natural forests, they cannot replace primary dipterocarp forests. Plantations cannot restore the biodiversity, environmental benefits, or economic rewards of old-growth forests. Most plantation logs are also not an adequate substitute to make plywood.

Reforestation—especially to protect watersheds and revive natural forests—has a poor record in Indonesia. Even according to official figures, Indonesia only replanted 1.35 million hectares between 1969 and 1989.[165] To ensure that companies replant, the government collects a nonrefundable fee of U.S.$22 per cubic meter of logs extracted.[166] This is placed in a reforestation fund. Companies are also supposed to allocate 1–5 percent of their profits for economic development of communities near the concession site.[167] Companies, however, frequently ignore reforestation fees. WALHI and the Legal Aid Foundation estimate that the government only collected 30 percent of these fees in the 1980s.[168] The small amount the government did collect was often squandered. In 1989, Forestry Minister Hasjrul Harahap admitted that out of Rp 600 billion collected, a mere Rp 15 million had actually gone to reforestation.[169] Today, with higher reforestation fees, the fund is larger, but it is mostly being used to build timber plantations, not to regenerate logged areas.

There are now 1.8 million hectares of plantations, mostly teak estates on Java. By the year 2000, the government plans to establish a total of 6.2 million hectares of timber estates.[170] This target may well be exceeded. By 1991, the government had already accepted applications for 12.5 million hectares of plantations.[171] Many environmentalists argue that these timber plantations are contributing to, rather than alleviating, forestry mismanagement. Certainly, serious problems have arisen. For example, the government only allows clear-cutting for plantations in nonproductive areas. But according to one report, "companies are not interested in barren land, when they can maximise profits by logging natural forests and then replant them with timber estates."[172] A concession holder claims that logging companies routinely evade the rules for establishing plantations by encouraging locals to degrade productive forest areas. These companies then claim that locals are destroying the forest, and it is therefore necessary to develop a plantation to protect the area and make it productive.[173]

Plantations and the Pulp and Paper Industry

Like the previous minister of forestry, Djamaludin is committed to developing huge plantations for pulp and paper. The government promotes pulp and paper plantations as an environmental and economic solution to depleting timber reserves. In 1991, Indonesia produced 1.1 million tons of pulp and 1.7 million tons of paper. Compared to other producers, Indonesia's output is still low. But with government support,

Indonesia plans to be one of the world's top ten pulp and paper producers by the year 2000.[174] Plans are also in the works to build or expand more than fifty pulp and paper mills by 2010. These mills will be supplied by plantations that will cover 10 percent of total land area.[175] The government is hoping foreign investment and aid will support these huge plantations.[176] Since private companies are wary of the risks, the expense, and the long-term commitment, the government, using the reforestation fund, generally takes 49 percent equity and provides soft loans.[177]

Many of the new pulp and paper mills are connected to military and political elites, particularly Suharto's patron-client network. Five of Indonesia's largest conglomerates—Sinar Mas, Raja Garuda Mas, Astra, Barito Pacific, and the Kalimanis Group—are already involved in pulp and paper operations.[178] The Sinar Mas Group, with annual revenues of U.S.$1.2–1.3 billion, has close links to the children and followers of Suharto. This conglomerate, under the control of the Chinese Indonesian Eka Tjipta Widjaja, is the largest producer of pulp and paper and a key force pushing further development. Prajogo's Barito Group is also deeply involved in pulp and paper operations. Prajogo, Suharto's daughter, Tutut, and the state forestry company P. T. Inhutani II are now developing a new pulp and paper mill in South Sumatra called P. T. Tanjung Enim Pulp & Kertas. The reforestation fund is providing generous subsidies. Eventually, around U.S.$2.66 billion will be invested in this project. This mill is expected to produce 1 million tons of pulp and 500,000 tons of paper. To maintain log supplies, between 300,000 to 500,000 hectares have been set aside as plantations. Another key force driving pulp and paper development is Hasan and his Kalimanis Group. Along with Suharto's son, Sigit Harjojudanto, Hasan is a major shareholder in Kertas Kraft Aceh, which operates a pulp and paper plant in Sumatra. As well, he controls P. T. Aspex Paper, a joint venture with a South Korean company. Even more important than these current operations, Hasan has ambitious plans to expand his control over the pulp and paper industry.[179]

State Attempts to Improve Timber Management

Since Djamaludin was appointed minister of forestry, the enforcement of logging guidelines has improved marginally.[180] As of December 1993, the government had rescinded sixty timber licenses. Many concession holders have reacted by simply abandoning their site. Instead of fining or forcing these companies to replant, the government appointed the state forestry companies P. T. Inhutani I, P. T. Inhutani III, and P. T. Inhutani V to rehabilitate these degraded areas.[181] In some cases, the government has taken over shares of timber companies with poor management records and then appointed a state official to the board of directors. By early 1994, the state had assumed control of 20 percent of the shares of twelve concession holders and 100 percent of the shares of another dozen.[182] State companies now control about 11 percent of Indonesia's forests.[183] As well, the Forestry Ministry has announced an "intelligence operation" to catch illegal loggers "in the act."[184] As a result, the government fined several major companies for breaching logging rules. Although these efforts are laudable, this campaign has done little to slow the rate of destructive extraction. So far the state "crackdown" has produced stern rhetoric but few concrete moves against major timber operators. This is hardly surprising. With powerful political and military ties, and with cooperation from key forestry officials, these companies are largely immune to pressure from the Ministry of Forestry. For example, in 1991 Barito Pacific Timber was fined Rp 11.1 billion (U.S.$5.4 million) for cutting nearly 100,000 cubic meters of logs outside their concession. The company, however, refused to comply, and it appears the fine will never be paid.[185]

Besides these attempts to improve enforcement and compliance, the government is also developing a timber certification program to boost state control of the timber industry. Indonesia's timber certification program will create an environmental label for timber from sustainable sources. The labeling criteria are still being hammered out. Apparently, the labeling process will work on a cradle-to-grave principle, accounting for all stages of production, including cutting techniques, concession management, and processing. Ideally, at each stage guarantees will be provided that the product is produced in a sustainable way.[186] The program will create local criteria for sustainable management—a practical checklist for loggers, processors, and government managers. Ecolabels for wood products will start from the year 2000,[187] then hopefully spread to all products. According to an NGO representative, developing an ecolabeling program has provided a window of opportunity to discuss with the Ministry of Forestry and concessionaires the criteria for sustainable forestry management. This program also intrigues concession holders and Apkindo, who see ecolabeling as a possible marketing tool.[188] Little foreign pressure has been applied for ecolabeling. Proponents of ecolabeling are aware that Indonesia's major wood markets—Japan, Taiwan, South Korea, and China—are indifferent to ecolabels. Advocates hope, however, that countries like Japan can be pressured or embarrassed into only importing wood with ecolabels.[189]

The main force behind ecolabeling is former state minister of the environment Emil Salim. He has a direct connection to the president and is quite influential; however, Hasan, who has a strained relationship with Salim, is more powerful. Fortunately for the program, Salim has a close relationship with the new minister of forestry, and has a "gentleman's agreement" with the president to establish the program.[190] Despite Salim's influence and the optimism of the NGOs involved, it is unlikely this program will succeed in the context of extensive military and political ties to timber operations. Nor is it likely that state implementation of certification guidelines will suddenly be better than the supervision and enforcement of current logging rules. Instead, it is more probable that business interests will capture this program to expand markets and divert attention from unsustainable management. Hasan is already rumored to be excited by the potential benefits of timber certification, and he is eager to start stamping plywood with an attractive logo that declares, "from a sustainable source." Keeping in mind the importance of patron-client relations, distorted management policies, low state capacity, and efforts to tackle omnipresent problems, the next section assesses the impact of Japan's shadow ecology on timber management.

Japanese Investment and Technology Transfers

The first Japanese link to large-scale commercial logging on Indonesia's outer islands was the Kalimantan Forest Development Corporation. Japanese trading and wood-based industries established this company in 1963 to supply the Indonesian state timber company, Perhutani, with equipment and technical support on credit. In exchange, Perhutani agreed to export at least 70 percent of its production to Japan. The Japanese government cooperated closely with the Forest Development Corporation. The president of the company was the former head of the Japanese Forestry Agency while the OECF provided 80 percent of all credit.[191]

The 1967 Indonesian Foreign Capital Investment Law triggered a wave of Japanese investment. In 1968, only nine Japanese companies had invested in Indonesia; by the late 1970s, there were over two hundred companies.[192] From 1967 to 1989, Japan accounted for 24 percent of total investment in Indonesia. The second largest investor, Hong Kong, was far behind at less than 9 percent of the total.[193] Although to a lesser extent than in other sectors, almost all major Japanese trading companies—including Mitsubishi, Marubeni, Itochu, Nissho-Iwai, Mitsui, and Sumitomo—invested in timber ventures in Indonesia. At the end of 1978, total Japanese investment in the Indonesian timber sector was U.S.$46.2 million, compared to U.S.$48.7 million from the United States, U.S$49.1 million from Malaysia, U.S.$53.0 million from Hong Kong, and U.S.$72.6 million from the Philippines.[194] Some of the Philippine companies were apparently backed by Japanese interests.[195] For joint timber ventures, the majority of Japanese corporations chose Indonesian partners based on their political, military, or bureaucratic connections, not their expertise or financial resources. For this reason, the Japanese company often supplied the equity of local partners.[196] As well, Japanese ventures tended to be smaller than American and British logging operations.[197]

Along with other MNCs, Japanese corporations provided technology that expedited rapid and destructive extraction of huge quantities of dipterocarp logs. For example, in East Kalimantan during the 1960s, many companies had limited equipment and tracts were often logged by hand. This frustrated Japanese buyers who wanted faster, more efficient extraction. To increase supply in East Kalimantan, Japanese buyers provided "credit for mechanization" and "by 1971 refused to accept hand-logged timber."[198] During this period, it was also common for sogo shosha to provide equipment in exchange for dipterocarp logs.[199] In addition, in the 1970s Japanese companies supported large-scale logging of fragile mangrove forests in Kalimantan and Sumatra. By the mid-1980s, around 4 percent of mangrove trees had been converted to wood chips, shipped mostly to Japan and Taiwan and manufactured into high-quality paper.[200] Today, Indonesia's mangrove forests are facing extinction.[201]

The Japanese government encouraged and supported corporate timber ventures in Indonesia. Both official development assistance and other official flows financed preliminary logging surveys and risky timber investments.[202] According to Nectoux and Kuroda, in the case of Kalimantan, the logging boom, "which appeared to be . . . provoked by market conditions, was in fact carefully engineered from Japan by public and private interests. The feasibility study and much of the necessary survey work were undertaken by . . . JICA's predecessor."[203] The OECF also supported commercial logging in Indonesia. Although since 1975 the OECF has mainly provided intergovernmental loans, initially it granted loans to Japanese firms involved in development projects in the South. From 1963 to 1981, almost three-quarters of OECF general forestry project loans went to Indonesia (forty-one of fifty-five projects), most at the height of the logging boom, 1969 to 1974. Although loan information is confidential, most trading companies likely received OECF loans during this period. For example, according to Urano, Mitsui received loans of ¥193 million for forestry development in Central Kalimantan and ¥510 million for forestry development in South Kalimantan. And Sumitomo Forestry received ¥1.3 billion for forestry development in East Kalimantan in a series of loans from 1970 to 1974.[204]

Besides loans to Japanese trading companies, OECF loans to the Indonesian government also expedited the timber boom. According to Urano, "although these were mainly loans to develop infrastructure such as electric power plants or transport facilities, there is little doubt that much of it was granted to promote the timber trade."[205] Because the content of and rationale for OECF loans are confidential, it is difficult to document links between general loans and timber extraction. A few leaks have occurred. A 1970 OECF report on loans for the construction of the Balikpapan-Samarinda road declares: "This area is famous for growing tropical lauan timber exported to Japan, and there is no doubt that [this project] will directly and indirectly promote the timber industry and prove immensely profitable to Japan through Japanese firms that operate locally."[206]

MITI also provided money to encourage Japanese corporations to invest in timber operations and import logs.[207] Meanwhile, the predecessor of JICA "conducted feasibility studies for infrastructure development (i.e., harbors, roads, and bridges) that were deemed important to Japan's timber trade and surveys to gather information necessary for timber operations (i.e., aerial photographs, topographical maps, and forest stock estimates)."[208] Of course, not all of these projects were designed solely to support timber extraction. But for many this was a key concern. In the case of the 1975 Banjarmasin Harbor Project, JICA's objective was "to improve harbor facilities in order to develop an area rich in timber resources into a production and distribution site mainly for the timber industry."[209] Besides surveys, JICA's Development Cooperation Fund, established in 1974, provided technical assistance and low-interest loans to Japanese timber firms involved in experimental forestry projects and facility upgrades. Although JICA does not disclose loan information, Mitsubishi, Mitsui, and Sumitomo Forestry have all apparently received loans for timber operations in Indonesia.[210] Finally, the EXIM Bank has granted loans to Japanese logging enterprises in Indonesia. Although most of this information is also restricted, between 1974 and 1980 the bank loaned almost ¥7 billion for timber-related projects in Indonesia, Malaysia, and Papua New Guinea.[211]

Like other MNCs, Japanese companies largely pulled out of Indonesia after the log export ban.[212] According to the Japan-Indonesian Entrepreneurs' Association, in 1988 only nine timber and woodworking joint ventures remained.[213] Prajogo, Indonesia's largest timber operator, assumed control of several Japanese concessions, including ones held by Marubeni and Mitsubishi. Even though these companies no longer participate directly in operations, they continue to have close ties. As Raphael Pura notes, "the Japanese, in effect, left the job of operating their remote concessions to Mr. Prajogo, while continuing to market his timber and help finance expansions."[214]

In 1989, Indonesia removed many restrictions on foreign investment.[215] This has led to increases in overall investment, but only a small amount has gone to timber enterprises. Today, little foreign investment is found in Indonesia's plywood industry: only five mills are joint ventures and all are controlled by Indonesians. Of these five, two are Japanese—one in East Java and one in Southern Sulawesi—and three are South Korean.[216] More foreign participation is found in the pulp and paper industry. In 1990, foreign investment in pulp and paper was U.S.$730 million out of a total of U.S.$8.75 billion. In 1991, five major pulp and paper joint ventures existed, accounting for 24 percent of production (42 percent of pulp and 17 percent of paper).[217]

While Japanese companies have invested only limited amounts in pulp and paper operations, these have been linked to environmental problems. For example, Marubeni invested U.S.$3 million in a mangrove chipping mill in Irian Jaya operated by P. T. Bintuni Utama Murni. In return, Marubeni has a ten-year contract to buy 300 thousand tons of wood chips annually. Environmentalists have strongly attacked this project, which is situated in an area that was once a national park. Even the Indonesian government has criticized P. T. Bintuni for poor management. In 1990, the government fined P. T. Bintuni U.S.$590 thousand and temporarily suspended its license for illegal logging. Apparently, however, this fine has not yet been paid.[218]

In recent years, Japanese corporations have made minor contributions to conservation projects in Indonesia. For example, the Keidanren Nature Conservation Fund provided ¥10 million to the Sulawesi Nature Conservation project.[219] In 1991, Sumitomo Forestry, along with

RETROF, the University of Tokyo, and the Indonesian Ministry of Forestry, established an experimental reforestation program in East Kalimantan. In the first five years, Sumitomo Forestry will spend about ¥50 million. The 100-hectare site is developing new techniques for planting indigenous dipterocarp in open spaces. Although this decreases survival rates, trees grow much faster, reaching cutting maturity in perhaps as little as thirty years. In the first year, the survival rate was only 30 percent, partly because of light rainfall. In the second year, with improved weather conditions and better planting techniques, the survival rate rose to 70–80 percent. This project is also trying to include local people, create employment, and reduce shifting cultivation.[220] Although commendable, compared to the lingering impact of past practices and the current rates of destructive logging, these efforts are inconsequential.[221]

Japanese ODA and Timber Management

Japan is the largest bilateral ODA donor to Indonesia, accounting for over 60 percent of bilateral Indonesian aid in 1993. In 1994, Indonesia received over 9 percent of Japanese bilateral ODA (only China and India received more).[222] Almost 38 percent of Indonesia's foreign loans are owed to Japan, compared to nearly 32 percent to multilateral institutions and a little more than 6 percent to the United States.[223] Unlike in the 1960s and 1970s, today little evidence exists that Japanese ODA is tied to commercial logging operations or securing timber supplies. Japanese aid now supports primarily commercial timber plantations and transferring processing technology and expertise. Although limited, JICA has also provided technical and financial support for natural forest regeneration, harvesting of less-utilized species, and prevention of forest fires. As of early 1994, nine Japanese ODA projects were ongoing in Indonesia, with most linked to plantations.[224] Compared to the severe problems facing Indonesia's timber industry, Japanese aid has had little impact on environmental protection or improving forest management.[225] Even though Japan is the largest contributor to Indonesian forestry ODA, accounting for around 35–40 percent of technical assistance, the total is still quite small. If timber prices incorporated environmental costs, it would far surpass the financial contribution of ODA.[226]

Besides inadequate forestry aid, general Japanese loan and technical cooperation projects in Indonesia do not adequately incorporate environmental objectives. Japanese aid still supports high-tech equipment purchases, with little regard for environmental implications and with little long-term support. As well, Japanese aid officials in Indonesia have little environmental expertise or ground-level knowledge and are reluctant to work with foreign environmental consultants.[227] Aid staff also apparently hesitate to work far away from amenities and avoid places like Irian Jaya.[228] Many of these aid officials insulate themselves, stay a short time, and learn little about Indonesia. Richard Forrest notes that even though "Japan is the leading provider of ODA to Indonesia, providing 12 times as much aid as the US, Japan has only 20 field staff there, less than one-fifth the total USAID [U.S. Agency for International Development] staff; in-country Japanese staff are responsible for 70 times as much aid money per person as USAID staff."[229] Senior Tokyo administrators compound these problems by dictating key decisions with minimal understanding of Indonesia's diverse cultures and ecosystems.[230] In terms of environmental awareness, one NGO activist claims that JICA is one of the worst aid agencies in Indonesia.[231] An Indonesian Ministry for the Environment official is less harsh, however, claiming that some improvements have been made to JICA projects in recent years.[232]

Japanese Log Imports from Indonesia: 1968–1985

Prior to the gradual log export ban from 1980 to 1985, sogo shosha thrived in the context of Indonesia's domestic political economy of timber. Generous foreign investment incentives, minimal timber royalties and license fees, schemes to evade forest charges and corporate taxes (including transfer pricing), widespread destructive and unsustainable logging, weak enforcement of logging rules, and complete disregard for reforestation, natural forest regeneration, and conservation allowed Japanese traders to purchase huge quantities of cheap logs to feed Japan's burgeoning tropical plywood industry. Through their control of the log trade chain and the flow of market information, sogo shosha had a major impact on Indonesian log production. In 1971, Indonesia replaced the Philippines as the main source of Japanese log imports. In that year, Japan accounted for over three-quarters of Indonesian log exports and imported about 60 percent of Indonesia's total log production.[233] The sogo shosha dominated this trade. In 1972, Mitsui & Company imported over 1 million cubic meters of logs, while Marubeni Corporation, Nissho Iwai Corporation, Itochu & Company (then C. Itoh & Company), and Nichimen Corporation all imported over half a million cubic meters of logs. Meanwhile, both Mitsubishi Corporation and Sumitomo Corporation imported close to half a million cubic meters.[234] Even these figures, however, underestimate the impact of sogo shosha because they ignore imports by affiliated firms. For example, in 1972 Sumitomo Forestry imported almost 400 thousand cubic meters of logs.

In 1974, Indonesian log exports to Japan peaked at almost 11.5 million cubic meters, accounting for 47 percent of total Japanese imports, over three-quarters of Indonesian log exports, and almost half of total Indonesian log production.[235] In that year, Mitsui & Company alone imported well over 1 million cubic meters of logs while Itochu & Company imported close to 1 million cubic meters. Meanwhile, Marubeni Corporation imported almost three-quarters of a million cubic meters, Mitsubishi Corporation imported over two-thirds of a million cubic meters, Nissho Iwai Corporation imported nearly two-thirds of a million cubic meters, and Nichimen Corporation and Sumitomo Corporation imported well over half a million cubic meters. In the same year, Sumitomo Forestry imported almost two-thirds of a million cubic meters of logs.[236] After 1974, Japanese log imports declined somewhat, averaging close to 9 million cubic meters per year from 1975 to 1980.[237] Over the period of Indonesia's log export boom from 1970 to 1980, Japanese companies imported almost 100 million cubic meters of logs, accounting for 59 percent of total log exports, and about 43 percent of Indonesia's total log production.[238]

In the early 1980s, as the Indonesian government implemented the log export ban, Japanese log imports from Indonesia fell sharply until ending in 1986. But since then Indonesian plywood exports to Japan have steadily increased. In 1989, Indonesia exported over 3 million cubic meters of plywood to Japan. From 1990 to 1992, this dropped to just below 3 million cubic meters before surging in 1993 to 3.7 million cubic meters.[239] In 1994, Indonesian plywood exports to Japan fell slightly to about 3.2 million cubic meters, comprising over 80 percent of total Japanese tropical plywood imports.[240] In 1995, Indonesian plywood exports to Japan again fell, to 3 million cubic meters.[241] Even in 1994 and 1995, however, Japan was by far Indonesia's largest market, accounting for over one-third of Indonesia's total plywood exports.[242]

Trade: Apkindo and the Battle for Japan's Plywood Market

Apkindo has flooded the Japanese market with cheap plywood.[243] To expand their market share, Indonesian processors produce plywood from high-quality logs. A sogo shosha official claims that "[for plywood,] Indonesia is stripping vast amounts of logs [of such high quality] that we in Japan can only dream of laying our hands on nowadays."[244] According to a representative from the JPMA Apkindo is a monopolistic, undemocratic organization ruled by Bob Hasan, which has a clear strategy to destroy Japan's plywood industry.[245] Apkindo sets export prices, establishes production quotas, and issues export licenses. It charges U.S.$15 per cubic meter of exported plywood and has made about U.S.$1 billion from this levy since the mid-1980s.[246] It also requires plywood exporters to use Karana Shipping Lines and Tugu Mandiri insurance company.[247] Apkindo has pushed processors to focus on designated markets, including Taiwan, South Korea, and Japan.[248] Apkindo has also pressured Indonesian processors to tailor plywood—especially kon-pane—for the Japanese market.

Hasan recently asserted: "We're the only guys in Southeast Asia who fight the sogo shoshas."[249] To bypass the import, transport, storage, and marketing services of the sogo shosha, in 1988 Apkindo established Nippindo to market Indonesian plywood in Japan.[250] Apkindo owns 95 percent of Nippindo and Kanematsu Trading owns 5 percent.[251] Today Japanese buyers must purchase plywood through Nippindo.[252] To break open the Japanese market, Nippindo has sold its plywood below world market prices.[253] The export price of Indonesian plywood to Japan is generally lower than to the rest of the world (although the average price of plywood exports to South Korea and Taiwan have been even lower than to Japan). In 1993, the average price of Indonesian tropical plywood on the world market—defined as plywood with at least one ply of tropical wood—was U.S.$259.97 per cubic meter. In that year, the average price of Indonesian plywood exported to Japan was U.S.$171.35 per cubic meter. In 1994, the average price of Indonesian plywood shipped to Japan was U.S.$370.92, while the average export price to the world market was U.S.$407.07 per cubic meter.[254] Obviously, in the immediate term, it would be more profitable for individual firms to export to markets other than Japan. Yet they have little choice. If the quota to Japan is ignored, Apkindo can decimate a company by refusing to allow future exports.[255]

Nippindo apparently makes huge profits, although as one Indonesian business leader notes, "Nobody knows how much Nippindo marks up."[256] So far, Nippindo has been remarkably successful. In 1994, total Japanese tropical plywood consumption was about 8.7 million cubic meters—around 3.8 million cubic meters from imports and the remainder from domestic production and reserve stocks.[257] In that year, Indonesian plywood accounted for over one-third of total Japanese tropical plywood consumption.[258] Part of the reason for Nippindo's remarkable success is the general Japanese perception that Indonesia is not an economic threat (unlike the United States) and the tendency of the Japanese government to stress protecting high-tech industries.[259]

Apkindo's and Nippindo's tactics demonstrate the vulnerability of Japanese processors who rely on overseas logs. As Apkindo undercuts plywood prices, as log prices rise, and as supplies fluctuate, many Japanese plywood processors have been driven out of business. Between 1990 and 1995, domestic plywood production dropped 40 percent.[260] Plywood factories have been closing every year in Japan. In April 1994, the JPMA had only one hundred members left. By the year 2000, the JPMA predicts that only sixty factories will remain.[261] Spurred by the success of Apkindo and Nippindo, Indonesia may use similar tactics to dominate the world pulp and paper industry. For now, pulp and paper projects are expanding quickly with few controls. Once economic momentum develops, however, there are plans to establish an overarching organization to control and guide the industry (perhaps modeled after Apkindo, perhaps even headed by Hasan).[262]

Japanese officials argue that Apkindo practices unfair trade. In the late 1980s, the JPMA persuaded the Japanese government to hold a bilateral conference to discuss Apkindo's export strategy. This conference produced no results. The JPMA has also appealed to the Fair Trade Commission of the General Agreement on Tariffs and Trade (GATT), but Apkindo is technically a nongovernmental organization and GATT has no jurisdiction.[263] Despite the growing power of Apkindo and Nippindo, the financial crisis of many Japanese processors, and the inability of the processing industry to push back the assault, Japanese plywood officials remain optimistic. According to several spokesmen, Apkindo's strategy of flooding Japan with cheap imports cannot continue, especially if Indonesia keeps Forestry Minister Djamaludin's promise to slash annual log production to 22.5 million cubic meters.[264] Despite the rapid loss of valuable commercial timber, Apkindo remains equally optimistic. According to a spokesman, high labor and tropical log costs and temperate plywood's inability to satisfy consumers will eventually lead to the collapse of Japan's plywood industry. Apkindo can then increase profit margins in Japan, which are now fairly low, especially for kon-pane.[265] Although it is uncertain who will be victorious in this plywood war, it seems clear that Indonesia's natural forests will sustain heavy casualties.

In the late 1970s, realizing that plywood processing was a sunset industry, Taiwan and South Korea dismantled plywood mills and exported used equipment to Indonesia.[266] But Japanese processors have stubbornly persevered. To protect and prolong the industry, the Japanese government and the private sector have tried to thwart Indonesia's plywood industry. For example, after the log export ban was announced, the Japanese ambassador, Japanese companies, JICA, and the OECF all lobbied to lift the ban. Although these tactics failed, the Japanese government continues to maintain stiff tariff and nontariff barriers to block plywood imports.

Japanese Tariff Barriers

Japan imposes a 10–15 percent tariff on plywood imports.[267] The Japanese government calculates the tariff based on a price that includes shipping and insurance costs. This makes Japan's import tariff higher than the more usual calculation based on a FOB (free on board) price. Northern tariffs on plywood reduce Indonesian exporters' profits and the Indonesian government's revenues. An official at the Indonesian National Development Planning Agency (Bappenas) claims that Apkindo exports high-quality plywood to Japan at prices 5–10 percent lower than to other countries to overcome tariff and nontariff barriers.[268] According to Hasan, "in many cases, the consuming country's tax revenue on a sheet of plywood is greater than the total growth of value in producing countries."[269] In 1991, Indonesia paid Japan U.S.$125 million in import duties on processed timber. These import charges deplete Indonesian revenue that, in theory, is essential for sustainable management. As former Forestry Minister Hasjrul Harahap argued, "if the import duties are lowered, the deductions from paying import duties can be allocated for the conservation of our tropical forests."[270] Besides the 10–15 percent tariff, Japan also has nontariff import barriers. The most important is the regulation that government projects must use timber with a Japan Agricultural Standard (JAS) certificate. The Japan Plywood Inspection Corporation issues these certificates based on quality. Indonesia has managed largely to overcome this nontariff barrier: fifty plywood mills now qualify for JAS certificates.[271]

Conclusion

Modern patron-client relations are a dominant feature of Indonesia's New Order government, binding together powerful political, military, bureaucratic, and corporate elites. Links between *pribumi* (indigenous or non-Chinese) state patrons and ethnic Chinese business clients are particularly important. Societal prejudice and regular backlashes against Chinese businesses create even weaker feelings of loyalty between ethnic Chinese and state elite than among pribumi Indonesians. Although these ties have been quite stable during the New Order, a sense of apprehension and uncertainty encourages ethnic Chinese business leaders to channel profits overseas.

President Suharto leads the largest and most powerful patron-client network with his family, friends, and key followers at the core. He provides protection, state funds, licenses, concessions, and access to the corridors of power in exchange for political loyalty, financial support, legitimacy, and stability. He has been especially careful to coopt or appease influential military generals by appointing officers to key state positions, awarding lucrative concessions and licenses, and supporting the business interests of military patron-client networks. Many of Suharto's clients also function as political, military, or bureaucratic patrons, building a base of power using their state position, wealth, and connections to Suharto. This process of clients acting as patrons contributes to patron-client ties pervading all levels of the state and society. This does not, however, translate into power flowing upward to a single summit; power is more diffuse, resting in pockets of patron-client clusters, pyramids, and networks—creating what Migdal calls a weblike society. For this reason, even though Suharto is clearly the most powerful state patron, he must judiciously cultivate and maintain support from key military, political, and bureaucratic leaders.

Although patron-client relations do not account for all political interaction, these ties at the state helm impair state policies and dilute control of middle- and lower-level state implementors. With little supervision, many implementors are absorbed by patron-client clusters, ignoring state rules in exchange for material or professional support. In some cases, state bureaus are captured by patron-client networks; instead of striving to implement state guidelines, these state tentacles work in the interests of private companies, perverting policies and debilitating state capacity to enforce regulations. For logging, distorted state forestry policies and the inability and unwillingness of the state to monitor and enforce timber regulations have driven destructive extraction and unsustainable management.

In the 1960s and 1970s, concessions were granted as gifts to appease or reward political and military elites. With little capital or knowledge, ethnic Chinese and multinational companies were hired to log these concessions. With almost no state supervision, and with technical and financial support from MNCs, huge quantities of logs were mined from the forests. Multinational log traders—especially sogo shosha—thrived in this setting. While the Indonesian state received a small portion of timber revenues, MNCs and Indonesian military, political, and bureaucratic elite made quick, easy money. At the same time, almost no effort was made to log areas on a sustainable basis or regenerate devastated areas.

The ban on log exports and the push to process plywood in the 1980s, and the moves to develop pulp and paper plantations in the 1990s, have done little to improve timber management. Today, commercial forests are under tremendous pressure. Few signs of improvement are evident despite a more assertive minister of forestry and government moves to improve logging management, establish an ecolabel for sustainable timber, increase collection of timber taxes and royalties, and crack down on illegal logging and smuggling. The government is also providing subsidies and pressuring companies to replant—not to regenerate commercial dipterocarp stands but to build huge timber plantations to supply an expanding pulp and paper industry. Instead of "reforestation," this policy contributes to "deforestation" as areas are cleared to establish plantations.

Concession operators—especially ethnic Chinese—wary of a sudden political upheaval and new leaders revoking concession rights, have few incentives for long-term management; instead, timber operators invest in real estate and stash money overseas. In addition, the state has little control over timber operations. As a result, legal concessions are badly managed, enrichment planting is limited, and illegal logging is rampant. According to NGO experts, illegal and legal logging have pushed annual log production to around 44 million cubic meters, well above even the government estimate of sustainable yield (31 million cubic meters), and two times higher than a recent World Bank estimate. Along with smuggling and schemes to evade timber taxes and royalties, illegal logging siphons state timber revenues. Forest charges are also remarkably low, and the state is now estimated to capture only 15–30 percent of timber rents. As long as powerful state patrons like Suharto protect timber clients like Hasan (Apkindo and the Kalimanis Group) and Prajogo (Barito Pacific Timber), and as long as state implementors follow the rules of patron-client networks, the state will be too weak to improve logging management, regardless of the content of actual policies or the rhetoric of state leaders.

While domestic political forces distort policies, undermine state revenue, and drive unsustainable extraction, shadow ecologies—especially Japan's—have bolstered and accelerated this process. In the 1960s and

1970s, Japanese ODA, technology transfers, investments, and log purchases had a catalytic impact on unsustainable logging. ODA funds supported commercial timber surveys, feasibility studies, logging infrastructure projects, and corporate timber investments. Although Japan was not the largest investor in the Indonesian timber sector in the 1970s, Japanese corporate credit, joint ventures, logging equipment, and technical advice were key forces that drove reckless logging. Even more important, sogo shosha—through their control of affiliated firms in the trade chain—imported immense quantities of logs from unsustainable sources and at prices that ignored environmental and social costs. As well as accelerating log production and expediting destructive logging, Japanese money, which deluged Indonesia after the 1967 Foreign Capital Investment Law, also provided critical financial slack to allow extensive patronage.

After log exports were banned in the mid-1980s, the key features of Japan's ecological shadow changed. Most Japanese companies withdrew or sold their shares in joint timber ventures. Today, there are few investments in Indonesian plywood or pulp and paper operations. Logging equipment is no longer shipped in substantial amounts, although some technological support continues for processing. ODA has also changed. Since the early 1980s, few JICA forestry projects or OECF loans have been connected to corporate logging ventures. Instead, ODA tends to emphasize commercial timber plantations. Although these are positive trends, Japanese ODA projects in Indonesia still have serious environmental problems. Few environmental experts are available; staff members have little field experience; and funds often support inappropriate technology purchases. In addition, decision-makers in Tokyo with little understanding of Indonesia's delicate outer island ecosystems exacerbate these problems. In fairness, there is limited Japanese government and corporate support for forest conservation and regeneration, but not nearly enough to dent deforestation rates.

Finally, since 1985, Japanese log imports have ceased while plywood imports have soared. For both logs and plywood, prices have been far below the cost of sustainable management, feeding voracious Japanese consumption habits. During the era of log exports, sogo shosha played a pivotal role in depressing prices, expanding export volumes, and promoting rapid, destructive logging. Today, these companies have been usurped by Apkindo. Under Hasan, Apkindo has flooded the Japanese market with cheap, high-quality plywood. This strategy—designed to destroy Japanese competitors—has been successful in bankrupting many Japanese processors. But it has also lowered prices, encouraged wasteful consumption, and fostered unsustainable timber management. At the same time, Japanese plywood tariffs have undercut Indonesian state and corporate revenue, further reducing potential funds for forest management and regeneration. In short, although some aspects of Japan's ecological shadow of timber have changed over the last thirty years, three critical components—low prices, wasteful consumption, and import tariffs on processed wood—remain constant. As a result, Japan's shadow ecology continues to provoke and support unsustainable timber extraction. This in turn fuels pervasive patron-client relations.

4 Japan, Clientelism, and Deforestation in East Malaysia

As in Indonesia, unsustainable logging has been a key cause of deforestation in East Malaysia over the last three decades. Wide areas are degraded and commercial log stocks are now perilously low. The environmental group Sahabat Alam Malaysia maintains that "Nowhere in the world are the forests being chopped with such ferocity and speed as in Sarawak."[1] Sabah has been logged with equal intensity. A 1990 ITTO report on Sarawak's timber industry claimed that if the "frenetic pace of logging continues at [the rate] of recent years, all primary forests will have been harvested in 11 years."[2] Even more dire predictions have been made for Sabah.

Links between top state patrons and timber operators in East Malaysia—similar to those in Indonesia—distort state policies, weaken state enforcement, and drive unsustainable logging. To maintain loyalty and support in fragmented societies, top political patrons grant timber concessions to key political and business clients. Many concession holders then hire contractors to manage logging operations; and contractors often use subcontractors to extract or process the timber. These multiple layers of responsibility reduce accountability and transparency, increasing the difficulty of enforcement and effective management. Timber profits fuel powerful patron-client networks. These networks are highly unstable, rupturing as political parties vie for power in East Malaysia's ethnically diverse landscape. As a result, concessions are frequently annulled as competing patron-client networks rise and fall. In this setting, incentives for long-term management or conservation are sorely lacking. Instead, concessionaires and timber companies race to extract as much timber as possible before tenuous political alliances and patron-client networks crumble. Timber mismanagement is aggravated further by poor supervision of middle- and lower-level state implementors. In exchange for money, gifts, and career opportunities, enforcement officers disregard concession rules, forge customs declarations, and ignore illegal logging and smuggling.

Unlike in Indonesia, Japanese aid and investment have not had a major impact on timber management in East Malaysia. Japanese ODA has been limited to a few infrastructure projects and minor technical assistance projects to support plantations (Sabah) and processing (Sarawak). Few major investments have been made in logging or timber processing. As well, unlike in Indonesia, Japanese import tariffs have not significantly reduced state revenues—although, as Sabah and Sarawak reduce log exports and increase plywood exports, import barriers have become relatively more important. Yet despite limited investment, aid, and import charges, Japan's shadow ecology has accelerated logging rates and bolstered unsustainable timber management. Thriving in the context of pervasive patron-client timber networks, Japanese companies, especially sogo shosha, have purchased giant quantities of logs, shipped them to Japan, and as with Indonesian logs, manufactured plywood and sawnwood. These logs have been extracted from unsustainable sources and sold at prices far below replacement or sustainable management costs. This is starkly revealed by the common Japanese practice of discarding kon-pane—made from trees that likely took a century or more to grow—after being used only a few times. To gain a deeper understanding of how patron-client ties have undermined forest management and facilitated unsustainable log exports to Japan, the next section sketches the evolution from traditional to modern clientelist relations in East Malaysia.

Patron-Client Relations in East Malaysia

In 1841, the British adventurer James Brooke was made Rajah of Sarawak after suppressing a rebellion against the Sultan of Brunei. Beginning in 1882, the British North Borneo Company administered Sabah. After World War II, Britain assumed formal control of East Malaysia. It is quite difficult to ascertain the nature of patron-client relations in Sarawak and Sabah before 1963, when the two states joined Malaya to form Malaysia. R. S. Milne claims that "Native chiefs and headmen, who existed in Sarawak and Sabah before the British came and who were institutionalized by them, sometimes functioned as patrons." In addition, he reasons that "where communications were good and the population was relatively dense and well organized (as among the coastal Malays in Sarawak), or where the degree of hierarchy was great, as among the 'aristocratic' Sarawak Kenyahs, patronage was probably fairly common."[3] Patron-client relationships also existed among the Chinese, with wealthy businessmen in the role of patrons. The Ibans of Sarawak probably had less-pervasive patron-client links because their society was relatively egalitarian.[4]

Near the end of the North Borneo Company rule in Sabah and the Brooke family reign in Sarawak, and throughout direct British colonial rule from 1946 to 1963, the populations of both states were "relatively unmobilized, the functions of government quite limited, and administrators in the field efficient and helpful, if paternalistic, within the restricted scope of their operations." Milne notes further that "life was not particularly unpredictable, nor personal security particularly tenuous."[5] Patron-client relations developed and flourished more as a result of a desire to obtain opportunities and benefits than as a need for protection. The British, in the latter part of their colonial rule, reshaped patron-client relations by appointing indigenous people to administrative positions, thus encouraging new patron-client links to form on a state rather than local scale. At the same time, indigenous people increasingly entered business, especially the timber industry, later becoming prominent state politicians.[6]

When Sabah and Sarawak joined Malaya in 1963, patterns of patron-client links were again altered as state and federal officials replaced British colonial administrators. New patron-client clusters and networks formed around state leaders while many old clientelist ties reshaped or dissolved. Patron-client networks also expanded as government institutions provided the resources to sustain large groups without deep loyalties or strong friendships.[7] Patron-client relations changed further with the start of directly elected state legislatures in 1967 in Sabah and 1969–70 in Sarawak. Patron-client networks became even larger, vertically linking urban areas to more remote rural areas. Milne claims that "dyadic patron-client relations now extended, in chain fashion, right to the top of state politics."[8] Large "peripheral" client followings became important during elections. Paying headmen to influence the voting of their clientele, buying votes, and swaying the allegiance of politicians with instrumental rewards were all evident by the 1967 election in Sabah and the 1969–70 election in Sarawak.[9]

Ethnicity (often distinguished by religion) and patron-client relations are closely linked in Sabah and Sarawak. Ethnic groups are generally divided into three categories: indigenous Muslims, indigenous non-Muslims, and nonindigenous. In Sarawak, indigenous Muslims (Malays and Melanaus) constitute 26 percent of the population; about 44 percent are indigenous non-Muslims (including Iban, Bidayuh, Kenyahs, and Kayans);[10] and 30 percent are nonindigenous (mostly Chinese).[11] Around 49 percent of Sabah's population are indigenous Muslims (Bajaus, Malays, and immigrants); 34 percent are indigenous non-Muslims (Kadazans and Muruts); and 16 percent are nonindigenous (primarily Chinese). The Kadazans are the largest ethnic group in Sabah, comprising 30 percent of the population. In total, just over half of the people in Sabah and a little more than a quarter in Sarawak are Muslims. Although some ethnic Chinese in Sabah have converted to Islam, most Chinese in East Malaysia follow a mixture of Confucianism, Christianity, and Buddhism. Indigenous non-Muslims are generally Christians or animists.[12]

Today, Sarawak and Sabah are ruled by multiethnic coalitions with some ethnically mixed political parties. In Sarawak, Malay and Melanau Muslims are the most powerful political and bureaucratic force. In Sabah, Christian Kadazans dominated from 1985 until early 1994. Since then, Malays, Muslims, and to a lesser extent ethnic Chinese have been pivotal forces in the coalition government. Given that no single ethnic or religious group can dominate politics in East Malaysia, patron-client networks that integrate elites from different ethnic groups and religious backgrounds, and which often crosscut official party lines, are crucial for maintaining power. This is particularly relevant in Sarawak given the many regional divisions among ethnic groups. Michael Leigh notes that the "peculiar ethnic complex, with three major groups, not one of which approaches a majority of the population, has facilitated accommodation in Sarawak." Political divisions within ethnic groups have encouraged compromise, "forcing the factions to seek allies outside their group in the quest for political power."[13] The situation in Sabah is quite similar. Bruce Gale argues that "questions of race, religion and class, relevant to the study of West Malaysian politics, are less important in Sabah than the existence of strong clientelist networks."[14]

Some of the most important patron-client links are between powerful indigenous politicians and Chinese business leaders. After Sarawak and Sabah joined Malaya, the general mainland pattern of Malay political power and Chinese economic influence was encouraged in the two new states. In most instances, indigenous political leaders assumed the role of patrons and the Chinese assumed the role of clients. Indigenous political patrons provided political protection and access to resources, licenses, and contracts in exchange for financial and electoral support from Chinese clients.

Patron-client ties in East Malaysia have been highly unstable since the first elections. One sign of this instability is frequent crossovers from one political party to another. For example, less than a year after the 1987 state election in Sarawak, six members of the Parti Bangsa Dayak Sarawak (PBDS or the Sarawak Dayak People's Party), which lost the election, were "bought over" by the ruling Barisan Nasional (BN or the National Front).[15] Changing alliances and party crossovers were such a problem in Sabah in the mid-1980s that an "anti-hop" law was passed forbidding politicians from switching parties without losing their seats.[16] This law was later struck down by the High Court, and shifting party allegiances dominated the 1994 election.[17] The Parti Bersatu Sabah (PBS or the United Sabah Party), under incumbent Chief Minister Joseph Pairin Kitingan, won this election by a slim margin. But defections—including his brother, Jeffrey Kitingan—toppled the government. According to some sources, "many of the defectors" were "enticed to change sides with money and promises of position."[18] Chinese business clients are particularly prone to change alliances. One author noted that the Chinese in Sarawak "go with whoever is the stronger, demanding more timber concessions in return for their support."[19]

Relations between the federal and state governments have contributed further to unstable and fluid patron-client clusters in East Malaysia. Francis Loh Kok Wah writes, "it is clear . . . that whosoever wishes to govern in Sarawak must receive the blessings and support of Kuala Lumpur."[20] In both states, federal pressure has contributed to political realignment. One example occurred in 1976 when the federal government engineered the downfall of Tun Mustapha Harun's government in Sabah and helped establish a new multiethnic coalition.[21]

In sum, compared to traditional ties, modern patron-client networks in Sabah and Sarawak are more unstable, particularly since the start of competitive elections. With the influx of immigrants, especially into Sabah, unstable "peripheries" have grown considerably in recent years.[22] Political relations with Kuala Lumpur have also contributed to fluid patron-client clusters: federal pressure can cause clusters to rupture and realign in an attempt to placate or gain support from Kuala Lumpur. Patron-client ties are now based less on loyalty, obligation, and honor and more on material benefits. A common feature of elections in East Malaysia is the downward flow of jobs and cash from patrons and the upward flow of votes from clients. As Michael Vatikiotis notes, "winning votes in Sabah is an expensive exercise; state politics is notoriously unpredictable and plagued by shifting loyalties and an appetite for cash."[23] Finally, a key characteristic of patron-client links in East Malaysia is the exchange of political favors by indigenous elite for financial and electoral support from Chinese business clients.

Timber in East Malaysia

Background

From 1919 to 1952, the British North Borneo Timber Company monopolized the timber industry in Sabah. During this period, the company logged limited quantities of high-grade hardwoods. In 1952, logging rates increased after three large foreign firms and eight local companies began operations.[24] Logging accelerated in the 1960s and 1970s. Sabah's log production rose from 2.8 million cubic meters in 1962 to 6.6 million cubic meters in 1970, to 11.1 million cubic meters in 1973, to a peak of 13.3 million cubic meters in 1978.[25] In 1973, primary forests covered 55 percent of Sabah; by 1983, this had dropped to 25 percent.[26] Large-scale logging began later in Sarawak than in Sabah, although by 1950, logging was an important part of Sarawak's economy.[27] As commercial log stocks diminished in Sabah in the 1980s, log production in Sarawak gained momentum. Two key factors have contributed to substantial increases in East Malaysian log extraction. First, Northern technology—including light and efficient chain saws, powerful tractors and winches, and bulldozers—has enabled rapid and easy logging, even in the hills.[28] Second, as commercial log stocks faded in the Philippines in the 1970s, and after Indonesia banned log exports in the early 1980s, massive Japanese log purchases have provided irresistible opportunities to make fast money. By the late 1980s, East Malaysia supplied approximately 90 percent of Japan's tropical log imports from Southeast Asia.

Commercial timber stocks differ in Sabah and Sarawak. In 1994, Sabah, with a total land area of 7.37 million hectares, had 4.40 million hectares of forests, covering almost 60 percent of the land area.[29] The state intends to maintain at least 50 percent of land area as permanent forest cover. Under Sabah's forest policy, 3.35 million hectares of forests, or 45.4 percent of the land area, are classified as forest reserves and under the control of the Forestry Department. Stateland forests, set aside for agricultural conversion or development projects, cover just over 1 million hectares and are not controlled by the Forestry Department. Around 30 percent of Sabah's land is cultivated or urbanized.[30] The forest reserves contain around 930 thousand hectares of protection forests and about

2.42 million hectares of commercial forests[31]—mostly lowland and hill dipterocarp forest set aside for sustainable timber production. Most commercial forests have already been logged. By 1993, loggers had harvested over 2 million hectares, and only 413 thousand hectares of primary forests remained in the commercial forests.[32] Moreover, remaining commercial logs are now largely in hill forests.[33]

The populations of Sarawak and Sabah are almost identical (1.7 million). Sarawak, however, is 60 percent larger than Sabah and is nearly as large as Peninsular Malaysia. Sarawak has 8.6 million hectares of forest, covering almost 70 percent of the total land area of 12.3 million hectares. The dominant forest type is mixed dipterocarp hill forest.[34] Only 600 thousand hectares, or 5 percent of land area, have been cultivated or urbanized. Six million hectares are designated as permanent forest estate and have been set aside for sustainable timber production.[35] Around 1 million hectares are classified as totally protected areas (wildlife sanctuaries and national parks). The rest is state land forest, areas that can be logged and then converted to agriculture or development projects.[36] As in Sabah, loggers have cut large amounts of valuable timber in Sarawak. From 1963 to 1985, timber companies logged 30 percent of Sarawak's forest area.[37] By 1989, only 4–5 million hectares of primary forests remained.[38]

The timber industry has been a crucial source of economic growth in both Sabah and Sarawak. From 1971 to 1976, the total value of timber exports from Sabah tripled and from 1977 to 1982 doubled.[39] Based mainly on log exports, Sabah's economy grew at an annual average rate of 8 percent from 1971 to 1983, at one point the highest in Southeast Asia.[40] Like Sabah, log exports have underpinned Sarawak's economy in the 1980s and early 1990s.[41] At the start of the 1990s, total log production declined somewhat in Sabah, to around 8.4 million cubic meters in 1990 and 8.1 million cubic meters in 1991, before shooting back up to 11.6 million cubic meters in 1992. In Sarawak, log production was over 18 million cubic meters in the late 1980s and still stood at 16.7 million cubic meters in 1993. Despite a log export ban in Sabah and greater export restrictions in Sarawak in 1994, East Malaysia continues to harvest large quantities of tropical logs. In 1993, Sabah's chief minister announced that annual log production would be reduced to 6 million cubic meters over the next few years.[42] Although the Sabah government considers 6 million cubic meters sustainable, according to the Malaysian Primary Industries minister, Sabah's annual sustainable yield may be as low as 3 million cubic meters.[43] Yet in 1994, Sabah produced almost 8 million cubic meters of logs. In that year, Sarawak harvested 16.3 million cubic meters (about 9.5 million cubic meters from the permanent forest estate and the rest from state land forest).[44] From 1995 to 2000, the Sarawak Forest Department plans to hold production in the permanent forest estate at about 9.5 million cubic meters and decrease extraction from state land forest to between 5 and 6 million cubic meters.[45] Sarawak maintains log production is now sustainable—a claim emphatically denied by environmentalists. Lord Cranbrook of the Nature Conservancy of England, who led the ITTO team that surveyed Sarawak's forests in 1989, estimated in the subsequent report that with proper management, sustainable production for Sarawak's entire forest area would be around 9.2 million cubic meters. Under current management practices, however, as he told the *New Scientist* in late 1994, sustainable production is more likely around 6.3 million cubic meters for the whole forest area and 4.1 million cubic meters for the permanent forest estate.[46]

While logging is the economic backbone of Sabah and a key resource in Sarawak, timber profits mainly benefit a small political, bureaucratic, and corporate elite. Only marginal amounts seep to outlying areas, mostly during elections as patron-client networks mobilize peripheral supporters. Cash payments by the state just before elections and straightforward "vote buying" redistribute a tiny portion of timber wealth in Sabah. In Sarawak, loggers sometimes put local leaders on retainer in exchange for support and an informal agreement to suppress complaints about environmental degradation.[47] Few native people, however, have benefited from logging. For example, even though much of Sarawak's logging is on traditional Iban land, Ibans have not prospered. According to Malaysian government figures, almost half of Iban households fall below the poverty line.[48] One reason is that Ibans, who are 95 percent rural, are not well integrated into patron-client clusters or networks, perhaps partially because of their historically egalitarian society. Although an awakening of Dayak (Iban and Bidayuh) consciousness, similar to Kadazan-Dusun in Sabah, may eventually bring the Dayak into the patron-client fold, to date these aspirations have been unsuccessful.[49]

Political power, patronage, and timber are inseparable in East Malaysia. Timber is more important to the economies of Sabah and Sarawak than to Indonesia or the Philippines. For this reason, virtually all political leaders have had extensive ties to timber operators, and profits from illegal and legal logging fund political parties and powerful patron-client networks.

State Patronage and Timber in Sabah

From 1967 to 1974, the United Sabah National Organization (USNO), under the firm grip of Tun Mustapha Harun, dominated Sabah politics. Based mainly on timber, Mustapha built an extensive patron-client network that superseded all others, allowing him to rule in an autocratic way. He controlled the state legislative assembly and the bureaucracy. Mustapha was also head of the Sabah Foundation. Under his leadership, the foundation—established in 1966 to support education and social projects—"was rapidly transformed to become a prime vehicle for administering state exploitation and development of timber resources, with the benefits being distributed on a patronage basis to political supporters."[50] To help win the 1974 election, Mustapha used his control over the foundation's timber profits to award all adult Sabah citizens M$60. He also used timber profits and concession licenses to appease and mute potential adversaries. According to Means, "patronage and the 'irregular' rewards of office were so great that the visible opposition to Mustapha's policies had been reduced to insignificance."[51] During this period, Mustapha's hold on Sabah was so tight that he was able to spend nine or ten months a year abroad, ruling through key clients such as Syed Kechik, director of the Sabah Foundation. The dominance of Mustapha's patron-client network allowed him to funnel a major portion of timber profits into his own pocket, supporting extravagant personal comforts and opulent homes in Australia and England. State funds also provided a luxurious official residence, a Boeing 707, and two executive jets.[52]

After the 1974 election Mustapha's control began to erode, in part as a result of an escalating dispute with the federal government over oil revenues. In 1975, under federal pressure, Mustapha "retired" and was replaced by his loyal follower, Said Keruak. From behind the scenes, Mustapha maintained power until April 1976, when USNO lost the election to Tun Fuad Stephens's Bersatu Rakyat Jelata Sabah (Berjaya) Party (Sabah United People's Party). In June 1976, Fuad Stephens's reign ended abruptly when he died in a plane crash. He was replaced by Harris Salleh who ruled a multiethnic coalition until 1985. Compared to the Mustapha years, Harris Salleh's government reduced extravagant waste and flagrant displays of personal wealth. Yet patron-client networks and state patronage were still central features of Harris Salleh's reign. Timber concessions and profits were at the core of many patron-client networks. By the early 1980s, Berjaya "perfected its techniques of retaining power through an emphasis on development projects, which tended to be distributed by political patriarchs and through patronage systems linked to the government." Berjaya easily won the 1981 election, in part "by a judicious distribution of projects and other benefits just prior to the election."[53] Foreign assistance provided crucial support for this extensive state patronage; by 1985 Sabah's foreign debt was M$2.7 billion.[54]

The Sabah Foundation has dominated Sabah's logging industry. In 1970, the foundation was granted a hundred-year license to 855 thousand hectares of forest, "to be developed on behalf of all citizens of the state." The foundation gained even more control in the late 1970s when it became "a statutory body of the state government."[55] In 1984, the foundation was awarded another large concession and it now controls close to 1 million hectares of forest, one-seventh of Sabah's land area.[56] The Sabah Foundation has had close ties to Japanese log traders. In 1986, the foundation extracted 1.2 million cubic meters of logs; 72 percent went to Japan.[57] Besides the Sabah Foundation, there are also some powerful private timber companies. Aokam Perdama Bhd, under the control of Teh Soon Seng, operates Sabah's largest timber processing plant. Aokam Perdama receives logs at preferential prices from Idris Hydraulic Bhd which controls a 190 thousand-hectare concession in Sabah. Idris Hydraulic has close connections to the United Malays National Organization (UMNO).[58]

Not surprisingly, top politicians have maintained tight control of the Sabah Foundation. From 1985 until March 1994, Sabah was ruled by the PBS, a multiethnic party led by Datuk Seri Joseph Pairin Kitingan, and dominated by Catholic Kadazans.[59] Even though Chief Minister Pairin was chairman of the foundation, one of his first decisions after gaining power was to appoint his brother, Dr. Jeffrey Kitingan, as director of the Sabah Foundation. In 1988, the PBS government formed Innoprise to handle the commercial affairs of the Sabah Foundation—including shipping, hotels, tourism, logging, and reforestation.[60] According to a spokesman, since then the foundation has concentrated on education and social issues, and stressed "self-reliance." Although scholarships are still available, the foundation no longer provides annual cash payments to all citizens over the age of twenty-one.[61] Opposition political parties ardently attacked the creation of Innoprise and the new emphasis on self-reliance. In 1990, Berjaya Secretary-General Datuk Haji Mohamed Noor Mansoor argued that "the creation of Innoprise has effectively put a tremendous amount of funds under the control of the PBS leader and his brother for distribution as patronage to selected supporters of the Kitingans."[62] In the same year, Berjaya Deputy President Datuk Lim Guan Sing claimed that the PBS was using Innoprise and the Sabah Foundation "for political patronage among its supporters."[63]

Political Leaders, Patronage, and Timber in Sarawak

Since 1966, the state ministers of forestry in Sarawak have all been from the Malay-Melanau elite and have been members of the Parti Pesaka Bumiputera Bersatu (PBB or the United Bumiputera Pesaka Party), the most powerful member of the current BN coalition government. Given that the state minister of forestry has the exclusive power to grant or deny timber concessions, "both between 1970–81 and ever since 1985, the Chief Ministers have jealously kept this portfolio in their own office: for it is a portfolio of extreme power."[64] State leaders have also maintained close links to lucrative log exports. According to Marcus Colchester, "all whole logs are exported through the company, Archipelago Shipping, an import-export company part-owned by the state and part-owned by a relative of the Chief Minister [Taib]."[65]

The most powerful patron in Sarawak is Chief Minister Datuk Patinggi Tan Sri Haji Abdul Taib Mahmud. The *Asian Wall Street Journal* describes him as one of Malaysia's most "flamboyant" politicians. He has a penchant for extravagant purchases, and owns a vintage Rolls-Royce, a mansion in Kuching, and a grand piano once owned by Liberace.[66] Timber underpins Taib's personal wealth and political power. The 1987 election in Sarawak provided a rare glimpse into his links to logging. During this campaign, former Chief Minister Tun Abdul Rahman Yaakub and his nephew, incumbent Chief Minister Taib, openly accused each other of using timber concessions and money to strengthen their political positions.[67] Their dispute was largely personal and factional: Rahman Yaakub was angry with Taib for not following his "advice" even though Rahman Yaakub had personally supported Taib's ascent to the chief ministership in 1981. Chief Minister Taib, in an attempt to weaken the political position of his increasingly critical uncle, froze twenty-five timber concessions worth about M$22.5 billion (U.S.$9 billion) that were linked to Rahman Yaakub's clientele. This sparked a public war to expose each others' links to timber money.[68] Taib's group provided documents indicating that Rahman Yaakub, during his tenure as chief minister, had "set up a very complex web using nominees and shell companies to cover up ownership of large tracts of the best timber in Sarawak."[69] It was divulged that all eight of Rahman Yaakub's daughters, many other family members, friends, and associates as well as his office staff had large timber holdings. Documents were also released that showed Chief Minister Taib had distributed similar amounts of timber concessions to his close family, friends, and clients.[70] In total, it was revealed that Taib and his clients controlled approximately 1.6 million hectares of timber while Rahman Yaakub and his clients controlled around 1.25 million hectares, which together comprise over 30 percent of Sarawak's total forest area.[71]

Chief Minister Taib's repeal of timber concessions held by Rahman Yaakub's group was an important reason behind Taib's subsequent landslide election victory. Rahman Yaakub's patron-client network lost its main source of patronage and numerous members defected, especially Chinese ones. Chief Minister Taib reportedly gained the support of many Chinese politicians by offering timber concessions to leaders of the Chinese-based Sarawak United People's Party.[72]

Other influential ministers in Sarawak also have direct links to timber concessions. For example, Datuk Amar James Wong Kim Min, president of the Sarawak National Party (SNAP)—a key member of the BN government—and minister of the Environment and Tourism, is head of Limbang Trading. This company controls about 300 thousand hectares of timber concessions in Sarawak. As minister of the Environment and Tourism, Datuk Wong has a well-known reputation for supporting logging and dismissing environmental degradation. In 1988, he explained that five years after logging primary forests, "all the animals are back . . . with more fruits and nuts than before . . . logging is good for the forest."[73] In the same interview, when the president of Survival International asked if he was concerned with the effect of deforestation on weather patterns, he replied, "We get too much rain in Sarawak; it stops me playing golf."[74] Limbang Trading has reportedly sold timber on the government's protected species list—a list established by the Select Committee on Fauna and Flora, chaired by Datuk Wong.[75]

In Sarawak, around half a dozen Malaysian Chinese companies control timber extraction.[76] These corporations supply financial and electoral support to top state leaders in exchange for concession licenses, political protection, and bureaucratic exemptions. Malaysia's largest timber operator is Datuk Tiong Hiew King. He heads the Rimbunan Hijau Group of companies which controls 800 thousand hectares of timber concessions and logging contracts in Sarawak.[77] Rimbunan Hijau also operates large logging ventures in Papua New Guinea, accounting for 60–80 percent of timber exports. The 1993 Chinese edition of *Forbes* magazine estimated Datuk Tiong's net worth at M$2 billion.[78] Datuk Tiong has powerful political ties. He is an appointed federal senator. He is also a key figure in the Sarawak United People's Party, and a close friend of former Sarawak Deputy Chief Minister Wong Soon Kai (who lost his seat in the September 1996 state election). He strongly backs Chief Minister Taib and the BN coalition government, and has secure links to local politicians. Taib's sister, Aisah Zainab Mahmud, and the Sarawak government are partners in one of his logging and plywood operations. In another logging venture, Datuk James Wong and Datuk Tiong are partners in a 180 thousand-hectare site near Limbang.[79] Datuk Tiong has also worked closely with Japanese companies. Japanese technical advisers have influenced the management of his plywood mills; through a Hong Kong affiliate, two of these advisers are minority shareholders in Tiong's timber empire. According to one source, Datuk Tiong's companies are "almost Japanese in their operations."[80]

Tan Sri Ting Pek Khiing is another powerful ethnic Chinese businessman in Sarawak. He is chairman of the Ekran Company which controls 600 thousand hectares of timber concessions in Sarawak. In early 1994, this company was awarded a contract to build the huge Bakun hydroelectric dam. This is the most expensive infrastructure project in Malaysian history. The dam will create a lake about the size of Singapore. Before flooding the area, Ekran will clear 80 thousand hectares of forest, producing 3–6 million tons of logs. Ekran officials estimate that profits from log exports and a planned wood chip plant could exceed M$2 billion. Moreover, according to Tan Sri Ting, because of the "pioneer status" of the project, "there will be tax exemptions for quite some time."[81] Tan Sri Ting has close ties to Chief Minister Taib and Prime Minister Datuk Seri Mahathir Mohamad. Taib's sons are minority shareholders in Ekran and in Pacific Chemicals Bhd, another Ting company.[82] These political ties were a critical factor behind the choice of Ekran to build the Bakun dam. According to the *Asian Wall Street Journal*, the deal was "negotiated privately in just a few weeks by [Tan Sri] Ting and powerful Sarawak Chief Minister Tan Sri Abdul Taib Mahmud, then approved by Dr. Mahathir and awarded without competitive bidding."[83] Prime Minister Mahathir confirmed this deal "a day after he attended a wedding dinner for Chairman Ting's son."[84]

Although domestic criticism has been muffled, "corrupt" East Malaysian politicians and timber tycoons have been condemned internationally. For this reason, state leaders—especially Sarawak's Chief Minister Taib—are sensitive to any international or domestic probes of Malaysian forestry management. The Sarawak government closely supervises NGOs (including tapping phones), and monitors foreign visitors, especially journalists and researchers. For the last twenty years, Sarawak has blacklisted journalists, academics, and NGO leaders, using the power over immigration to bar unwanted visitors.[85] Despite these measures, criticism of East Malaysian forestry management mounted in the late 1980s and early 1990s. In 1992, the federal and state governments launched a campaign to suppress domestic environmental critics—in particular the Penan of Sarawak—and to flood the world media with positive images of Malaysian environmental management. When announcing the campaign, the federal primary industries minister declared: "If the reputation of Malaysia is not protected by giving the right information and counter arguing against ecocolonialistic attitude[s], such misinformation will in the end affect the country's economy."[86]

Pervasive clientelist ties between top state patrons and timber operators weaken supervision of state implementors, distort formal policies, and undermine state capacity to enforce regulations. This does not mean that formal institutions and policies can be ignored. Despite dismal enforcement, public policies can still have important consequences.[87] But they must be seen as existing alongside informal, unstable, instrumental arrangements that drive destructive logging, protect illegal loggers and smugglers, undercut tax and royalty collection, place concessions in the hands of a small, unaccountable elite, and distort policies to encourage processing, reforestation, plantations, and concession management.

Role of Formal Institutions, Regulations, and Policies

Background

Sabah and Sarawak both have exclusive jurisdiction over forestry management. The federal government is restricted to financing research and development, providing technical assistance and training, issuing export licenses,[88] and approving large foreign investments.[89] As well, under the federal Environment Quality Act, state logging companies are required to conduct environmental impact assessments. State governments are responsible for compliance, however, and so far no logging company has ever bothered to submit a report.[90]

Under the 1957 Land Code and the 1954 Forest Ordinance, all forested areas in Sarawak are owned by the state.[91] Responsibility for forestry policy and enforcement, and issuing and canceling timber concessions, rests primarily with the Sarawak Forest Department, while timber tax and royalty policies are formulated by the Chief Minister's Office.[92] The Sarawak Timber Industry Development Corporation (STIDC) negotiates with foreign investors. Harwood, a subsidiary of STIDC, monitors log export quotas and timber concessions. Since the beginning of 1993, STIDC has taken charge of approving timber export licenses from the Ministry of International Trade and Industry.[93]

In Sabah, responsibility for timber management is divided among the Sabah Foundation (through Innoprise), the Forestry Department, and the Chief Minister's Office. The exact duties of each institution are unclear, although generally both the Sabah Foundation and the Chief Minister's Office grant and revoke concessions, the Chief Minister's Office determines royalty policy, and the Forestry Department controls and enforces harvest regulations outlined in specific licenses, the 1968 forest enactment (and 1984 and 1992 amendments), and the 1969 forest rules.[94] The Forestry Department is only involved in minor reforestation projects, primarily for research.[95]

Logging Guidelines in East Malaysia

In Sabah, 2 million hectares have been carved into timber concessions.[96] Three main kinds of licenses are issued for logging: concessions, special licenses, and annual licenses. The Sabah Foundation grants concessions, usually from 21 to 25 years and between 20 thousand and 80 thousand hectares. In 1989 there were eleven concession holders. Special licenses are valid for five years and can be renewed for another one to five years. There were ninety-three special licenses in 1989.[97] Annual licenses are renewable one-year agreements. There were 500 in 1986.[98] In theory, Sabah timber operators, including the Sabah Foundation, use the Malayan Uniform System.[99] All commercial trees above a forty-five centimeter diameter are cut in one logging operation. The stand is then left to regenerate naturally—usually sixty to eighty years—before the next harvest. To facilitate natural replacement, climbers and seedlings, which compete with valuable species, are often poisoned.[100] In recent years, Sabah's management problems have been compounded now that lowland forests are largely depleted and loggers have moved to "highland areas where seedlings are less profuse."[101] In Sarawak, companies use a selective logging system similar to Indonesia's but with a shorter cutting cycle of twenty-five years.[102]

Although problems with formal logging guidelines exist in both Sabah and Sarawak, in practice timber companies quickly remove the most valuable logs with little regard for official regulations. State supervision and enforcement of logging rules are poor. Many forestry enforcement officers ignore violations in exchange for money or gifts. Problems are aggravated by a lack of staff.[103] For example, in the Keningau region of Sabah, one forestry official is responsible for an average area greater than 10 thousand hectares.[104]

Poorly controlled companies ignore silvicultural treatment and logging rules, reenter concessions too quickly, and do irreparable damage.[105] In Sabah as much as 75 percent of trees remaining after logging are damaged.[106] As in Indonesia, logged areas are vulnerable to slash-and-burn farmers and forest fires. In 1983, 20 percent of Sabah's forested land burned—85 percent of this area had been logged.[107] East Malaysian companies also illegally extract logs from protected forest areas and state land forest. In Sabah the government reported ninety-three cases of illegal logging, royalty evasions, and violations of timber regulations in the first ten months of 1993.[108] The government likely reports or discovers a small fraction of illegal activities. According to a Sabah logger, before the export ban illegal logs accounted for about 30 percent of total log exports.[109] As well, East Malaysia is a common exit point for illegal Indonesian and Philippine logs. Although no systematic documentation is available, sporadic evidence suggests that Japanese companies purchase illegal logs. For example, in 1992 the Sabah Forestry Department discovered more than 600 illegal logs in Japan.[110]

Tax and Royalty Policies

Royalty policies in East Malaysia have been more effective than environmental protection policies. State governments keep all timber royalties, export taxes, and license fees, a sharp contrast to the 5 percent of oil revenues allotted to Malaysian states. Over the last two decades, timber charges—especially on log exports—have generated substantial revenues in Sabah and Sarawak.[111] From 1980 to 1989, the forestry sector accounted for about 60 percent of Sabah's revenue; 95 percent came from royalties and taxes on log exports.[112] In the early 1990s, the forestry sector accounted for more than half of Sabah's revenue and around one-third of Sarawak's.

Through aggressive royalties and export taxes, Sabah has captured a significant portion of timber rents.[113] Nevertheless, informal agreements among politicians, bureaucrats, and timber operators have siphoned substantial amounts of potential state revenues. To lower forest charges, logging companies—often in collusion with customs officials and enforcement officers—forge species types, underdeclare the value and volume of exports, and falsify the degree of processing.[114] In many cases, timber executives simply report to customs a price or quantity lower than the one agreed on with the importer. In exchange for accepting these forged declarations, customs officials receive kickbacks. Importers—often sogo shosha—ignore these irregularities as long as "their supplies reach them at the agreed prices and quantities."[115] Besides these "sophisticated" schemes, companies sometimes dodge customs and covertly deliver logs to offshore ships.[116] As a result of these practices, one Sabah insider claimed in the mid-1980s that "two out of every five ships leaving here have not paid duty."[117] According to some sources, 30–40 percent of Sabah log exports were improperly documented in the early 1990s, contributing to substantial losses of royalties for the state government. In 1991, one Sabah logging group alone was alleged to be slipping out the equivalent of ten to fifteen vessels a month during busy periods, with an annual market value estimated by the *Far Eastern Economic Review* at U.S.$100 million. The same article estimated that in Sarawak these practices may be even more widespread.[118]

Under Malaysian law, federal timber revenue, which is collected by the Inland Revenue Department, is limited to corporate and personal income tax on timber profits. East Malaysian companies routinely practice transfer pricing to evade these taxes. Ethnic Chinese corporations in both Sarawak and Sabah sell logs to "home" companies, often in Hong Kong. These logs are priced at the cost of extraction. As a result, the local company's books show no profits, and the company pays no taxes. The Hong Kong company then sells the logs at market prices, in many cases to a sogo shosha (the logs generally "leave" East Malaysia only on paper). Profits appear in the Hong Kong books, where taxes are low. These profits are placed in a Hong Kong bank; the East Malaysian company then borrows an equivalent amount with interest payments equal to the interest earned in Hong Kong. Because the money "returns" as a loan, it is tax exempt.[119]

Political Concessionaires, Chinese Clients, and Subcontracts

In Sarawak all uncultivated land—except designated forest reserves, communal forests, and national parks—can be licensed by the state government as logging concessions.[120] Control over concession licenses is a critical source of power for patron-client networks. According to Philip

Hurst, "it is an open secret that timber concessions are handed out in East Malaysia as a means of strengthening political allegiances or as rewards for favours."[121] One study declared that in Sarawak, "political elites' control over awarding [logging] licences gives them the means to maintain and tighten their grip on state power—by alternately rewarding their cronies and followers, and buying off their political rivals and opponents."[122] Powerful political concession holders rely on ethnic Chinese contractors with the equipment and expertise to manage timber sites.[123] These ties are at the core of many patron-client clusters. Political patrons gain financial, political, and electoral support while Chinese business clients reap huge profits.

The central role of concessions in binding together patron-client clusters has contributed to overexploitation. In Sarawak, 60 percent of all land has been granted as timber concessions "on a scale which has no relation to the sustainable capacity of [timber] resources and with little regard for management prescriptions on the number and size of trees cut."[124] As well, patron-client links contribute to contracting arrangements in East Malaysia that reduce accountability and transparency, especially when concessions are granted to nominees.[125] In Sarawak Chinese contractors often make subcontracting arrangements. Subcontractors, many of whom are connected to local leaders, provide employees and equipment. To appease local opposition to destructive logging practices and the poor treatment of many native loggers, "there is evidence of some native leaders and even communities being paid off for making deals with timber concessionaires and especially with logging operators."[126] These complex contracting arrangements obscure lines of responsibility and make the enforcement of timber management rules much harder.[127] In 1993, Kuala Lumpur pushed state governments to stop awarding timber concessions to companies or individuals with no logging expertise.[128] According to foresters, this would "help eliminate unnecessary sub-contracting, reduce corruption and payment of under-counter money, control illegal logging . . . ensure higher efficiency . . . [and] in the long term, generate higher revenues for the state governments."[129]

Unstable patron-client ties contribute to a sense of uncertainty, which provides strong incentives to mine timber concessions quickly. It is fairly common for powerful leaders in East Malaysia to revoke concessions and licenses as political winds shift. For example, when Datuk Harris Salleh became chief minister of Sabah in 1976, he "cancelled concessions granted by his predecessor, covering 12 percent of the total forest area under license."[130] After Pairin's PBS Party ousted the ruling Berjaya Party under Harris Salleh in the 1985 Sabah election, timber patronage was again redistributed. The constant threat for concessionaires and contractors of being labeled "corrupt" further increases uncertainty. The overlap of "modern" legal institutions and "traditional" relations of power has created a situation where timber patronage is an "open secret," yet the threat of being labeled "corrupt" constantly exists. Charges of corruption clearly do not undermine authority in East Malaysia in the same way as in many Western democracies. For example, even after Chief Minister Taib was linked to widespread corruption and nepotism during the 1987 election in Sarawak, he still won easily. Nevertheless, corruption charges can undermine the stability of patron-client clusters and networks, especially when used as a tactic by the federal government to undermine state leaders or when used as a strategy by state politicians to "embarass" their opponents.[131]

Unpredictable political settings and unstable patron-client networks contribute to a serious problem of capital flight. Chinese timber clients, concerned about future economic trends, the fall of their patron, and racial backlashes, stash a significant portion of timber proceeds overseas, especially in Hong Kong. In addition, although ethnic Chinese loggers have made some investments in wood processing, they have made almost none in long-term forest management. Loggers perceive the industry as too volatile, perhaps even doomed.[132]

Log Export Restrictions and Processing Policies

In 1979, to reduce log exports and encourage domestic processing of sawn timber and plywood, Sabah established export quotas. But compared to Indonesia these were lenient and not well enforced.[133] This changed suddenly at the start of 1993 when Kuala Lumpur used its power over export licenses to prevent logs from leaving Sabah.[134] Officially, the federal government claimed that the ban was necessary to enhance environmental protection and promote domestic wood processing. It appears, however, to have been primarily motivated by Prime Minister Mahathir's desire to undermine Chief Minister Pairin's key source of patronage, topple his power base, and establish a more cooperative state government.[135] Before the ban, Japan had accounted for around 70 percent of Sabah log exports.[136] The move surprised Japanese plywood processors, spinning many into a financial crisis.[137] Kuala Lumpur lifted the ban in April 1993, after escalating log prices began to hamper wood processing in Peninsular Malaysia, and after receiving complaints and pressure from Japan's wood processing industry and the Japanese government.[138] The Sabah government, however, then struck back at Kuala Lumpur and imposed its own ban on log exports.[139] The Japanese government and corporations tried to convince Sabah to lift this ban, but the Pairin government stood firm.[140]

Sabah state revenues have remained stable since the ban on log exports. To offset lost export charges on logs, the government increased local processing fees.[141] The government and companies have also benefited from an increase in the price of sawn timber, which doubled in the first four months of the ban.[142] The ban on log exports has provided a crucial boost to Sabah wood processors. Before the ban, only 105 out of 164 sawmills were operating; many were functioning at half of their production capacity. Plywood and veneer mills were also operating well below capacity.[143] After the ban, Sabah plywood, veneer, and sawnwood mills all increased output, absorbing logs once destined for export.[144] As a result, in 1994 total log production was only 1.3 million cubic meters lower than it was in 1993.[145]

Despite stable government revenues and an increase in processing output, Sabah's ban on log exports has had few economic or environmental benefits. Log production is still far above sustainable levels, and little improvement has been made in the management of concessions. The total capacity of Sabah's plywood and veneer mills is over 11 million cubic meters. With production now set at about 8 million cubic meters, logs are in chronic short supply,[146] thus creating strong incentives to process illegal logs. As well, in the absence of international competitors, the Sabah Sawmilling Industries Association (SSIA) appears to be suppressing log prices.[147] In addition, as in Indonesia, the ban will likely protect and foster inefficient processors, putting even more pressure on commercial log stocks.[148] Finally, much of Sabah's sawn timber is little more than logs with their corners shaved, providing almost no value-added economic benefits. This "sawn" timber is then exported overseas and processed again.[149] In many ways, Sarawak has been the main beneficiary of Sabah's log export ban. In 1993 and the first quarter of 1994, Sarawak's logging industry thrived as log prices increased.[150]

Unlike in Indonesia since 1985 and Sabah since 1993, Sarawak has tried to balance log exports with incentives and restrictions to promote wood processing. Beginning in 1988, the government set aside 10 percent of logs for processing; in 1992, this was increased to 17 percent. Despite higher prices for log exports, since the beginning of 1993 Sarawak has made even more aggressive moves to promote processing.[151] To guarantee logs and stable prices for local processors, in early 1994 the state-controlled Harwood Company was made the sole distributor of local logs.[152] As well, in 1993 the government gave generous royalty rebates on logs manufactured in Sarawak,[153] and reserved around 36 percent of logs for local processors.[154] By the year 2000 the government intends to set aside 50 percent of logs for local processors.[155] No plans have been made, however, to ban log exports.[156] According to a government spokesman, foreign demand keeps log prices high, and log exports generate critical foreign exchange. Furthermore, around 60 percent of workers who manufacture wood are already Indonesian; creating more processing jobs would not boost Sarawak's economy.[157] So far, unlike in Sabah, Japan has not overtly pressured the Sarawak government to reduce log export restrictions. Local loggers, however—perhaps backed by Japanese companies—have lobbied to reduce export restrictions.[158]

With the help of government subsidies and protection, in 1994 Sarawak had 47 plywood and veneer mills and 208 sawmills.[159] Processed timber production has been steadily rising. For example, total plywood production in 1992 was 535 thousand cubic meters; by 1994 it had increased to 1.35 million cubic meters.[160] As in Sabah and Indonesia, however, many processing plants operate below capacity. For example, in early 1993 plywood mills were functioning at 60–70 percent of capacity.[161]

Conservation, Reforestation, and Timber Plantations

Informal links and personal agreements among forestry officials, concession holders, and logging companies sap the ability of the forest departments in Sabah and Sarawak to enforce conservation and reforestation policies. In Sarawak, "a great many forestry officials themselves are believed to have shares in the licensed companies, generally through relatives and nominees, and they thus have a vested interest in maximising short-term returns to the company rather than in assuring the careful management of State forest estate."[162] Logging companies in East Malaysia extract logs from national parks, state parks, and wildlife sanctuaries, which, according to the Malayan Nature Society, cover about "2 percent of Sarawak's land area and 3.6 percent of Sabah."[163] In Sabah, forestry officials are alleged to ignore illegal logging in exchange for "favours."[164] Of course, some forestry officials do try to enforce regulations, but they have had little success. The cumulative effect of these informal practices has contributed to minimal regeneration of natural forests, illegal logging in conservation areas, and ineffective reforestation projects.

In Sabah, corporations invest little in natural forest regeneration or timber plantations. Since concession licenses are linked to unstable patron-client networks, both domestic and foreign investors are wary of long-term commitments. As a timber exporter succinctly explained, companies "want to be sure that after investing . . . huge sums of money, the timber will be theirs. There is still much uncertainty over this aspect."[165] For this reason, most reforestation is conducted by the state government—especially the Sabah Foundation (through Sabah Softwoods Sdn Bhd) and the Sabah Forestry Development Authority.[166] There are now 300 thousand hectares of state timber plantations in Sabah, mostly fast-growing acacia mangium.[167]

Unlike Indonesia and Sabah, Sarawak has no plans to reforest concession sites or develop commercial timber plantations. Only about 10 thousand hectares of degraded land have been replanted in the permanent forest estate, mainly for conservation. According to the government, slash-and-burn farmers destroyed most of these areas.[168] In the Forest Department's view, plantations or reforestation are inherently unnecessary because areas are logged selectively. Instead, it is more important to improve silvicultural techniques.[169]

Recent Attempts to Improve Timber Management

During the last couple of years, the federal and state governments have introduced policies to tackle illegal logging and smuggling, destructive timber extraction, and tax and royalty evasion. In 1993 the federal government amended its National Forestry Act to improve enforcement of timber management rules and curb illegal logging. The revised law increases fines for logging violations, stipulates mandatory jail sentences of up to twenty years for illegal loggers, and permits the armed forces to be deployed in the forests. However, although this law provides important signals to East Malaysia, as one opposition member of Sarawak's legislature noted, "No federal forestry ordinance is strictly enforceable in Sarawak."[170]

In the early 1990s Sabah and Sarawak both imposed stiffer penalties to deter illegal loggers. Under Sabah's 1992 amendment to the Forest Enactment, illegal loggers face jail terms of up to seven years and fines of M$100,000.[171] In late 1993 the Sarawak state legislature passed the Forests (Amendment) Bill, stipulating a mandatory one-to-five-year prison sentence for illegal loggers.[172] Both states have also tightened rules and bolstered enforcement units to combat illegal loggers. In 1993, Sabah Forestry Department director Datuk Miller Munang announced that air force aerial surveys would be used to monitor illegal logging.[173]

Sarawak is particularly concerned with the smuggling of logs reserved for local processing, especially as log prices increased after the log export ban in Sabah. To combat this problem, in 1993 the Sarawak government called on members of the JLIA to reject illegal logs.[174] At the same time, Sarawak's Forest Department recruited 300 more enforcement officers, many of whom are former soldiers. Their task is to "undertake round-the-clock checking of all log export points, regular patrols in the jungle, mount raids and ambushes where necessary and make regular checks on logging camps, rafts and barges in transit and log ponds."[175] The State Enforcement Unit of the Sarawak Forest Department also established floating checkpoints at all export locations. Ships and barges transporting logs are now inspected just before leaving. In addition, the Enforcement Unit plans on surprise checks of ships loading logs offshore.[176] As an incentive to boost enforcement, Sarawak forestry officers now receive 50 percent of the total value of confiscated illegal logs.[177] To further hinder illegal loggers, in early 1994, Sarawak banned transporting logs on some rivers at night.[178]

Even though monetary incentives, more enforcement officers, stiffer penalties, and tighter regulations appear to be important steps to improve timber management, in the setting of pervasive state links to timber operators, these moves are likely to have little impact on large companies. When announcing plans in 1993 to combat illegal logging, the Sarawak forestry director Datuk Leo Chai argued that most illegal loggers were local people, not major companies. As he explained, "there are few organised illegal logging groups in the state because they cannot bring their logging machinery into the forest without being detected."[179] The failure of past campaigns to tackle illegal logging and tax evasion demonstrates the impunity of commercial timber companies in East Malaysia. In 1991 a former manager of a major Sabah timber group publicly alleged that his company had extracted logs from restricted areas, forged species types, and distorted log measurements, costing the state millions of Malaysian dollars. He claimed that Sabah forestry officials participated in these illegal activities. In response, Chief Minister Pairin announced a low-key campaign to halt illegal logging and royalty evasion. These efforts, however, had little impact on major timber firms.

Instead, "small operators served as the scapegoats." These "small operators were mostly businessmen believed to be unable to pay customary gratuities to forestry officials."[180]

To increase state capacity to monitor exports and improve royalty collection rates, Sabah officials are now considering a proposal to hire a British firm, Inchcape, to check timber export and import documents. Inside Sabah, Inchcape would replace forestry and customs officials who verify volumes, tree diameters, species type, and tax and royalty assessments. Inchcape would also place inspectors in key importing countries, including Japan. According to Miller Munang, "the global approach—checking shipments at both ends—is the best way to plug the leak in the state coffers."[181] Given that foreigners are not linked to patron-client networks and are not involved in political struggles, Inchcape inspectors in theory could be far more effective than current state officials. But state leaders and implementors who receive timber proceeds are unlikely to allow this to occur. It is more likely that Inchcape's proposal will be scuttled or that Inchcape inspectors will become pawns of the ruling elite to legitimize current practices.

In the early 1990s, the federal Inland Revenue Department began a campaign to stop transfer pricing by East Malaysian timber firms. According to federal Primary Industries minister Datuk Lim Keng Yaik, even though transfer pricing is exceedingly difficult to prove, in 1992 Inland Revenue forced numerous Sarawak timber companies to pay outstanding taxes, including one large conglomerate that had to pay M$100 million. He claims that, as a result, transfer pricing has dropped to a "bearable minimum."[182] In late 1993 the federal police and Inland Revenue authorities searched Sarawak's Rimbunan Hijau Group (led by Datuk Tiong) for evidence of tax evasion. Although the results of the investigation were not disclosed, ample reason exists to be suspicious of Tiong. According to the financial records of Tiong's major company, Rimbunan Hijau Sdn Bhd, from 1976 to 1991 the company made an after-tax profit of a mere M$9.68 million on total revenues of M$3.2 billion. As a result, Rimbunan Hijau Sdn Bhd only paid M$20 million in federal corporate taxes.[183] Compared to state initiatives, the Inland Revenue Department has had a far greater impact on large companies, perhaps because East Malaysian corporate links to federal authorities are often weaker than those to state leaders.

In the midst of Malaysia's vigorous campaign to reduce international criticism of its environmental practices, it is difficult to wade through the rhetoric to document concrete changes in timber management.

Overall, marginal improvements have been made, especially in hindering transfer pricing. But East Malaysia is still far from reaching sustainable timber management. Harvesting rates are falling, but this appears to be a response to declining timber stocks rather than to better management. With powerful political patrons protecting major loggers, and with customs and forestry enforcement officers integrated into timber-based networks, large timber companies have largely escaped the "crackdown." When illegal loggers or smugglers are nabbed, they tend to be small-time operators or local swidden farmers. Sim Kwang Yang, a member of parliament from Sarawak, succinctly summarized the current campaign to improve timber management: "On paper, there is a sluggish move in the direction of reduced logging under international pressure."[184] Keeping in mind domestic patron-client politics and timber policies in East Malaysia, I now turn to assess Japan's ecological shadow of tropical timber.

Japanese ODA in East Malaysia

The Japan International Cooperation Agency and the Japanese Overseas Economic Cooperation Fund have channeled only a small amount of technical assistance and loans to Sabah forestry projects.[185] The OECF has not provided any concessional loans to help finance plantation schemes[186] and JICA currently has no projects in Sabah nor does it have plans for future assistance.[187] JICA's last major forestry aid project in Sabah, the Reafforestation Technical Development and Training Project, began in 1987 and expired in March 1994. This project was operated jointly by JICA and the state-controlled Sabah Forestry Development Authority (SAFODA). The state government provided funding, while JICA supplied experts on reforestation, equipment (such as bulldozers, front-end loaders, and fire-fighting equipment), and training in Japan. The main purpose of the project was to enhance planting techniques and train forestry personnel in silvicultural methods for timber plantations. The research concentrated on acacia mangium—a fast-growing Australian hardwood imported to Sabah in the 1960s—although some preliminary research was done on dipterocarp. Today, SAFODA controls this project, training new recruits using the knowledge and equipment supplied by JICA.[188]

According to SAFODA and JICA officials, the SAFODA-JICA project was a resounding success.[189] SAFODA, created in 1976, had made minimal headway in replanting in its first decade. But with JICA's advice and equipment, by 1993 SAFODA had planted 25 thousand hectares of acacia mangium and 8 thousand hectares of rattan.[190] SAFODA has no ambitious plans to expand and only expects to plant around 2 thousand hectares every year.[191] To date, only a few thousand hectares of acacia mangium have been harvested. Most plantation logs have been sold to South Korea.[192]

JICA-SAFODA research on cross-breeding and silvicultural techniques improved the quality of acacia mangium plantations in Sabah. Trees are taller, straighter, grow faster, and have fewer blemishes. But compared to the problems confronting Sabah forestry managers, these efforts are minor. The project itself was quite small; only four, or sometimes five, JICA researchers worked at the project. Moreover, even if acacia mangium becomes an important "agricultural commodity" that is able to thrive in degraded areas, it cannot replace the biodiversity and environmental benefits of natural forests or sufficiently substitute for the commercial value of dipterocarp logs. Also, it is unclear whether these plantations will actually reduce pressure on natural forests. In theory, plantations can create employment and provide an alternative wood source in severely degraded areas. But in practice, as in Indonesia, timber companies often maximize profits by clearing natural forests before establishing plantations.[193]

Japan has provided no major loans or grants for Sarawak forestry projects.[194] There is now one major technical assistance project. In April 1993, JICA launched the Effective Wood Utilization Research Project and Timber Research and Technical Training Center. Four long-term Japanese experts advise eight Sarawak counterparts. As well, some Japanese specialists visit for one or two months. As part of this project, two or three researchers from Sarawak will study in Japan every year. In its first year, JICA spent ¥150 million. JICA's budget for 1994–95 was around ¥67 million. This project is designed to provide equipment, technology, and advice to improve the efficiency of domestic processing. At present, Sarawak processors discard or burn 40–50 percent of logs. JICA's project is also supposed to encourage loggers to extract lesser-quality, lesser-known species. Better wood utilization, coupled with improved efficiency, will waste less wood and presumably reduce pressure on commercial species in the natural forests.[195] Although these efforts are laudable, as in Sabah, compared to the problems of timber management, JICA's overall financial and technical contribution has been inconsequential.[196]

Japanese Corporate Investment in East Malaysia's Timber Industry

In Sabah, Japanese companies have invested minimal amounts in logging and processing.[197] As of December 1993, eleven wood processing companies were in Sabah with Japanese equity. These mills include veneer, plywood, sawn timber, and molding.[198] Japanese investment is not likely to increase in the near future. Since the log export ban and the reduction in log output to 8 million cubic meters, Japanese investors have become even more reluctant to invest in Sabah forestry projects.[199] Furthermore, Sabah timber operators have become disillusioned with joint ventures. According to a Sabah business executive, local companies are wary of joint ventures with Japan because many of them lost money in the past. He argues that two main factors account for this poor track record. First, some Japanese partners manipulated timber prices and undercut profit margins of joint ventures. In these cases, the Japanese joint venture partner, after consulting with their "home" company, sold logs below the international market price to enhance the profits and economic stability of the corporate group. Second, joint ventures often have lower production efficiency. Japanese (as well as U.S. companies) have a tendency to manage workers within their own cultural prism. As a result, Sabah workers, who may for example respond poorly to anger, are less productive.[200] Sabah's dominant timber operator, the Sabah Foundation, has moved away from joint ventures. For example, Sinoru Sdn Bhd, a wood processing plant in Sandakan, was originally a joint venture with Japan's Yuasa Trading Company. In 1989, however, after fifteen years as a joint venture, the foundation gained full control.[201]

Most Japanese companies have avoided direct investments in logging in Sarawak. The few Japanese Sarawak logging joint ventures have not been particularly successful. For example, Itochu's joint logging venture with Limbang Trading Company (owned by James Wong) was a public relations fiasco. A scandal erupted after it was disclosed that the company's logging roads had been funded by JICA and the EXIM Bank of Japan.[202] Itochu withdrew in 1987 after intense public criticism, which included a debate in the Japanese Diet. A few Japanese wood processing joint ventures have also been established in Sarawak. In total, there have been about half a dozen, all with guarantees of access to the Japanese market.[203] Both Sarawak's Ministry of Resource Planning and the Sarawak Timber Industry Development Corporation have urged Japanese companies to invest in processing.[204] But these firms have shown little interest.[205] Rather than participate directly, these companies, especially sogo shosha, prefer to purchase logs, and when necessary provide credit, equipment, and technical advice to facilitate logging.[206]

Japanese Companies and Conservation in East Malaysia

Japanese companies have not participated in conservation or improving forestry management in Sabah.[207] In the last few years, Sabah officials have tried to prompt major sogo shosha—including Sumitomo, Itochu, and Marubeni—to provide assistance for forestry management and conservation. But so far there has been no response.[208] The Sabah Foundation, which is now developing techniques and training personnel for enrichment planting in logged areas, has received some support from two utility companies, the New England Power Service and the Dutch Electricity Generating Board, but nothing from Japan.[209] According to a Sabah forestry official, Japanese companies seem far more concerned with developing new techniques to make temperate plywood than with ensuring a sustainable yield of tropical timber.[210] Japanese firms also have not invested in timber plantations in Sabah. In 1993, Sumitomo, acting as a broker for two paper companies in Japan, began negotiations for a large, joint-venture plantation project. These companies, however, eventually lost interest.[211] Japanese corporate executives are wary of the long-term commitments, financial risks, unclear land tenure, sudden political or policy changes, and world fluctuations in pulp and paper prices.[212]

Poor harvesting techniques and inefficient processors waste valuable wood and increase the pressure on commercial timber stocks. Although Japanese corporations have provided some equipment and technical advice for Sabah loggers and processors, no systematic effort has been undertaken to enhance processing efficiency, recover timber waste, or improve cutting methods.[213] Instead, sogo shosha have sent technicians to Sabah to guarantee that logs and sawn timber meet Japan's rigid cutting and manufacturing stipulations. These technicians ensure that the best timber reaches the Japanese market. According to a senior Sabah timber executive, they are not concerned with the process, only the end result.[214] In Sarawak—where processors waste as much as 50 percent of logs—Japanese companies have also done little to improve efficiency. One exception is a Japan-Sarawak joint venture to produce Sarawak's first medium-density fiberboard (MDF) plant. Construction began in 1994 and production is expected to begin in 1996. The plant has five partners: Daiken Corporation of Japan (50 percent equity), Itochu (20 percent), the Sarawak Timber Industry Development Corporation (15 percent), the Sarawak company Proexcel (10 percent), and Datuk Wong's Limbang Trading Company (5 percent). The joint venture company, Daiken Sarawak Sdn Bhd, received a U.S.$50 million loan from the EXIM Bank of Japan. To make MDF, this plant will use wood scraps from plywood mills and sawmills. The company hopes to export 80–100 thousand cubic meters of MDF by the end of this century.[215]

Environmentalists around the world have attacked Sarawak for its forest management and treatment of aboriginal peoples. They have also strongly criticized Japanese companies. Some of the harshest criticism has been leveled at Mitsubishi. To counteract these critics, sogo shosha have increased funding for public relations and made token contributions to forest conservation in Sarawak, but few serious efforts have been made to improve timber management.[216] For example, Mitsubishi partially funds the Bintulu project, a research experiment to recreate a natural rain forest.[217] According to a professor at the University of Tokyo, of all the recent corporate "conservation" projects, the Bintulu project is designed the most for "show."[218]

Japanese Timber Purchases from East Malaysia

Japan's primary impact on East Malaysia's timber industry has been as a log buyer. Sogo shosha have thrived in the clientelist states of East Malaysia, using their control over the trade chain and the flow of market information to import massive amounts of inexpensive logs from unsustainable sources. These cheap logs have allowed Japanese plywood processors to prosper, which in turn has stimulated wasteful tropical timber consumption. Given that the quality of wood in Sabah is higher than in Sarawak, after commercial log stocks eroded in the Philippines and as demand soared, sogo shosha turned first to Sabah.[219] Besides supplying credit and equipment (often in exchange for logs), these companies provided powerful financial incentives that escalated log production in Sabah. In 1965, out of a total of 9.3 million cubic meters of Southeast Asian log imports, Japan imported 2.8 million cubic meters from Sabah and 644 thousand cubic meters from Sarawak. In that year, Japan imported about two-thirds of Sabah's total log production.[220] By 1969, Japanese log imports from Sabah had climbed to over 4 million cubic meters. In the same year, Japan imported 1.9 million cubic meters of logs from Sarawak. In 1978, Japan imported around 21.8 million cubic meters of Southeast Asian logs: 9.2 million cubic meters came from Sabah and only 1.5 million cubic meters came from Sarawak. As Sabah logs became less abundant in the 1980s, and after Indonesia's log export ban, Japanese log purchases from Sarawak increased substantially. By 1987, Japan's log imports from Southeast Asia had dropped to 13.7 million cubic meters. Sabah accounted for 7.0 million cubic meters and Sarawak accounted for 5.5 million cubic meters.[221]

From 1979 to 1988, Sabah exported an annual average of around 9 million cubic meters of logs, worth more than U.S.$5.5 billion.[222] During the height of Sabah's log exports from 1972 to 1987, Japan imported about 61 percent of total log production and accounted for nearly 70 percent of total log exports.[223] After 1987 Japanese log imports from Sabah steadily declined. In 1988, Japan imported 5.4 million cubic meters of Sabah logs. By 1991, Japanese log imports from Sabah had dropped to around 2.6 million cubic meters, although this accounted for about three-quarters of Sabah's total log exports.[224] In 1993, as a result of the log export ban, Japanese log imports from Sabah plummeted to less than 300 thousand cubic meters. From 1987 to 1992, Japanese plywood, sawn timber, and veneer imports from Sabah increased only marginally. In 1988 Japan imported 213,700 cubic meters of sawn timber, 200 cubic meters of plywood, and 80,200 cubic meters of veneer. In 1992, Japan imported 444,496 cubic meters of sawn timber, 14,965 cubic meters of plywood, and 201,616 cubic meters of veneer.[225] Since the log export ban, sawn timber and veneer imports have decreased. In 1995, Japan imported 89,133 cubic meters of veneer and 306,633 cubic meters of sawn timber, although plywood imports increased to 321,018 cubic meters.[226] As a result of these changes, total Japanese timber imports from Sabah (in roundwood equivalent) fell from nearly 7.5 million cubic meters in 1987 to 2.9 million cubic meters in 1992, to below 1.5 million cubic meters in 1995.[227]

As Sabah's log exports decreased from 9.4 million cubic meters in 1987 to 3.4 million cubic meters in 1991, Sarawak increased log exports from 12.6 million cubic meters in 1987 to 15.9 million cubic meters in 1990.[228] As logs became less accessible in Sabah, Japanese corporations turned to Sarawak. In 1988, Japan imported 5.3 million cubic meters of logs from Sarawak. Japanese log imports from Sarawak climbed to 6.7 million cubic meters in 1990 and then dropped slightly in 1991 and 1992 to around 6.5 million cubic meters. With greater restrictions on log exports, Japanese log imports decreased even further, to 4.9 million cubic meters in 1993 and 3.9 million cubic meters in 1995.[229] Although less than in Sabah in the 1970s, from 1989 to 1995 Japanese companies imported around one-third of Sarawak's total log production.[230] These companies, however, are by far the most important log buyers, accounting for over half of Sarawak's log exports from 1993 to 1995.[231]

Since the late 1980s, Japan has slightly increased sawn timber and veneer imports from Sarawak, while plywood imports have increased significantly. In 1987, Japan imported 10,723 cubic meters of sawn timber, 2 cubic meters of plywood, and 47,848 cubic meters of veneer. In 1992, Japan imported 54,668 cubic meters of sawn timber, 45,300 cubic meters of plywood, and 18,449 cubic meters of veneer.[232] In 1995, Japan imported 77,429 cubic meters of sawn timber, 60,101 cubic meters of veneer, and 591,665 cubic meters of plywood. As a result of these changes, total Japanese timber imports from Sarawak (in roundwood equivalent) increased from almost 6 million cubic meters in 1987 to around 6.5 million cubic meters in 1992. In 1995, however, export restrictions reduced total Japanese timber imports to around 5.5 million cubic meters (in roundwood equivalent).[233]

Japan, Tariff Barriers, Log Prices, and Sustainable Management

As East Malaysian plywood exports to Japan increase, Japanese import tariffs reduce timber revenues and in theory, as in Indonesia, siphon money that could support sustainable management.[234] Also as in Indonesia, the prices Japanese companies pay for East Malaysian logs and processed timber are far below the cost of sustainable management. One angry Malaysian columnist wrote, "Japan is gobbling our trees because they are dirt cheap. A jungle tree which took hundreds of years to grow is cheaper in Japan than a softwood pine that took only 20 years to grow. That's why Japan is using Malaysian timber for junk furniture and throw-away construction frames."[235] Without prices that reflect environmental costs, sustainable management is unlikely. Barney Chan, spokesman for the Sarawak Timber Association (STA) argues, "If you give tropical timber a higher value, it allows us to harvest it in a fashion more friendly to the environment. We have all along been saying to the West: put your money where your mouth is. If you want to save the rainforest, give us a better price for timber."[236] In theory, Chan is correct. Japan's extensive purchases have played a key role in driving unsustainable logging. But increasing prices is not an automatic solution. In a setting where particularistic, rent-seeking patron-client networks undermine state capacity to enforce rules and distort state policies, higher prices may simply add incentives to extract logs recklessly and make quick money.

Conclusion

Patron-client politics and timber in East Malaysia are intricately connected: patron-client relations shape timber resource distribution and management while timber binds many of these links together. Modern patron-client networks have large, fluid peripheries. Compared to traditional relations, they are based less on loyalty and honor and more on self-interested material exchange. This contributes to highly unstable ties that frequently rupture as political parties contest elections and jockey for control. This creates an unpredictable atmosphere that encourages fast, destructive logging. Political leaders have used timber concessions and profits to build and hold together multiethnic patron-client networks and appease and coopt potential adversaries. As a result, patron-client ties strongly influence the allocation of concessions, licenses, and contracts, determining who primarily benefits from logging profits, and contributing to a complex distribution system that decreases transparency and accountability necessary for environmental management. Patron-client ties to timber operators at the top of the state also dilute political will and weaken state supervision of forestry and enforcement officers. In this context, timber-based patron-client networks are able to capture or coopt bureaus of the state. This contributes to many state implementors ignoring customs and management regulations in exchange for gifts, money, and career opportunities. In short, informal, particularistic relations are a critical force shaping formal timber institutions, policies, and regulations in the clientelist states of East Malaysia.

Sabah, which began large-scale logging before Sarawak, now has grave forestry problems. Poor management, weak enforcement, political links to logging concessions, unstable patron-client ties, and constant disputes with the federal government have contributed to overlogging and forest degradation. The dominance of the state-controlled Sabah Foundation—rather than enabling the state to tackle unsustainable logging—has contributed to mismanagement as timber profits have been channeled to powerful political patrons such as Chief Ministers Mustapha, Harris Salleh, and Pairin. The 1993 ban on log exports and the moves to tackle poor harvesting practices and illegal logging have done little to improve timber management. Annual log production has dropped; but this is more a result of declining commercial timber stocks than of better forest management.

Sarawak has similar problems, but with a later start and more forest resources, there are still considerable areas of valuable commercial timber. Based on timber concessions and profits, top politicians such as Chief Minister Taib and Environment and Tourism Minister James Wong have built personal fortunes and powerful patron-client networks. These networks have distorted state policies and undermined state capacity and willingness to enforce timber regulations. Private-sector timber companies—such as the Rimbunan Hijau Group (Datuk Tiong) and the Ekran Company (Tan Sri Ting)—are protected by political patrons and assisted by forestry and enforcement officers. As a result, these corporations continue to extract unsustainable amounts of logs, ignore logging rules, conduct illegal logging and smuggling, elude state royalties and federal income taxes, and disregard conservation and silvicultural treatments. In the short term, since Sabah's log export ban, Sarawak has benefited from higher log prices. But these prices still fall far short of the costs of sustainable management. In addition, as in Indonesia and Sabah, government moves to build a domestic processing industry are unlikely to promote sustainable logging. With similar political forces driving mismanagement, and Japanese corporate purchases expediting overcutting, Sarawak appears headed down the same trail as Sabah, with Indonesia not far behind.

Unlike in Indonesia, Japanese ODA and investment have had minor implications for East Malaysian timber management. Japanese tariff barriers have also had less impact on state and corporate revenues, although since 1993 these have become relatively more important. Nevertheless, Japan's shadow ecology has expedited the process of East Malaysian deforestation. Sogo shosha have provided equipment, advice, and credit that has facilitated unsustainable logging. But Japan's greatest impact has been as a log trader. In the context of pervasive clientelism, sogo shosha—through structural and financial arrangements with firms in the log trade chain and through access to current market information—have procured large amounts of cheap logs from unsustainable sources. From 1972 to 1987, Japan accounted for almost 70 percent of Sabah's log exports. After exhausting much of Sabah's valuable commercial logs, Japanese traders turned to Sarawak. Japan now accounts for over half of Sarawak's log exports. These purchases have provided incentives for destructive logging and crucial funds for patron-client networks. They have also contributed to a sharp fall in primary forest cover. Japan now has less impact on timber management in Sabah. But past log purchases—at prices far below the costs of sustainable management—have left Sabah scrambling to find the funds and resources to save what remains of their timber industry.

Having analyzed the implications of patron-client relations for timber management, it is interesting to speculate on the possible impact of declining timber resources on patron-client relations, given that in Sabah and Sarawak these two issues are virtually inseparable: a change in one will certainly result in a change in the other. Given that patron-client clusters are bound together largely by timber profits, at the very least, depletion of timber resources will force patron-client clusters to reshape and realign, and perhaps more ominously, could destabilize the political system. Patron-client links now provide an essential source of stability and means of cooperation among the diverse ethnic and religious groups. If timber revenues evaporate, many patron-client links will dissolve and quite possibly could realign along religious or ethnic lines, especially given that an economic crisis will likely accompany the collapse of the timber industry. Another result of the loss of timber revenue could be increased calls from Sabah and Sarawak for greater autonomy from the federal government in Kuala Lumpur, especially in terms of control over oil revenues. Kuala Lumpur is, however, unlikely to concede control over this key resource and serious disputes could arise.[237]

5 Japan, Patron-Client Politics, and the Collapse of the Philippine Timber Industry

As in Indonesia and East Malaysia, commercial loggers have been a key force behind deforestation in the Philippines. Poor selective cutting techniques, illegal extraction, and logging roads have cleared and degraded primary forests, making these areas more accessible to slash-and-burn farmers and more susceptible to devastating fires. In these ways, commercial loggers have not only degraded vast areas but also have triggered the process that has stripped much of the Philippines.[1] During the 1970s and 1980s, on average 2.5 percent of Philippine forests disappeared every year, three times the rate of worldwide tropical deforestation.[2] Over this time more than 80 percent of the remaining primary forests vanished. Today, forests only cover around 20 percent of the Philippines.[3] If illegal and legal logging continue at the current rate, almost all old-growth forests will disappear over the next decade.[4]

This chapter begins the ascent to the conclusion. Because the Philippines is deeper in the spiral of deforestation, an analysis of its past and current trends sheds light on the future of the forests of Indonesia and East Malaysia. After World War II, ubiquitous patron-client networks at the top and middle levels of the state debilitated state capacity and willingness to enforce timber policies. In the 1950s and 1960s Congress members used timber profits and licenses to reward clients and finance expensive electoral campaigns. In the 1970s, President Ferdinand Marcos (1965–86) built a large, dominant patron-client network, especially after declaring martial law in 1972. As Marcos battled to remain supreme in the societal web of clientelist relations, he allowed rent-seeking, particularistic patron-client clusters to thrive at all levels of the state and society. On an unbelievable scale and at a frantic pace, powerful patrons and well-connected clients plundered natural resources to support extravagant whims and opulent lifestyles. In this setting, poorly supervised, demoralized state implementors were absorbed by timber-based patron-client networks. State bureaus were captured by private interests; rather than enforcing management principles, the Philippine clientelist state protected and facilitated rapid and destructive logging.

After the fall of Marcos in 1986, key patron-client ties at the top of the state dissolved. Many realigned, however, and formidable timber-based networks still exist, especially in the middle level of the state and in the outer regions. In many ways, post-Marcos elites have restored the politics of the 1950s and 1960s, when politicians battled for votes and political parties riddled by patron-clientelism jockeyed for control. Unlike the 1950s and 1960s, however, timber stocks are no longer sufficient to sustain large patron-client networks, and top state elites now have fewer ties to timber operators. This has contributed to an incremental increase in state capacity and willingness to manage the forests. But pervasive patron-client ties in the middle level of the state, especially in regional areas, still distort timber policies and undermine state enforcement. As a result, although marginal improvements in state management have been made, the Philippine clientelist state is still unable to enforce concession guidelines, collect taxes and royalties, prevent illegal logging, and ensure adequate conservation, reforestation, and regeneration of natural forests.

From the 1950s to the mid-1970s, with minimal state control over loggers and with Philippine patrons and timber clients receiving lucrative profits, Japanese log traders—backed by strategic investments and credit to firms involved in the log trade—purchased vast quantities of cheap logs from unsustainable sources, accelerating the process that led to the environmental wasteland of the late Marcos years. Today there are few Japanese corporate investments or timber purchases. Nevertheless, the residue of Japan's ecological shadow of timber compounds the problems facing Filipino managers. Filipinos are now absorbing the costs of substantial profits reaped by Japanese companies in the past. State managers must cope with and pay for the consequences of extensive deforestation, including soil erosion, river siltation, flash floods, climatic instability, and inadequate timber stocks.[5] Burdened by past environmental abuse by Filipino elites and their Northern allies, it is hardly surprising that current managers are struggling to find the funds and means to preserve the scattered primary forests and reforest the swaths of degraded areas. One obvious place to look is Japan. But current Japanese ODA does not compensate for past practices. At present, JICA provides no technical cooperation projects or grants. Instead, the Japanese government has emphasized "environmental loans." But these have major flaws. In the case of the Forestry Sector Program Loan (U.S.$120 million from 1988–92), rather than reviving the environment, this loan will eventually add even more pressure to extract and export natural resources to acquire foreign exchange and repay the national debt. To provide a foundation for understanding the domestic political economy of forest management and the past and current impact of Japan's ecological shadow, the next section explains key changes to Filipino patron-client relations, concentrating on shifts prior to 1972, changes after Marcos declared martial law in 1972, and realignments after Corazon Aquino became president in 1986.

Traditional and Modern Patron-Client Relations

Traditional patron-client relations in the Philippines are multifarious, asymmetrical, personal, noncontractual, and grounded in a strong cultural norm of reciprocal obligation (*utang na loob*). As in most of rural Southeast Asia, these ties initially developed between landowners and tenant farmers. Landowners provided agricultural fields, credit, security, and prestige in exchange for loyalty, obedience, labor, and collective power. These ties persisted for decades, often crossing generations of both patron and client families. After World War II, with the onslaught of "modernization"—that is, urbanization, a market economy, a larger middle class, more educational opportunities, social upheavals, changes to agricultural production, and an expanding bureaucracy—patron-client networks became larger and more complex. These networks integrated people with diverse occupational backgrounds and from all levels of society.[6] Shopkeepers, rice dealers, employers, labor leaders, bureaucrats, and local politicians became patrons. As the bureaucracy expanded, patrons increasingly relied on the state as a source of patronage. In this new setting, patron-client ties—although still personal, informal, and asymmetrical—became based more on direct exchange of state resources and less on loyalty, reciprocal obligation, family wealth, and feelings of shame. These large, material-based patron-client networks are more unstable than traditional ties as patrons and clients switch allegiances to maximize opportunities. Modern networks often dissolve when a patron dies or loses political or economic clout. Today, modern networks are pervasive, although some traditional ties still remain, mostly in outlying areas. Alliances between these modern patron-client networks create factions, often generating strong cleavages among Filipino elite.[7]

Political and corporate activities are often organized around families. Some families even maintain their own bank. In the 1960s about 400 families dominated the Philippines. By the end of the 1970s, this had dropped to around sixty families.[8] Filipino families are built on both real and ritual kinship ties. *Compadrazgo*, or ritual kinship, joins families of similar socioeconomic rank as well as poor families to wealthier ones. These ties are often cemented by a member of an influential family acting as a godfather (*compadre*) for a child of a less-powerful family. Families strive to secure the strongest godfather possible. Marcos was reportedly a godfather for around 20 thousand people.[9] Because Filipino families include the relatives of both spouses as well as ritual ties, families are often quite large. This has important implications for modern patron-client links. Compared to other Southeast Asian countries, Filipino patron-client networks tend to have stronger feelings of loyalty and reciprocity.[10] Even distant family members are supported, contributing to rampant corporate and government nepotism. As well, the "strength of blood and ritual kinship ties discourages trust among non-family members," and encourages an "us" verses "them" attitude.[11] Finally, the large size of Filipino families makes it difficult to distinguish between patron-client networks and families; in many cases, a family is the core of a patron-client network.[12]

Patron-Client Relations (1898–1972)

After the United States colonized the Philippines in 1898, more and more patrons exploited bureaucratic connections and resources to obtain benefits for their clientele. As the bureaucracy grew, especially after independence in 1946, "congressmen and senators, the president and close associates, influential businessmen, members of the press, bureau directors and office chiefs all made telephone calls, wrote letters of recommendation or personally accompanied their protégés to agencies where vacancies and new positions were available."[13] As more patrons relied on state resources to sustain their networks, bureaucratic appointments, licenses, and funds were increasingly allocated based on personal contacts rather than on competitive bids or exams.[14] In the 1950s and 1960s, loyal Congress members—especially from the government party—gained informal powers to appoint followers to bureaucratic positions. Through this clientele and their control over the budget, political leaders dominated the bureaucracy. Instead of functioning on principles of merit and efficiency, bureaucratic decisions and policies were overwhelmed by particularistic, opportunistic patron-client interaction. In this setting, "departmental secretaries, bureau directors, and office division chiefs—themselves recruited from among the party—faithful clients and political protégés, or clients of heavy financial contributors—mediated between their own clients and the more powerful politicians."[15] Patron-client networks, often capitalizing on low state wages, captured tentacles of the state, debilitating the state as it battled societal interests for control over the rules of the game. This created a weak state, "unable to collect more than a small share of the GNP in taxes, effectively regulate powerful economic groups, or efficiently distribute social services."[16] Not surprisingly, the state also lacked the political will, requisite attitudes, and institutional capacity to manage natural resources on a sustainable basis.

Before 1972 patron-client interaction overwhelmed political parties and elections. Federal politicians focused on distributing patronage and maintaining close links to "lower-level political leaders who had personal followings and hence votes they could deliver 'at will.'"[17] Congress became a forum to carve slices of patronage. Political parties were essentially "hierarchies of patron client networks."[18] As a result, political alliances were often held together by patron-client ties rather than by ideological beliefs. Elections were "plagued by factionalism, by party switching, by rebels who contested the official party candidates, and by independent candidates."[19] In this setting, many clients exchanged their votes for money, gifts, and jobs. As well, financial backers of victorious politicians often received senior administrative posts. Elections were expensive and political power was often limited to wealthy families.[20] The 1969 election apparently cost 1 billion pesos (P), nearly one-quarter of that year's national budget. By this time elections were so expensive, they "trigger[ed] massive government deficits and ultimately the devaluation of the peso."[21]

Marcos as Supreme Patron (1972–1986)

After Marcos declared martial law in 1972, his family and clients (cronies)—especially from his home province of Ilocos Norte—consolidated control over the distribution of patronage.[22] Rather than dispersing "the national network of patron-client relations," Marcos maneuvered to centralize control over these networks. To increase his power, he decided "to become 'supreme godfather' and acquire the personal wealth that would reinforce that role. He eliminated his competitors at the national level and strengthened his own position in regions and provinces by dealing more directly with the *barangay*" (the smallest unit of local government).[23]

Friends, followers, and relatives of Ferdinand and Imelda Marcos received government credit, licenses, tax exemptions, monopolistic contracts, classified government information, and privileged access to foreign aid and joint ventures. Funds from the World Bank, the International Monetary Fund, and Northern commercial banks and bilateral donors—especially the United States and Japan—fueled pervasive patronage. In 1991 the Philippine solicitor general alleged that Japanese firms—including Mitsui, Nissho Iwai, Marubeni, and Sumitomo—channeled U.S.$55 million of aid money to Marcos's bank accounts in Hong Kong and Switzerland.[24] In this setting, Marcos and his clients—including Herminio Disini and Ricardo Silverio (manufacturing), Eduardo Cojuangco (coconuts), Antonio Floirendo (bananas), and Roberto Benedicto (sugar)—built immense personal and corporate fortunes.[25] Marcos alone hoarded a staggering U.S.$5 to U.S.$10 billion.[26] Much of the wealth of Marcos's patron-client network was invested or hidden overseas, often in Swiss bank accounts and Northern real estate, especially in the United States.[27]

Marcos justified martial law as necessary to purge corrupt officials and establish a "New Society." At first, state patronage abated and state capacity to develop policies and enforce rules appeared to increase; but by late 1973 widespread patronage had resurfaced. Although Marcos encased the martial law years in anticorruption rhetoric, few concrete changes resulted. For example, in 1975 Marcos fired more than 2 thousand "corrupt" officials, including judges, cabinet members, senior administrators, and middle-level bureaucrats. However, "it was soon discovered that many who were 'dismissed' had already retired or died. And many charges against the more influential were 'discovered' to have been 'unfounded.' Acute observers opined that those actually dismissed were those with poor connections."[28] Patronage reached phenomenal levels over the next decade. The Commission on Audit estimated that bribes accounted for 10 percent of GNP between 1975 and 1980.[29]

The military was the backbone of martial law, providing Marcos with an effective tool to suppress dissent. Marcos promoted loyal generals, retired reluctant followers, and judiciously distributed patronage to senior officers—including top positions in state corporations.[30] In addition, many military officers became middle-level patrons, and "speeding applications and cutting red tape often became a colonel's rather than a congressman's function."[31] As a result, the military establishment developed a vested interest in preserving the status quo. As David Wurfel notes, "whether profiting or sacrificing, all officers were becoming enmeshed more deeply in increasingly centralized patronage networks. School ties and ethnicity created factions, but ultimately it was the superpatron who provided material benefits, and so even factions were organized by patronage."[32] By linking key generals to his patron-client network and allowing middle-level officers to skim personal benefits, Marcos maintained solid control over the military, although there were certainly rumblings from some junior officers who advocated greater efficiency and less corruption.

Under Marcos, the bureaucracy was emasculated by rent-seeking patron-client networks. Martial law undercut legislative patrons, increasing the scope and power of local and intermediate bureaucratic patrons and intrabureaucratic patron-client units.[33] Bureaucratic patron-client networks proliferated as Marcos placed clients in strategic positions, rewarded loyal followers, and punished dissidents.[34] By the mid-1970s, competitive exams were used to fill only 35 percent of government positions. Political manipulation of bureaucrats and flagrant accumulation of personal profits by state leaders lowered bureaucratic morale and justified similar activities among state implementors. As a result, instead of working to promote state objectives, bureaucrats from top to bottom worked to maximize particularistic goals and personal profits.[35]

Marcos used patronage and loyal clients to control outlying regions. By 1979, Marcos had appointed 26 percent of the country's mayors. In 1981, Imelda Marcos introduced the Movement for Livelihood and Progress to provide interest-free "loans" to the "poor." In effect, this program provided cash to loyal local leaders and their clients. Loan procedures were ignored and few were repaid. According to Wurfel, "the style of the program created the impression of a patroness distributing largesse; few perceived the money as repayable."[36] Even though Marcos extended his patron-client network down to the villages, this did not increase the total amount of patronage distributed to rural areas. With fewer elections—and with few restrictions on the manipulation of election results—rural areas actually received less patronage.[37]

Patron-Clientelism and the Fall of Marcos

In the twentieth century, Filipino government leaders have faced two contradictory pressures that shape their legitimate right to rule: traditional demands by clients for particularistic benefits and a legal regime that precludes the use of public office for private profit. Politicians must maneuver in a minefield between "acceptable legal bounds" and "acceptable levels of patronage." In this setting, too much patronage can undermine legitimacy, as can too little. When the interest of *one* network supersedes all else, material exchanges, rather than supporting stability and legitimacy, can spiral "out of control" and corrode elite support. Throughout the 1970s, as a result of reasonable economic growth and substantial international funding, most Filipino economic elites supported Marcos. But increasingly blatant patronage by state-owned firms and the personal extravagance of key allies—including Imelda Marcos[38]—began to undermine the economy in the early 1980s. International creditors lost confidence in Marcos, the economy stagnated, and opposition from Filipino economic elites mounted.[39] As his legitimacy eroded, Marcos responded with "massive outlays to insure the loyalty of local elites."[40] But without international support or a vibrant economy, Marcos could no longer sustain his vast network and still appease state and societal dissidents. By the time "People Power" vaulted Corazon Aquino to the presidency in 1986, Marcos and his clients, in their desperate bid to hold together their unwieldy patron-client network, had plundered and decapitated the state.

Patron-Client Networks and Patronage Since 1986

The Aquino government (1986–92) restored key features of pre–martial law politics, including the pre–1973 constitution, many former politicians, and pervasive, decentralized state patronage.[41] After Marcos fell, his network fragmented. But instead of dissipating, these ties realigned and power dispersed among rival networks. Although Aquino was not personally "corrupt," and despite public anticorruption campaigns, she was unable to undercut systemic state patronage. She could not even purge the bureaucracy; instead, "it was filled to overflowing by some of her less-respected allies."[42] Since Fidel Ramos became president in 1992 he has also encased his reign in flamboyant campaigns to eradicate state patronage.[43] But like Aquino, he has had little success. Today, patron-client networks permeate the state and weaken state capacity to develop and implement policies. Informal material exchanges persist; personal links to political and bureaucratic patrons remain a decisive factor in obtaining state licenses, contracts, and tax breaks; and personal contacts—rather than objective judicial or police procedures—continue to shape the interpretation and enforcement of laws. Not surprisingly, patron-client relations still dominate resource management. As Paul Hutchcroft vividly explains, "once again, as in the pre–martial law years, a decentralized polity simply gives *more* oligarchs a chance to claw for the booty of state."[44] Along similar lines, David Kummer argues that Filipino politics remains "basically a form of 'institutionalized looting,' with the main purpose of public office being to enrich oneself and one's followers."[45]

Voter attitudes, a cultural proclivity to view transactions as personal and to feel obligated to reciprocate, cynical views of politicians and state laws, low bureaucratic salaries, and general poverty contribute to the persistence of patron-client ties and state patronage. Many Filipinos "expect their votes to be rewarded concretely with better roads and schools, with government jobs, and with 'a little help' when confronting stubborn officials or unreasonable regulations. Politicians who do not comply or who, for lack of influence in the right places, cannot comply, soon find themselves officeless."[46] As a result, members of Congress often focus on securing "pork barrel" projects for their constituencies rather than debating and drafting national or regional socioeconomic development policies.

The clash between traditional values and modern (American) legal and political norms contributes to flagrant violations of laws and to a cynical public view of the state. According to David Timberman, "the conflict between traditional and modern values is exemplified by the contradictory tendency of Filipinos to pass laws and regulations against corruption and nepotism (in a desire to be 'modern'), even though the norms of traditional society, which emphasize kinship ties, reciprocity, and personal loyalty, compel almost everyone to ignore or violate these laws."[47] This has contributed to government campaigns to purge corrupt officials, and to incessant charges of corruption by opposition parties, NGOs, and the media. However, although token scapegoats are sometimes punished, only marginal progress has been made in curbing the use of public office for private gain. As Timberman notes, "it is a paradox of Philippine politics that corruption is assumed to be endemic to politics and government, but at the same time 'exposing' corruption is a time-tested political tactic and guaranteed vote-getter."[48] This has undermined public faith in legal institutions and government regulations.

A cultural tendency to perceive transactions as personal reinforces patron-client ties between state officials and societal members. In this cultural prism, "routine political, bureaucratic, or business transactions considered in the West to be *im*personal (such as voting, applying for a permit or license, or entering into a business contract) are instead considered to be *personal* interactions involving favors or other unspecified obligations."[49] Carl Landé's observation in the 1960s is still valid: "when a congressman proudly 'gives' a town a new chapel or bridge, few may know or care whether the money came from his own pocket or from the government."[50] As a result, patron-client links flourish as people feel obliged to individual state representatives rather than to the state itself. Low state salaries—undercut by inflation and general poverty—further strengthen patron-client ties. James Rush argues that in poor countries like the Philippines, almost everyone searches vigilantly for ways of "getting a little more." For this reason, "from top to bottom, civil servants are often entangled in relationships of mutual assistance with others outside government." Few people are working for the "common good," and state laws are often sacrificed for personal profit.[51]

In sum, there is surprising continuity across postwar political regimes in the Philippines. In the 1950s and 1960s, particularistic, rent-seeking patron-client networks—often centered in Congress—battled for votes and control of state levers to distribute patronage. During this period, power was dispersed among central, regional, and local patrons. Using the tools of martial law, Marcos centralized the allocation of patronage in the 1970s. Although he relied heavily on support from international financiers, the military, and less-powerful patrons throughout the country, Marcos managed to eliminate or appease many competing patron-client units. He was deposed in 1986 after resources grew scarce and he could no longer sustain his unwieldy patron-client network. Today, power is again dispersed among rival patron-client units—many with a powerful economic "family" at the core. These have ties to the president, members of Congress, key corporate leaders, military officers, bureaucrats, and leaders in the outlying provinces. Although these three periods have obvious distinctions, all are characterized by one dominant feature: patron-client units battling for access to and control over state patronage.

Patrons and Timber

From the 1950s to the mid-1980s, extensive ties between senior state officials and timber operators distorted management policies and drove destructive and excessive logging. During the Marcos years, top political and military leaders—including Defense Secretary Juan Ponce Enrile and Armed Forces Chief of Staff General Fabian Ver—were involved in illegal logging and smuggling.[52] Powerful timber operators—Alfonso Lim and Herminio Disini among them—were key Marcos clients.[53] The Marcos family also owned several timber companies. These clientelist ties at the top of the state weakened supervision of state implementors, undermining state capacity to enforce timber regulations and collect forest charges. The state was unable to protect and rehabilitate the forests, and deforestation was rampant.

After the fall of Marcos, patrons and clients scrambled to form new alliances. A remarkable number survived. A University of the Philippines resource specialist lamented, "With the change of government [in 1986], many of us were hopeful that things would change—only to find out that a new group of politicians close to Malacanang [the presidential palace] has again served as sponsor . . . showing that the control of natural resources is power and that the game goes on."[54] Today, numerous Congress members, provincial governors, and local mayors have past or present links to timber companies.[55] The career of Palawan timber magnate Jose "Pepito" Alvarez illustrates how many timber operators linked to Marcos survived the transition to Aquino. After working for about ten years for a Japanese timber company in Indonesia, Alvarez moved to the heavily forested province of Palawan. Alvarez developed close ties to Teodoro Pena, the Minister of Natural Resources and Marcos's key Palawan client. Pena arranged for Alvarez to obtain two concessions covering 168 thousand hectares, 61 percent of Palawan's productive forest. In exchange, Alvarez supported Pena's bid for a seat in the legislature. Alvarez's links to Marcos were reinforced by his father-in-law, a key Marcos client in Mindanao.

According to photos taken by former workers, Alvarez's main company, Pagdanan, has logged illegally, clear-cut forest areas, and limited reforestation "to the sides of roads."[56] But by adroitly switching patrons after Marcos fell and judiciously distributing patronage, Alvarez has remained largely immune from state sanctions. In the 1987 congressional election Alvarez abandoned Pena and backed Ramon Mitra, who later became a presidential candidate and Speaker of the House. Alvarez financed Mitra's political party and reportedly gave him a ranch house in Palawan. Besides cultivating close ties to Mitra, Alvarez has prudently maintained links to Palawan's other congressman (David Ponce de Leon), provincial military officers, business leaders who control the two newspapers and one radio station in Palawan, local government officials, and even Palawan's Catholic bishop.[57] According to Robin Broad and John Cavanagh, Alvarez is typical of many powerful loggers in the post-Marcos era: they simply "shifted their allegiance and economic backing from Marcos to politicians in Aquino's camp."[58]

As a result of these realignments, loggers still have leverage over political decisions and policies, especially in the outer regions and among state enforcement officers. But at the highest levels their power has diminished. Aquino had no apparent ties to loggers and pushed for better environmental management.[59] Changes to the political positions and the timber interests of the three main candidates in the 1992 presidential election—Mitra, Eduardo Cojuangco, and Ramos—demonstrate the waning influence of loggers at the top of the state. During the 1992 presidential campaign, Mitra, who in the past had been a staunch supporter of logging, publicly condemned destructive and illegal loggers, and—although he still defended Alvarez—called for a total logging ban. This sharp reversal of his previous environmental views likely reflected the growing concern among Filipino voters with floods, soil erosion, and environmental degradation. Whereas Mitra has indirect ties to the timber industry, Cojuangco—a former Marcos client—has direct links. He is president of International Hardwood and Veneer Corporation (Interwood) and director of Eastern Plywood Company and Santa Clara Plywood Company. In 1992, after DENR found evidence of illegal logging, Cojuangco—despite controlling a corporate empire—was unable to prevent the suspension of Interwood's license.[60]

Ramos has also had direct ties to destructive logging. He held shares in Greenbelt Wood Products, a company chaired by his father until he died in 1986. Greenbelt violated numerous timber regulations, even after March 1991, when its concession license officially expired. According to one report for the government, Greenbelt has an "image of invincibility . . . with apparent blessings of . . . some patrons in Manila. With its vast resources and influence, it was able to put up its own security force . . ."[61] Before the 1992 presidential election, Ramos severed his direct ties to the timber industry and divested his shares in Greenbelt. He then made environmental protection a key part of his 1992 presidential platform. Since winning this election, Ramos has responded to some environmental concerns. At the start of his term, under intense media and congressional pressure, he replaced his political ally Edelmiro Amante as secretary-designate of DENR after the media publicized Amante's close links to Mindanao timber companies. Ramos then accepted a recommendation by a coalition of environmental groups and appointed Angel C. Alcala as the new DENR secretary. In his first four years as president, Ramos supported moves to curb illegal logging and smuggling, increase reforestation, and improve forest management.

The weakening of ties between loggers and top state leaders does not signal a fundamental change in Filipino patron-client politics. Rather, it reflects the collapse of the timber industry: with fewer valuable logs, there is simply less patronage to sustain powerful timber-based patron-client networks. As Horacio Severino aptly notes, although it would be gratifying to perceive the changing balance of power as a victory for NGOs and environmental groups, "just as likely, the diminished influence of the loggers in our society has simply coincided with the disappearance of much of our country's forests."[62]

As timber-based patron-client ties to top politicians erode, as potential profits decline, and as attitudes supporting environmental protection strengthen, state capacity to manage the forests has increased marginally. As we will see in the next section, since 1986 the state has slashed the number of logging licenses, gathered more accurate data and information, and made notable strides in reforestation. But pervasive patron-client links among politicians, military officials, and bureaucratic implementors still distort policies and thwart enforcement. As a result, illegal logging is common, companies evade taxes and timber royalties, numerous reforestation sites have failed, timber processors are inefficient, and selective logging bans—including one to protect the last primary forests—are almost meaningless. Even the laudable move to allow communities to manage forest areas is undermined by local patron-client networks that struggle to promote particularistic goals.

Forestry Policies and Patron-Client Politics

Background

The Philippines has around 7 thousand islands and a total land area of 30 million hectares. The state owns all land classified as forests. After independence in 1946, forests covered about three-quarters of the Philippines.[63] Partly driven by Northern trade and technology, and partly by government incentives, large logging operations began in the Philippines in the 1950s. By the 1960s, as log purchases from Japan soared, annual deforestation climbed to 300 thousand hectares. In 1968, log production peaked at over 11.6 million cubic meters, and log exports accounted for around one-third of total Philippine export earnings. In the early 1970s, log production held steady at about 10 million cubic meters. As valuable timber stocks grew scarce, and as demand from Japan dropped sharply, log extraction declined in the 1970s.[64] By the early 1980s annual deforestation had fallen to 150 thousand hectares. By 1990 annual deforestation was less than 100 thousand hectares as a result in part of fewer logging concessions, more reforestation, selective logging bans, and most important, fewer forests to deforest.

The government classifies 15.88 million hectares, or 53 percent of total land area, as forest lands. But there is more likely less than 5.9 million hectares, and it "is going down as fast as fire, axe and chainsaw allow."[65] Of this, 3.91 million hectares are dipterocarp forests; about 800 thousand hectares of these forests are undisturbed.[66] According to an ecologist with the Institute of Church and Social Issues, every year another 50 thousand hectares of primary forests disappear.[67] At the beginning of 1992, the government banned logging in all primary forests to slow the rapid loss of old-growth forests. Logging is now allowed only in "adequately stocked residual forests."[68]

After Aquino took control in 1986, the duties of the Ministry of Natural Resources were expanded to include environmental protection and the ministry was renamed the Department of Environment and Natural Resources. DENR is responsible for regulating, monitoring, and protecting forest land, issuing timber license agreements (TLAs), enforcing selective logging guidelines, and ensuring adequate reforestation.[69]

Aquino first appointed Ernesto Maceda as DENR secretary, despite previous allegations of corruption. According to Marites Danguilan Vitug, "the DENR post was Cory Aquino's 'thank you' gift to Maceda for his big role in her victory."[70] Maceda's tenure lasted only nine months, ending after the November 1986 attempted coup. Maceda was replaced by human rights lawyer, Fulgencio Factoran, following interim Secretary Carlos Dominguez. Factoran had a profound impact on the department and, until his term ended in June 1992, was a key force behind efforts to improve state timber management. He restructured forest management within the department, curtailing the powers of the Bureau of Forest Development (BFD)—the core of many patron-client networks linked to poor enforcement in the past. The BFD was renamed the

Forest Management Bureau, and operational officials were integrated into DENR's "line structure."[71] In addition, Factoran's group pushed forestry staff into the field, decentralized some power to lower levels of the department and regional offices, and put more emphasis on social and community forestry programs. After Factoran stepped aside, DENR undersecretary Ricardo Umali acted briefly as interim secretary until Ramos appointed Angel Alcala. Alcala continued in the tradition of Factoran and pressed hard for better enforcement and forestry management until he was replaced in mid-1995. But like Factoran, he faced formidable obstacles, including his own recalcitrant department.

Timber Concessionaires and Legal Logging

As in Indonesia and Sarawak, in theory, Philippine companies are supposed to follow selective logging rules and conduct appropriate enrichment planting and silvicultural treatments. But, in practice, loggers—with protection from political, bureaucratic, and military officials—have rarely adhered to these rules and many timber concessions have been devastated.[72] In the 1950s and 1960s, licenses were usually granted for one to ten years. By 1960, 5.5 million hectares of forests were carved into logging concessions; by 1971, loggers controlled 10.6 million hectares, over one-third of the total land area.[73] To obtain and renew licenses, logging companies often placed influential politicians on their boards of directors. Many timber concessions, licenses, and contracts were directly connected to political patrons. The electoral turbulence of the 1950s and 1960s—and shifts in the composition and size of patron-client networks—contributed to an uncertain and unpredictable atmosphere for loggers. Most companies considered their licenses to be tentative, contributing to quick and destructive harvesting techniques.

During martial law, Marcos issued timber licenses and "special logging permits" to reward loyal followers, enrich his family, and appease influential dissidents. Military officers, key political and economic elites, and Muslim dissidents were granted lucrative logging sites. In 1972 alone, Marcos distributed over 12 thousand special logging permits.[74] Often license holders did not have the expertise or equipment to log concessions and many employed ethnic Chinese subcontractors.[75] A typical concession was 40–60 thousand hectares, although key Marcos clients controlled areas larger than 100 thousand hectares, the nominal constitutional limit.[76] These loggers made enormous profits. The Haribon environmental group estimates that from 1972 to 1988, Filipino companies logged 8.57 million hectares, for a total profit of U.S.$42.85 billion; 3.88 million hectares were primary forests.[77]

Extensive links between top state leaders and timber operators weakened supervision of state enforcement officers and lowered state morale in the Marcos years. Instead of working for the state, many middle- and lower-level officials worked to promote their own interests. According to a former Bureau of Forest Development bureaucrat, "because the leadership was corrupt, the rank and file employees were not afraid to be corrupt."[78] In exchange for money, gifts, and job opportunities, enforcement officers often ignored blatant violations of selective logging rules. Former DENR secretary Maceda claimed that 90 percent of forestry bureaucrats in the Marcos era were corrupt.[79] In this setting, the few state officials who tried to uphold the law confronted formidable systemic barriers.

In the 1970s, Marcos extended the time limit for timber concession licenses to twenty-five years. At the same time, however, he fostered an unpredictable setting by threatening to cancel licenses to control his timber clients. The tenuous position of loggers was aggravated by the arbitrary power of Marcos's top client in the forest bureaucracy, Edmundo Cortes, director of the Bureau of Forest Development from 1975 to 1986. As a result, longer concession licenses had little practical impact because loggers realized their license depended on the grace of Marcos and Cortes. Few bothered with long-term management.[80] According to Vitug, if loggers "were out of favor with Cortes and Malacañang [the presidential palace], their TLA would surely be cancelled. The application of the law was subjective."[81]

Since 1986, DENR has suspended, canceled, or refused to renew numerous timber licenses. Between 1987 and June 1992, this reduced the number of timber license agreements from 143 to 32 and the annual allowable cut from 6.03 million cubic meters to just over 1 million cubic meters. By February 1995, there were only thirty license holders with a combined annual cut of less than 900 thousand cubic meters.[82] From 1986 to 1994, log production fell from 3 million cubic meters to less than 1 million cubic meters. This appears to indicate that DENR moves to cancel timber licenses successfully reduced log production. But with fewer valuable commercial forests, the drop in production was largely inevitable. Prior to 1986, log production was already decreasing steadily, from 10.2 million cubic meters in 1973, to 6.2 million cubic meters in 1980, and to 3.1 million cubic meters in 1985.[83] Since 1987 DENR has also not granted any new logging licenses, and there are apparently no plans to issue licenses in the future.[84] Instead, DENR is promoting community-based industrial forest plantations "to maintain wood supply and to provide alternative livelihood for wood-dependent communities."[85] As of December 1993, DENR had awarded 176 industrial forest management agreements. According to Human Rights Watch/Asia, "many of these [industrial forest management areas] are now operated by the same individuals and corporations who were responsible for abuses linked to TLAs in the past."[86]

As a result of DENR's moves to reduce legal logging, timber operators face the constant possibility that the government will revoke or cancel their licenses with no concrete explanation. As one study notes, "The national government . . . has the tendency to cancel leases on areas peremptorily, sometimes without due process. Many TLA holders continually fear the cancellation of their leases as political circumstances change, with the consequent loss of their fixed investments in processing plants, infrastructure, and forest development in their areas."[87] As in the past, this induces timber operators to extract logs as fast as possible. In this context, loggers routinely ignore silvicultural treatments, enrichment planting, and selective logging rules.[88] Although poor management of legal concessions is certainly a problem, as the government cuts the number of licenses, illegal logging is an even greater factor driving contemporary deforestation.

Illegal Logging

Illegal loggers—often protected by politicians, military leaders, police officers, and bureaucrats—are chopping down the few remaining primary forests and destroying the national parks and wildlife sanctuaries.[89] Although illegal logging is often blamed on destitute villagers, in many cases influential officials and timber company executives—who skim most of the profits on lucrative illegal log sales—protect and encourage these people.[90] In Samar, even though logging was banned in 1989, timber companies extract logs "through a web of allies ranging from politicians to local officials and even communist rebels."[91] In 1989, a World Bank report estimated that illegal logging may be roughly equivalent to legal logging.[92] In the same year, a Senate committee claimed that destructive and illegal logging cost the Philippines U.S.$5 million every day.[93] In 1991, the Economist Intelligence Unit estimated that the Philippine illegal timber trade was worth U.S.$800 million a year.[94] More recently, Congressman Renato Yap claimed that illegal logs account for about half of annual Philippine timber consumption—estimated at 2.5 million cubic meters.[95]

Military officers have protected and profited from illegal logging.[96] As well, in some cases, members of the Civilian Armed Forces Geographical Unit, a paramilitary force of about 15 thousand civilians under army supervision, "are used by politicians and businessmen to escort their illegally cut logs."[97] Federal, provincial, and local politicians and judges also shield illegal loggers. In 1990, the government established a Department of Justice Task Force on Illegal Logging to prosecute illegal loggers and corrupt DENR officers. The chairman of the task force, Alvin Go, "has received telephone calls from senators, congressmen and judges indirectly asking him not to proceed with some cases."[98] In Basilan, Governor Gerry Saluppudin is one of the most powerful loggers. According to one inside source, "that's why illegal logging activities in the area are very hard to stop."[99] In Isabela, former Governor Faustino Dy—whose family has close ties to logging companies—candidly admits that "there are violations which could not be avoided because regulations of the Department of Environment and Natural Resources are difficult to comply with. Sawmill operators may lose money if they follow DENR rules to the letter."[100]

Since 1986 the government has tried to curb illegal logging. DENR has canceled concessions, confiscated illegal logs, strengthened laws, and prosecuted cases. In 1987, to increase state capacity to monitor illegal logging, the government began rewarding informers 30 percent of the value of seized logs.[101] In early 1994, the Presidential Anticrime Commission and DENR established a special task force to tackle "big-time" illegal loggers.[102] Before 1987 no one had been convicted of illegal logging; yet by the middle of 1991, twenty-eight people had been convicted, including city councillors and the wife of a senior military officer.[103]

Despite these modest results, pervasive links between local DENR officers and timber operators continue to undermine the state's ability to halt illegal logging. From 1987 to 1992, the government investigated 443 cases of improprieties at DENR—fifty officials were disciplined; six were fired.[104] Local enforcement officers routinely ignore and even assist illegal logging.[105] In Cagayan, the former regional director of DENR, Rogelio Bagayan, concedes: "We have problems of collusion (between government officials and loggers); we have to transfer staff or force them out."[106] In 1990, DENR punished or relocated local forestry officers in Isabela after an undercover team found strong evidence of collaboration between illegal loggers and provincial DENR officials. After this crackdown, illegal logging was temporarily reduced, but by early 1991, "illegal logging activities [had] resumed with a vengeance."[107] According to Senator Heherson Alvarez, "it is very difficult to enforce [laws in Isabela] because everybody is involved."[108] Local DENR officials, linked to patron-client timber networks, have also undercut central DENR investigations. For example, in 1992, after a successful government raid of Super Mahogany Plywood Corporation, local DENR allies apparently tampered with crucial evidence.[109] Of course, not all DENR officials are "corrupt" or members of patron-client networks. Some are competent and idealistic and work hard for the state (which presumably supports better timber management). These officials, however, face grave dangers from other state officials as well as powerful economic elites. In 1993 alone, several DENR officials and employees were apparently killed by illegal loggers.[110]

To sever links between local DENR officials and timber operators, former DENR Secretary Alcala suspended and reshuffled personnel. This created a backlash from recalcitrant departmental staff. In late 1993, the ombudsman began investigating graft and corruption charges against Alcala and Undersecretary Ben Malayang III. These charges, which were leveled by a former DENR assistant secretary whom Alcala fired for anomalies in the campaign to halt illegal logging, were apparently part of a campaign to topple Alcala.[111] In February 1994, the DENR employees' union called for Alcala's resignation, arguing he had destroyed morale and abused his authority.[112] As a result of this internal resistance, Alcala made only incremental progress in weakening links between timber operators and DENR staff before he was replaced as DENR Secretary by Victor Ramos on July 1, 1995.

Besides ties between forestry officials and timber operators, remote concessions and a lack of institutional resources further hamper DENR's ability to curb illegal logging. Monitoring illegal logging is exceedingly difficult. The Philippines has only 4 thousand forest guards.[113] Palawan, which contains one-third of the remaining primary forests, has just 135 guards. Enforcement problems have increased even more since the closure of U.S. military bases.[114] The navy is unable to patrol the jagged coastline. Even when surveillance units pinpoint smugglers, by the time the navy reaches the site, it is often too late.[115] In Cagayan, DENR has "neither the helicopters nor boats to conduct patrols with and soldiers who are supposed to enforce the law often connive with loggers."[116] In Samar, DENR has "no guns, no radios, no boats, and only 250 guards to roam the jungles, where they are usually terrorized by armed men or rebels."[117] In Bukidnon, DENR officials confessed in 1989 that "We are unable to control the illegal loggers."[118]

DENR is also unable to trace the volume of logs extracted and compare this with allowable cuts. To monitor harvests, DENR issues a certificate of timber origin. There are two serious problems with these certificates. First, companies bribe officials to ignore or alter certificates. Second, companies duplicate certificates which are then stamped by local DENR officials. Without a computerized system, DENR cannot trace these documents.[119] An additional problem is DENR's reliance on timber companies to provide transportation, accommodation, and, in some cases, protection from surprise attacks by the communist New People's Army (NPA).[120] These close ties to timber companies subvert the independence and objectivity of DENR inspectors.

Smuggling

Under Marcos, domestic companies—often with the participation or knowledge of customs officials and foreign firms—smuggled huge quantities of logs overseas. Former DENR Secretary Maceda "estimated that between 1974 and 1980, U.S.$960 million worth of timber was smuggled out of the country by friends and associates of President Marcos."[121] Many illegal logs landed in Japan. Official Japanese customs records show that in 1981 Japan imported 1.4 million cubic meters of Philippine logs; but for the same period, according to Philippine records, only 365,441 cubic meters were shipped to Japan.[122] In 1984, Japanese companies imported 938 thousand cubic meters of Philippine logs, over 400 thousand cubic meters more than the official export quota. In 1985, 257 thousand cubic meters of undocumented Philippine logs were imported into Japan. In 1986, under the new government, the discrepancy between Japanese import and Philippine export figures dropped to 85 thousand cubic meters. But even in 1987, after the total ban on log exports, "35,000 cubic meters of 'unexplained' logs left the Philippines for export to Japan."[123] Although it is difficult to prove, Japanese companies likely colluded with Filipino loggers to smuggle logs and falsify export documents.[124] Through these practices timber operators exceeded their allowable cut, evaded export and corporate taxes, and stashed foreign exchange earnings overseas. Today, most illegal logs are consumed in the country.[125] Although some timber is smuggled overseas, especially to Taiwan, there do not appear to be substantial shipments. It is unlikely that Japanese traders are still involved in smuggling syndicates. Potential profits are now too low to risk sabotaging newly crafted corporate images.[126]

Tax and Royalty Evasion

Marcos provided timber licenses to key clients for a paltry fee of P 1. For a long time, the main source of government logging revenue was remarkably low royalties based on the volume extracted. In 1983, this was only P 20 per cubic meter.[127] Between 1979 and 1982, the government collected only U.S.$170 million in export taxes and timber royalties, a mere 11.4 percent of potential timber rents.[128] The excess profits flowed to a small elite, often linked to Marcos. In the late 1980s, Haribon president Junie Kalaw vividly explained: "In the past 15 years we have had only 470 logging concessionaires . . . . The average profit on logging is 100,000 pesos per hectare after you've paid all expenses. When you total this, it would amount to about [U.S.] $42 billion, more than our foreign debt, that came from the forest and this money went to 470 people. The process created poverty for 17 million people around the forest areas."[129]

Despite negligible forest charges, during the height of log exports, Filipino companies used elaborate schemes to conceal overcutting and evade royalties and taxes. With the help of forestry and customs officials, companies forged export documents, preparing one for the foreign port (often in Japan) that stated the true volume of logs and one for Filipino authorities that underdeclared the volume (often the allowable cut). The foreign company paid a front company in Hong Kong the full value of the logs. The Hong Kong company then paid the Filipino company the value of the underdeclared shipment. The difference was generally diverted to a foreign bank or used to finance overseas operations.[130]

A 1989 World Bank report estimated that the Philippine government—through royalties and taxes—collected only 9–14 percent of potential timber rent in the late 1980s.[131] In 1991, forest fees were increased substantially and are now 25 percent of market price (this includes an environmental fee of P 500 per cubic meter of logs extracted, first imposed in 1990).[132] But without better collection these higher charges will make little difference. Since 1986, tax evasion has continued to be an acute problem. According to Antonio Carpio, a key anticorruption activist in the Ramos government, tax evaders are disabling economic development and driving the deficit. One company alone—Fortune Tobacco under the control of beer and tobacco billionaire Lucio Tan—avoided paying P 7 billion in taxes from 1986 to 1993.[133]

Log Export Restrictions, Bans, and Processing Policies

Unlike in Indonesia, where strong political will and business cooperation created a stringent log export ban, in the Philippines, strong societal resistance, weak state capacity, and diluted and inconsistent direction from top state leaders have distorted and delayed policies to restrict log exports, ban logging, and promote domestic processing. In 1973, the Marcos government announced a log export ban to be phased in over three years. This was never enforced, and in 1975 Marcos proclaimed a selective log export ban. This selective ban enabled Marcos to award timber clients with export quotas and deny smaller and recalcitrant companies log export profits. It also fostered widespread illegal logging and smuggling as companies skirted these new regulations.[134]

In 1986, log exports were finally banned. In 1987, the government announced that it would not issue any new timber licenses. In 1989, sawn timber exports were banned; in the same year, logging was banned in provinces with less than 40 percent tree cover, in theory, stopping logging in sixty-five of seventy-three provinces. But as one report bluntly stated, "None of these bans have been enforced."[135] In 1992, the government banned logging in all remaining primary forests. But like so many government initiatives, the state has been unable to enforce this law. Since 1986, the Congress has made numerous unsuccessful attempts to pass a total ban on logging. Yet even if a total ban is eventually passed—if previous selective bans are any indication—this will have little impact on the rate of destructive logging.

The Marcos administration provided incentives to process logs. Although processed wood production increased, these policies protected small, inefficient plywood, veneer, and sawnwood mills.[136] The value of processed wood exports (mainly sawn timber and plywood) reached U.S.$317 million in 1979. By 1982, however, exports had dropped and the number of plants had decreased: sawmills from 325 to 190, plywood mills from 209 to 35, and veneer mills from 23 to 11.[137] At the end of the Marcos era, processed wood exports were still quite low. In 1986 the Philippines exported 495 thousand cubic meters of sawn timber, 256 thousand cubic meters of plywood, and 50 thousand cubic meters of veneer.[138] Today, the Philippines does not have a major wood processing industry. In 1994, total sawnwood production was 408 thousand cubic meters, a 44 percent decrease from 1991. Of this, companies exported around 30 thousand cubic meters. In the same year, plywood production was 258 thousand cubic meters (about 20 percent less than in 1991), and veneer plants manufactured 39 thousand cubic meters (around 28 percent lower than in 1991).[139]

Local Power and Forest Management

The 1991 Local Government Code allocated more powers to local governments, including powers to manage forests. Given that forest degradation directly affects villagers, decentralized control could potentially improve management. The author of the code, Aquilino Pimentel, argues that "resistance from local environmental groups will make local officials think twice. This will affect their votes. . . . It is easier to monitor corruption on a local level. In the national office, the official hides in the bowels of the bureaucracy."[140] But Pimentel may be overly optimistic. Already signs have begun to appear that local leaders are using their new powers to distribute patronage. Vitug claims that "among some NGOs, especially those that work with community-managed forests, there is a downcast feeling. They are apprehensive that some politicians will recklessly issue stewardship contracts and permits to cut trees to favored supporters. The field is wide open to abuse."[141] Community involvement is clearly vital for effective management. But it is equally apparent that effective checks must be placed on self-interested local patrons and clients.

Conservation, Reforestation, and Timber Plantations

Until 1986, conservation and reforestation policies were largely ineffective. A 1988 study showed that the Bureau of Forest Development—which claimed that it had reforested 272 thousand hectares—only *successfully* replanted 70 thousand hectares.[142] In 1986, the Philippines began a national forestation program (NFP) to replant 1.4 million hectares by the end of the year 2000. The goal is to reforest an annual average of about 100 thousand hectares. Initial progress was slow: in 1986, 33 thousand hectares were reforested; in 1987, 40 thousand hectares; in 1988, 64 thousand hectares. In September 1988, DENR began implementing the ADB-OECF First Forestry Sector Program Loan and reforestation accelerated.[143] According to DENR, 190 thousand hectares were reforested in 1990, dropping to around 93 thousand hectares in 1991, and about 40 thousand hectares in 1992. As of 1992, in total just over 1.35 million hectares had been replanted. The government reforested almost 950 thousand hectares, timber concessionaires accounted for just over 310 thousand hectares, and private-sector organizations planted the rest.[144]

Since the late 1980s, DENR has promoted forestry management at the local level by encouraging communities and NGOs to participate as managers as well as to monitor and enforce rules. Serious difficulties, however, have arisen. The government has had problems persuading local people—especially marginal forest dwellers—to participate, given that "results" are often far in the future. As well, leases have been too short and little money has been provided to maintain and protect reforested areas. Even more troublesome, reforestation has been undercut by patron-clientelism. While discussing DENR's reforestation efforts during his term, former DENR secretary Factoran admitted: "We had to make a political decision. We chose to distribute reforestation funds to congressional districts to make congressmen cooperate."[145] As well, NGOs and "community groups" have formed spontaneously to take advantage of the funding; there has been wide evidence of abuse.[146] DENR officials and local politicians who siphon funds have also undermined reforestation. DENR officials have been linked to "ghost" reforestation sites, accepting bribes and gifts from contractors, and demanding a percentage of profits from reforestation contractors.[147] During Factoran's term as DENR secretary (1986–92), "about 15 percent of the funds spent [on reforestation] may have gone to the pockets of some DENR officials, politicians and parties contracted to reforest."[148]

DENR is now trying to improve reforestation. The most important initiative is the Second Forestry Sector Program, which attempts to build on the lessons and successes of the First Forestry Sector Program (1988–92).[149] The Second Forestry Sector Program is funded by an Asian Development Bank U.S.$100 million project loan and U.S.$29 million from the Philippine government. Because this is a project loan, the ADB approves all subprojects.[150] This program aims to develop 93 thousand hectares of community forests, 55 thousand hectares of integrated reforestation sites, and 22 thousand hectares of critical watershed restoration. Under this program DENR only grants reforestation contracts to local residents. These are long-term agreements designed to encourage villagers to plant various indigenous species. To discourage fraudulent NGOs from taking advantage of reforestation contracts, NGOs are compensated for services to local contractors. The fund is also designed to protect 800 thousand hectares of primary forests.[151]

The Philippines and Japan's Shadow Ecology

The North has expedited large-scale logging in the Philippines since the Spanish colonial period. During the seventeenth and eighteenth centuries, Cebu was logged extensively to build Spanish galleons. During the American colonial period log extraction increased, driven in part by American technology, advice, financing, and market demand. After World War II, Northern investment, technology, and trade further facilitated and accelerated destructive logging.[152] Japanese log purchases were a particularly virulent force, although Japanese money and technology were also important.

Japanese Investment and Technology

Japanese investment surged during martial law. In December 1973, Japan and the Philippines signed the Treaty of Amity, Commerce, and Navigation. From almost no investment prior to 1972, by 1978 Japan accounted for 21 percent of all Philippine investments approved by the Central Bank.[153] After the rapid appreciation of the yen following the Plaza Agreement in 1985, Japanese investment soared worldwide. In the Philippines, from 1985 to 1990 Japanese investment increased 891 percent, from U.S.$25.9 million to U.S.$256.7 million.[154] Despite these substantial increases, in the early 1990s, the Philippines still accounted for less than 1 percent of total Japanese investment.[155] Japanese investors are wary of political instability, unreliable power supplies, inadequate infrastructure, and rampant crime. In 1991, Japanese companies invested U.S.$203 million in the Philippines, compared to U.S.$1.19 billion in Indonesia, U.S.$925 million in Hong Kong, U.S.$880 million in Malaysia, and U.S.$807 million in Thailand.[156]

Direct Japanese investment was less important in triggering the Philippine logging boom in the 1960s than the Indonesian boom in the 1970s. In the case of the Philippines, American companies—such as Weyerhauser and Georgia-Pacific—provided much of the advice and equipment necessary for large-scale logging during the 1950s.[157] Nevertheless, Japanese companies were still a key force driving extraction. To guarantee log supplies—yet minimize risks and maintain a low profile—sogo shosha provided credit in exchange for logs or held minority shares in local Philippine companies.[158] These arrangements accelerated destructive logging. According to Suzuki, "In cases where the Philippine side could not supply enough capital to make up 60 percent, the Japanese side would provide the difference through the back-door.... These back-door funds, often accounting for as much as 30 percent of the total, could not be insured. As a result the Japanese side endeavoured to recover the uninsured amount as quickly as possible, contributing to the extremely rapid exploitation of concession areas."[159]

Through minority shares, sogo shosha had significant influence over the sale and price of logs. As Nectoux and Kuroda note, in many cases, "Japanese control of logging interests [was] obtained not through corporate ownership, but by financing an operation, supplying equipment, purchasing logs and controlling export operations."[160] As with almost all timber companies in the Philippines prior to 1986, companies with Japanese shareholders logged areas illegally, forged export documents, ignored silvicultural and reforestation duties, evaded royalties and taxes, and were protected by powerful political elites.[161] Today, sogo shosha have little interest in the sparse, inaccessible stands of commercial timber. Some small Japanese companies have minority shares in lumber processing, rattan furniture, and chopstick mills.[162] But unlike in the past—when sogo shosha facilitated rapid, large-scale, and often destructive logging in primary forests—these investors do not have a major impact on the overall structure or sustainable management of the timber industry.

Japanese Trade

Japan's greatest impact on Philippine timber management has been massive purchases of logs from unsustainable sources and far below replacement or effective management costs. Sogo shosha prospered in the Philippines as pervasive clientelist ties drove unsustainable and reckless logging. In the 1950s and 1960s, the Philippines was the primary source of Japanese tropical log imports. Over this period—as Japan used more and more dipterocarp logs to make cheap plywood, especially konpane—sogo shosha log purchases provided potent financial incentives that propelled destructive, rapid harvests.[163] In 1950, the Philippines accounted for 92.4 percent of Japanese log imports from Southeast Asia, although the total volume was only 111 thousand cubic meters. In 1961, Japan imported 3.7 million cubic meters of Philippine logs, accounting for almost two-thirds of Japanese log imports and over half of total log production in the Philippines.[164] In 1965, Japan imported 5.63 million cubic meters of Philippine logs (again over half of total Philippine log production).[165] By 1969 Japanese log imports from the Philippines had soared to 7.92 million cubic meters, although this now only comprised 46.6 percent of Japan's total log imports from Southeast Asia.[166] In that year, however, this accounted for a remarkable 72 percent of total Philippine log production.[167]

In the early 1970s, as accessible, high-quality Philippine logs became increasingly scarce, and as Japanese demand soared, Japanese companies shifted to Sabah and Indonesia. Many Filipino loggers—in some cases financed by Japanese companies—also moved to Indonesia.[168] In 1971, Indonesia surpassed the Philippines as Japan's key source of tropical logs. By 1973, Indonesia and Sabah supplied around 69 percent of Japanese log imports from Southeast Asia. In that year, Japanese imports of Philippine logs had dropped to 5.9 million cubic meters, although this still accounted for about 58 percent of total Philippine log production.[169] Throughout the Philippine logging boom (1964–73), Japan imported 63.7 million cubic meters of Philippine logs, around 62 percent of total Philippine log production.[170]

Japanese traders moved to new log sources in the mid-1970s as valuable and accessible Philippine logs became scarcer. In 1976, Japan only imported 1.7 million cubic meters of Philippine logs, a mere 7.6 percent of Japan's total Southeast Asian log imports. Over the next ten years, Japanese companies—including sogo shosha such as Nissho Iwai, Sumitomo, Marubeni, Mitsui, Mitsubishi, and Itochu—continued to purchase Philippine logs, although far less than during the logging boom. In 1983, Japan only imported around 648 thousand cubic meters of Philippine logs.[171] After the log export ban in 1986, Japanese legal timber imports from the Philippines were reduced to small amounts of processed wood.

From the 1950s to the mid-1980s, processed wood accounted for a minor portion of total Japanese timber imports from Southeast Asia. For example, in 1984 Japan only imported 151 cubic meters of plywood from the Philippines.[172] Even after the ban on log exports, in 1990 Philippine plywood exports to Japan were still inconsequential: 2,842 cubic meters, 0.1 percent of Japan's total plywood imports. By 1993, Japan imported even less, a mere 723 cubic meters of plywood, which represented a negligible portion of Japan's total tropical plywood imports of 3.86 million cubic meters.[173] As a result, unlike in Indonesia, Japanese tariff barriers on plywood have not had a major impact on Philippine timber management.

Even though Japan no longer imports Philippine logs and only buys a small amount of processed wood, past log purchases far below the costs of regeneration or sustainable management contribute to significant contemporary economic, social, and environmental problems. The Philippines is now struggling to regenerate degraded forests and tackle concomitant environmental disasters, including floods, soil erosion, siltation, and rural poverty. Filipino managers cannot find the funds to absorb all these costs and still protect the remaining primary and secondary forests. One logical source of funds is Japanese development assistance.

Japanese Forestry and "Environmental Aid"

Japanese aid to the Philippines increased substantially in the 1970s, providing an important financial pillar for Marcos's patronage network. From 1970 to 1976, Japanese development loans swelled from 7 percent to 19 percent of total Philippine loan assistance, rising in absolute terms from U.S.$23.5 million to U.S.$308.4 million. Japan is now the largest bilateral aid donor to the Philippines, accounting for 56.8 percent of bilateral Philippine aid in 1993. In 1994 around 6 percent of bilateral Japanese ODA went to the Philippines.[174] From 1989 to 1994, annual Japanese bilateral aid to the Philippines averaged around U.S.$648 million.[175]

Until 1988 only a small amount of Japanese aid had gone to the Philippine forestry sector. From 1976 to 1992, a JICA technical cooperation project—the Forestry Development Project Watershed Management in the Pantabangan area—provided assistance with Philippine reforestation techniques. As well, from 1985 to 1988, JICA conducted a development study of the Cagayan River watershed to help formulate a forest management plan. JICA also provided one grant in 1978 (¥1.05 billion) and two in 1984 (¥1.07 billion and ¥103 million) to construct forestry buildings and fight forest fires.[176] Today, no JICA technical cooperation forestry projects exist in the Philippines, although a coordinator is examining possibilities.[177]

During the Aquino administration, international donors loaned substantial sums for DENR projects to protect the environment and rehabilitate and reforest degraded areas. Between 1979 and 1988, the Bureau of Forest Development was the primary recipient of only one loan and had a secondary role in eight others, in total implementing about U.S.$60 million. In contrast, between 1988 and 1992, DENR received loans worth

U.S.$731 million, accounting for a major portion of Philippine development assistance. The OECF provided a large share of these loans. The two largest loans were the 1988–92 Forestry Sector Program Loan from the ADB (U.S.$120 million) and the OECF (U.S.$120 million) and the 1991 Environment and Natural Resources Sector Adjustment Loan (ENR-SECAL) from the World Bank (U.S.$234 million) and the OECF (U.S.$100 million).[178] DENR also implemented grants and grant-funded projects from USAID, several UN organizations, and numerous Northern governments. To understand the environmental impact of Japanese development assistance, the next section evaluates the 1988–92 Forestry Sector Program Loan.

The Philippines now has more than 10 million hectares of degraded forest land. To reforest this area would cost about U.S.$7.8 billion. The ADB-OECF Forestry Sector Program Loan was intended to reforest 358 thousand hectares over five years, "a first step on a long and expensive journey toward restoring the nation's wealth."[179] The OECF accepted ADB guidelines and procedures for this loan, remaining in the background and providing yen credit.[180] Yet the OECF is still responsible for any repercussions, even if by default. Although many of the principles and concepts behind this loan were laudable, and even though some areas were reforested, there were significant drawbacks.

Prior to 1988, the Bureau of Forest Development had conducted most reforestation, often hiring local residents to plant and nurture the trees. The 1988–92 Forestry Sector Program Loan took a different tack, using contracts to include corporate, community, nongovernmental, and family groups in managing forest areas. In theory, contractors were paid based on the survival of their trees: if 80 percent of the trees survived after three years, then the contractor would be fully paid.[181] In some cases, contractors established effective forest plantations. Successful contractors tended to be family contractors, genuine "community contractors" (a group of residents), or committed NGOs that worked closely with locals.[182]

Despite these scattered accomplishments, numerous reforestation sites failed. Sometimes trees died, sometimes contractors never planted trees, and sometimes local residents burned the area. In some cases, contractors reached less than 20 percent of their target.[183] Several studies have estimated that after three years less than 40 percent of trees had survived. The scope and speed of reforestation under the Forestry Sector Loan contributed to problems, including poor supervision by DENR (which tended to involve paperwork rather than on-site inspections), misunderstandings, and insufficient training for contractors.[184] Patron-clientelism further distorted the potential benefits of this loan. Contractors often had few connections to the community and local inhabitants were hired as low-wage planters instead of being active participants. Many contractors lived in the provincial capital; instead of links to the community, they had personal ties to DENR officials. Reforestation funds were used for bureaucratic patronage and "corruption" was common. DENR officials siphoned funds by awarding reforestation contracts to "fictitious" people.[185] Although perhaps somewhat exaggerated, one scholar estimated that sixty percent of the Forestry Sector Loan was "lost" and only forty percent went into reforestation.[186]

Besides mixed environmental results, the Forestry Sector Program Loan has major economic drawbacks. The agreement stipulated that the loan be placed in the Central Bank to establish a "peso account" to fund DENR's contract reforestation program. Foreign exchange was supposed to be used to purchase *essential* foreign products. According to Frances Korten, however, many "items eligible for financing were for the use of loggers and wood industry enterprises, some of which were the cause of the deforestation that the loan was presumably trying to reverse."[187] The annual interest rate for the OECF loan—after an initial seven-year grace period—is 2.7 percent.[188] This must be repaid in yen after twenty-five years. Although on the surface these are soft terms, as the yen appreciates, repayment will become increasingly onerous. This expands the Philippine debt, adding even more pressure to generate foreign exchange by exporting natural resources.[189] As Korten notes, "lending that couples the environmental agenda with foreign exchange . . . is likely to accelerate the very damage it is intended to reverse."[190] Even though Japan considers this loan part of its environmental aid, the concept "environmental loan" is an oxymoron.[191]

Conclusion

Politics in the post-Marcos era is remarkably similar to previous political regimes as tenacious patron-client networks battle for access to and control over state resources. Many timber-based patron-client networks that dissolved in the wake of Marcos realigned in the Aquino years. But with less valuable commercial timber, fewer quick profits, and greater voter concern with environmental degradation, ties between top state leaders and timber operators are now more tenuous and brittle. In this setting, the state has pushed harder to tackle timber mismanagement and rein in "corrupt" state implementors. The state has canceled, suspended, or refused to renew many timber licenses; made scattered attempts to punish illegal loggers and their state allies; and, with support from international donors, increased reforestation of degraded land. Yet with fewer primary forests, the decline in legal log production from 1987 to 1994 was largely inevitable, following a trend that began in the mid-1970s. Moreover, intrinsic problems remain. As in the past, as state leaders fight to maintain stability and control, they are unable or unwilling to break pervasive clientelist ties among local political and military leaders, middle-level state officials, enforcement officers, and timber operators. These links distort state policies and allow timber-based patron-client networks to capture state bureaus, thereby crippling state capacity to enforce rules and collect taxes. As a result, poor logging techniques, inadequate silvicultural treatments, extensive illegal logging in primary forests and national parks (estimated to be equivalent to legal production), insufficient reforestation, and low state timber revenues continue to drive deforestation.

Post-Marcos Philippines also highlights the significant residual effects of ecological shadows. Japanese trade, technology, and investment now have little direct impact on timber management. But past Japanese log purchases at prices far below the cost of sustainable management have left severe environmental scars. Rebuilding a viable commercial timber industry will necessitate finding the funds and means to replace lost forests while still paying for concomitant environmental damage, including extensive soil erosion and climate changes that reduce agricultural productivity and produce calamitous floods. Japanese aid has done little to offset the environmental impact of past practices. There are currently no technical cooperation projects or grants in forestry. Instead, Japan has provided "environmental loans." Although these yen loans have supplied foreign exchange and financed a few successful reforestation and conservation sites, severe problems remain. In the case of the ADB-OECF First Forestry Sector Program Loan, a large portion of the money was wasted by administrators and contractors, or siphoned by bogus NGOs, local political and military leaders, and DENR officials. Moreover, the concept "environmental loan" is flawed; rather than offsetting Japanese past practices, these loans will eventually create even more pressure to extract and export natural resources to service the accompanying debt.

6 Conclusion: Japan's Ecological Shadow of Tropical Timber in Southeast Asia

Patron-client politics and ecological shadows of national economies create a context that supports and accelerates destructive and illegal logging and hampers efforts to implement sustainable management in Southeast Asia. Legal loggers extract excessive amounts and typically damage one-third to two-thirds of the trees left after harvesting. Illegal loggers are equally destructive, further damaging legal concessions, harvesting outside concession borders, and cutting in parks, watersheds, and wildlife sanctuaries. As a result, much of Southeast Asia's forests are now degraded. Without stronger restraints on legal operations and aggressive moves to halt illegal ones, loggers will degrade the remaining old-growth forests in the Philippines and East Malaysia within a decade and in Indonesia within three decades.

Japan's ecological shadow has been, by far, the most intense, although of course other ones have also helped ignite the process of deforestation in Southeast Asia. Building on previous chapters, the conclusion compares and evaluates the impact of Japan's ecological shadow of tropical timber across the clientelist states of Southeast Asia. Nine intertwined generalizations emerge that suggest a bleak future for Southeast Asia's forests. First, coupled with international markets and conventional economic calculations, Southeast Asian patron-client politics have generally magnified Japan's ecological shadow. Second, Japanese companies, particularly sogo shosha, have avoided tropical timber investments, especially in plantations, reforestation, and conservation. Third, these reluctant investors are aggressive and resilient traders that thrive on purchasing large quantities of cheap logs extracted from unsustainable sources. As log stocks inevitably decline, or after governments restrict log exports, these traders have simply moved to new areas. Fourth, these companies have facilitated and supported illegal logging, smuggling, and transfer pricing.

Fifth, while sogo shosha dominate the log trade, Apkindo (Indonesian Wood Panel Association) controls trade in tropical plywood. Using its monopolistic powers, Apkindo exports huge quantities of cheap high-grade plywood, especially to Japan, where Apkindo has bankrupted many plywood processors. These tactics have had significant economic costs, which have been aggravated by import tariffs in countries like Japan. Environmental costs have been even greater. Sixth, large import volumes, international markets that ignore environmental and social costs, Southeast Asian domestic policies, financial and structural arrangements of sogo shosha, and Apkindo's aggressive export tactics have depressed log prices and stimulated wasteful consumption of tropical timber. Coupled with illegal logging and schemes to evade forest fees, these factors have also depleted Southeast Asian state revenues that, in theory, are essential for sustainable management. Seventh, Japan's impact is indirect and only part of the complex process driving unsustainable logging. Effective reforms must tackle both the underlying and proximate causes of forest degradation. For this reason, log export bans and higher log and plywood prices have not improved timber management. Eighth, the intensity and components of Japan's ecological shadow have shifted over time and across states. Yet even after Japan no longer purchases significant amounts of tropical timber—such as in Sabah and the Philippines—the effects of past practices continue to undercut sustainable management. Finally, new Japanese official development assistance policies and corporate overseas environmental policies have done little to offset the residual and proximate repercussions of Japan's ecological shadow of tropical timber.

Patron-Client Politics and Timber Mismanagement

Japan's ecological shadow, Southeast Asian policies, and patron-client networks are interlocked. Japan's ecological shadow of tropical timber constricts Southeast Asian decisions and generates short-term financial incentives for destructive and illegal timber operators and their political, bureaucratic, and military patrons. Japanese corporate leaders are generally not members of Southeast Asian patron-client timber networks. But Japanese money is often crucial for the survival of these networks.

As Southeast Asian leaders battle to survive in societal webs of patron-client ties, modern clientelist networks flourish at all levels of the state and society.[1] At the top of the state, powerful patrons—such as Indonesian President Suharto and Sarawak Chief Minister Taib—have built potent patron-client networks with family, friends, and loyal supporters at the core. Top political patrons provide security, state resources, licenses, and concessions in exchange for political support, financial backing, legitimacy, and stability. In many cases, political, bureaucratic, and military clients also act as patrons, using their ties to top state leaders as a power base. These ties do not contribute to all power flowing to the top. Instead, power is diffused among patron-client clusters, pyramids, and networks, creating weblike societies. As a result, powerful patrons like Suharto and Taib—as well as patrons in the middle of the state—judiciously distribute patronage to reward and appease key political, military, bureaucratic, regional, and local elites. Quite naturally, patron-client networks often absorb state enforcement officers. These officials then ignore regulations in exchange for money, support, or security. In some cases, patron-client networks even capture state bureaus which then promote the interests of patrons rather than implement official state policies and rules. Limited supervision and pervasive patron-client exchange relations also contribute to simple "corruption," where military, police, customs, and forestry officials accept bribes without being absorbed by patron-client networks.

Patron-client relations are of course only one form of political, bureaucratic, or social interaction. But these dominate timber management in Southeast Asia. State patrons have granted logging concessions to reward followers, or, in some cases, appease potential opponents. These pervasive links distort state policies, contribute to a small elite prospering from timber profits, create multiple layers of subcontractors that reduce accountability, generate an unpredictable atmosphere that encourages quick and destructive extraction, subvert supervision of state implementors, and thwart state enforcement of timber regulations. Huge and remote concessions, along with small forest departments with limited financial and technical resources, further hamper effective forest management. Shielded by state patrons, timber operators, including Indonesia's Bob Hasan and Prajogo Pangestu (P. T. Barito Pacific Timber), and Sarawak's Datuk Tiong Hiew King (Rimbunan Hijau Group) and Tan Sri Ting Pek Khiing (Ekran Company), have made fortunes. With political protection, limited state supervision, little pressure to conserve or regenerate natural forests, and uncertain futures, legal loggers have quickly mined concessions and sold large quantities of cheap logs, especially to Japan.

Illegal logging is equally troublesome. In Indonesia, illegal loggers are linked to all levels of the state, from senior leaders down to local administrators, customs officials, and forestry staff. Some of these logs are smuggled overseas (often through East Malaysia), though perhaps more important, inefficient local mills process these logs and then export legal products. Illegal logging and smuggling have also been a serious problem in East Malaysia and the Philippines. One Sabah logger estimated that prior to the log export ban illegal logs comprised around 30 percent of total log exports. In 1989, a World Bank study estimated that illegal logging in the Philippines was equivalent to legal logging. Despite the 1986 log export ban, according to the Economist Intelligence Unit, the Philippine annual illegal trade in timber was worth U.S.$800 million in the early 1990s. In 1994, a Filipino congressman asserted that illegal logs accounted for around half of Philippine timber consumption.

Besides illegal logging and smuggling, poorly designed and inadequate forest fees have allowed concession holders to make substantial profits. A World Bank study calculated that the Philippine government only captured 9–14 percent of timber rents in the late 1980s. The nongovernmental organization WALHI estimated that the Indonesian government collected only 15–17 percent of potential timber rents in the early 1990s. The rest went to private companies. Transfer pricing, tax evasion, and schemes to lower forest charges and export fees have further reduced state revenues and increased private profits. In Sabah in the early 1990s, for example, 30–40 percent of total log exports may have been recorded inaccurately to evade government charges. Similar estimates have been made for Sarawak. Inadequate forest fees and poor collection rates effectively subsidize inefficient processors and allow exporters to sell timber at low prices. This also encourages loggers to harvest their concessions quickly, before the government improves enforcement or suddenly increases royalties, license fees, or export taxes. The tendency to extract logs as fast as possible is reinforced by concern among logging operators (often ethnic Chinese clients) that, if their patron loses power, the new government will revoke their concessions. As well, this uncertainty encourages logging companies to channel profits overseas.

Patron-client ties have also undermined recent plans to increase the collection of state taxes and timber royalties, and crack down on illegal logging and smuggling. Southeast Asian governments now have stricter policies. For example, illegal loggers in Sabah and Sarawak now face long jail sentences and stiff fines. But so far these policies have had little impact. Major timber operators, protected by state patrons and aided by state implementors, have remained unscathed. Southeast Asian governments have also announced plans to expand reforestation and regenerate natural forests.[2] As in Indonesia, however, governments have used "reforestation" to build immense fast-growing timber plantations, or as in the Philippines, reforestation money has been hijacked by patron-client networks.[3]

Clientelist politics and ineffective policies have generally magnified Japan's ecological shadow of tropical timber. The inability and unwillingness of Southeast Asian states to charge and collect sufficient forest fees, rampant illegal and destructive logging, disregard for conservation and natural forest regeneration, and inadequate and inappropriate reforestation have allowed Japan to consume vast quantities of cheap logs and plywood. International markets and conventional economic indicators that ignore environmental and social costs have further aggravated these environmental effects. These forces and policies have also distorted Japanese corporate investments and government aid projects.

Japanese Companies: Reluctant Investors

Except in Indonesia in the late 1960s and 1970s, Japanese companies have avoided major direct investments in logging and timber processing.[4] Today, as accessible and valuable tropical logs become increasingly scarce, as Japan's plywood industry fades, and as environmental criticism mounts, Japanese investors are even less interested in Southeast Asia's timber operations.[5] They now provide few technical advisers or long-term lines of credit.[6] Even with the rapid appreciation of the yen since the mid-1980s, there is almost no Japanese investment in the timber industries in East Malaysia and the Philippines, and only a small amount in wood processing and pulp and paper in Indonesia.[7] Japanese plywood processors also have no plans to relocate to Southeast Asia, despite the financial struggles of many mills in Japan.[8]

Japanese companies are even more reluctant to finance or participate in major conservation or reforestation projects. Several factors inhibit Japanese investment. Sogo shosha tend to avoid long-term commitments essential for effective reforestation or sustainable timber operations. Yuta Harago of WWF Japan succinctly explains: "They are basically traders, not investors. So they aren't obliged to think in terms of 30-year projects."[9] In addition, environmentalists and the media tend to scrutinize and fervently criticize timber joint ventures. On the other hand, even though the economic and environmental consequences may be far greater, it is more difficult to develop sensational stories about purchasing practices, distribution structures, and import and consumer prices. Southeast Asian politics also curb Japanese corporate investment. Although clientelist states have been natural prey for sogo shosha log traders, they provide little security for investors. Japanese companies are wary of sudden political shifts that could undercut concession licenses or change informal rules that allow quick, profitable logging. As well, naturally firms do not want to sink money into poorly managed, likely doomed, timber operations.

Japanese Log Traders: Persistent Buyers

Sogo shosha need intense ecological shadows to survive as trade intermediaries. These companies account for the majority of tropical log imports. Even more important, they dominate the tropical log trade chain and Japanese plywood processors, who absorb about three-quarters of Japanese tropical log imports.[10] To facilitate and organize the tropical log trade, they work at low profit margins, charging small commissions to finance and coordinate firms involved in the trade chain. To remain viable at low profit margins, they import huge volumes. Intense competition among sogo shosha to generate the largest sales turnover reinforces the emphasis on import volumes over profits.[11] Sogo shosha have stimulated and maintained demand for log volumes through financial and structural arrangements with producers, wholesalers, retailers, and consumers and by monitoring market information, absorbing exchange rate fluctuations and short-term losses, aggressively searching for new sources of cheap logs, and assisting domestic plywood processors. To increase the speed and volume of log harvests, they have supplied funds, equipment (chainsaws, bulldozers, and road machinery), and technical advice to Southeast Asian producers, often in exchange for logs or guaranteed purchasing deals. These arrangements and tactics have depressed import and consumer prices, further elevating demand. In addition, these companies have apparently manipulated prices. As a buffer against sudden changes in log prices or quantities, sogo shosha store a two to three-month supply of tropical logs in Japan.[12] When necessary, they have apparently used these reserves to flood the Japanese market and lower log prices.[13]

Over the last forty years, sogo shosha log traders have thrived in the clientelist states of Southeast Asia. Cheap log imports have enabled these companies to maintain a viable tropical log trade chain, build and protect a substantial tropical plywood industry, and fuel Japanese construction. These log sales have also stoked Southeast Asian patron-client networks, adding to the fantastic wealth of state patrons and their timber clients. At no time have sogo shosha considered the source or long-term environmental effects of log imports.[14] Instead, as supplies have dwindled, or after Southeast Asian governments have restricted exports, these traders have simply moved to new sources. The Philippines was the first country to attract these traders. In the 1950s, the Philippines accounted for over 85 percent of Japanese log imports from Southeast Asia. In the first half of the 1960s, Philippine logs accounted for two-thirds—and Sabah for just under one-third—of Japanese log imports from Southeast Asia. Japanese log imports from the Philippines increased throughout the 1960s, peaking at the end the decade. In the 1970s, however, as accessible Philippine primary forests became scarce, and as Japanese consumption of tropical logs surged, Japanese traders increasingly turned to Sabah, Indonesia, and to a lesser extent Sarawak.

In 1970, the Philippines was still Japan's largest source of tropical logs. In that year, Japan imported 7.5 million cubic meters of logs from the Philippines, 6.1 million cubic meters from Indonesia, 4.0 million cubic meters from Sabah, and 1.9 million cubic meters from Sarawak. In 1971, Indonesia replaced the Philippines as Japan's key source of logs. In 1973, Japanese tropical log imports from Southeast Asia peaked at 26.7 million cubic meters. In that year, Japan imported 42.1 percent from Indonesia, 27.4 percent from Sabah, 22.1 percent from the Philippines, and 4.7 percent from Sarawak. After 1973, Japanese log imports gradually declined as accessible, cheap log stocks dwindled and as Japan's plywood industry contracted. By 1980, total Japanese log imports from Southeast Asia had dropped to 18.9 million cubic meters: 45.6 percent from Indonesia, 33.3 percent from Sabah, 11.8 percent from Sarawak, and 5.7 percent from the Philippines.

As Indonesia slashed log exports in the early 1980s, Japanese traders maintained a steady supply from Sabah and boosted log imports from the lower-grade forests of Sarawak. In 1987, after the complete ban on Indonesian and Philippine log exports, East Malaysia accounted for over 90 percent of Japan's total log imports from Southeast Asia: 7.0 million cubic meters from Sabah and 5.5 million cubic meters from Sarawak. In the late 1980s, as accessible, high-quality commercial forests became increasingly scarce in Sabah, Japanese traders turned even more to Sarawak. In 1988, Japan imported 5.4 million cubic meters of logs from Sabah and 5.3 million cubic meters from Sarawak. Japanese log imports from Sabah then fell sharply, from 4.6 million cubic meters in 1989 to 2.1 million cubic meters in 1992 to less than 300 thousand cubic meters in 1993 after the log export ban early that year. Meanwhile, Japanese log imports from Sarawak climbed to around 6.7 million cubic meters in 1989 and 1990, then fell slightly over the next two years. As the Sarawak government imposed greater log export restrictions, Japanese log imports decreased even further after 1992, falling to 3.9 million cubic meters in 1995. Despite this decrease, however, from 1993 to 1995, Sarawak still accounted for over 65 percent of Japanese log imports from Southeast Asia (including Papua New Guinea and the Solomon Islands) and 60 percent of total tropical log imports.[15]

To partially replace tropical logs from East Malaysia, Japanese traders have turned to Papua New Guinea and the Solomon Islands.[16] From 1992 to 1995, PNG and the Solomon Islands accounted for over one-quarter of Japanese log imports from Southeast Asia.[17] Despite these moves, however, Japanese tropical log imports have continued to decline as hardwood supplies diminish throughout the Asia-Pacific region, as Japan's recession impedes builders, as Japan imports more tropical plywood, and as plywood processors refine techniques to make softwood plywood.[18] As a result of all these changes, in 1995 Japan imported only 5.9 million cubic meters of Southeast Asian logs (including PNG and the Solomon Islands). (See figure 6.1.)

As in the Philippines from the 1950s to the 1980s, Indonesia from the late 1960s to the early 1980s, and Sabah from the 1960s to the early 1990s, sogo shosha provide powerful economic incentives for destructive and unsustainable logging in the old-growth forests of Sarawak, PNG, and the Solomon Islands.[19] Japan now accounts for over half of Sarawak's log exports, far more than the next largest importers: Taiwan (15.9 percent); South Korea (8.8 percent); and China (7.0 percent). In addition, plywood imports from Sarawak are increasing; in 1995, Japan accounted for 36.7 percent of Sarawak's total plywood exports (592 thousand cubic meters), two times more than China, the next largest importer.[20] Despite international pressure to curb illegal and destructive loggers, from 1990 to 1995, annual legal log production in Sarawak averaged almost 18 million cubic meters, about the same as in 1989.[21] Although log production in 1995 was around 2 million cubic meters lower than in 1989, according to Lord Cranbrook (who led the 1989 ITTO survey of Sarawak's forests), under current practices it is still two and a half times higher than sustainable levels. From 1992 to 1995, Japan imported on average 1.6 million cubic meters of logs from PNG and 344 thousand cubic meters from the Solomon Islands, accounting for around half of total log production in both countries.[22] In 1994, Japanese log imports from PNG were three times higher than in 1990.[23] Not surprisingly, PNG log production more than doubled in the first half of the 1990s, from 1.45 million cubic meters in 1990 to over 3 million cubic meters since 1993.[24] In the Solomon Islands,

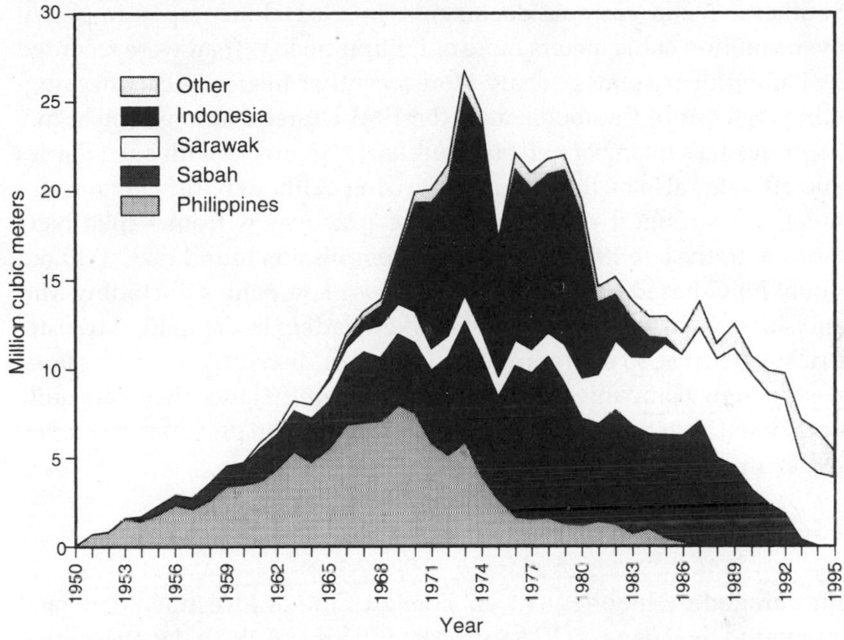

Figure 6.1
Japanese log imports from Southeast Asia (South Seas), 1950–95
Other includes PNG, the Solomon Islands, Vietnam, Burma, Laos, Cambodia, and other minor exporters in the region.
Source: tables 6 and 7 (see appendix).

as Japanese log imports increased from about 188 thousand cubic meters in 1991 to 381 thousand cubic meters in 1995, log production from the natural forests has also shot up, increasing from 381 thousand cubic meters in 1991 to around 826 thousand cubic meters in 1995.[25] Annual log production in the Solomon Islands is now well over sustainable production, estimated at 275 thousand cubic meters.[26] At 1995 production levels, the Solomon Islands—which relies on timber exports for half of its total export earnings—will deplete its commercial timber stocks in thirteen years. If log production continues to increase at the current rate, this will occur in less than a decade.[27]

Japan, Illegal Logging, Smuggling, and Transfer Pricing

Besides these legal log purchases, Japanese companies have cooperated with—and likely participated in—smuggling syndicates, and schemes to alter volumes, species, extent of processing, and log diameters on

Southeast Asian customs documents. In 1981 alone, Japan imported over 1 million cubic meters more of Philippine logs than were recorded by Philippine customs officials. More recently, Mitsui was caught smuggling logs out of Cambodia after the 1993 United Nations' embargo.[28] Sogo shosha's financial and structural arrangements with subsidiaries and affiliates also facilitate transfer pricing. Although difficult to document, the strongest evidence of these practices is from Papua New Guinea. In the late 1980s, the Barnett Commission found that "Without doubt PNG-based subsidiaries of Japanese companies [including Mitsubishi and Nissho Iwai] are the market leaders in the field of transfer pricing. Because so many are either openly or discreetly owned by Japanese parent companies with exclusive buying rights they can quite openly sell their timber under value and the hidden profit can be reaped higher up the corporate chain."[29]

From Log Traders to Plywood Consumers

Encouraged by Indonesia's 1967 Foreign Capital Investment Law and supported by Japanese ODA, in the late 1960s and 1970s, Japanese companies invested in logging in Indonesia, especially in Kalimantan. Along with other foreign investors and donors, Japanese technology, funds, and advice supported large-scale logging operations. During the 1970s, Japan imported over 40 percent of Indonesia's total log production. Sogo shosha dominated this trade. For example, from 1972 to 1974, Mitsui alone imported almost 3.4 million cubic meters of Indonesian logs.[30] These investments and purchases triggered a logging boom. Log production increased from 5.5 million cubic meters in 1968 to over 26 million cubic meters in 1973. From 1973 to 1980, Indonesia's annual log production averaged 23.7 million cubic meters.[31]

Sogo shosha now have little influence on the Indonesia-Japan timber trade. But Japanese consumers still have a crucial impact on Indonesian forest management as Apkindo floods Japan with plywood. To capture Japan's plywood market and destroy Japanese processors, Apkindo—which sets plywood prices, assigns export quotas, and issues export licenses—has exported inexpensive high-grade plywood. Apkindo has also exploited Japan's wasteful consumption patterns, "encouraging" processors to manufacture kon-pane suitable for the Japanese market. As well, Apkindo established Nippindo to import plywood directly, thus bypassing sogo shosha's financial, transport, import, and storage services. Nippindo sells plywood below world market prices, which in turn depresses international plywood prices.[32] In terms of sales, Nippindo has been remarkably successful. In the early 1980s, Japan imported almost no tropical plywood. Yet from 1990 to 1995, Japan imported an annual average of more than 3 million cubic meters of Indonesian plywood, the bulk of Japan's total tropical plywood imports.[33] As a result of Apkindo's aggressive export strategy, in 1995, in roundwood equivalent, Japan imported 6.9 million cubic meters of Indonesian plywood, more than total tropical log imports.[34]

Japan's plywood industry has had severe economic problems as Apkindo bombards the market with cheap plywood, as tropical log stocks disappear,[35] as Japanese processing costs rise, as Japan's recession impedes builders, and as Southeast Asian states restrict log exports, sometimes, as in Sabah, with no warning. In the mid-1980s, domestic Japanese processors supplied around 90 percent of total tropical plywood consumption; by 1994, this had dropped below 50 percent.[36] This trend will likely continue. According to the Japan Plywood Manufacturers' Association, by the year 2000, forty of the remaining hundred Japanese plywood mills will fold.[37]

Using similar tactics, Apkindo has also undercut plywood processors in South Korea and Taiwan.[38] By 1991, Apkindo controlled over three-quarters of the world plywood trade, although this fell to about two-thirds in the mid-1990s, largely as a result of greater Malaysian plywood exports. Apkindo's tactics have had severe economic and environmental costs. Plywood prices not only ignore environmental and social costs but also underestimate the full economic costs of extraction, production, and transportation. Indonesian state revenue losses have been compounded by import tariffs, including Japan's 10–15 percent tariff on plywood.[39] Inefficient and wasteful plywood processors—who produce about 10 million cubic meters of plywood per year—put great pressure on Indonesia's primary forests. The International Tropical Timber Organization calculates that Indonesian log production was 35 million cubic meters in 1994. A 1996 World Bank report estimates that it is now over 40 million cubic meters. And NGOs claim it is more likely around 44 million cubic meters, two times higher than a recent World Bank estimate of sustainable production.[40]

Low Prices, Inadequate Revenue, and Wasteful Consumption

Southeast Asian state policies, patron-client networks, and sogo shosha financial and structural arrangements all contribute to low tropical timber prices. Low prices are reinforced by markets and economic measures that ignore environmental and social costs. Stumpage prices assume that primary forests are essentially free. They reflect extraction and transportation costs, and ignore the investment, manpower, and time it would take to regrow a tree, and the social and environmental costs of degrading the forest ecosystem.[41] Low tropical timber prices, coupled with illegal logging, smuggling, inadequate timber fees, and poor enforcement of timber taxes and royalties, deplete Southeast Asian state revenues that, in theory, are essential for sustainable management. A 1991 ITTO study showed that "producer countries captured only 9 percent of the final product price (comprising production costs, government revenues and profits) . . . when exporting raw logs. . . . The remaining 91 percent went to consumer countries." In some cases, forest charges to assess the value of a standing tree were less than 1 percent of the final price.[42] Log and plywood exporters have generated sufficient funds to satisfy rent-seeking patron-client networks but not nearly enough to reflect the environmental and social costs of logging.

Low tropical log and plywood prices stimulate wasteful consumption.[43] Higher prices would create incentives for "conscientious consumption" and recycling. Although public campaigns that explain the causes and effects of tropical deforestation, or put pressure on companies to treat tropical timber as a limited and valuable resource, may help reshape wasteful consumption patterns, it is vital that consumer prices reflect these attitudes. In Japan, it is often more economical to purchase a new product than to reuse or recycle hardwood furniture, tropical plywood and sawnwood, and kon-pane.[44] As a result, Japanese construction companies generally discard kon-pane after a few uses.[45] Houses and apartments made partially from tropical plywood and sawnwood are often torn down after twenty or thirty years. And when people move to a new home, hardwood furniture is often simply thrown away. Cheap timber imports have also helped Japan protect its own forests. In 1991, the Organization for Economic Cooperation and Development estimated that Japan extracted only 53 percent of their annual growth, allowing a significant net increase in forest cover.[46] Today, around two-thirds of Japan is covered in forests; about 41 percent of these forests are planted. As a result, Japan is one of "the most heavily forested countries in the world."[47]

Japan: An Indirect Force

The impact of Japan's ecological shadow of tropical timber is indirect—a shadow that constricts options, undermines sustainable management, and provides incentives for destructive and illegal logging. It is part of a complex array of intertwined indirect and proximate forces that drive timber mismanagement in Southeast Asia. Alone, this shadow is not a "cause" of deforestation. For this reason, log export bans have not improved forest management in Southeast Asia. In the Philippines, illegal loggers still pose a great threat to the remaining primary forests. In Sabah, legal log production was over 9 million cubic meters in 1993 and almost 8 million cubic meters in 1994, well over the estimate of annual sustainable yield by the Malaysian Primary Industries minister (3 million cubic meters). Meanwhile, in Indonesia, there are now far too many inefficient processors—often with close links to state patrons—who firmly resist moves to lower production to sustainable levels. Indonesian log production is now at least 8 million cubic meters higher than at the peak of the log export boom.[48]

Reforming specific elements of trade will also not automatically improve timber management. For example, in theory, export and consumer prices must fully internalize environmental and social costs to increase Southeast Asian state revenues and foster sustainable consumption. But Southeast Asian clientelist states are unable, or at least unwilling, to collect forest fees or control illegal and destructive loggers. Although higher prices would likely reduce wasteful consumption, without first gaining control of particularistic, rent-seeking patron-client networks, higher prices could well create even stronger incentives to extract illegal logs or mine legal concessions as timber operators make even more quick money. This apparently occurred in the Philippines in the early 1990s, when higher log prices stimulated illegal logging rather than better management.[49]

Ecological Residues

The intensity and nature of Japan's ecological shadow of tropical timber have shifted over time and across states as valuable and accessible log stocks wane, as Southeast Asian states ban or restrict log exports, as international market prices fluctuate, as more Japanese plywood processors go bankrupt, and as the Japanese government and corporations shift priorities. Yet all of Southeast Asia must cope with the residual and cumulative effects of past practices. The deepest scars are in Sabah and the Philippines. During the height of Philippine logging (1964–73), Japan imported over 60 percent of total Philippine log production. Even as Philippine log exports fell sharply from 1974 to 1986, Japan still accounted for close to half of total Philippine log exports.[50] Over 80 percent of the Philippines' remaining primary forests disappeared in the 1970s and 1980s. Today, there is relatively little old-growth forest left, and the Philippine legal commercial timber industry has collapsed. In 1994, Philippine log production was less than 1 million cubic meters, about 10 million cubic meters lower than from 1967 to 1969, when log production peaked.[51]

From 1972 to 1987, Japan consumed over 60 percent of Sabah's total log production, contributing to a sharp fall in Sabah's primary forests, from over half of total land area in 1973 to one-quarter in 1983. In both Sabah and the Philippines, the effects of these log purchases have swamped the effects of Japanese investment, ODA, and conservation projects, leaving these states without sufficient funds to revive their commercial timber industries and tackle the economic, social, and environmental consequences of extensive deforestation, and the corresponding problems of soil erosion, local climate changes, flash floods, siltation, lower agricultural productivity, and increased poverty. In the Philippines, the annual cost of soil erosion alone is more than a half a billion U.S. dollars.[52] Japanese aid—which can be seen as partially derived from economic growth propelled by unsustainable resource imports—is a logical source of funds to tackle environmental problems, regenerate degraded forests, replant cleared areas, and protect the remaining old-growth forests. But current Japanese aid projects have done little to offset the ecological impact of past practices.

Japanese Aid and Tropical Forests

Under pressure from the international community, Japan rapidly increased the quantity of ODA in the 1970s and 1980s. Today, Japan is the world's largest bilateral aid donor and the major contributor to the Asian Development Bank. This aid has provided vital scientific and technical assistance to many Southern countries. But even though Japanese aid has certainly provided benefits, it has also entailed environmental costs. As with all Northern donors, Japan's ODA has promoted and supported its overseas business and strategic goals. Indicative of Japan's attitude is an unpublished 1980 report by the Ministry of Foreign Affairs that defines ODA as "the cost of building an international order to secure Japan's overall national security."[53]

Particularly in Indonesia from 1969 to 1974, general Japan International Cooperation Agency technical assistance and Japanese Overseas Economic Cooperation Fund loans—such as support for roads and ports—facilitated unsustainable log exports. JICA and the OECF also funded projects that supported destructive logging, including forest surveys and inventories, logging feasibility studies, and logging equipment transfers. As well, JICA and OECF funds helped offset risky investments by Japanese log traders. Few JICA programs are now linked to commercial loggers or log exporters. JICA has also developed new environmental sections and guidelines. Partially as a result, tropical forest policies now focus more on regenerating natural forests, protecting watersheds and old-growth forests, maintaining biodiversity, replanting degraded land, and establishing social and community forest programs. But serious problems remain. JICA's environmental guidelines are vague and ambiguous. JICA still supports questionable "reforestation" projects, including large-scale industrial timber estates in Indonesia. And perhaps most important, only a negligible amount of JICA funds actually support projects to regenerate natural forests, develop social and community forestry, and conserve old-growth forests.[54]

Along similar lines as JICA, the OECF and the EXIM Bank of Japan have also expanded their environmental departments and developed procedures to consider environmental factors when evaluating loan applications. This has contributed to more refined rhetoric, but to no obvious changes to forestry loans. Although it is difficult to be certain, since OECF and EXIM Bank environmental procedures and evaluations are shrouded in secrecy, few loan requests seem to be rejected for environmental reasons.[55] OECF and EXIM Bank environmental departments appear more concerned with avoiding scandals than promoting environmental management in the South.

Broader problems with Japanese ODA hinder attempts to incorporate environmental and social factors into grants, technical cooperation, and loans. Despite some commendable principles, Japan's new environment law and ODA guidelines are ineffective. Numerous clauses are ambiguous, and there are no concrete enforcement mechanisms or penalties. Moreover, little coordination or cooperation exists among key ministries—the Ministry of International Trade and Industry, the Ministry of Foreign Affairs, the Ministry of Finance, the Economic Planning Agency, the Environment Agency, and the Forestry Agency—or the two implementing agencies, JICA and the OECF. Convoluted guidelines and a fragmented aid structure impede environmental reviews and obscure accountability. Aid staff with little environmental expertise, field experience, or in-depth knowledge of the diverse cultures and ecosystems of Southeast Asia further aggravate environmental miscalculations. The emphasis on concessional loans—which comprise over half of Japan's

ODA, more than any other donor's—also thwart environmental objectives. Finally, effective Japanese aid projects are undermined by continuing links to Japanese companies, recipient ambivalence and apathy toward environmental protection, poor cooperation with NGOs and communities, and minimal supervision of aid funds.[56]

In FY1994, 14.2 percent of Japanese ODA was allocated as "environmental aid." There are also clear problems with this aid. The definition of environmental aid is ambiguous. These funds have in part been derived by simply reclassifying traditional projects. Moreover, "environmental loans" have accounted for the majority of this aid. Under MITI guidance, environmental aid has focused on exporting environmental technology to tackle industrial pollution, especially urban water and sewage management. As a result, except in the Philippines, only a small portion has funded conservation, reforestation, or tropical forest management.[57]

Even in the Philippines, however, Japanese environmental loans—like the 1988–92 Forestry Sector Program Loan—have had marginal environmental rewards and considerable economic penalties. In the case of the Forestry Sector Program Loan, the economic burden is compounded by the failure of many reforestation sites, contractors and government officials who wasted funds, patron-client networks that siphoned substantial portions (perhaps as much as 60 percent), and the steady appreciation of the yen. Eventually, these loans will create even greater pressure on the state to export resources to service the debt.[58]

Japanese Corporate Environmental and Forest Policies

In the late 1980s, international criticism of the overseas environmental impact of Japanese firms mounted. To counter these attacks, the major sogo shosha developed new environmental guidelines and departments. Keidanren also proclaimed a nonbinding global environmental charter. This public relations campaign has contributed to a profusion of glossy brochures and refined corporate environmental rhetoric. It has also funded a few forest conservation projects—such as Sumitomo Forestry's project to replant an indigenous forest in East Kalimantan and Mitsubishi's project to recreate a natural rain forest in Sarawak—and contributed to modest support for reforestation, especially through research at Japanese universities.[59] But these measures appear designed more to deflect environmental critics than to improve overseas environmental management. Little evidence exists of concrete changes to Japanese trade practices or to the attitudes of corporate leaders.[60] Corporate environmental officials tend to ignore, dispute, or dismiss as irrelevant the environmental impact of corporate structures, consumption, prices, and past practices.[61]

Japanese Policies to Reduce Tropical Timber Consumption

At the beginning of the 1990s, as part of the campaign to deflect criticism of Japan's overseas environmental practices, the Japanese government and major corporations announced plans to reduce tropical timber consumption. The Japan Building Contractors' Society and the Japan Plywood Manufacturers' Association set nonbinding targets to use less tropical wood, especially kon-pane (30–35 percent over five years). The Japan Lumber Importers' Association established import guidelines. The Construction Ministry developed new codes to encourage builders to substitute alternative materials for tropical timber. The Forestry Agency announced that it would track log imports by specific companies, require companies to submit five-year import projections, and encourage traders to import logs from sustainable sources. The national government and several municipal governments also proclaimed plans to reduce tropical timber consumption, especially the use of kon-pane for public projects.[62]

These policies have had little impact. Since 1990, tropical log imports have dropped. But this is a result of fewer valuable and accessible log stocks, log export restrictions and bans, the collapse of many Japanese plywood processors, and Japan's recession. More important, although tropical timber consumption fell from the mid-1970s to the late 1980s, it has declined only slightly since 1990. The drop in tropical log imports has been largely offset by drawing on log reserves and by greater tropical plywood imports.[63] As a result, in 1991 and 1994, Japan imported about the same quantity of tropical timber (in roundwood equivalent).[64] Moreover, from 1990 to 1995, total tropical plywood consumption has remained fairly stable.[65]

Overall, recent Japanese corporate and government moves to address the environmental impact of overseas activities have not altered the fundamental impact of Japan's ecological shadow of tropical timber. Japanese government reforms have focused on reshaping the least potent element—ODA—and even these have only made marginal improvements. Meanwhile, Japanese corporate environmental departments and guidelines, and revised rules to integrate environmental factors into corporate decisions, have produced more sophisticated rhetoric and token forest conservation but few concrete changes to purchasing practices or consumption patterns. Japanese plywood producers, sogo shosha, and powerful government departments either ignore or superficially address the key factors that support and accelerate destructive logging in Southeast Asia: corporate financial and structural arrangements; log and plywood imports from unsustainable sources; timber prices far below replacement or sustainable management costs; wasteful consumption; import tariffs; and the cumulative effects of past practices. It is not surprising that Japanese government officials and corporate leaders are diverting attention away from these factors. Import tariffs and low tropical log prices are crucial for the survival of Japan's plywood industry. Cheap tropical plywood, especially kon-pane, supports Japan's powerful construction industry. And low log prices, massive import volumes, and wasteful consumption are essential for the ability of sogo shosha to function as effective trade intermediaries.

The inability of Southeast Asian clientelist states to impede destructive loggers, collect timber revenues, and enforce regulations, and the current and residual impact of Japan's ecological shadow of tropical timber cast an ominous darkness over the forests of Southeast Asia. International markets and other ecological shadows add to the pall over these forests. In this setting, it is hardly surprising that loggers—seeking quick profits and protected by state patrons—irreparably degrade old-growth forests, destroy commercial concessions, illegally log parks and conservation zones, and export unsustainable volumes of timber. Fundamental reforms are essential to alter shadow ecologies and strengthen Southeast Asian state capacity.[66] But there will be no easy solutions. At a minimum, effective reforms will require the North to sacrifice money, Southeast Asian states to sacrifice some sovereignty, extensive South-North dialogue, and a plethora of innovative international and domestic policies and structures. The international community must also confront Southeast Asian political forces driving unsustainable logging. This may well be impossible in a world that jealously guards artificial borders, relentlessly pursues economic growth and higher consumption, and invariably protects powerful corporations and state patrons. If so, Southeast Asia's primary forests will soon disappear.

Appendix: Statistical Tables

Given slightly different estimates, data origins, and definitions, statistics for tropical timber production, exports, and imports vary somewhat depending on the source. For consistency, when possible, this book uses recent International Tropical Timber Organization (ITTO) or Japanese government statistics. Otherwise, figures come from the governments of the Phillipines, Indonesia, Malaysia, and the states of Sabah and Sarawak, or from the Food and Agriculture Organization (FAO). Also note that ITTO figures for 1995 are forecasts and will be revised in the *Annual Review and Assessment of the World Tropical Timber Situation 1996*.

Table 1
Total Japanese tropical hardwood imports, 1990–95 (1,000 cubic meters)

	1990	1991	1992	1993	1994	1995
Logs	11,321	10,402	10,990	8,324	7,632	6,550
Sawn	1,375	1,013	1,248	1,805	1,642	1,500
Veneer	650	250	192	239	160	132
Plywood	2,810	2,941	2,882	3,864	3,791*	4,074*

See Table 5 for similar estimates of Japan's tropical log imports.
*Japan's two main sources of tropical hardwood plywood are Indonesia and Malaysia. According to the Sarawak Campaign Committee, in 1994 Japan imported 3.228 million cubic meters of plywood from Indonesia and 508 thousand cubic meters from Malaysia. In 1995 Japan imported 3.018 million cubic meters from Indonesia and 970 thousand cubic meters from Malaysia. Sarawak Campaign Committee, "Japan's Tropical Timber Imports in 1994 and 1995," *Mori no Koe*, no. 8, sent by Glen Barry at Ecological Enterprises.
Sources: ITTO, *Annual Review and Assessment of the World Tropical Timber Situation 1993–1994* (Yokohama, Japan: ITTO, 1995), p. 54; and ITTO, *Annual Review and Assessment of the World Tropical Timber Situation 1995* (Yokohama, Japan: ITTO, 1996), p. 48.

Table 2
Total Japanese tropical hardwood imports in roundwood equivalent, 1990–95 (1,000 cubic meters)

	1990	1991	1992	1993	1994	1995
Logs	11,321	10,402	10,990	8,324	7,632	6,550
Sawn	2,475	1,823	2,246	3,249	2,956	2,700
Veneer	1,235	475	365	454	304	251
Plywood	6,463	6,764	6,629	8,887	8,719	9,370
Total	21,494	19,464	20,230	20,914	19,611	18,871

Conversion rates (cubic meters of roundwood per cubic meters of processed timber product): multiply by 1.8 for sawnwood; 1.9 for veneer; and 2.3 for plywood.
Calculated from ITTO, *Annual Review 1993–1994*, p. 54; and ITTO, *Annual Review 1995*, p. 48.

Table 3
Total Japanese tropical hardwood production, 1990–95 (1,000 cubic meters)

	1990	1991	1992	1993	1994	1995
Logs	0	0	0	0	0	0
Sawn	1,000	1,000	1,364	1,050	1,030	1,009
Veneer	307	303	274	218	181	166
Plywood	6,145	6,062	5,477	4,576	3,988	3,688

Sources: ITTO, *Annual Review 1993–1994*, p. 54; and ITTO, *Annual Review 1995*, p. 48.

Table 4
Total Japanese apparent tropical hardwood consumption, 1990–95 (1,000 cubic meters)

	1990	1991	1992	1993	1994	1995
Logs	11,321	10,402	13,010	9,811	9,071	7,816
Sawn	2,368	2,013	2,674	2,917	2,721	2,557
Veneer	957	979	495	508	375	290
Plywood	8,950	8,997	9,176	9,609	8,703	8,669

The ITTO defines apparent domestic consumption as "Production + Imports − Exports +/− Stock Change (if reported)."
Sources: ITTO, *Annual Review 1993–1994*, p. 54; and ITTO, *Annual Review 1995*, p. 48.

Table 5
Major sources of Japanese tropical log imports, 1990–95 (1,000 cubic meters)

	1990	1991	1992	1993	1994	1995
Malaysia	10,169.6	9,045.7	8,426.8	5,216.2	4,463.2	3,902.0
Papua New Guinea (PNG)	625.9	819.0	1,161.2	1,754.7	1,932.1	1,586.0
Solomon Islands	227.6	187.5	309.5	346.4	338.3	381.0
Burma	16.7	12.6	12.9	76.9	22.3	17.0
Vietnam	14.4	23.1	9.7	0.0	0.0	—
Cambodia	9.9	21.6	36.1	24.5	5.5	—
Laos	14.1	3.0	13.2	13.6	40.7	30.0
Philippines	23.4	2.3	0.0	2.0	0.0	—
Vanuatu	0.0	0.0	0.0	4.0	0.0	—
Africa	126.3	95.9	99.5	506.9	—	531.0
Latin America	3.9	2.4	2.6	2.9	—	—
Total	11,231.8	10,213.1	10,071.5	7,948.1	7,632.0*	6,455.0**

*The total figure for 1994 is from ITTO, *Annual Review 1995*, p. 48. This presumably includes imports from major and minor sources.
**1995 data are from the Sarawak Campaign Committee, "Japan's Tropical Timber Imports in 1994 and 1995."
Sources: Data from the Japanese Lumber Importers' Association (JLIA), received by the author, May 1995; figures for Africa and Latin America are from JATAN, "Asia-Pacific Forests," p. 2, from data from the Japan Tariff Association.

Table 6
Japanese tropical log imports from Southeast Asia (South Seas), 1950–69 (million cubic meters)

Year	Philippines	Sabah	Sarawak	Indonesia	Other	Total
1950	0.111	0.008	0.000	0.000	0.000	0.119
1951	0.436	0.009	0.000	0.000	0.000	0.445
1952	0.538	0.014	0.000	0.000	0.000	0.552
1953	1.256	0.042	0.000	0.005	0.000	1.303
1954	1.249	0.129	0.000	0.006	0.000	1.384
1955	1.846	0.160	0.000	0.018	0.000	2.024
1956	2.357	0.273	0.000	0.021	0.000	2.651
1957	2.050	0.384	0.000	0.010	0.000	2.444
1958	2.746	0.539	0.019	0.004	0.000	3.308
1959	3.431	0.869	0.106	0.005	0.016	4.427
1960	3.475	1.025	0.100	0.017	0.045	4.662
1961	3.662	1.622	0.300	0.017	0.052	5.646
1962	4.371	1.754	0.267	0.013	0.056	6.461
1963	5.443	2.161	0.352	0.024	0.106	8.086
1964	5.017	2.296	0.371	0.059	0.097	7.840
1965	5.632	2.806	0.644	0.105	0.098	9.285
1966	6.758	3.614	1.277	0.213	0.154	12.016
1967	7.042	3.885	1.431	0.502	0.238	13.098
1968	7.110	3.660	1.931	0.955	0.249	13.905
1969	7.915	4.077	1.911	2.723	0.372	16.998

Source: JLIA data collected by JATAN, in Mariko Urano, "Commercial Exploitation of Indonesian Tropical Forests by Japan," in JANNI, *Reshaping "Development": Indonesia-Japan Relation from Grassroots' Perspective,* Proceedings of the INGI Kanagawa Symposium (Tokyo: Japan NGO Network on Indonesia, 1993), p. 54.

Table 7
Japanese tropical log imports from Southeast Asia (South Seas), 1970–95 (million cubic meters)

Year	Philippines	Sabah	Sarawak	Indonesia	Other*	Total
1970	7.542	3.960	1.872	6.091	0.585	20.050
1971	5.701	4.130	1.472	8.181	0.627	20.111
1972	5.136	5.409	1.377	8.977	0.738	21.637
1973	5.896	7.309	1.251	11.231	1.008	26.695
1974	3.886	6.997	0.951	11.450	0.891	24.175
1975	2.853	5.598	0.702	7.298	0.522	16.973
1976	1.692	8.490	1.738	9.656	0.591	22.167
1977	1.501	8.138	1.487	9.272	0.546	20.944
1978	1.559	9.212	1.496	8.986	0.539	21.792
1979	1.264	8.200	2.268	9.769	0.582	22.083
1980	1.073	6.306	2.260	8.639	0.663	18.941
1981	1.418	5.471	2.917	4.138	0.784	14.728
1982	1.308	6.442	4.049	2.453	0.869	15.121
1983	0.648	6.238	4.075	2.111	0.807	13.879
1984	0.935	5.483	4.256	1.328	0.941	12.943
1985	0.510	5.892	5.395	0.137	1.061	12.995
1986	0.264	6.019	4.778	0.000	1.056	12.117
1987	0.027	6.980	5.494	0.000	1.154	13.655
1988	0.033	5.351	5.260	0.000	1.001	11.645
1989	0.052	4.641	6.683	0.000	1.184	12.560
1990	0.023	3.420	6.749	0.000	0.909	11.101
1991	0.002	2.577	6.468	0.000	1.067	10.114
1992	0.000	2.064	6.363	0.000	1.543	9.970
1993	0.002	0.293	4.923	0.000	2.222	7.440
1994	0.000	0.000	4.463	0.000	2.339	6.802
1995	0.000	0.000	3.902	0.000	2.022	5.924

*Other includes PNG, the Solomon Islands, Vietnam, Burma, Laos, Cambodia, and other minor exporters in the region.

Sources: JPMA, *Plywood Industry in Japan* (Tokyo: JPMA, 1993), pp. 24–25; JPMA, *Plywood Industry in Japan* (Tokyo: JPMA, April 1994), p. 8; and data from the JLIA, received by the author, 4 April 1994, and May 1995. Also see François Nectoux and Yoichi Kuroda, *Timber from the South Seas: An Analysis of Japan's Tropical Environmental Impact* (Gland, Switzerland: WWF International, 1989), figure B7, p. 118. Figures for 1995 are from the Sarawak Campaign Committee, "Japan's Tropical Timber Imports in 1994 and 1995."

Table 8
Total Indonesian log production and log exports, 1961–93 (million cubic meters)

Year	Total log production	Total log exports
1961	3.944	—
1962	4.023	—
1963	4.023	—
1964	4.100	0.135
1965	4.150	0.150
1966	4.300	0.295
1967	4.800	0.531
1968	5.500	1.333
1969	7.000	3.685
1970	10.700	7.834
1971	13.705	10.822
1972	16.821	13.354
1973	26.197	18.500
1974	23.120	16.873
1975	15.800	12.532
1976	23.200	17.695
1977	22.330	18.560
1978	26.620	19.200
1979	24.860	17.800
1980	27.559	14.884
1981	23.334	6.201
1982	22.448	3.104
1983	25.448	2.993
1984	26.958	1.724
1985	23.500	0.027
1986	27.400	0.027
1987	31.200	0.063
1988	34.800	0.140
1989	36.700	0.068
1990	32.000	0.048
1991	35.400	0.048
1992	35.850	na
1993	35.500	na

Sources: Production data, FAO data, International Economic Data Bank, the Australian National University, Canberra (product no. 1604, sawlogs + veneer logs, nonconiferous); FAO, *FAO 1991 Yearbook: Forest Products 1980–1991* (Rome: FAO, 1993), p. 71; FAO, *1983 Yearbook of Forest Products 1972–1983* (Rome: FAO, 1985), p. 132; FAO, *1975 Yearbook of Forest Products 1964–1975* (Rome: FAO, 1977), p. 75; and *FAO 1993 Yearbook: Forest Products 1982–1993* (Rome: FAO, 1995), p. 83.

Table 9
Total Indonesian plywood exports and production, 1973–93 (million cubic meters)

Year	Total plywood exports	Total plywood production
1973	0.000	0.009
1974	0.000	0.024
1975	0.001	0.107
1976	0.013	0.214
1977	0.017	0.279
1978	0.070	0.424
1979	0.117	0.624
1980	0.245	1.001
1981	0.759	1.552
1982	1.232	2.487
1983	2.106	3.138
1984	3.021	3.600
1985	3.964	4.615
1986	4.607	5.750
1987	5.648	6.400
1988	6.372	7.733
1989	8.039	8.784
1990	8.244	8.250
1991	8.635	9.600
1992	8.654	10.100
1993	8.904	10.050

Sources: FAO data, International Economic Data Bank, the Australian National University, Canberra (product no. 1640, plywood); and FAO, *FAO 1993 Yearbook*, pp. 170, 178.

Table 10
Total Indonesian tropical hardwood production, 1990–95 (1,000 cubic meters)

	1990	1991	1992	1993	1994	1995
Logs	36,000	37,000	37,500	37,000	35,000	34,000
Sawn	8,632	7,500	7,200	6,800	6,700	6,500
Veneer	44	50	55	55	50	50
Plywood	8,860	9,958	10,550	10,689	9,836	9,500

Sources: ITTO, *Annual Review 1993–1994*, p. 57; and ITTO, *Annual Review 1995*, p. 51.

Table 11
Total Indonesian tropical hardwood exports, 1990–95 (1,000 cubic meters)

	1990	1991	1992	1993	1994	1995
Logs	0	0	0	0	0	0
Sawn	615	936	711	639	308	300
Veneer	40	31	30	13	10	10
Plywood	8,502	8,970	9,761	9,724	8,852	8,500

Sources: ITTO, *Annual Review 1993–1994,* p. 57; and ITTO, *Annual Review 1995,* p. 51.

Table 12
Total Sabah log production and exports, 1959–95 (million cubic meters)

Year	Total log exports	Total log production
1959	1.386	1.563
1960	1.771	2.165
1961	2.254	2.631
1962	2.465	2.804
1963	2.975	3.464
1964	3.348	3.585
1965	3.797	4.163
1966	4.856	5.555
1967	5.322	5.709
1968	5.797	5.909
1969	6.188	6.201
1970	6.150	6.561
1971	6.558	6.953
1972	7.708	8.527
1973	10.144	11.104
1974	9.733	10.031
1975	8.991	9.120
1976	12.061	12.589
1977	12.337	12.979
1978	13.127	13.291
1979	10.332	10.841
1980	8.510	9.064
1981	9.361	11.732
1982	9.950	11.739
1983	9.495	11.991
1984	7.340	10.505
1985	8.442	10.757
1986	8.218	9.811
1987	9.449	12.174

Table 12
continued

Year	Total log exports	Total log production
1988	—	—
1989	—	9.494
1990	—	8.443
1991	3.400	8.163
1992	—	11.633
1993	—	9.300
1994	0.144*	7.965
1995	0.119*	na

*plantation logs
Sources: Sabah Forestry Department, *Forestry in Sabah* (Sandakan: Sabah Forestry Department, 1989), p. 139; and Malaysian Timber Council, Statistics, http://www.mtc.com.my.

Table 13
Total Sarawak log exports, 1977–85 (million cubic meters)

Year	Total log exports
1977	3.5
1978	4.2
1979	6.1
1980	6.7
1981	6.9
1982	8.3
1983	9.2
1984	9.0
1985	10.5

Source: SEALPA (Southeast Asian Lumber Producers' Association), in Yasuko Higuchi and Norio Umahashi, "The Campaign Against 3rd World Forest Resources Exploitation by Japan," in Sahabat Alam Malaysia, ed., *Forest Resources Crisis in the Third World*. Proceedings of the conference, "Forest Resources Crisis in the Third World," 6–8 September 1986, Sahabat Alam Malaysia, 1987, p. 376.

Table 14
Total Sarawak log production and exports, 1989–95 (million cubic meters)

Year	Total log exports	Total log production
1989	—	18.163
1990	15.900	18.838
1991	15.800	19.411
1992	14.800	18.848
1993	9.100	16.735
1994	8.417	16.318
1995	7.745	16.000

Sources: 1990, 1991, Sarawak Timber Industry Development Corporation (STIDC), *Statistics of Timber and Timber Products. Sarawak 1993* (Kuching: STIDC, 1993); 1992, Sarawak Timber Association (STA), supplied to author; 1993 and 1994 export data, STA data, from the *Nippon Mokuzai Shimbun,* supplied by the Sarawak Campaign Committee; production data (1989–94) and 1995 log export figure, Malaysian Timber Council, statistics, http://www.mtc.com.my; 1995 log production, "Shorter Harvest Period Boosts Sarawak's Log Output," *Star,* 19 April 1996, Reuter Business Briefing.

Table 15
Total Philippine log production and log exports, 1961–93 (million cubic meters)

Year	Total log production	Total log exports
1961	6.940	—
1962	7.115	—
1963	—	—
1964	9.130	—
1965	10.015	—
1966	7.843	—
1967	11.114	—
1968	11.584	—
1969	11.005	—
1970	10.680	—
1971	10.600	—
1972	10.446	6.858
1973	10.190	7.759
1974	7.332	4.693
1975	8.441	4.596
1976	8.646	2.331
1977	7.873	2.047
1978	7.169	2.200
1979	6.578	1.248
1980	6.212	1.154
1981	5.280	1.683

Table 15
continued

Year	Total log production	Total log exports
1982	4.462	1.590
1983	4.283	1.017
1984	3.785	1.323
1985	3.124	0.679
1986	3.039	0.427
1987	3.346	0.210
1988	3.157	0.176
1989	2.773	0.101
1990	2.155	0.004
1991	1.558	0.004
1992	0.798	na
1993	0.685	na

Sources: FAO data, International Economic Data Bank, the Australian National University, Canberra (product no. 1604, sawlogs + veneer logs, nonconiferous); FAO, *FAO 1993 Yearbook,* p. 83; FAO, *FAO 1991 Yearbook,* p. 71; FAO, *1983 Yearbook of Forest Products,* p. 132.

Table 16
Total Philippine tropical hardwood production, 1990–95 (1,000 cubic meters)

	1990	1991	1992	1993	1994	1995
Logs	2,502	1,919	1,438	1,022	940	865
Sawn	841	726	647	440	408	378
Veneer	49	54	80	65	39	23
Plywood	397	321	331	273	258	244

Sources: ITTO, *Annual Review 1993–1994,* p. 57; and ITTO, *Annual Review 1995,* p. 51.

Notes

Introduction: Ecological Shadows

1. Interview, College of Forestry, University of the Philippines at Los Banos, 1 February 1994. Also see Mark Poffenberger and Roger D. Stone, "Hidden Faces in the Forest: A 21st Century Challenge for Tropical Asia," *Sais Review* 16, no. 1 (winter 1996), p. 204. Dipterocarp forests are dominated by trees from the Dipterocarpaceae family. These forests contain Southeast Asia's main commercial species.

2. Evelyne Hong, *Natives of Sarawak: Survival in Borneo's Vanishing Forest* (Pulau Pinang, Malaysia: Institut Masyarakat, 1987), pp. 128–129, cited in Harold Brookfield, Lesley Potter, and Yvonne Byron, *In Place of the Forest: Environmental and Socio-economic Transformation in Borneo and the Eastern Malay Peninsula* (Tokyo: United Nations University Press, 1995), p. 101.

3. Interviews, World Wide Fund for Nature (WWF) Malaysia, Petaling Jaya, 10 March 1994.

4. Robert Repetto, *The Forest for the Trees? Government Policies and the Misuse of Forest Resources* (Washington, DC: World Resources Institute, 1988), p. 56; and Malcolm Gillis, "Malaysia: Public Policies and Tropical Forest," in Malcolm Gillis and Robert Repetto, eds., *Public Policies and the Misuse of Forest Resources* (Cambridge: Cambridge University Press, 1988), p. 141.

5. Calculated from table 12.

6. This estimate is made by the economist Rizal Ramli. Summarized in "Timber: An Economic Dilemma," *Economic and Business Review Indonesia*, no. 98 (26 February 1994), p. 9. Large secondary forests (logged primary forests) will of course remain.

7. In some cases, loggers clear-cut forests, although this is generally limited to areas designated for agriculture or development projects (e.g., hydroelectric dams).

8. See Peter Dauvergne, "The Politics of Deforestation in Indonesia, *Pacific Affairs* 66, no. 4 (winter 1993–94), pp. 497–518.

9. This book focuses on trade in "forest products" (timber) as defined by the International Tropical Timber Agreement: "tropical hardwood saw and veneer logs, sawnwood, veneer, and plywood." ITTO (International Tropical Timber Organization), *Annual Review and Assessment of the World Tropical Timber Situation 1995* (Yokohama: ITTO, 1996), p. 1.

10. For brevity, the term Southeast Asia refers primarily to Indonesia, East Malaysia, and the Philippines. For Japanese log import statistics, "Southeast Asia" also includes Papua New Guinea and the Solomon Islands. This region is known as the South Seas in Japan.

11. Over these times, Japan imported 271.48 million cubic meters of logs while these three areas produced 509.77 million cubic meters. Calculated from tables 6, 7, 9, 12, and 15. This calculation is based on Japanese import data, Food and Agriculture Organization (FAO) production data, and Sabah Forestry Department data; and as with other figures in this book that draw on different statistical sources, this should be considered a rough estimate.

12. Calculated from tables 7 and 14.

13. Calculated from ITTO, *Annual Review 1995*, p. 57; and ITTO, *Annual Review and Assessment of the World Tropical Timber Situation: 1993–1994* (Yokohama: ITTO, 1995), p. 52.

14. For brevity, this book refers to these sogo shosha as: Mitsubishi, Mitsui, Itochu, Sumitomo, Marubeni, and Nissho Iwai.

15. Summarized in Lee Smith, "Japan: Does the World's Biggest Company Have a Future?" *Fortune* (7 August 1995), Reuter Business Briefing.

16. Calculated from tables 5 and 7.

17. See table 7 and figure 6.1.

18. The estimate of Apkindo's control over world trade in tropical plywood is calculated from ITTO, *Annual Review 1995*, p. 57.

19. Calculated from tables 1 and 5. Roundwood equivalent is the "'under-bark' log volume which would have been necessary to obtain one unit of volume of the processed product." François Nectoux and Yoichi Kuroda, *Timber from the South Seas: An Analysis of Japan's Tropical Environmental Impact* (Gland, Switzerland: WWF International, 1989), p. 127.

20. Calculated from table 10.

21. The World Bank estimate of sustainable production is summarized in Jim Della-Giacoma, "Indonesia Says Improving Logging Practices," (20 May 1996), Reuter News Service, Reuter Business Briefing.

22. See tables 2 and 4.

23. Sustainable timber production is defined as doing nothing that will "irreversibly reduce the potential of the forest to produce marketable timber." Duncan Poore, "The Sustainable Management of Natural Forest: the Issues," in Duncan Poore, ed., *No Timber Without Trees: Sustainability in the Tropical Forest*. A study for ITTO. (London: Earthscan, 1989), p. 5. Poore explains this concept in detail.

24. The Asian Development Bank is sometimes portrayed as being under Japan's thumb. Yet it is simplistic to equate bank policies with Japanese interests. According to a bank official, Japan does not shape policy; rather, the Japanese government has "piggybacked" intellectually on the policies of the bank. Interview, ADB official, Manila, 31 January and 4 February 1994. Similar comments were made about Japan's influence over the ITTO. Interview, ITTO official, Tokyo, 6 April 1994.

25. See, for example, Patricia Adams, *Odious Debts: Loose Lending, Corruption, and the Third World's Environmental Legacy* (Toronto: Earthscan Canada, 1991); and Susan George, *The Debt Boomerang: How Third World Debt Harms Us All* (London: Pluto Press, 1992).

26. For recent studies that analyze the impact of one or more of these factors on tropical forests, see Poffenberger and Stone, "Hidden Faces in the Forest," pp. 203–219; Nancy Lee Peluso, Peter Vandergeest, and Lesley Potter, "Social Aspects of Forestry in Southeast Asia: A Review of Postwar Trends in the Scholarly Literature," *Journal of Southeast Asian*

Studies 26, no. 1 (1 March 1995), pp. 196–218; Brookfield, Potter, and Byron, *In Place of the Forest*; R. Gerard Ward and Elizabeth Kingdon, eds., *Land, Custom and Practice in the South Pacific* (Cambridge: Cambridge University, 1995); Christine Padoch and Nancy L. Peluso, eds., *Borneo in Transition: People, Forests, Conservation and Development* (Selangor, Malaysia: Oxford University Press, 1995); Nancy Lee Peluso, *The Impact of Social and Environmental Change on Forest Management: A Case Study from West Kalimantan, Indonesia*. Community Forestry Case Study Series, no. 8 (United Nations: FAO, 1995); Nigel Sizer and Richard Rice, *Backs to the Wall in Suriname: Forest Policy in a Country in Crisis* (Washington, DC: World Resources Institute, 1995); Charles Victor Barber, Nels C. Johnson, and Emmy Hafild, *Breaking the Logjam: Obstacles to Forest Policy Reform in Indonesia and the United States* (Washington, DC: World Resources Institute, March 1994); D. M. Taylor, D. Hortin, M. J. G. Parnell, and T. K. Marsden, "The Degradation of Rainforests in Sarawak, East Malaysia, and Its Implications for Future Management Policies," *Geoforum* 25, no. 3 (1994), pp. 351–369; Dauvergne, "The Politics of Deforestation"; Nels C. Johnson and Bruce Cabarle, *Surviving the Cut: Natural Forest Management in the Humid Tropics* (Washington, DC: World Resources Institute, 1993); Lesley Potter, "The Onslaught on the Forests in South-East Asia," in Harold Brookfield and Yvonne Byron, eds., *South-East Asia's Environmental Future: The Search for Sustainability* (Tokyo: United Nations University Press/Oxford University Press, 1993), pp. 103–123; Norman Myers, *The Primary Source: Tropical Forests and Our Future* (updated for the 1990s) (New York: W. W. Norton, 1992); Nancy Lee Peluso, *Rich Forests, Poor People: Resource Control and Resistance in Java* (Berkeley: University of California Press, 1992); Nancy Lee Peluso, "The Political Ecology of Extraction and Extractive Reserves in East Kalimantan, Indonesia," *Development and Change* 23, no. 4 (October 1992), pp. 49–74; Lesley Potter, "Environmental and Social Aspects of Timber Exploitation in Kalimantan, 1967–1989," in Joan Hardjono, ed., *Indonesia, Resources, Ecology, and Environment* (Singapore: Oxford University Press, 1991); George Marshall, "FAO and Tropical Forestry," *Ecologist* 21 (March/April 1991), pp. 66–72; James Rush, *The Last Tree: Reclaiming the Environment in Tropical Asia* (New York: Asia Society, 1991); Marcus Colchester, "The International Tropical Timber Organization: Kill or Cure for the Rainforests?" *Ecologist* 20 (September/October 1990), pp. 166–173; David M. Kummer, *Deforestation in the Postwar Philippines* (Chicago: University of Chicago Press, 1991); Chris Elliot, *Tropical Forest Conservation* (Gland, Switzerland: WWF International, 1991); Philip Hurst, *Rainforest Politics: Ecological Destruction in South-East Asia* (London: Zed Books, 1990); Mark Poffenberger, ed., *Keepers of the Forest: Land Management Alternatives in Southeast Asia* (Hartford: Kumarian Press, 1990); Charles Victor Barber, "The State, the Environment, and Development: The Genesis and Transformation of Social Forestry Policy in New Order Indonesia." Doctoral dissertation (Berkeley: University of California, 1989); Poore, ed., *No Timber Without Trees*; Todd K. Martens, "Ending Tropical Deforestation: What Is the Proper Role for the World Bank?" *Harvard Environmental Law Review* 13 (1989), pp. 485–515; Repetto, *The Forest for the Trees?*; Gillis and Repetto, eds., *Public Policies*; Rob A. Cramb, "Shifting Cultivation and Resource Degradation in Sarawak: Perceptions and Policies," *Review of Indonesian and Malaysian Affairs* 22, no. 1 (winter 1988), pp. 115–149.

27. Raymond L. Bryant, "Political Ecology: An Emerging Research Agenda in Third-World Studies," *Political Geography* 11 (January 1992), p. 16.

28. Jim MacNeill, Pieter Winsemius, and Taizo Yakushiji, *Beyond Interdependence: The Meshing of the World's Economy and the Earth's Ecology* (New York: Oxford University Press, 1991), pp. 58–59. The relative influence of specific elements that shape the impact of a shadow ecology on resources in the global commons, especially the effect on the atmosphere, differ somewhat from those that shape resources in other sovereign states. This book emphasizes factors that involve interstate relations.

29. International Institute for Sustainable Development (IISD), main contributors, David Runnalls and Aaron Cosbey, *Trade and Sustainable Development: A Survey of the Issues and a New Research Agenda* (Winnipeg: IISD, 1992), p. 22, from United Nations Development Program, *Human Development Report 1992* (New York: Oxford University Press, 1992), p. 204.

30. The term ecological shadow should not be confused with the concept of ecological footprint—defined as "the total area of productive land and water required on a continuous basis to produce all the resources consumed, and to assimilate all the wastes produced, by that population, wherever on Earth that land is located." William E. Rees, "Ecological Footprints: Making Tracks Toward Sustainable Cities," from *People and Planet Magazine*, in http://www.iisd.ca/linkages/consume/brfoot.html. A shadow ecology refers exclusively to the environmental impact of a national economy on external resources, while an ecological footprint usually refers to the impact of individuals, towns, or cities. The concept of an ecological footprint loses its analytical power if it is pushed to discuss country-level effects.

31. This is the title of MacNeill, Winsemius, and Yakushiji, *Beyond Interdependence*.

32. See Ivan L. Head, *On a Hinge of History: The Mutual Vulnerability of South and North* (Toronto: University of Toronto Press, 1991).

33. This is generally accepted by the South. Northern assistance—especially technology transfers on noncommercial terms—has been a priority for developing countries during international environmental negotiations. Gareth Porter and Janet Welsh Brown, *Global Environmental Politics* (Boulder, CO: Westview Press, 1991), p. 129.

34. Much of this research was sparked by the World Commission on Environment and Development, *Our Common Future* (Oxford: Oxford University Press, 1987).

35. For example, Teresa Hayter, *Exploited Earth: Britain's Aid and the Environment* (London: Earthscan, 1989).

36. William M. Adams, *Green Development: Environment and Sustainability in the Third World* (London: Routledge, 1990), p. 166, quoted in Bryant, "Political Ecology," p. 16.

37. Bryant, "Political Ecology," p. 16. See Czech Conroy and Miles Litvinoff, eds., *The Greening of Aid: Sustainable Livelihoods in Practice* (London: Earthscan, 1988). Conroy and Litvinoff provide thirty-four cases of aid projects with positive environmental consequences.

38. Numerous influential studies argue that the diffusion of environmentally sound technology is critical for Southern sustainable development. For example, see World Commission on Environment and Development, *Our Common Future*, p. 87; and Linda Starke, *Signs of Hope: Working Towards Our Common Future* (Oxford: Oxford University Press, 1990), p. 165.

39. For a general discussion of the relationship between technology and the environment, see Amitav Rath and Brent Herbert-Copley, *Green Technologies for Development: Transfer, Trade and Cooperation* (Ottawa: International Development Research Center [IDRC], 1993).

40. Martin Khor Kok Peng, "North-South Relations Revisited in Light of UNCED," briefing paper for UNCED, no. 8, 1991, p. 6. For a critique of the environmental impact of Northern technology transfers, see Ecologist, "Mainstream Solutions," *Ecologist* 22, no. 4 (July/August 1992), pp. 187–192.

41. Nazli Choucri, "Multinational Corporations and the Global Environment," in Nazli Choucri, ed., *Global Accord: Environmental Challenges and International Responses* (Cambridge, MA: MIT Press, 1993), p. 220.

42. For example, see Pamela Wellner, "A Pipeline Killing Field: Exploitation of Burma's Natural Gas," *Ecologist* 24, no. 5 (September/October 1994), pp. 189–193; Brewster Kneen, "The Invisible Giant: Cargill and Its Transnational Strategies," *Ecologist* 25, no. 5 (September/October 1995), pp. 195–199; Amiya Kumar Bagchi, "The GATT Final Act—A Declaration of Rights of TNCs," *Third World Resurgence*, no. 46 (June 1994), pp. 26–29; and the articles in Charles S. Pearson, ed., *Multinational Corporations, Environment, and the Third World: Business Matters* (Durham, NC: Duke University Press, 1987).

43. Roger D. Stone and Eve Hamilton, *Global Economics and the Environment* (New York: Council on Foreign Relations Press, 1991), pp. 42–43.

44. Charles Arden-Clarke, "An Action Agenda for Trade Policy Reform to Support Sustainable Development: A United Nations Conference on Environment and Development Follow-up," in Durwood Zaelke, Paul Orbuch, and Robert F. Housman, eds., *Trade and the Environment: Law, Economics and Policy* (Washington, DC: Island Press, 1993), p. 72.

45. For example, see Tom Wathen, "A Guide to Trade and the Environment," pp. 3–22 and Charles S. Pearson, "The Trade and Environment Nexus: What Is New Since '72?" pp. 23–32, in Zaelke, Orbuch, and Housman, eds., *Trade and the Environment*; Patrick Low, "International Trade and the Environment: An Overview," pp. 1–14 and Judith Dean, "Trade and the Environment: A Survey of the Literature," pp. 15–28, in Patrick Low, ed., *International Trade and the Environment* (Washington, DC: World Bank, 1992); and IISD, *Trade and Sustainable Development*. Recent articles include: Andrea C. Durbin, "The North South Divide," *Environment* 37 (September 1995), pp. 16–20, 35; Steve Charnovitz, "Improving Environmental and Trade Governance," *International Environmental Affairs* 7, no. 1 (winter 1995), pp. 59–91; Graciela Chichilnisky, "North-South Trade and the Global Environment," *American Economic Review* 84, no. 4 (September 1994), pp. 851–874; Richard Eglin, "GATT and Environment," *Ecodecision*, no. 8 (March 1993), pp. 34–36; Daniel C. Esty, "Beyond Rio: Trade and the Environment," *Environmental Law* 23, no. 2 (1993), pp. 387–396; and Alex Trisoglio and Kerry ten Tate, "Systemic Integration of the Environment and Trade," *Ecodecision*, no. 8 (March 1993), pp. 23–28.

46. Hal Kane, "Managing Through Prices, Managing Despite Prices," in Zaelke, Orbuch, and Housman, eds., *Trade and the Environment*, p. 58.

47. Zaelke, Orbuch, and Housman, eds., *Trade and the Environment*, p. xiv.

48. For a discussion of the links between Northern consumption of luxury goods and Southern environmental degradation and human suffering, see Martin Khor Kok Peng, "The Global Environment Crisis: A Third World Perspective," briefing paper for UNCED, no. 5, 1991; Jyoti Parikh and Kirit Parikh, "Consumption Patterns: The Driving Force of Environmental Stress," Bombay, Indira Gandhi Institute of Development Research, 1991, in NGONET 0795, computer database of the Alternative Conference at UNCED, Rio de Janeiro, 1992; and Bunker Roy, "Population or Over-Consumption: Which Is Destroying the World?" India, 1992, in NGONET 1251.

49. Kane, "Managing Through Prices," p. 60.

50. Although perhaps extreme, the Center for Science and Environment in New Delhi estimates a mature tree in India is worth U.S.$50,000. Alan Thein Durning, "Let's Put a Proper Price on Trees," *International Herald Tribune* (3 February 1994).

51. MacNeill, Winsemius, and Yakushiji, *Beyond Interdependence*, pp. 37, 21. For more detail, see Stewart Hudson, "Trade, Environment and the Pursuit of Sustainable Development," in Low, ed., *International Trade*, pp. 55–64.

52. For a discussion of the links between Southern subsidies and resource depletion, see Edward B. Barbier, Joanne C. Burgess, and Anil Markandya, "The Economics of Tropical Deforestation," *Ambio* 20, no. 2 (April 1991), p. 55.

53. Charles Arden-Clarke, "South-North Terms of Trade: Environmental Protection and Sustainable Development," *International Environmental Affairs* 4, no. 2 (spring 1992), p. 124.

54. Internalizing environmental and social costs into resource prices should help stabilize prices because these costs are inherently stable.

55. See Arden-Clarke, "South-North Terms of Trade," pp. 122–137. For a strong critique of "environmental economics"—especially the disregard for values and rights—see Ecologist, "Mainstream Solutions," pp. 173–179. In my view, pointing to the need for prices to internalize environmental costs is not a monstrous vision reducing people and culture to money. Rather, it accepts that money is necessary to implement policies to protect the environment.

56. Philippine Department of Environment and Natural Resources, *The Philippine Natural Resources Accounting Project: Executive Summary* (Quezon City: Department of Environment and Natural Resources, 1991), p. 1.

57. Robert Repetto, *Promoting Environmentally Sound Economic Progress: What the North Can Do* (Washington, DC: World Resources Institute, 1990), p. 3.

58. Roefie Hueting, Peter Bosch, and Bart de Boer, *Methodology for the Calculation of Sustainable National Income* (Gland, Switzerland: WWF International, 1992), p. 5. The authors use the term "environmental burden" to measure the impact of consumption on overseas resource depletion and environmental change.

59. Edward B. Barbier, Joanne C. Burgess, Timothy M. Swanson, and David W. Pearce, "The Economic Linkages Between the International Trade in Tropical Timber and the Sustainable Management of Tropical Forests," *Final Report*. ITTO Activity PCM (XI)/4, 19 March 1993, pp. iv, v.

60. See Peter Dauvergne, "A Model of Sustainable International Trade in Tropical Timber," forthcoming, *International Environmental Affairs* 9, no. 1 (winter 1997).

61. Ibid.

62. Rachel A. Crossley, "A Preliminary Examination of the Economic and Environmental Effects of Log Export Bans." Draft manuscript. Central Forestry Team, Natural Resources Division. (Washington, DC: World Bank Environment Department, 1994), cited in Sizer and Rice, *Backs to the Wall in Suriname*, p. 25.

63. For example, Rachel Crossley argues that "the limited amount of analysis on the impacts of removing [log export bans] shows that without introducing countervailing policies, there could be substantial negative effects on the environment, although the economic effects would undoubtedly be positive." Crossley, "A Preliminary Examination," p. 2.

64. See Dauvergne, "A Model of Sustainable International Trade in Tropical Timber."

Chapter 1: Japan's Shadow Ecology

1. Robert M. Orr, Jr. and Bruce M. Koppel, "A Donor of Consequence: Japan as a Foreign Aid Power," in Bruce Koppel and Robert M. Orr, Jr., eds., *Japan's Foreign Aid: Power and Policy in a New Era* (Boulder, CO: Westview Press, 1993), pp. 2–3. On changes to Japanese aid in the late 1980s, see "Beware the Helping Hand," *Economist* (15 July 1989), pp. 12–14. For a succinct summary of the evolution of Japanese aid, see William L. Brooks and Robert M. Orr, Jr., "Japan's Foreign Economic Assistance," *Asian Survey* 25, no. 3 (March 1985), pp. 322–340.

2. "Japan Funds to Developing Nations Hit Record," *Jiji Press Newswire* (26 September 1995), Reuter Business Briefing.

3. Japanese Ministry of Foreign Affairs, *Japan's ODA: Annual Report 1995* (Tokyo: Association for Promotion of International Cooperation, February 1996), p. 100. For a discussion of Japanese aid in ASEAN, see Alan Rix, "Managing Japan's Aid: ASEAN," in Koppel and Orr, eds., *Japan's Foreign Aid*, pp. 19–40; and Robert Orr, Jr., "The Rising Sun: Japan's Foreign Aid to ASEAN, the Pacific Basin and the Republic of Korea," *Journal of International Affairs* 41 (1987/88), pp. 39–62.

4. For articles on Japanese ODA in the Philippines, see Akira Takahashi, "From Reparations to Katagawari: Japan's ODA to the Philippines," in Koppel and Orr, eds., *Japan's Foreign Aid*, pp. 63–90; and Filologo Pante, Jr. and Romeo A. Reyes, "Japanese and U.S. Aid to the Philippines: A Recipient-Country Perspective," in Shafiqul Islam, ed., *Yen for Development: Japanese Foreign Aid and the Politics of Burden-Sharing* (New York: Council on Foreign Relations Press, 1991), pp. 121–136. For Indonesia, see Jeff Kingston, "Bolstering the New Order: Japan's ODA Relationship with Indonesia," in Koppel and Orr, eds., *Japan's Foreign Aid*, pp. 41–62.

5. Japanese Ministry of Foreign Affairs, *Japan's ODA 1993* (Tokyo: Association for Promotion of International Cooperation, 1994), p. 17.

6. For a description of JICA, see Robert M. Orr, Jr., *The Emergence of Japan's Foreign Aid Power* (New York: Columbia University Press, 1990), pp. 47–50, for the OECF, pp. 45–47.

7. OECF, *OECF Annual Report 1993* (Tokyo: OECF, 1993), pp. 3, 37. From 1961 to the end of March 1993, Indonesia, Thailand, the Philippines, and Malaysia absorbed 40.9 percent of OECF loans. Ibid., p. 37.

8. Richard Forrest and Yuta Harago, *Japan's Official Development Assistance (ODA) and Tropical Forests* (Gland, Switzerland: WWF International, 1990), p. 8.

9. Although officially in FY1990 31.5 percent of bilateral aid funded infrastructure projects, Hiroshi Kanda claims it was actually around half. Hiroshi Kanda, "A Big Lie: Japan's ODA and Environmental Policy," *AMPO: Japan-Asia Quarterly Review* 23, no. 3 (1992), p. 42.

10. For background on JICA activities, see JICA, *For the Future of the Earth* (Tokyo: JICA, 1992).

11. The distinction between OECF aid loans and EXIM loans is in many ways purely definitional—a small change in the Development Assistance Committee (DAC) guidelines of the Organization for Economic Cooperation and Development could easily eliminate a large percentage of OECF "aid" and swell EXIM "loans." For this reason, it is logical to consider EXIM loans—although not officially part of ODA—alongside a discussion of

government overseas economic assistance. For a description of DAC guidelines for economic assistance qualifying as ODA, see Orr and Koppel, "A Donor of Consequence," p. 16, footnote 3.

12. EXIM Bank of Japan, *The Export-Import Bank of Japan: Annual Report 1993* (Tokyo: EXIM Bank of Japan, 1993), p. 8.

13. EXIM Bank of Japan, *Guide to the Export-Import Bank of Japan* (Tokyo: EXIM Bank of Japan, February 1994), p. 1.

14. It should be emphasized that "few of the problems the Japanese development program faces are unique." Alan S. Miller and Curtis Moore, *Japan and the Global Environment* (College Park, MD: Center for Global Change, University of Maryland, 1991), p. 20.

15. During interviews in 1994, environment-oriented aid bureaucrats at the OECF and JICA expressed frustration with omnipresent administrative obstacles. For a critique of ODA administration, see chapter 3 in Alan Rix, *Japan's Foreign Aid Challenge: Policy Reform and Aid Leadership* (London: Routledge, 1993); for aid policy, see chapter 4.

16. The weakest central actor, the EPA, generally remains neutral or sides with the finance ministry. Orr and Koppel, "A Donor of Consequence," p. 6. The role of these actors is discussed by Toru Yanagihara and Anne Emig, "An Overview of Japan's Foreign Aid," in Islam, ed., *Yen for Development*, pp. 53–58.

17. Interview, forestry consultant, Japan Overseas Forestry Consultants Association (JOFCA) and United States Agency for International Development (USAID), 3 February 1994.

18. Quoted in Orr, *The Emergence of Japan's Foreign Aid Power*, p. 50.

19. "In 1990 each ODA administrator in Japan was responsible for an average of U.S.$6.35 million in funds—far more than aid staff in any other nation." Richard Forrest, "Japanese Aid and the Environment," *Ecologist* 21 (January / February 1991), p. 29.

20. Interview, senior official, JICA, Tokyo, 12 April 1994.

21. Forrest, "Japanese Aid and the Environment," p. 29.

22. JICA provides loans when projects do not qualify for OECF or EXIM Bank of Japan loans. For details, see JICA, *Support for Japanese Enterprises in Developing Countries: Long-Term, Low-Interest Financing System* (Tokyo: JICA, undated); and JICA, *Development Loan and Investment Program* (Tokyo: JICA, 1991).

23. Forrest, "Japanese Aid and the Environment," p. 27. For more detail, see Richard Forrest, *Japanese Economic Assistance and the Environment: The Need for Reform* (Washington, DC: National Wildlife Federation, 1989).

24. Orr and Koppel, "A Donor of Consequence," p. 3.

25. Forrest, "Japanese Aid and the Environment," pp. 29–30.

26. JICA technology transfers are often far too advanced. Two factors make this difficult to overcome: Japanese technicians are more comfortable with advanced equipment; and developing countries often *insist* on the most advanced equipment. Interview, Office of Overseas Environmental Cooperation, Environment Agency, Tokyo, 5 April 1994.

27. Orr and Koppel argue that "request-based" aid has "left Japanese firms open to charges of manipulating requests more conducive to corporate rather than recipient inter-

ests." Orr and Koppel, "A Donor of Consequence," p. 9. As well, it "falls prey to the desires of ruling elites in developing countries who request large-scale, ultramodern 'showcase' projects often irrelevant to the greatest needs of the people." Forrest and Harago, *Japan's Official Development Assistance*, p. 12.

28. See Forrest, "Japanese Aid and the Environment," pp. 26–27.

29. For a general critique of Japanese aid, see Mera Koichi, "Problems in the Aid Program," *Japan Echo* 16, no. 1 (1989), pp. 13–18, an abridged translation of "*ODA wa 'senshinkoku kurabu no sankahi' de wa nai,*" *Economic Today* (summer 1988), pp. 88–97.

30. Forrest and Harago, *Japan's Official Development Assistance*, p. 4.

31. Ibid.

32. Rix, *Japan's Foreign Aid Challenge*, p. 190 and p. 8. He examines these changes throughout his book.

33. Although funding for NGOs has increased slightly, compared to the overall aid budget, it is still "minuscule." David Potter, "Assessing Japan's Environmental Aid Policy," *Pacific Affairs* 67, no. 2 (summer 1994), p. 203.

34. Although officially much of Japanese aid has been untied, informal ties to business are still widespread, especially for yen loans. Orr and Koppel, "A Donor of Consequence," p. 10; and Koichi, "Problems in the Aid Program," p. 14.

35. Interview, senior JICA official, Tokyo, 12 April 1994.

36. Japanese Ministry of Foreign Affairs, *Japan's ODA 1993*, p. 175. Japan's environmental aid policy—based on declarations at the 1989 Paris summit and the 1991 London summit—is outlined in ibid., pp. 176–191.

37. Forrest and Harago, *Japan's Official Development Assistance*, p. 13.

38. Japanese Ministry of Foreign Affairs, *Japan's ODA 1993*, table II-22, p. 180.

39. Potter, "Assessing Japan's Environmental Aid Policy," p. 206.

40. Louise do Rosario, "Green at the Edges," *Far Eastern Economic Review* (hereafter *FEER*) (12 March 1992), p. 39.

41. Japanese Ministry of Foreign Affairs, *Japan's ODA 1993*, p. 178. Also see Japanese Ministry of Foreign Affairs, *Japan's ODA: Annual Report 1995*, p. 189. Considering the links between Southern debt and environmental problems, it is debatable whether any loan should be labeled "environmental aid."

42. "ODA Should Be Used to Guard the Environment, Panel Says," *Japan Times* (27 May 1992), p. 7.

43. OECF, *OECF Annual Report 1993*, p. 18.

44. Shigeaki Fujisaki, "Environmental Issues in Developing Countries and the Role of ODA," *Japan Review of International Affairs* 7, no. 1 (winter 1993), p. 75.

45. *Asahi Shimbun*, 17 January 1993, in Potter, "Assessing Japan's Environmental Aid Policy," p. 201.

46. Government of Japan, The Basic Environment Law law no. 91, 1993, effective 19 November 1993. For an overview of the new law, see Hidefumi Imura, "Japan's Environmental

Balancing Act: Accommodating Sustained Development," *Asian Survey* 34, no. 4 (April 1994), pp. 355–368.

47. Government of Japan, The Basic Environment Law.

48. Interview with one of the drafters of the 1993 Basic Environment Law, Environment Agency, Global Environment Department, Tokyo, 9 June 1994.

49. do Rosario, "Green at the Edges."

50. Interview, MITI official, Environmental Policy Division, Tokyo, 27 April 1994.

51. MITI, "The New Earth 21," internal document, supplied by a MITI official, April 1994.

52. *ICETT* (Yokkaichi, Japan: International Center For Environmental Technology Transfer, June 1993).

53. MITI, "Green Aid Plan," internal document, supplied by a MITI official, April 1994.

54. For background, see *RITE* (Tokyo: Research Institute of Innovative Technology for the Earth, March 1992).

55. MITI, and the Agency of Industrial Science and Technology, *New Sunshine Program* (Tokyo: New Sunshine Program Promotion Headquarters, 1993), p. 4.

56. These signs must be examined warily because, for favorable publicity, it is sometimes useful for the more powerful ministries to make it look like the environment agency is involved in decisions, perhaps even at the helm. Interview, Friends of the Earth, Tokyo, 25 May 1994.

57. Interview, Office of Overseas Environmental Cooperation, Environment Agency, Tokyo, 5 April 1994.

58. Tsuneyuki Morita, "Environmental and Natural Resource Accounting in Japan," CIDIE (Committee of International Development Institutions on the Environment) Workshop on Environmental and Natural Resource Accounting, UNEP (United Nations Environment Programme) Headquarters, Nairobi, 1992, p. 2. The Economic Planning Agency and the Ministry of Agriculture, Forestry, and Fisheries are also studying resource accounting. Ibid., p. 1.

59. Rix, *Japan's Foreign Aid Challenge*, p. 125.

60. Interview with one of the drafters of the Basic Environment Law, Environment Agency, Global Environment Department, Tokyo, 9 June 1994. Also see Kunitoshi Sakurai, "Japan's New Government and Official Development Assistance," *INTEP Newsletter*, no. 3 (October 1993), p. 1.

61. Based on several interviews, Global Environment Department, Environment Agency, Tokyo, 9 June 1994.

62. According to one source, it is a defensive, inflexible agency linked closely to sogo shosha. Interview, Friends of the Earth, Tokyo, 25 May 1994.

63. While these are all positive proposals (although plantations must be managed with great care), as we will see in later chapters, the forestry agency has not actively pursued these goals.

64. My summary is based on Forrest and Harago, *Japan's Official Development Assistance*, pp. 10–11.

65. Rix, *Japan's Foreign Aid Challenge*, p. 125.

66. Interview, OECF Environment and Social Development Division, Tokyo, 11 April 1994. Also see OECF, *OECF Environmental Guidelines* (Tokyo: OECF, 1989). For a review of OECF environmental projects, see OECF, *OECF and the Environment* (Tokyo: OECF, 1993).

67. Interview, OECF official, Tokyo, 11 April 1994. The OECF has suspended projects after severe criticism by environmentalists and NGOs, although these suspensions were not based on violations of OECF environmental guidelines. Examples include the Sardar Sardovar dam project in India (1990), the Mindanao geothermal power project in the Philippines (1991), and the U.S.$80 million loan for the Calaca II power plant in Luzon (1992). Potter, "Assessing Japan's Environmental Aid Policy," p. 202.

68. Forrest and Harago, *Japan's Official Development Assistance*, p. 8.

69. Rix, *Japan's Foreign Aid Challenge*, pp. 125–126. Rix's evaluation is based on *Operational Guidance on OECF Loans*, March 1991, Tokyo, p. 19.

70. Quoted in Rix, *Japan's Foreign Aid Challenge*, p. 126.

71. As of April 1994, no revisions had been published.

72. Interview, senior official, Environment Section, EXIM Bank of Japan, Tokyo, 11 April 1994. The Ministry of Finance has shown little interest in environmental issues. According to one source, officials are "arrogant and authoritarian" and unlike the other ministries, not even a superficial attempt is made to bother with public relations. Interview, Friends of the Earth, Tokyo, 25 May 1994.

73. Revealingly, I was unable to obtain statistics on the number of applications rejected at this stage. Although unverifiable, an EXIM Bank of Japan official claimed that loan applications are almost never turned down because, if bank officials consider the project environmentally unsound, the loan is quietly, informally rejected; the applicant then formally withdraws the request to save face.

74. Interview, senior official, Environment Section, EXIM Bank of Japan, Tokyo, 11 April 1994.

75. One indication is the rationale for reviewing the logging project in Sarawak. A central concern was the publicity and scrutiny given to logging in Sarawak, not specific problems with the loan proposal. Interview, senior official, Environment Section, EXIM Bank of Japan, Tokyo, 11 April 1994.

76. Interview, senior JICA official, Tokyo, 12 April 1994.

77. Hiroshi Enomoto, JICA, Division of the Environment, "Environmental Cooperation and the Japan International Cooperation Agency," *INTEP Newsletter*, no. 4 (February 1994), pp. 6–7.

78. A summary of Forrest and Harago, *Japan's Official Development Assistance*, pp. 6–7.

79. Potter, "Assessing Japan's Environmental Aid Policy," p. 208.

80. Kanda, "A Big Lie," p. 45.

81. Interviews, senior official, Forestry Cooperation Division, JICA, Tokyo, 12 April 1994; and senior official, International Forestry Cooperation Center, Forestry Agency, Ministry of Agriculture, Forestry, and Fisheries, Tokyo, 19 April 1994. Social forestry projects emphasize broad social aspects, whereas community forestry projects tend to be small, community-based projects.

82. These data were provided by an official at the Forestry Cooperation Division, JICA, Tokyo, 12 April 1994.

83. Interview, senior official, Forestry Cooperation Division, JICA, Tokyo, 12 April 1994.

84. Ibid.

85. Interviews, environmental consultants, Bogor Indonesia, 24 February 1994.

86. Forrest, "Japanese Aid and the Environment," pp. 31–32.

87. See Kanda, "A Big Lie," p. 44; and Forrest, "Japanese Aid and the Environment," p. 31.

88. "Japan Funds to Developing Nations Hit Record," *Jiji Press Newswire* (26 September 1995), Reuter Business Briefing. Even in 1987 Japanese private investment, commercial loans, and official aid amounted to U.S.$22.5 billion, a quarter of all Northern financing in the South. Forrest, "Japanese Aid and the Environment," p. 24.

89. This is a key theme of the articles in Koppel and Orr, eds., *Japan's Foreign Aid*.

90. Forrest, "Japanese Aid and the Environment," p. 26.

91. Wendy Dobson, *Japan in East Asia: Trading and Investment Strategies* (Singapore: Institute of Southeast Asian Studies, 1993), p. 67.

92. The Japan Foreign Trade Council lists sixteen sogo shosha. The media often refers to nine (the six largest, plus Itoman and Company Ltd., Kanematsu-Gosho Ltd., and Nichimen Corporation). The other seven are: Chori Company Ltd., Kawasho Corporation, Kinsho-Mataichi Corporation, Nozaki & Company Ltd., Okura & Company Ltd., Toshoku Ltd., and Toyo Menka Kaisha Ltd. Max Eli, translation by Michael Capone, Tristam Carrington-Windo, and Charles Foot, *Japan Inc.: Global Strategies of Japanese Trading Corporations* (London: McGraw-Hill, 1990), pp. 102–103. As well, there are a large number of specialized trading companies. For details on Itochu, see "Japan: Itochu Corporation," Hoover's Company Profile Database, The Reference Press, Inc., (3 August 1995), Reuter Business Briefing; and http://www.iijnet.or.jp/ITOCHU/.

93. Eli, *Japan Inc.*, p. 103.

94. Michael Y. Yoshino and Thomas B. Lifson, *The Invisible Link: Japan's* Sogo Shosha *and the Organization of Trade* (Cambridge, MA: MIT Press, 1986), p. 2. Also see Alexander K. Young, *The Sogo Shosha: Japan's Multinational Trading Companies* (Boulder, CO: Westview Press, 1979), chapter 1; and Kiyoshi Kojima and Terutomo Ozawa, *Japan's General Trading Companies* (Paris: OECD, 1984), chapter 2.

95. Mitsubishi is connected to the Mitsubishi Group; Mitsui to the Mitsui Group; Sumitomo to the Sumitomo Group; Itochu to the Dai-ichi Kangyo Bank Group; Marubeni to the Fuyo Group; and Nissho Iwai to the Sanwa Bank Group. Kojima and Ozawa, *Japan's General Trading Companies*, p. 21; and Eli, *Japan Inc.*, p. 9. As well, sogo shosha sometimes have links to companies outside their group. Hafiz Mirza, "The Past, Present and Future of the *Sogo Shosha*," in Howard Cox, Jeremy Clegg, and Grazia Ietto-Gillies, *The Growth of Global Business* (London and New York: Routledge, 1993), p. 67.

96. Yukio Ohnuma, "Sogo-Shosha and the Human Factor," *Japan Update* (November 1992), p. 18.

97. The largest sogo shosha have over 140 overseas offices, and trade between 20 thousand and 30 thousand different products. Yukio Ohnuma, "Trading Their Way to the Top," *Japan Update* (October 1992), p. 20.

98. Eli, *Japan Inc.*, pp. 107–113.

99. Yoshino and Lifson, *The Invisible Link*, p. 2. Although sogo shosha are still major traders, they are increasingly diversifying their activities. In Asia, they focus on small, risky investments and technology transfers. They now hold equity in numerous companies. For example, "Mitsui and Mitsubishi each have 180 ventures in Thailand; Itochu has 170 in China." Henny Sender, "The Sun Never Sets," *FEER* (1 February 1996), p. 47. They also facilitate and coordinate investment by Japanese and other Asian companies. For example, Itochu helped the Japanese firm Asahi invest in a beer brewery in China in late 1995, making Asahi the largest beer brewer in China. Using similar broker skills, Marubeni recently helped the Indonesian Salim Group establish a textile plant in China. (The Salim Group is controlled by Liem Sioe Liong, also known as Sudono Salim.) Ibid. Also see "Japan: Japan's Trading Companies—Sprightly Dinosaurs?" *Economist* (11 February 1995), Reuter Business Briefing.

For background on recent trends among sogo shosha, see Hideo Udagawa, "Dawning of a New Age for the Sogo Shosha Traders," *Tokyo Business Today* (January 1992), pp. 54–57; Alan T. Shao and Paul Herbig, "The Future of Sogo Shosha in a Global Economy," *International Marketing Review* 10, no. 5 (1993), pp. 37–55; Namiko Katsuki, "Putting Their Energy into Energy," *Tokyo Business Today* (February 1994), pp. 36–37; Sam Jameson, "Trading Companies Power Tokyo's Economic Expansion," *Daily Yomiuri* (Los Angeles Times World Report) (11 June 1994), p. 8A; Taketoshi Yamazaki, "*Sogo Shosha* Take Over as Top Venture Capitalists," *Tokyo Business Today* (February 1995), pp. 22–23; Ichiishi Iwao, "Sogo Shosha: Meeting New Challenges," *Journal of Japanese Trade and Industry* 14, no. 1 (1995), pp. 16–18; and Paul Herbig, *Marketing Japanese Style* (Westport, Connecticut: Quorum Books, 1995), pp. 219–240.

100. The quote is from "Japanese Trading Companies: The Web Rips," *Economist* (8 August 1992), p. 68. The import and export statistics are from Smith, "Japan: Does the World's Biggest Company Have a Future?"

101. "Japan: Japan's Trading Companies—Sprightly Dinosaurs?"

102. Jaakko Poyry Oy, World Bank commissioned study, *Tropical Deforestation in Asia and Market for Wood*. Annex V, Tropical Wood Markets in Japan. (Finland: Jaakko Poyry Oy, 1992), p. v/25; and Peter Dauvergne, *Major Asian Tropical Timber Traders and Overseas Corporate Investors: Current Trends* (Ottawa: Government of Canada, Department of Foreign Affairs and International Trade, November 1995), pp. 20–22.

103. Yoshino and Lifson, *The Invisible Link*, pp. 37, 50.

104. Yoshino and Lifson, *The Invisible Link*, p. 50.

105. Jaakko Poyry Oy, *Tropical Deforestation*, Annex V, p. v/29.

106. Nectoux and Kuroda, *Timber from the South Seas*, p. 64.

107. Lawrence B. Krause and Sueo Sekiguchi, "Japan in the World Economy," in Hugh Patrick and Henry Rosovsky, eds., *Asia's New Giant: How the Japanese Economy Works* (Washington, DC: Brookings Institution, 1976), quoted in Nectoux and Kuroda, *Timber from the South Seas*, p. 64.

108. Both quotes are from Jaakko Poyry Oy, *Tropical Deforestation*, Annex V, p. v/30. To some extent, sogo shosha's control over the log trade and plywood industry has started to erode as larger Japanese construction, furniture, and plywood companies no longer need, or can afford, their services. This trend will likely continue over the next decade as Japan's plywood industry fades. See Dauvergne, *Major Asian Tropical Timber Traders*, p. 22.

109. Sogo shosha profit margins have declined since the 1960s and 1970s, when profit margins were around 3 percent. For example, Mitsubishi's 1994 profit margin was a mere 0.12 percent. Smith, "Japan: Does the World's Biggest Company Have a Future?"

110. See Yoshino and Lifson, *The Invisible Link*.

111. According to Nectoux and Kuroda, "rather than concentrating on long-term—or even short-term—returns of high-value products, [trading companies] are often prepared to use the 'grab it and run' strategy." Nectoux and Kuroda, *Timber from the South Seas*, p. 64.

112. Hundreds of specialized Japanese trading companies are involved in log and lumber imports. But sogo shosha have accounted for the majority of tropical log imports. See Nectoux and Kuroda, *Timber from the South Seas*, pp. 62, 65; and Mariko Urano, "Commercial Exploitation of Indonesian Tropical Forests by Japan," in JANNI (Japan NGO Network on Indonesia), *Reshaping "Development": Indonesia-Japan Relation from Grassroots' Perspective* [sic]. Proceedings of the INGI Kanagawa Symposium (Tokyo: Japan NGO Network on Indonesia, 1993), p. 71. For example, in 1990, Mitsubishi, Nissho Iwai, Marubeni, Itochu, and Nichimen all imported over 1 million cubic meters of tropical timber. Mitsui imported over 700 thousand cubic meters and Sumitomo Corporation imported over 500,000 cubic meters. (These figures are in roundwood equivalent.) From JATAN, cited in K.S. Jomo, "Malaysian Forests, Japanese Wood: Japan's role in Malaysia's deforestation," in K.S. Jomo ed., *Japan and Malaysian Development: In the shadow of the rising sun* (London: Routledge, 1994), p. 190. Even these figures, however, likely underestimate the extent of sogo shosha log imports because they do not take into account the log imports of affiliated firms. In 1990, for example, Sumitomo Forestry imported over 1 million cubic meters of tropical timber (in roundwood equivalent). Ibid. (Since 1991, sogo shosha, the Japan Lumber Importers' Association, and the Japanese government no longer release import figures for specific corporations.)

113. For a succinct overview of the impact of sogo shosha on log production in Southeast Asia (including Papua New Guinea and the Solomon Islands), see Peter Dauvergne, "Japanese Trade and Deforestation in Southeast Asia," in Rodolphe De Koninck and Christine Veilleux, dirs. [eds.], *L'Asie du Sud-Est face à la mondialisation: les nouveaux champs d'analyse/ Southeast Asia and Globalization: New Domains of Analysis* (Québec: GÉRAC [Research and Study Group on Contemporary Southeast Asia], Université Laval, 1996).

114. Choucri, "Multinational Corporations and the Global Environment," p. 212.

115. Yoichi Nakamura, "The Ecobusiness Logic," *AMPO: Japan-Asia Quarterly Review* 23, no. 3 (1992), p. 56. Also see Tomoya Inyaku, "A Step Forward? Debt-for-Nature Swaps," *AMPO: Japan-Asia Quarterly Review* 23, no. 3 (1992), p. 48.

116. Keidanren, *Towards Preservation of the Global Environment*, tentative translation (Tokyo: Keidanren, 27 May 1992), p. 1. MITI has also encouraged businesses to "formulate voluntary plans on the environment." MITI, "Voluntary Plans for the Environment" (12 October 1992), internal document, supplied by a MITI official, April 1994, p. 2.

117. See Keidanren, *Keidanren Global Environment Charter* (Tokyo: Keidanren, April 1991).

118. Interview, Global Environment Department, Keidanren, Tokyo, 7 April 1994.

119. Keidanren, "Keidanren Policy and Activities for 1994," internal document. Tentative translation (Tokyo: Keidanren, 4 January 1994), p. 3.

120. Many Japanese academics, NGO representatives, and even government insiders are quite critical of the charter. Interviews, Tokyo, April to July 1994. Besides developing the charter in 1992, Keidanren also established the Nature Conservation Fund to finance nature conservation projects, particularly in tropical rain forests. Although commendable,

the amount distributed is still relatively small. In its first year, the fund supplied ¥100 million to projects in Palau, Sulawesi, Tanzania, Ecuador, and Vietnam. In FY1994, the fund provided ¥114.5 million to seventeen projects. See Keidanren, "Keidanren Nature Conservation Fund Makes First Pledge to Conservation Projects," internal document (Tokyo: Keidanren, undated, acquired by the author April 1994); and Asako Murakami, "Keidanren to Bolster Efforts of Environment NGOs," *Japan Times* (3 January 1995), p. 10.

121. Interview, Mitsubishi Corporation, Environmental Affairs Department, Tokyo, 5 April 1994. This department was created in 1990.

122. For example, see Marubeni, "Guidelines on Global Environmental Issues," internal document (Tokyo: Marubeni, 1991).

123. A spokesman was unable to provide a single example of a project rejected for environmental reasons. Interview, Department of Global Environment, Itochu Corporation, Tokyo, 12 April 1994. For details on Itochu's environmental guidelines and the environmental management and assessment system, see Itochu, "Global Environment Problem and Itochu Corporation," internal document (Tokyo: Department of Global Environment, 30 November 1993).

124. Marubeni, *Marubeni Corporation: Annual Report 1993* (Tokyo: Marubeni, 1993), p. 35.

125. This point was made most cogently by an official at Keidanren, Tokyo, 7 April 1994.

126. *New York Times* (10 May 1993).

127. Based on interviews at the Environment Departments of Mitsubishi, Marubeni, Nissho Iwai, and Itochu, Tokyo, April–June 1994. Also see Nissho-Iwai, "Environment 21: Nissho-Iwai Corp.," internal document (Tokyo: Environmental 21 Division, Nissho-Iwai, 12 February 1991).

128. There are government plans to increase assistance for large-scale reforestation in degraded areas. Government of Japan, *National Action Plan for Agenda 21*, internal document supplied by a MITI official (Tokyo: Government of Japan, January 1994), p. 62.

129. Corporate brochures now call for advice and equipment to improve the efficiency of Southern wood processors—a move that would presumably reduce wood waste and decrease some of the pressure on tropical forests. For example, see Marubeni, "Friendly to Forests and to Our Mother Planet," internal document (Tokyo: Marubeni, undated); Marubeni, *Earth Conscious* (Tokyo: Marubeni, March 1994); and Sumitomo Forestry, *Sumitomo Forestry: Annual Report 1993* (Tokyo: Sumitomo Forestry, 1993), p. 4.

130. Interviews, senior officials, RETROF, Tokyo, 27 April 1994.

131. RETROF, "Research Association For Reforestation of Tropical Forest," internal document (Tokyo: RETROF, October 1991).

132. Marubeni, *Earth Conscious*, p. 7. Also see Marubeni, "Friendly to Forests." At the same time as publicly declaring "new" purchasing practices, sogo shosha downplay their role, claiming that local slash-and-burn farmers are the key cause of deforestation while the timber trade has little global impact. Makoto Inoue, "Who's Killing the Rain Forests?" *Japan Views Quarterly* (autumn/winter 1992), p. 12. This view was confirmed during interviews at Keidanren, Mitsubishi, Itochu, Nissho Iwai, Sumitomo Forestry, and Marubeni, Tokyo, April–June 1994.

133. Japan Building Contractors' Society, "Methods to Reduce the Consumption of Plywood Forms Which Use Tropical Timber," internal document (Tokyo: Building Contractors' Society, Board of Directors, 19 February 1992). Kon-pane accounts for about 35 percent of total Japanese tropical wood consumption. Roger A. Sedjo, A. Clark Wiseman, David J.

Brooks, and Kenneth S. Lyon, *Changing Timber Supply and the Japanese Market*. Discussion paper 94–25. (Washington, DC: Resources for the Future, 1994), p. 17.

134. Government of Japan, "Japan's Paper for Proposed Progress Towards the Year 2000 Target," presented at the International Tropical Timber Council, November 1991, pp. 3–5. Also see "Lumber Importers Issue Rain Forest Guidelines," *Daily Yomiuri* (5 December 1991).

135. "Wholly or partly softwood plywood is 15% of total plywood production last year," *Japan Lumber Reports*. Published by *Japan Forest Products* journal, 198 (9 September 1994), p. 1; and Government of Japan, "Japan's Paper for Proposed Progress Towards the Year 2000 Target," p. 5. Japanese plywood makers claim that the move to softwood logs is motivated by environmental concerns. But it is far more likely an attempt to survive the onslaught of cheap Indonesian plywood and more expensive hardwood logs, and to prepare for the future collapse of tropical log stocks.

136. Interview, JATAN, Tokyo, 26 May 1994; and Jaakko Poyry Oy, *Tropical Deforestation*, Annex V, p. v/5.

137. Summarized in Yoichi Kuroda, "The Tropical Forest Crisis and the Future Course of Japanese Society," *Research on Environmental Disruption Toward Interdisciplinary Cooperation* (special edition, Global/International Environmental Problems 2, Iwanami Shoten, July 1991), p. 6.

138. Government of Japan, "Japan's Paper for Proposed Progress Towards the Year 2000 Target," p. 6. Not surprising, Japanese corporations hesitate to connect low prices with environmental concerns. Keidanren's environmental charter does not address incorporating environmental costs into price. Interview, Global Environment Department, Keidanren, Tokyo, 7 April 1994. In the case of Sumitomo Forestry, officials argued that tropical timber prices have actually been quite high—particularly in 1993—and there is no evidence of insufficient funds for reforestation or sustainable management. Interviews, Green Environmental Research R & D Division, Sumitomo Forestry, Tokyo, 20 April 1994.

139. Government of Japan, "Japan's Paper for Proposed Progress Towards the Year 2000 Target," pp. 5–6.

140. For example, the Tokyo metropolitan government announced in 1992 that it would reduce tropical kon-pane use by 50 percent by 1995 and 70 percent by 1997. It is, however, not mandatory and no implementing measures have been created. Interview, JATAN, Tokyo, 26 May 1994.

141. Government of Japan, *National Action Plan for Agenda 21*, p. 62.

142. Calculated from table 2.

143. The ITTO forecasted that Japanese plywood consumption would remain almost the same in 1995 (8.67 million cubic meters.) See table 4.

Chapter 2: A Model of Resource Management in Clientelist States

1. As noted in the introduction, although scholars have analyzed links between multilateral financial institutions and forestry mismanagement, little attention has been paid to the environmental impact of peaceful interaction between states.

2. Environmentalists sometimes point to political corruption as a key factor in resource mismanagement. But this has generally taken the form of accusations, without any refer-

ence to concrete political conditions or societal arrangements in these countries. Until recently, academic analysis has largely ignored the impact of politics on environmental change. This is discussed by Michael Redclift, *Sustainable Development: Exploring the Contradictions* (London: Methuen, 1987); and Adams, *Green Development*. One exception is Piers Blaikie, *The Political Economy of Soil Erosion in Developing Countries* (London: Longman, 1985).

3. "Clients are not . . . slaves, serfs or indentured labour. They too have valued assets—their support and their numbers—and patrons can take neither for granted." John Waterbury, "Clientelism Revisited," *Government and Opposition* 14, no. 2 (1979), p. 224.

4. Carl H. Landé, "The Dyadic Basis of Clientelism," in Steffen W. Schmidt, Laura Guasti, Carl H. Landé, and James C. Scott, eds., *Friends, Followers, and Factions: A Reader in Political Clientelism* (Berkeley: University of California Press, 1977), p. xiv.

5. See James C. Scott, "Patron-Client Politics and Political Change in Southeast Asia," *American Political Science Review* 66, no. 1 (March 1972), pp. 91–113; and Waterbury, "Clientelism Revisited," pp. 217–228.

6. For Sabah and Sarawak, see R. S. (Robert Stephen) Milne, "Patrons, Clients and Ethnicity: The Case of Sarawak and Sabah in Malaysia," *Asian Survey* 13, no. 10 (October 1973), pp. 891–907. For Japan, see Peter Cheng, "Political Clientelism in Japan: The Case of 'S,'" *Asian Survey* 28, no. 4 (April 1988), pp. 471–483. Cheng argues that the Japanese bureaucracy contains significant patron-client relations despite the security and prosperity of Japanese bureaucrats.

7. Jean C. Oi, "Communism and Clientelism: Rural Politics in China," *World Politics* 37, no. 2 (January 1985), p. 263.

8. Landé, "The Dyadic Basis of Clientelism," p. xv.

9. Scott, "Patron-Client Politics," pp. 96–97.

10. See Robert Kaufman, "The Patron-Client Concept and Macro-Politics: Prospects and Problems," *Comparative Studies in Society and History* 16, no. 1 (June 1974), pp. 284–308.

11. Shmuel N. Eisenstadt and Luis Roniger, "The Study of Patron-Client Relations and Recent Developments in Sociological Theory," in Shmuel N. Eisenstadt and René Lemarchand, eds., *Political Clientelism, Patronage and Development* (London: Sage, 1981), p. 276. Also see Shmuel Eisenstadt and René Lemarchand, "Introduction," in ibid., p. 2.

12. For a discussion of the trend toward, and merits of, middle-range theory, see Howard J. Wiarda, "Toward the Future: Old and New Directions in Comparative Politics," in Howard J. Wiarda, ed., *New Directions in Comparative Politics*, revised ed., (Boulder, CO: Westview Press, 1991), pp. 221–250.

13. Christopher Clapham, "Clientelism and the State," in Christopher Clapham, ed., *Private Patronage and Public Power: Political Clientelism in the Modern State* (London: Frances Pinter, 1982), p. 30.

14. Landé, "The Dyadic Basis of Clientelism," p. xix.

15. Scott, "Patron-Client Politics," p. 92.

16. Structural-functionalism is especially prone to this problem.

17. Scott, "Patron-Client Politics," p. 92.

18. Kaufman, "The Patron-Client Concept," p. 301.

19. René Lemarchand, "Political Clientelism and Ethnicity in Tropical Africa: Competing Solidarities in Nation Building," *American Political Science Review* 66, no. 1 (March 1972), p. 68.

20. Anthony Hall, "Patron-Client Relations: Concepts and Terms," in Schmidt, Guasti, Landé, and Scott, eds., *Friends, Followers, and Factions*, p. 512.

21. Lemarchand rightly stresses this point. Lemarchand, "Political Clientelism and Ethnicity in Tropical Africa," pp. 68–90.

22. Kaufman, "The Patron-Client Concept," p. 286.

23. Jean-François Medard, "The Underdeveloped State in Tropical Africa: Political Clientelism or Neo-Patrimonialism?" in Clapham, ed., *Private Patronage*, p. 168.

24. A few recent studies are available. For example, see Jonathan Fox, "The Difficult Transition from Clientelism to Citizenship: Lessons from Mexico," *World Politics* 46, no. 2 (January 1994), pp. 151–184; the collection of articles in Luis Roniger and Ayse Gunes-Ayata, eds., *Democracy, Clientelism and Civil Society* (Boulder, CO: Lynne Rienner, 1994), pp. 1–18; Carlene J. Edie, *Democracy by Default: Dependency and Clientelism in Jamaica* (London: Lynne Rienner, 1991); Robert Gay, "Community Organization and Clientelist Politics in Contemporary Brazil: A Case Study from Suburban Rio de Janeiro," *International Journal of Urban and Regional Research* 14 (December 1990), pp. 648–666; Eliphas Mukonoweshuro, "Ethnicity, Class and Clientelism in Sierra Leone Politics: A Methodological Critique," *Plural Societies* 20 (September 1990), pp. 65–91; and Cheng, "Political Clientelism in Japan," pp. 471–483.

25. Luis Roniger, *Hierarchy and Trust in Modern Mexico and Brazil* (New York: Praeger, 1990), p. xiii.

26. Rush, *The Last Tree*, pp. 30–32.

27. Paul D. Hutchcroft, "Oligarchs and Cronies in the Philippine State: The Politics of Patrimonial Plunder," *World Politics* 42, no. 3 (April 1991), p. 423.

28. Gordon P. Means, *Malaysian Politics: The Second Generation* (Singapore: Oxford University Press, 1991), pp. 298–299. In the context of Malaysia, Means claims that "By the time of Dr. Mahathir, the patronage system had not only grown enormously, but it included many intermediate layers of middlemen in a more extensive and institutional system of rewarding loyalty and political support." Ibid., p. 305.

29. Foreign corporations often supply a key ingredient for modern patron-client ties—money—but foreign business executives, including the Japanese, are generally not directly involved in patron-client exchange relations.

30. Scott, "Patron-Client Politics," p. 105. At the same time, however, "in the midst of this change, old-style patrons thrive." Ibid.

31. Ibid., p. 107.

32. Means, *Malaysian Politics*, p. 317. The inherent instability of modern ties makes it virtually impossible to categorize and specify the membership of different patron-client networks—a monumental task even in ideal circumstances—because these continually dissolve and realign as patrons die or lose control of key resources.

33. This is a broad generalization. A more-detailed description of modern patron-client relations in Indonesia, Malaysia, and the Philippines is provided in chapters 3–5. For background on traditional patron-client relations in Southeast Asia, see Shmuel N. Eisenstadt

and Luis Roniger, *Patrons, Clients, and Friends: Interpersonal Relations and the Structure of Trust in Society* (Cambridge: Cambridge University Press, 1984), Indonesia, pp. 122–127, and the Philippines, pp. 127–130.

34. Max Weber, *Economy and Society*, eds., Guenther Roth and Claus Wittich (New York: Bedminster Press, 1968), vol. 3, p. 1041, quoted in Hutchcroft, "Oligarchs and Cronies," p. 415.

35. Medard, "The Underdeveloped State in Tropical Africa," p. 170.

36. See Harold Crouch, "Patrimonialism and Military Rule in Indonesia," *World Politics* 31, no. 4 (July 1979), pp. 571–587. Neopatrimonialism is similar to the model of a bureaucratic polity. For example, see Fred W. Riggs, *Thailand: The Modernization of a Bureaucratic Polity* (Honolulu: East-West Center Press, 1966); and John L. S. Girling, *The Bureaucratic Polity in Modernizing Societies*, Occasional Paper No. 64 (Singapore: Institute of Southeast Asian Studies, 1981).

37. See Hutchcroft, "Oligarchs and Cronies," pp. 414–450.

38. Bruce Gale, *Politics and Public Enterprise in Malaysia* (Singapore: Eastern Universities Press, 1981), pp. 4–10.

39. Neopatrimonial studies have accurately pointed to pervasive links between political and military patrons and business clients as a key feature of Southeast Asian politics and an important means for societal groups to share in the spoils of office. But no major neopatrimonial studies have examined how these links shape state capacity to enforce rules and laws.

40. Michael Dove persuasively argues that elites must be held responsible for the destruction of tropical rain forests, even if many actors are involved in the actual process. Michael R. Dove, "Marketing the Rainforest: 'Green' Panacea or Red Herring?" *Asia-Pacific Issues: Analysis from the East-West Center*, no. 13 (Honolulu: East-West Center, 1994), pp. 1–8.

41. To help dodge this problem, Hutchcroft uses the term "patrimonial features." See Hutchcroft, "Oligarchs and Cronies," pp. 414–417.

42. It is commonly accepted in the literature on state-society relations in Southeast Asia that state patrons channel extensive patronage to individuals and groups in society. This is seen as the main route for societal input into otherwise strong states. See Dwight Y. King, "Indonesia's New Order as a Bureaucratic Polity, a Neopatrimonial Regime or a Bureaucratic-Authoritarian Regime: What Difference Does It Make?" in Benedict Anderson and Audrey Kahin, eds., *Interpreting Indonesian Politics: Thirteen Contributions to the Debate*. Interim Reports Series, publication no. 62 (Ithaca, NY: Cornell University, 1982), p. 113; and Andrew MacIntyre, *Business and Politics in Indonesia* (Sydney: Allen and Unwin, 1990), p. 8. What is not commonly recognized is that these pervasive patron-client ties between the state and society have profound implications for the capacity of the state to enforce laws.

43. The following summary is based on Joel S. Migdal, *Strong Societies and Weak States: State-Society Relations and State Capabilities in the Third World* (Princeton: Princeton University Press, 1988). Also see Joel S. Migdal, "A Model of State-Society Relations," in Wiarda, ed., *New Directions*, pp. 45–58.

44. Migdal, *Strong Societies and Weak States*, see prologue, footnote 2, and pp. 19–20.

45. The distinction between state and nonstate organizations is an analytical device; in reality, the difference is often blurred.

46. Migdal, *Strong Societies and Weak States*, prologue, p. xvii.

47. Ibid., p. 4, prologue, xiii.

48. Ibid., p. 173.

49. Migdal, "A Model of State-Society Relations," p. 56. Also see Migdal, *Strong Societies and Weak States*, p. 40.

50. Migdal, *Strong Societies and Weak States*, pp. 30, 27–28, 33, 31.

51. Ibid., pp. 135, 28.

52. Ibid., pp. 37, 138, 265.

53. Ibid., p. 182.

54. Some interpretation and latitude are necessary when using Migdal's ideas, definitions, and concepts because I am studying Southern resource management whereas he focuses on social policy. I try to maintain the spirit of his work, even though my emphasis is somewhat different.

55. In my view, this is a congruous addition to Migdal's work. He argues that states can be both strong and weak, depending on the activity—what he calls the "duality of states." Migdal, *Strong Societies and Weak States*, p. 9.

56. Many political analysts of Southeast Asia emphasize the critical impact of extensive patron-client relations. For example, see David Wurfel, *Filipino Politics: Development and Decay* (Quezon City: Ateneo de Manila University Press, [also published by Cornell University Press], 1988); Crouch, "Patrimonialism and Military Rule in Indonesia," pp. 571–587; Scott, "Patron-Client Politics," pp. 91–113; Riggs, *Thailand*; and Gale, *Politics and Public Enterprise in Malaysia*. As Gale notes, "the Southeast Asian region provides many examples of regimes in which weak political institutions exist together with pervasive patrimonial or patron-client structures. Thailand, Indonesia, and the Philippines are perhaps the best examples." Gale, *Politics and Public Enterprise in Malaysia*, p. 11. Sabah and Sarawak can be added to this list of best examples.

57. For example, see John Duncan Powell, "Peasant Society and Clientelist Politics," *American Political Science Review* 64 (June 1970), pp. 411–426. Some authors have also called this a clientele system.

58. Given that state capacity and the impact of patron-client networks changes across different policies, for this work the term "clientelist state" refers only to the management of natural resources. For other policies, clientelist forces may be less significant in shaping state capacity.

59. Since the New Order was established by General Suharto in the mid-1960s, the state has become increasingly centralized and now dominates policy *formation*. For this reason, most academic studies portray the Indonesian state as dominating society. For a summary, see MacIntyre, *Business and Politics*, pp. 6–21. Specific examples include Benedict Anderson, "Old State, New Society: Indonesia's New Order in Comparative Historical Perspective," *Journal of Asian Studies* 42, no. 3 (May 1983), pp. 477–496; Donald K. Emmerson, "Understanding the New Order: Bureaucratic Pluralism in Indonesia," *Asian Survey* 23, no. 11 (November 1983), pp. 1220–1241; the bureaucratic-authoritarian model by King, "Indonesia's New Order," pp. 104–117; and Karl D. Jackson, "Bureaucratic Polity: A Theoretical Framework for the Analysis of Power and Communications in Indonesia," in Karl Jackson and Lucien Pye, eds., *Political Power and Communications in Indonesia* (Berkeley: University of California Press, 1978). This conventional view has been challenged some-

what by Andrew MacIntyre's 1990 study that shows that, since the mid-1980s, business has gained limited input into developing legislation, regulations, and specific policy measures; see MacIntyre, *Business and Politics*. He does not, however, look closely at enforcement. As we will see in the next chapter, state domination of the process of forming resource policy does not translate into effective implementation.

60. Theoretical models that concentrate on the process of policy development and decision making—such as corporatism or bureaucratic authoritarianism—tend to portray a strong state. For overviews, see Douglas A. Chalmers, "Corporatism and Comparative Politics," in Wiarda, ed., *New Directions*, pp. 59–81; and John D. Martz, "Bureaucratic-Authoritarianism, Transitions to Democracy, and the Political-Culture Dimension," in Wiarda, ed., *New Directions*, pp. 199–220. In my view, these studies overestimate the ability of Southern states to control the distribution and management of natural resources.

61. For a discussion of how comparative politics theories could strengthen comparative studies of environmental policymaking, see Sheldon Kamieniecki and Eliz Sanasarian, "Conducting Comparative Research on Environmental Policy," *Natural Resources Journal* 30 (spring 1990), pp. 321–339.

62. Migdal, "A Model of State-Society Relations," pp. 54–55. Also see Migdal, *Strong Societies and Weak States*, p. 31.

63. Migdal, *Strong Societies and Weak States*, p. 138.

64. According to one critic of the Philippine state, an example is General Orlando Soriano. Marites Dañguilan Vitug, *Power from the Forest: The Politics of Logging* (Manila: Philippine Center for Investigative Journalism, 1993), pp. 108–110.

65. A second characteristic of the "politics of survival" is "dirty tricks" such as torture or "illegal" imprisonment. See Migdal, *Strong Societies and Weak States*, pp. 223–226.

66. Ibid., p. 240.

67. Ibid., p. 227.

68. Ibid., pp. 238, 241.

69. Migdal calls this the "Triangle of Accommodation." Ibid., p. 249.

70. For a more general discussion, see ibid., pp. 141, 245.

71. Ibid., p. 256. Of course, for Migdal, all nonstate organizations have the potential to capture a section of the state.

72. This argument is the same as Migdal's, although he is referring generally to social fragmentation rather than to patron-client relations. See ibid.

Chapter 3: Japan, Patron-Client Politics, and Timber Mismanagement in the Outer Islands of Indonesia

1. Adam Schwarz, "Banking on Diversity," *FEER* (28 October 1993), p. 58.

2. Commercial trees in the Philippines, Sabah, Sarawak, and Indonesia are mostly from the family Dipterocarpaceae. In Indonesia, the common commercial name for this timber is meranti, and in the Philippines, lauan.

3. Gareth Porter writes: "While Indonesian forestry officials claim that commercial logging accounts for only 10 percent of annual deforestation, the actual figure may be at least twice that. . . . Moreover, if the estimated 70 thousand to 100 thousand hectares of forest lost in forest fires is also attributable to destructive logging, logging could account directly for more than 25 percent of Indonesia's annual deforestation. Combined with its indirect impact on forests, commercial logging may account for as much as 75 percent of Indonesia's forest loss." Gareth Porter, "The Environmental Hazards of Asia Pacific Development: The Southeast Asian Rainforests," *Current History* 93, no. 587 (December 1994), p. 431.

4. The World Bank estimates that annual deforestation is 1.1 million hectares. World Bank, *Indonesia: Sustainable Development* (Washington, DC: World Bank 1993), p. 7, cited in Colin MacAndrews, "Politics of the Environment in Indonesia," *Asian Survey* 34, no. 4 (April 1994), p. 374.

5. For a more general analysis of the impact of Indonesian political forces on deforestation, see Dauvergne, "The Politics of Deforestation in Indonesia," pp. 497–518.

6. Karl D. Jackson, "Urbanization and the Rise of Patron-Client Relations: The Changing Quality of Interpersonal Communications in the Neighbourhoods of Bandung and the Villages of West Java," in Jackson and Pye, eds., *Political Power and Communications*, p. 346. The Javanese dominate state positions in Indonesia. It is therefore logical to focus on how patron-client ties evolved on Java even though most commercial timber is on the outer islands. For a detailed study of the evolution of traditional patron-client relations in South Sulawesi, see Heddy Shri Ahimsa Putra, "The Politics of Agrarian Change and Clientelism in Indonesia: Bantaeng, South Sulawesi, 1883 to 1990." Doctoral dissertation (New York: Columbia University, 1993).

7. Karl D. Jackson, "The Political Implications of Structure and Culture in Indonesia," in Jackson and Pye, eds., *Political Power and Communications*, p. 34.

8. Jackson, "Urbanization," p. 349.

9. Ibid., p. 344. My terminology differs slightly from Jackson's. He calls traditional patron-client relations "traditional authority relations" and modern patron-client relations either "patronage" or simply "patron-client relations." Our meanings, however, are essentially identical.

10. Ibid., pp. 349, 350.

11. Jackson, "Urbanization," passim, although see in particular, p. 390.

12. Jackson, "Bureaucratic Polity," p. 3.

13. Ibid., p. 14. For extensive details on traditional and modern patron-client relations in Indonesia, see Karl D. Jackson, *Traditional Authority, Islam, and Rebellion: A Study of Indonesian Political Behavior* (Berkeley: University of California Press, 1980), especially chapter 8.

14. I assume that the values and customs of precolonial Indonesia have important implications for current practices. For a supporting view, see Harry J. Benda, "Democracy in Indonesia," in Anderson and Kahin, eds., *Interpreting Indonesian Politics*, pp. 13–21.

15. G. McGuire and Bob Hering, "The Indonesian Army: Harbingers of Progress or Reactionary Predators?" in Christine Doran, ed., *Indonesian Politics: A Reader* (North Queensland: James Cook University, 1987), p. 211.

16. Theodore M. Smith, "Corruption, Tradition, and Change," *Indonesia* 11 (April 1971), pp. 25–26.

17. This helps explain why anticorruption campaigns generally fail. Of course, as one would expect in any diverse society, some Indonesians—especially university students—are quite critical of rampant legal violations.

18. For a discussion of the impact of cultural cleavages on Indonesian politics, see Donald K. Emmerson, *Indonesia's Elite: Political Culture and Cultural Politics* (Ithaca, NY: Cornell University Press, 1976).

19. For example, around 75 percent of key positions in the military are held by Javanese. Leo Suryadinata, *Military Ascendancy and Political Culture: A Study of Indonesia's Golkar* (Athens, OH: Ohio University Center for International Studies, 1989), p. 1.

20. A 1989 survey showed that 163 of the top 200 Indonesian firms are controlled by ethnic Chinese. MacIntyre, *Business and Politics*, p. 263, footnote 19.

21. For more detail on the impact of attitudes on Indonesian forestry management, see Dauvergne, "The Politics of Deforestation in Indonesia," pp. 506–507.

22. Jackson, "Bureaucratic Polity," p. 14.

23. For overviews of the New Order period, see Michael R. J. Vatikiotis, *Indonesian Politics Under Suharto: Order, Development and Pressure for Change* (London: Routledge, 1993); Hal Hill, ed., *Indonesia's New Order: The Dynamics of Socio-economic Transformation* (St Leonards, Australia: Allen and Unwin, 1994); and R. William Liddle, *Leadership and Culture in Indonesian Politics* (Sydney: Asian Studies Association of Australia in association with Allen and Unwin, 1996).

24. See David McKendrick, "Indonesia in 1991, Growth, Privilege and Rules," *Asian Survey* 32, no. 2 (February 1992), p. 108. According to MacIntyre, DPR committees have some influence. MacIntyre, *Business and Politics*, pp. 31–35. Some signs suggest that the DPR is becoming more important. See John McBeth, "Loyal House: But Parliament Is Becoming More Animated," *FEER* (8 September 1994), pp. 32–34.

25. For a study of Golkar, see David Reeve, *Golkar of Indonesia: An Alternative to the Party System* (Singapore: Oxford University Press, 1985).

26. Army personnel have not been placed at the village level. But local officials sometimes receive military training, and their loyalty is monitored. Donald K. Emmerson, "The Bureaucracy in Political Context: Weakness in Strength," in Pye and Jackson, eds., *Political Power and Communications*, pp. 103–104.

27. Measures have been taken to control the political influence of these groups. University student organizations were banned in the late 1970s. The 1985 Law on Social Organizations (Ormas) severely restricts the activities of NGOs. The media is regularly censored and many newspapers and magazines have been closed for being too critical of the government.

28. For details, see Henny Sender, "New Boys' Challenge," *FEER* (1 April 1993), pp. 72–75.

29. King, "Indonesia's New Order," p. 108.

30. See "In Suharto's Shadow," *Economist* (9 May 1992), pp. 33–34; Adam Schwarz, "All Is Relative," *FEER* (30 April 1992), pp. 54–58; Adam Schwarz, *A Nation in Waiting: Indonesia in the 1990s* (St Leonards, NSW, Australia: Allen and Unwin, 1994), pp. 133–161; Henny Sender, "Bambang's Challenge," *FEER* (5 September 1996), pp. 56–58; and Geoff Hiscock, "Wealth sprouts on Suharto family tree," *Australian* (10 October 1996), pp. 25, 29.

31. Interview, environmental consultant, Bogor Indonesia, 24 February 1994. Richard Robison notes that key Suharto supporters, including Liem Sioe Liong, Bob Hasan, and

Prajogo Pangestu, continue to receive "state bank credit on quite a massive scale given the credit squeeze which should have choked this source." Richard Robison, "The middle class and the bourgeoisie in Indonesia," in Richard Robison and David S.G. Goodman, eds., *The New Rich in Asia: Mobile phones, McDonald's and middle-class revolution* (Routledge: London and New York, 1996), p. 92.

32. Schwarz, "All Is Relative," p. 54.

33. Quoted in Steven Erlanger, "For Suharto, His Heirs Are Key to Life After '93," *New York Times International* (11 November 1990), p. Y11.

34. Crouch, "Patrimonialism and Military Rule in Indonesia," p. 578. Also see Herbert Feith, "Political Control, Class Formation and Legitimacy in Suharto's Indonesia," in Doran, ed., *Indonesian Politics*, pp. 221–234.

35. Rapid economic growth and oil exports have been vital for the stability of the New Order. Crouch argues that with "huge sums available for patronage distribution, the regime was in a position to reward its supporters royally; at the same time it could make dissidence very costly for its critics." Harold Crouch, *The Army and Politics in Indonesia*, revised ed. (Ithaca: Cornell University Press, 1988), p. 355. Writing in the early 1970s, Willem F. Wertheim argued that under Suharto, patron-client relations were eroding, especially at the lower levels of society. He predicted that insurgency and revolution similar to China's would occur unless the government implemented radical land reform. In my view, part of the reason for his inaccurate forecast is that patron-client links that cut across and weaken class ties have not diminished but have flourished. For a discussion of Wertheim's work, see Feith, "Political Control," pp. 229–231.

36. Jackson, "The Political Implications," p. 36.

37. Privately, some officials do criticize the extensive business links to Suharto's children. Donald K. Emmerson, "Indonesia in 1990: A Foreshadow Play," *Asian Survey* 31, no. 2 (February 1991), p. 185. As well, orthodox Muslims have been critical of his close ties to Chinese corporations.

38. Erlanger, "For Suharto, His Heirs Are Key to Life After '93."

39. Richard Robison, "Toward a Class Analysis of the Indonesian Military Bureaucratic State," *Indonesia*, no. 25 (April 1978), pp. 17–39; Richard Robison, *Indonesia: The Rise of Capital* (Sydney and London: Allen and Unwin, 1986); and Schwarz, *A Nation in Waiting*.

40. As attitudes change, and business is no longer perceived as a lower-class activity, "a number of fairly large *pribumi* [indigenous or non-Chinese] Indonesian businesses have developed, particularly those with connections to the presidential family." MacAndrews, "Politics of the Environment," p. 372.

41. Ernst Utrecht, "Indonesia's Foreign Private Corporate System, Past and Present," in Doran, ed., *Indonesian Politics*, p. 184.

42. Two examples are: the anti-Chinese focus of the 1974 riots following Japanese Prime Minister Tanaka's visit to Jakarta and the Chinese pogroms in Central Java in 1980. Since the late 1980s, the Islamic revivalist movement has rekindled anti-Chinese feelings. John McBeth, "Challenges of Progress," *FEER* (28 April 1994), p. 46. Apparently, a "prominent target" during the riots in Jakarta in July 1996 "were Chinese-owned car dealerships and banks." Vedi R. Hadiz, "Riots underline woes of the elites," *Australian* (16 August 1996), p. 37.

43. Go Gien Tjwan, "The Chinese in Indonesia, Past and Present," in Doran, ed., *Indonesian Politics*, p. 93.

44. Schwarz, *A Nation in Waiting*, p. 282. Also see Harold Crouch, "Generals and Business in Indonesia," *Pacific Affairs* 48, no. 4 (winter 1975–76), pp. 519–540.

45. Emmerson, "The Bureaucracy in Political Context," p. 104.

46. Crouch, *The Army and Politics*, p. 357.

47. Jackson, "Bureaucratic Polity," p. 13. Also see Ulf Sundhaussen, "The Military: Structure, Procedures, and Effects on Indonesian Society," in Jackson and Pye, eds., *Political Power and Communications*, pp. 45–81. In recent years, the number of cabinet members with military background has declined, and now almost half of the twenty-seven provincial governors are civilians. One study showed that "from a peak of 25,000 in 1967, officers seconded to *dwi-fungsi* [dual function] positions had dropped to 13,000 in 1986 and to about 9,500 by 1992." McBeth, "Challenges of Progress."

48. Ruth T. McVey, "The Post-Revolutionary Transformation of the Indonesian Army Part I," *Indonesia*, no. 11 (April 1971), pp. 152–153, quoted in McGuire and Hering, "The Indonesian Army," p. 209.

49. Crouch, "Generals and Business in Indonesia," p. 523.

50. Ibid., pp. 523–524. As a result of this strategy, officers have prospered in the New Order far more than the lower ranks. Ernst Utrecht, *The Indonesian Army: A Socio-Political Study of an Armed, Privileged Group in the Developing Countries* (Townsville: James Cook University, 1980), pp. 100–101. For details on the military's involvement in business, see Robison, *Indonesia: The Rise of Capital*, chapter 8.

51. Utrecht, *The Indonesian Army*, p. 103.

52. Emmerson, "The Bureaucracy in Political Context," pp. 82–83, 90–91, 100.

53. Colin MacAndrews, "The Structure of Government in Indonesia," in Colin MacAndrews, ed., *Central Government and Local Development in Indonesia* (Singapore: Oxford University Press, 1986), p. 33.

54. Jackson, "Bureaucratic Polity," p. 13.

55. See Loekman Soetrisno, "Patron-Client Relationships," *Economic and Business Review Indonesia*, no. 98 (26 February 1994), p. 18.

56. Ruth T. McVey, "The Beamtenstaat in Indonesia," in Anderson and Kahin, eds., *Interpreting Indonesian Politics*, p. 88.

57. Jackson, "Bureaucratic Polity," p. 15. For details on Pertamina, see Sundhaussen, "The Military," pp. 53–54; and Emmerson, "The Bureaucracy in Political Context," pp. 112–116. For details on Bulog's management of rice in the 1970s, see Bruce Glassburner, "Indonesia's New Economic Policy and Its Sociopolitical Implications," in Jackson and Pye, eds., *Political Power and Communications*, pp. 147–149.

58. Jackson, "Bureaucratic Polity," p. 15.

59. Ibid., p. 16. Crouch argues that foreign aid and investment and rising oil prices have provided critical funding for massive state patronage and regime stability. Crouch, "Patrimonialism and Military Rule in Indonesia," pp. 178–179.

60. For a discussion of Japanese corruption in Indonesia, see Yoko Kitazawa, "Japan-Indonesia Corruption," *AMPO: Japan-Asia Quarterly Review* 8, no. 1 (1976), parts I and II.

61. Utrecht, "Indonesia's Foreign Private Corporate System," p. 184.

62. *AMPO: Japan-Asia Quarterly Review,* Special Issue on "Japanese Transnational Enterprises in Indonesia" 12, no. 4 (1980), p. 49.

63. Rush, *The Last Tree,* p. 35.

64. Jackson, "The Political Implications," p. 35.

65. Poor policy implementation is reinforced by a cultural suspicion of action. Jackson argues that "as designing plans is relatively passive while implementation requires action, attention and high status go with the former rather than the latter. Progress in bureaucracies is often impressive until the moment when implementation is required." Ibid., p. 39. An example is the 1982 Environmental Management Act which contains an impressive set of principles. There are, however, still no implementing regulations. According to MacAndrews, "Without these regulations, cases taken to court under this Act have often been dismissed for lack of an adequate legal basis." MacAndrews, "Politics of the Environment," p. 379, footnote 16.

66. See MacIntyre, *Business and Politics,* p. 3. He argues that business leaders have had greater leverage over policy formulation since the mid-1980s, partially because of more *pribumi* Indonesian businesses. MacIntyre focuses on legislation—on the content of policy. He examines how business groups have fought to overturn regulations (e.g., spinning industry), have resisted the introduction of specific measures (e.g., pharmaceutical industry), and have attempted to convince the state to introduce legislation (e.g., insurance industry). He does not, however, look closely at problems with enforcement, where businesses simply ignore or skirt regulations and laws.

67. Around 82 million hectares are rain forests.

68. These figures were supplied by a professor at Bogor Agricultural University, Faculty of Forestry, Bogor Indonesia, 25 February 1994. These figures are essentially the same as those used by the Ministry of Forestry. For government forestry data, see Indonesian Ministry of Forestry, *Indonesia and the Management of Its Forests* (Jakarta: Republic of Indonesia, 1992); Indonesian Ministry of Forestry, *The Timber Industry in Indonesia* (Jakarta: Republic of Indonesia, 1992); Indonesian Ministry of Forestry, *The Indonesian Tropical Rain Forest Conservation Areas* (Jakarta: Republic of Indonesia, 1990).

69. Both of these estimates are outlined in WALHI (Indonesian Forum for the Environment) and YLBHI (Indonesian Legal Aid Foundation), *Mistaking Plantations for the Indonesia's Tropical Forest* [sic] (Jakarta: Wahana Lingkungan Hidup Indonesia [WALHI], 1992), p. 11. Also see Sandra Moniaga, "Status of Forest Resources in Indonesia," in JANNI, *Reshaping "Development,"* pp. 39–42. For a range of estimates, see Jill M. Blockhus, Mark R. Dillenbeck, Jeffrey A. Sayer, and Per Wegge, eds., "Conserving Biological Diversity in Managed Tropical Forests," proceedings of a workshop held at the IUCN General Assembly Perth, Australia, 1990. (Gland, Switzerland: World Conservation Union (IUCN)/ITTO, 1992), pp. 45–46.

70. SKEPHI, *Forest Management Is Inefficient,* position paper for Austrian Parliament (Jakarta: SKEPHI, 1993), p. 2.

71. Summarized in Rush, *The Last Tree,* p. 36.

72. In 1983, the directorate-general of Forestry of the Ministry of Agriculture became a ministry and was named the Ministry of Forestry.

73. See Malcolm Gillis, "Indonesia: Public Policies, Resource Management, and the Tropical Forest," in Gillis and Repetto, eds., *Public Policies,* pp. 50–51; and Malcolm Gillis, "Mul-

tinational Enterprises and Environmental and Resource Management Issues in the Indonesian Tropical Forest Sector," in Pearson, ed., *Multinational Corporations, Environment, and the Third World*, pp. 76–78.

74. Raphael Pura, "Rapid Loss of Forest Worries Indonesia," *Asian Wall Street Journal* (hereafter *AWSJ*) (3 February 1990), p. 10.

75. WALHI and YLBHI, *Mistaking Plantations for the Indonesia's Tropical Forest*, p. 12.

76. For an interview with Hasan, see John Vidal, "High Stakes in the Rainforest," *Guardian* (19 October 1990).

77. Adam Schwarz, "Timber Troubles," *FEER* (6 April 1989), p. 86. For background on Apkindo, see "Indonesia: Plywood Exports Tumble Due To Declining Prices," *Jukarta Post* (12 August 1995), Reuter Business Briefing; "Indonesia: Apkindo to Help Government in Marketing," *Jakarta Post* (3 July 1995), Reuter Business Briefing; and "No Plywood Boycott Claims Bob Hasan," *Economic and Business Review Indonesia*, 24 (27 August 1994), pp. 40–41.

78. Interview, senior official, Bappenas (Badan Perencanaan Pembangunan Nasional), Indonesian National Development Planning Agency, Jakarta, 4 March 1994. Hasan also has close ties to Suharto's children. He is in business with Suharto's sons, Hutomo Mandala Putra (known as Tommy), Sigit Harjojudanto, and Bambang Trihatmodjo. For details, see Hiscock, "Wealth sprouts on Suharto family tree."

79. This official claimed that Hasan is motivated primarily by a desire to build his "empire," and although he sometimes sounds "green," he has little concern for environmental issues. Confidential interview, senior Indonesian official, Jakarta, 3 March 1994

80. For a critical account of Barito Pacific Timber, see SKEPHI, *Setiakawan: A Call for International Solidarity on Indonesian Tropical Forest Issues*, no. 10 (January–June 1993), pp. 53–55.

81. A leaked 1991 memo from Prajogo to Suharto illustrates their close relationship. In this memo, Prajogo asked Suharto to encourage the forestry minister, Hasjrul Harahap, to "facilitate the paperwork and financing for an industrial-tree plantation in South Sumatra." According to *FEER*, Suharto responded by jotting a note to Hasjrul on the memo that "he should fulfil all of Prajogo's requests." Jonathan Friedland and Adam Schwarz, "Risks on Paper," *FEER* (12 March 1992), p. 44.

82. Raphael Pura, "Timber Tycoon Confronts His Critics," *AWSJ* (27 August 1993), p. 8.

83. Prajogo's timber holdings are discussed in ibid., pp. 1, 8; Raphael Pura, Stephen Duthi, and Richard Borsuk, "Plywood Tycoon May Purchase Malaysian Firm," *AWSJ* (3 February 1994), pp. 1, 4; and Adam Schwarz, "Forest Framework," *FEER* (12 March 1992), p. 44.

84. Pura, "Timber Tycoon Confronts His Critics."

85. Robison, "Toward a Class Analysis," p. 28. These companies were backed by Chinese and foreign funds.

86. In the early 1970s, ITCI's major shareholders included the most powerful generals of the New Order. According to Hurst, ITCI's concession was in effect a "pay-off from Suharto for the loyalty of Indonesia's military elite." Hurst, *Rainforest Politics*, p. 34.

87. Based on ITCI (International Timber Corporation Indonesia), *PT. International Timber Corporation Indonesia* (Jakarta: ITCI, 1992); Rush, *The Last Tree*, pp. 36–37; Pura, "Rapid Loss of Forest Worries Indonesia"; and Erlanger, "For Suharto, His Heirs Are Key to Life After '93."

88. Confidential interview, senior Indonesian official, Jakarta, 3 March 1994.

89. According to the *Jakarta Post*, "in recent years, the ministry [of forestry] has tightened supervision to prevent illegal logging, and over-logging by concessionaires, but the move has so far resulted mostly in distorted log markets." "Importing Logs," *Jakarta Post* (17 January 1996), Reuter News Briefing.

90. For details on TPI, see Hurst, *Rainforest Politics*, pp. 16–17. For a critique of Indonesian selective logging rules, see Gillis, "Indonesia: Public Policies," pp. 63–65.

91. "Importing Logs," *Jakarta Post* (17 January 1996), Reuter News Briefing.

92. WALHI and YLBHI, *Mistaking Plantations for the Indonesia's Tropical Forest*, pp. 59–60.

93. See Barbier, Burgess, and Markandya, "The Economics of Tropical Deforestation," p. 57.

94. Despite needing subcontractors, concessions were still excellent "presents" because profits were huge and fast. Interview, Bogor Agricultural University, Faculty of Forestry, Bogor Indonesia, 28 February 1994.

95. Urano, "Commercial Exploitation," p. 50.

96. "Indonesia to Reduce Tree Cutting to Help Preserve Rainforests," *Japan Times* (27 July 1994), p. 18.

97. Charles Zerner, *Legal Options for the Indonesian Forestry Sector* (Jakarta: Ministry of Forestry, Government of Indonesia, and FAO, Indonesia UTF/INS/065/INS, Forestry Field Studies Field Document, no. VI-4, 1990), p. 10.

98. Adam Schwarz, "Emerald Forest," *FEER* (7 February 1991), p. 51; and interview, senior Indonesian official, Jakarta, 3 March 1994. There is also a shortage of staff. An International Institute for Environment and Development (IIED) study claimed that the Forestry Ministry would need ten times more field staff to monitor logging concessions adequately. Summarized by Mark Poffenberger, "Facilitating Change in Forest Bureaucracies," in Poffenberger, ed., *Keepers of the Forest*, p. 101.

99. Edith Terry, "Indonesia's Disappearing Jungle," *Globe and Mail* (14 October 1989), p. A2.

100. According to James Rush, "timber harvesting goes on largely unchecked by either self-imposed conservation measures or by state vigilance." Rush, *The Last Tree*, p. 36.

101. Summarized in WALHI and YLBHI, *Mistaking Plantations for the Indonesia's Tropical Forest*, p. 59.

102. Quoted in Schwarz, "Forest Framework," p. 45. SKEPHI is strongly critical of forestry management in Indonesia. See SKEPHI, *Selling Our Common Heritage: Commercialization of Indonesian Forest* (Jakarta: SKEPHI, 1990); SKEPHI, *Forest Problem in Indonesia Issues & Solution* (Jakarta: SKEPHI, 1989). SKEPHI also publishes a journal that focuses on Indonesian forestry mismanagement. For example, SKEPHI, *Setiakawan: A Call for International Solidarity on Indonesian Tropical Forest Issues*, no. 4–5 (January–June 1990), provides a detailed account of the impact of development in Irian Jaya.

103. Quoted in Pura, "Rapid Loss of Forest Worries Indonesia."

104. For a list of these studies, see Potter, "Environmental and Social Aspects of Timber Exploitation," pp. 182–183. For general background on deforestation and timber extraction on the island of Borneo, see Harold Brookfield and Yvonne Byron, "Deforestation and Tim-

ber Extraction in Borneo and Malay Peninsula," *Global Environmental Change* 1, no. 1 (December 1990), pp. 42–56.

105. Summarized in Hurst, *Rainforest Politics*, p. 17.

106. Summarized in Schwarz, "Emerald Forest"; and Schwarz, "Forest Framework."

107. Peyton Johnson, "Fire in the Mother Lung," *CERES FAO* 24, no. 3 (May–June 1992), p. 34; and SKEPHI, *Forest Fire Profile in Indonesia* (Jakarta: SKEPHI, 1992). SKEPHI is critical of the lack of Northern assistance in combating these fires. SKEPHI, *Setiakawan: A Call for International Solidarity on Indonesian Tropical Forest Issues*, no. 7 (January–June 1992), pp. 44–46.

108. See "Burning Rainforest Spreads Pall Over Southeast Asia," *Vancouver Sun* (18 October 1994), p. A17; and S. Jayasankaran and John McBeth, "Hazy Days," *FEER* (20 October 1994), pp. 66–67.

109. Even the *Jakarta Post* recently declared that "illegal logging, with the support of local security officials, is rampant in several areas." "Importing Logs," *Jakarta Post* (17 January 1996), Reuter News Briefing.

110. According to a WALHI representative, many senior Indonesian forestry academics are funded by timber money and therefore are unwilling to document extensive illegal logging. Interview, WALHI, Jakarta, 3 March 1994.

111. Calculated from table 10.

112. A forestry academic claimed that NGO estimates of illegal logging were "plausible." Interview, Bogor Agricultural University, Faculty of Forestry, Bogor Indonesia, 28 February 1994.

113. According to local forestry service data, loggers smuggle between 50 thousand to 100 thousand cubic meters of illegal timber every year from West Kalimantan to East Malaysia. SKEPHI, *Setiakawan: A Call for International Solidarity on Indonesian Tropical Forest Issues*, no. 11 (July–September 1993), pp. 31–33.

114. Interview, environmental consultant, Bogor Indonesia, 24 February 1994; and Nectoux and Kuroda, *Timber from the South Seas*, p. 73.

115. *Asian Timber* (January 1993), p. 9.

116. Debra J. Callister, *Illegal Tropical Timber Trade: Asia Pacific* (Cambridge: Traffic International, 1992), p. 30.

117. This incongruity is partially a result of poor coordination between the Ministry of Forestry and the Ministry of Industry. The Ministry of Industry sets the capacity of plywood mills, stressing intense production to maintain rapid economic growth. Interview, Bogor Agricultural University, Faculty of Forestry, Bogor Indonesia, 28 February 1994.

118. "Production of Plywood Not to Rise—Djamaludin," *Jakarta Post* (29 December 1995), Reuter Business Briefing. Forestry Minister Djamaludin speculated in January 1996 that the government may import logs—perhaps from Burma, Vietnam, or the Solomon Islands—to supply Indonesian plywood processors. "RI Considers Possibility of Importing Logs," *Jakarta Post* (13 January 1996), Reuter Business Briefing.

119. Interview, Indonesian concessionaire, Jakarta, 3 March 1994.

120. "Indonesia: Apkindo Defends Good Prospects of Plywood Trade," *Jakarta Post* (11 January 1995), Reuter Business Briefing; and ITTO, *Annual Review 1993–1994*, p. 6. Over this period the government also predicts that loggers will extract 3.7 million cubic meters from natural conversion forest, 2.7 million cubic meters from timber estates, and 8.7 million cubic meters from private land. "Timber: An Economic Dilemma," *Economic and Business Review Indonesia* 98 (26 February 1994), p. 8.

121. Barbier, Burgess, Bishop, and Aylard, *The Economics of the Tropical Timber Trade*, p. 83; and Elvin T. Choong, Rubini Atmawidjaja, and Suminar S. Achmadi, "The Forest Products Industry in Southeast Asia: An Emphasis on Indonesia," *Forest Products Journal* 43, no. 5 (May 1993), p. 46.

122. Gillis, "Indonesia: Public Policies," pp. 59–60; and Barbier, Burgess, and Markandya, "The Economics of Tropical Deforestation," pp. 56–57.

123. Repetto, *The Forest for the Trees?*, p. 43. For more details, see Gillis, "Indonesia: Public Policies," pp. 85–98. "Rent, by definition, is a value in excess of the total costs of bringing trees to market as logs or wood products, including the cost of attracting necessary investment. That cost may include a risk premium that reflects uncertainties about future market and political conditions, so there are inevitably doubts about the exact magnitude of available rents." Robert Repetto, "Overview," in Gillis and Repetto, eds., *Public Policies*, p. 18.

124. Summarized in Adam Schwarz, "Timber Is the Test," *FEER* (23 July 1992), p. 36.

125. WALHI and YLBHI, *Mistaking Plantations for the Indonesia's Tropical Forest*, pp. 20–21; and interview, WALHI, Jakarta, 3 March 1994. Estimates of timber rent captured by the government range from a low of 8–15 percent by WALHI to a high of 83 percent by a government consultant. Most studies fall in a range between 20–30 percent. For a list of studies, see Dudung Darusman, "The Economic Rent of Tropical Forest Utilization in Indonesia," a paper presented at the National Seminar on the Economic Aspect of the Forestry Business in Indonesia, the Association of Forest Concessionaires and the Ministry of Forestry, Jakarta, 6–7 October 1992, p. 17. In 1994, the Indonesian government increased the reforestation fee from U.S.$10 to U.S.$22. In theory, this should increase the amount of timber rent the government captures.

126. Indonesian Ministry of Forestry and FAO, *Indonesian Tropical Forestry Action Programme: Executive Summary* (Jakarta: Government of Indonesia and the United Nations, 1991), p. 44.

127. Robison, "Toward a Class Analysis," p. 33.

128. Summarized in SKEPHI, *Setiakawan: A Call for International Solidarity on Indonesian Tropical Forest Issues*, no. 11 (July–September 1993), p. 31.

129. SKEPHI, *Setiakawan: A Call for International Solidarity on Indonesian Tropical Forest Issues*, no. 8 (July–September 1992), p. 3.

130. The significant impact of Southern investment—and increasingly trade—on Indonesian timber management suggests an important area for future research: contrasting the impact of Southern and Northern MNCs on resource management. For a preliminary comparison of the environmental impact of Northern and Southern MNCs on Indonesian timber management, see Gillis, "Multinational Enterprises," pp. 84–86.

131. Ibid., p. 73.

132. See Economic and Social Commission for Asia and the Pacific, *Transnational Corporations and the Tropical Hardwood Industry of Indonesia*, United Nations, Joint CTC/ESCAP Unit on Transnational Corporations, Working Paper No. 16, Bangkok, 1981, pp. 1–2.

133. Calculated from table 8.

134. A. J. Leslie, The Government-TNC Relationship in Tropical Timber Concession Contracts, unpublished paper (1980), summarized in Economic and Social Commission for Asia and the Pacific, *Transnational Corporations*, p. 5.

135. Hurst, *Rainforest Politics*, pp. 2, 10.

136. This greatly reduced Indonesian state timber revenues. Gillis, "Indonesia: Public Policies," pp. 67–69.

137. Gillis, "Multinational Enterprises," p. 68.

138. Ibid., pp. 74–76.

139. Gillis, "Indonesia: Public Policies," p. 69. To evade export and income taxes both national and foreign firms were involved in undervaluing timber exports, including those to Japan. Gillis, "Multinational Enterprises," p. 68.

140. See table 8.

141. In 1992, the "ban" on log exports was lifted and replaced by astronomical taxes on log exports. This in effect maintains the ban.

142. Interview, senior official, Bappenas, Jakarta, 4 March 1994. According to this government spokesman, more companies now replant to ensure future supplies for their mills.

143. Brookfield, Potter, and Byron, *In Place of the Forest*, p. 103.

144. William B. Wood, "Tropical Deforestation: Balancing Regional Development Demands and Global Environmental Concerns," *Global Environmental Change* 1, no. 1 (December 1990), p. 34. Also see table 9.

145. Calculated from ITTO, *Annual Review 1995*, p. 57.

146. Calculated from ibid., p. 51.

147. Around 2.5 million people work directly in the timber industry and 1.2 million work in related industries such as glue manufacturing. In 1990, plywood exports accounted for 14 percent of total foreign exchange earnings. M. Bob Hasan, keynote address, "Prospects for Plywood into the 21st Century," *Proceedings of the World Conference on Tropical Plywood* (Jakarta: ITTO, December 1991), p. 24. It is important to note, however, that government and corporate statistics exaggerate the economic benefits of timber processing given that "primary forest assets are established without cost. Harvesting depreciates what is a valuable stock but the economic accounting of timber operations does not include this depreciation as a cost." Zerner, *Legal Options*, p. 5.

148. Interview, senior official, Bappenas, Jakarta, 4 March 1994.

149. In Japan, processing efficiency is between 55 and 70 percent; in Indonesia it is between 40 and 50 percent. In fairness to Indonesian processors, although this discrepancy is partly a result of better Japanese technology, expertise, and policies, it is also partly a result of differences in the quality of logs. Japanese processors import high-quality logs, whereas local Indonesian mills often use logs from the surrounding area, naturally decreasing efficiency. Interview, Japan Plywood Inspection Corporation, Tokyo, 8 April 1994.

150. Carlos Alberto Primo Braga, "Tropical Forests and Trade Policy: The Cases of Indonesia and Brazil," in Low, ed., *International Trade*, p. 190. Although I have no substantive evidence, a government spokesman claims that many processing mills have become more efficient since the mid-1980s. Interview, senior official, Bappenas, Jakarta, 4 March 1994.

151. Barber, Johnson, and Hafild, *Breaking the Logjam*, p. 44.

152. Holly Lindsay, "The Indonesian Export Ban: An Estimation of Foregone Export Earnings," *Bulletin of Indonesian Economic Studies* 25, no. 2 (August 1989), pp. 111–123.

153. Quoted in Schwarz, "Timber Is the Test."

154. Calculated from table 8.

155. See tables 8 and 10.

156. Calculated from table 10.

157. Joseph Viandrito, "Bob Hasan Speaks Up," *Indonesia Business Weekly* 3, no. 16 (3 April 1995), p. 31.

158. Jim Della-Giacoma, "Indonesia Says Improving Logging Practices," Reuter News Service, Reuter Business Briefing.

159. Ibid.

160. Porter, "The Environmental Hazards of Asia Pacific Development," p. 431.

161. The FAO figure is summarized in Schwarz, "Timber Is the Test." The World Bank study is summarized in Barber, Johnson, and Hafild, *Breaking the Logjam*, p. 43. The Indonesian Ministry of Forestry estimates that annual sustainable yield for Indonesia's 64 million hectares of production forest is around 30 million cubic meters. Interview, Bogor Agricultural University, Faculty of Forestry, Bogor Indonesia, 28 February 1994; and ITTO, *Annual Review 1993–1994*, p. 6.

162. "Timber: An Economic Dilemma," *Economic and Business Review Indonesia*, p. 9.

163. Quoted in "Shades of Green," *Economist* (18 April 1992), p. 38.

164. Interview, Bogor Agricultural University, Faculty of Forestry, Bogor Indonesia, 28 February 1994. Also see WALHI and YLBHI, *Mistaking Plantations for the Indonesia's Tropical Forest*, pp. 18–19.

165. Indonesian Department of Information, *Indonesia 1990: An Official Handbook* (Jakarta: Department of Information, Republic of Indonesia, 1990), p. 229. WALHI and YLBHI estimate that by 1990, 1.2 million hectares—or 4 percent of logged areas—had been replanted. WALHI and YLBHI, *Mistaking Plantations for the Indonesia's Tropical Forest*, p. 13.

166. Indonesia, Ministry of Forestry, "Resource Rent and Implications for Sustainable Forest Management," Sector Study Working Paper No. 3, ADB Project Preparation Technical Assistance No. 1781-INO (Jakarta: Ministry of Forestry, 1994), summarized in Sizer and Rice, *Backs to the Wall in Suriname*, p. 12. In the 1980s, this was U.S.$4 and later U.S.$7 per cubic meter of timber extracted, refundable after reforestation. In the early 1990s, the reforestation fee was U.S.$10 per cubic meter.

167. "Timber: An Economic Dilemma," *Economic and Business Review Indonesia*, p. 6.

168. WALHI and YLBHI, *Mistaking Plantations for the Indonesia's Tropical Forest*, p. 30.

169. Summarized in Rush, *The Last Tree*, p. 38.

170. See Indonesian Ministry of Forestry, directorate-general of Reforestation and Land Rehabilitation, *The Development of Industrial Forest Plantation (HTI)* (Jakarta: Republic of Indonesia, 1993), p. 4.

171. WALHI and YLBHI, *Mistaking Plantations for the Indonesia's Tropical Forest*, p. 23.

172. Down to Earth, *Pulping the Rainforest: The Rise of Indonesia's Paper and Pulp Industry*, Down to Earth, the International Campaign for Ecological Justice in Indonesia, Special Report No. 1, July 1991, p. 6.

173. Interview, Indonesian concessionaire, Jakarta, 3 March 1994.

174. Jonathan Friedland, "Aiming for a Market," *FEER* (18 April 1991), p. 50.

175. Down to Earth, *Pulping the Rainforest*, p. 2; and WALHI and YLBHI, *Mistaking Plantations for the Indonesia's Tropical Forest*, pp. 3, 24.

176. In 1990 the forestry minister announced: "We're opening our country. If you want to invest in these man-made forests, you are welcome." Quoted in Raphael Pura, "Indonesia Sees Tree Estates as a Cure-All," *AWSJ* (6 February 1990), p. 8.

177. Interview, Bogor Agricultural University, Faculty of Forestry, Bogor Indonesia, 25 February 1994; and Down to Earth, *Pulping the Rainforest*, p. 9. The low rate of private investment in plantations is aggravated by a legitimate fear that a sudden political change could nullify state licenses.

178. Friedland, "Aiming for a Market."

179. See Down to Earth, *Pulping the Rainforest*, pp. 22–25, 29–32.

180. Based on numerous interviews: Environmental Research Center, Bogor Agricultural University, Bogor Indonesia, 25 February 1994; environmental consultant, Bogor Indonesia, 24 February 1994; Sumitomo Forestry Company, Ltd., Tokyo, 20 April 1994. According to one optimistic source, he is open-minded, clean, powerful, an effective manager, and knowledgeable about forestry issues. Interview, Bogor Agricultural University, Faculty of Forestry, Bogor Indonesia, 28 February 1994. Another source claimed that he is honest and independent, and unlike almost everyone else, he has not been "bought" by Hasan. Interview, senior official, Bappenas, Jakarta, 4 March 1994. He also appears more willing to work with NGOs. Interview, WALHI, Jakarta, 3 March 1994.

181. Her Suharyanto, "HPH [Concession] Holders Take Money and Run," *Indonesian Business Weekly* 1, no. 51 (3 December 1993), p. 16.

182. "The Price of Non-Compliance," *Economic and Business Review Indonesia* 98 (26 February 1994), p. 8.

183. "State Firms Urged to Manage 50 Percent of RI Forests," *Jakarta Post* (5 February 1996), Reuter Business Briefing.

184. "Indonesia Will Send Spies to Hunt Down Illegal Loggers," *Japan Times* (18 November 1992), p. 21.

185. Schwarz, "Forest Framework," p. 45.

186. Interview, environmental consultant, Bogor, Indonesia, 24 February 1994.

187. This promise was made by Forestry Minister Djamaludin. "Indonesia to Reduce Tree Cutting to Help Preserve Rainforests," *Japan Times*, 27 July 1994, p. 18.

188. Interview, WALHI, Jakarta, 3 March 1994. For a critique of ecolabeling, see SKEPHI, *Setiakawan: A Call for International Solidarity on Indonesian Tropical Forest Issues*, no. 11 (July–September), 1993, pp. 44–46.

189. Interview, WALHI, Jakarta, 3 March 1994; and interview, ecolabeling program, Jakarta, 4 March 1994.

190. Ibid.

191. Urano, "Commercial Exploitation," pp. 67–69.

192. For general background on Japanese economic links with Indonesia in the 1970s, see Yoshi Tsurumi, "Japanese Investments in Indonesia: Ownership, Technology Transfer, and Political Conflict," in Gustav F. Papanek, *The Indonesian Economy* (New York: Praeger Publishers, 1980), pp. 295–323; and J. Panglaykim, *Indonesia's Economic and Business Relations with ASEAN and Japan* (Jakarta: Center for Strategic and International Studies, 1977). For a study of Japanese MNCs in Indonesia during this period, see *AMPO: Japan-Asia Quarterly Review,* Special Issue on "Japanese Transnational Enterprises in Indonesia," pp. 3–54.

193. Hiroyoshi Kano, "The Structure of Japan-Indonesia Relations and the Relations of NGOs of Both Countries," in *Reshaping "Development,"* p. 13.

194. Directorat Jenderal Kehutanan, *Kehutanan Indonesia 1978* (Bogor: October 1979), cited in Gillis, "Multinational Enterprises," p. 73.

195. Interview, senior professor, University of the Philippines at Los Banos, 1 February 1994.

196. Yoshi Tsurumi, *A Report Submitted to the Harvard Advisory Group* (Jakarta: Bappenas, October 1973), pp. 13–14, in Robison, "Toward a Class Analysis," p. 29. For a list of Japanese investments in Indonesia prior to the log export ban, see Urano, "Commercial Exploitation," table 5, pp. 72–73. The following are a few examples of large Japanese timber investments: until 1986, Mitsubishi controlled 80 percent of P. T. Balikpapan Forest Industries Ltd.; until 1978, Tomen owned 49 percent of P. T. East Kalimantan Timber Industries; until its license was canceled in 1978, Mitsui held 45.5 percent of P. T. Kalimantan Forest and controlled P. T. Palembang Timber Development Company Ltd. until 1985.

197. Malcolm Gillis, "The Logging Industry in Tropical Asia," in Julie Sloan Denslow and Christine Padoch, eds., *People of the Tropical Rain Forest* (Berkeley: University of California Press, 1988), p. 179.

198. Potter, "Environmental and Social Aspects of Timber Exploitation," p. 182. For background on the early years of the timber boom in East Kalimantan, see Chris Manning, "The Timber Boom with Special Reference to East Kalimantan," *Bulletin of Indonesian Economic Studies* 7, no. 3 (November 1971), pp. 30–60.

199. Urano, "Commercial Exploitation," table 5, pp. 72–73.

200. Miguel D. Fortes, "Mangroves and Seagrass Beds in East Asia: Habitats Under Stress," *Ambio* 17, no. 3 (1988), pp. 207–213, summarized in Nectoux and Kuroda, *Timber from the South Seas,* p. 81.

201. In 1990 Forestry Minister Hasjrul Harahap announced that without strong conservation measures, of the remaining 4.3 million hectares of Indonesian mangrove forests, 1 million hectares would soon disappear. "One million ha of RI's mangrove forests threatened with extinction," *Jakarta Post* (8 October 1990). As with all Ministry of Forestry statistics, environmentalists consider the estimate of 4.3 million hectares of mangrove forests highly exaggerated. Hurst claims that only 1 million hectares of mangrove forests remain. Hurst, *Rainforest Politics,* p. 3.

202. Urano, "Commercial Exploitation," footnote 30, p. 74.

203. Nectoux and Kuroda, *Timber from the South Seas*, p. 79. Of course, other MNCs also accelerated logging in East Kalimantan. For a general discussion of the role of multinational corporations in East Kalimantan's timber industry, see William B. Wood, "Two Boom Cities in the Resource Frontier: An Indonesian Case Study," *Asian Geographer* 5, no. 1 (1986), pp. 25–41.

204. Urano, "Commercial Exploitation," pp. 82–83.

205. Ibid., p. 83.

206. OECF, "Report of the Indonesian Project Mission of 1970," quoted in ibid., p. 83.

207. For a list of MITI projects, see ibid., table 6, p. 76.

208. Ibid., p. 75.

209. JICA, *JICA Annual Report*, 1976, quoted in ibid.

210. Ibid., pp. 75–78.

211. Yoichi Kuroda, "Commercial Exploitation of Indonesian Tropical Forests by Japan," in JANNI, *Reshaping "Development,"* p. 44; and Urano, "Commercial Exploitation," p. 85.

212. Sumitomo Forestry was one of the few Japanese companies to remain in Indonesia after the log export ban, although on a much smaller scale than in the 1970s when it had interests in over twenty firms connected to the timber industry. Nectoux and Kuroda, *Timber from the South Seas*, p. 79. For a list of Japanese timber investments in the 1980s, see ibid., appendix C, pp. 120–121.

213. Summarized in SKEPHI, *Setiakawan: A Call For International Solidarity on Indonesian Tropical Forest Issues*. A Special Edition on Japan's Role in the Timber Industry, no. 3 (November–December 1989), p. 18.

214. Pura, "Timber Tycoon Confronts His Critics."

215. "Suharto and the Reins of Power," *Economist* (17 November 1990), p. 38. In June 1994, the government lifted even more restrictions.

216. Interview, Asosiasi Panel Kayu Indonesia (Apkindo), Jakarta, 1 March 1994.

217. WALHI and YLBHI, *Mistaking Plantations for the Indonesia's Tropical Forest*, pp. 27, 6.

218. Down to Earth, *Pulping the Rainforest*, p. 35; and MacKerron, *Business in the Rain Forests*. Five Japanese companies have also invested in Chipdeco, a mangrove chipping plant in East Kalimantan.

219. Keidanren, "Keidanren Nature Conservation Fund Makes First Pledge to Conservation Projects."

220. Interviews, senior officials, Sumitomo Forestry Company Ltd., Tokyo, 20 April 1994; Sumitomo Forestry, Ministry of Forestry (Republic of Indonesia), P. T. Kutai Timber Indonesia, and the University of Tokyo, *Research Report on the Sebulu Experimental Forest: 1992*, July 1993; and Sumitomo Forestry, "Tropical Rain Forest Regeneration Project Gets Under Way in Indonesia," *Greengraph: Sumitomo Forestry Newsletter* 1 (March 1992), pp. 1–2.

221. Japanese corporations have provided no assistance for large-scale programs for the Ministry for the Environment. Interview, State Ministry for the Environment, Jakarta, 3 March 1994.

222. Japanese Ministry of Foreign Affairs, *Japan's ODA: Annual Report 1995*, pp. 6, 102. For a study of Japanese ODA in Indonesia, see Hadi Soesastro, *Japan's ODA and Indonesia: Resource Security Aid?* (Jakarta: Center for Strategic and International Studies, 1991).

223. Arief Budiman, "Human Rights, Foreign Aid and People to People Cooperation," in JANNI, *Reshaping "Development,"* p. 28.

224. Seven were grants for a total of approximately U.S.$15 million. Two were loans for a total of about U.S.$22 million. For a list, see Indonesian Ministry of Forestry, "Daftar Proyek Bantuan Luar Negeri (On-going Projects), Departemen Kehutanan (Tahun Anggaran 1993/1994), and the Evaluation of CGIF Questionnaire Proyek of On-Going Forestry Foreign Cooperation Project as of October 1993," supplied by an official at the Indonesian Ministry of Forestry, Jakarta, 1 March 1994. For more details on JICA forestry projects in Indonesia, see JICA, *Environment* (Jakarta: Indonesia Office, 1993), pp. 12–19.

225. Of course, Japanese aid has had some positive implications—for example, a 1991 OECF loan to upgrade eighteen environmental research facilities. The money was used to improve facilities, buy books and equipment, and educate staff. Interview, Environmental Research Center, Bogor Agricultural University, Bogor Indonesia, 25 February 1994.

226. Interview, Center for International Forestry Research (CIFOR), Bogor Indonesia, 2 March 1994.

227. Interviews, environmental consultants, Bogor Indonesia, 24 February 1994.

228. Interview, Indonesian Ministry of Forestry, Bureau of International Cooperation and Investment, Jakarta, 1 March 1994. In contrast, a Japanese official claimed that JICA has difficulty convincing senior Indonesians to study in the field. Interview, coordinator of JICA Indonesia, Jakarta, 1 March 1994.

229. Forrest, "Japanese Aid and the Environment," p. 29.

230. Interviews, environmental consultants, Bogor Indonesia, 24 February 1994.

231. Interview, Asian Wetlands Bureau, Bogor Indonesia, 2 March 1994.

232. Interview, State Ministry for the Environment, Jakarta, 3 March 1994.

233. Calculated from tables 7 and 8.

234. Urano, "Commercial Exploitation," table 4, (based on data from the JLIA), p. 71.

235. Calculated from tables 7 and 8.

236. Urano, "Commercial Exploitation," table 4, (based on data from the JLIA), p. 71.

237. Calculated from table 7.

238. Over these eleven years, total Indonesian log production was 230.91 million cubic meters. Calculated from tables 7 and 8.

239. These data were supplied by an official at Apkindo, Jakarta, 1 March 1994.

240. Calculated from table 1.

241. Sarawak Campaign Committee, "Japan's Tropical Timber Imports in 1994 and 1995," *Mori no Koe*, no. 8, sent by Glen Barry at Ecological Enterprises.

242. Calculated from table 11.

243. For a succinct overview of the environmental and economic impact of the Japan-Indonesia trade in tropical plywood, see Dauvergne, "Japanese Trade and Deforestation in Southeast Asia."

244. Quoted in Urano, "Commercial Exploitation," p. 92.

245. Interview, senior official, JPMA, Tokyo, 8 April 1994.

246. "The Plywood Paradox: What Has Gone Wrong?" *Economic and Business Review Indonesia,* no. 149 (18 February 1995), p. 9.

247. "Apkindo's All-Encompassing Role," *Indonesia Business Weekly* 3, no. 12 (6 March 1995), p. 8.

248. Vincent Lingga, "Indonesia: Apkindo's Export Monopoly Is Outdated," *Jakarta Post* (27 October 1994), Reuter Business Briefing.

249. Quoted in Raphael Pura, "Indonesian Plywood Cartel Under-Fire as Sales Shrink," *AWSJ* (23 January 1995).

250. In 1988 Japanese companies accounted for almost 96 percent of total Indonesian plywood imports to Japan. By 1990 Japanese companies only accounted for about 53 percent. Calculated from table 10, in Urano, "Commercial Exploitation," based on data from the JLIA.

251. In the early 1990s, Apkindo established other marketing arms similar to Nippindo, including: Celandine Company Ltd. in Hong Kong to channel exports to China and Taiwan; Fendi Wood in Singapore to handle Singapore and Europe; and Indo Kor Panels Ltd. in Hong Kong to funnel exports to South Korea. According to Indonesian plywood company executives, these marketing wings generally charge exporters U.S.$5 to U.S.$6 per cubic meter of plywood. Lingga, "Indonesia: Apkindo's Export Monopoly Is Outdated."

252. In most cases, Apkindo forbids direct contact between importers and Indonesian plywood processors. Instead, buyers must contact Apkindo's marketing wings. Vincent Lingga, "Indonesia: Plywood Exports Fall in Wake of Apkindo Tug of War with Korea," *Jakarta Post* (27 October 1994), Reuter Business Briefing; and Lingga, "Indonesia: Apkindo's Export Monopoly Is Outdated."

253. Numerous knowledgeable sources in and outside Indonesia confirmed that Apkindo is suppressing prices to bankrupt Japanese plywood competitors and capture this lucrative market.

254. Nageri Munthe, "Plywood Exports Hit Hurdle," *Indonesia Business Weekly* 3, no. 33 (31 July 1995), p. 13. Apkindo strongly denies that it exports plywood to Japan below world market prices.

255. Interview, senior official, Bappenas, Jakarta, 4 March 1994. In response to a question on how he maintains discipline, Hasan remarked, "I sign the approval for revoking a company's export licence." Quoted in "Shades of Green," pp. 28, 30. In 1994 and 1995 government and business leaders publicly criticized Apkindo for contributing to a sharp drop in plywood prices and a decline in Indonesian plywood exports. For example, see "Indonesia: M. Hasan Defends Export Monopoly Over Plywood," *Jakarta Post* (20 March 1995), Reuter Business Briefing; "Indonesia: Apkindo Faulted for Export Drop," *Jakarta Post* (16 February 1995), Reuter Business Briefing; Viandrito, "Bob Hasan Speaks Up," p. 31; and Gary Nageri Munthe and Rin Hindryati, "Apkindo Under Fire," *Indonesia Business Weekly* 3, no. 12 (6 March 1995), pp. 4–7. Apkindo argues that the decline in plywood prices is

primarily a result of the Japanese and South Korean recessions and Malaysian tactics to flood the market with underpriced plywood.

256. Raphael Pura, "Some Believe Apkindo Is Too Powerful," *AWSJ* (23 January 1995).

257. See tables 1, 3, and 4.

258. Calculated from tables 1 and 4. A large portion of Indonesian plywood is kon-pane. According to an Apkindo official, Indonesia supplied about 70 percent of Japanese kon-pane consumption in the early 1990s. Interview, Apkindo, Jakarta, 1 March 1994.

259. Interview, senior official, Bappenas, Jakarta, 4 March 1994.

260. Calculated from table 3.

261. Senior executive, JPMA, Tokyo, 8 April 1994.

262. Interview, senior official, Bappenas, Jakarta, 4 March 1994.

263. Interview, senior official, JPMA, Tokyo, 8 April 1994. The United States also accused Apkindo of violating the GATT and American antitrust laws. Jaakko Poyry Oy, World Bank Commissioned Study, *Tropical Deforestation in Asia and Market for Wood*. Annex II, Wood Supply From Indonesia. (Finland: Jaakko Poyry Oy, 1992), p. II/54.

264. Interviews, JLIA, Tokyo, 4 April 1994; JPMA, Tokyo, 8 April 1994; Japan Plywood Inspection Corporation, Tokyo, 8 April 1994.

265. Interview, Apkindo, Jakarta, 1 March 1994.

266. Interview, CIFOR, Bogor Indonesia, 2 March 1994.

267. The 15 percent tariff is for plywood that is less than six millimeters thick. If the thickness is more than six millimeters then the import duty is 10 percent. *Asian Timber* (October 1994), p. 9. Logs are not charged an import duty.

268. Interview, senior official, Bappenas, Jakarta, 4 March 1994.

269. Hasan, "Prospects for Plywood," p. 16.

270. Quoted in "Jakarta Receives US$1.9 b in New Loans from Japan for Development," *Star* (15 September 1992), p. 16.

271. Interview, Apkindo, Jakarta, 1 March 1994; and interview, senior official, Japan Plywood Inspection Corporation, Tokyo, 8 April 1994.

Chapter 4: Japan, Clientelism, and Deforestation in East Malaysia

1. Quoted in Hurst, *Rainforest Politics*, p. 102.

2. Summarized by Rowley, "Logged Out," *FEER* (13 December 1990), p. 72. For the ITTO report, see ITTO, "The Promotion of Sustainable Forest Management: A Case Study in Sarawak, Malaysia," report submitted to the International Tropical Timber Council, ITTC (VIII)/7, 7 May 1990, especially p. 35.

3. Milne, "Patrons, Clients and Ethnicity," p. 898.

4. Ibid., pp. 898–899.

5. Ibid., p. 896.

6. These included Tun Fuad Stephens and Tun Mustapha Harun in Sabah and Datuk Amar James Wong Kim Min in Sarawak. R. S. (Robert Steven) Milne and K. J. Ratnam, *Malaysia—New States in a New Nation* (London: Frank Cass, 1974), pp. 316–318.

7. Means, *Malaysian Politics*, pp. 298–299.

8. Milne, "Patrons, Clients and Ethnicity," p. 899.

9. See Milne and Ratnam, *Malaysia—New States in a New Nation*, for a discussion of these practices.

10. The Bidayuh and Orang Ulu are sometimes grouped with the Iban and called Dayaks.

11. The role of Sarawak's ethnic groups in politics is discussed in Jayum A. Jawan, *The Ethnic Factor in Modern Politics: The Case of Sarawak, East Malaysia*, Occasional Paper No. 20 (University of Hull: Center for South-East Asian Studies, 1991). For a specific discussion of the Sarawak Chinese, see John M. Chin, *The Sarawak Chinese* (Kuala Lumpur: Oxford University Press, 1981).

12. Diane K. Mauzy and R. S. (Robert Stephen) Milne, *Malaysia: Tradition, Modernity and Islam* (Boulder, CO: Westview Press, 1986), p. 68.

13. Michael B. Leigh, *The Rising Moon: Political Change in Sarawak* (Sydney: Sydney University Press, 1974), pp. 162, 161.

14. Bruce Gale, "Politics at the Periphery: A Study of the 1981 and 1982 Election Campaigns in Sabah," in Bruce Gale, ed., *Readings in Malaysian Politics* (Selangor, Malaysia: Pelanduk Publications, 1986), p. 25.

15. Marcus Colchester, *Pirates, Squatters and Poachers: The Political Ecology of Dispossession of the Native Peoples of Sarawak* (London: Survival International, INSAN [Institut Analisa Sosial, Malaysia] 1989), p. 32.

16. Michael Vatikiotis, "Disarray in the Ranks," *FEER* (10 September 1992), pp. 24–26.

17. See "PBS Wins By Two Seats," *Borneo Post* (20 February 1994), p. 1.

18. Michael Vatikiotis, "Dominant Front," *FEER* (31 March 1994), p. 18. Also see Michael Vatikiotis, "Settling Scores," *FEER* (24 March 1994), p. 23.

19. Suhaini Aznam, "Murmurs in the Forest," *FEER* (27 July 1989), p. 30.

20. Francis Loh Kok Wah, "Early Elections In Sarawak?: Understanding Electoral Politics in Sarawak," *Aliran* 11, no. 7 (1990), p. 5.

21. Mauzy and Milne, *Malaysia*, p. 117.

22. Many of these immigrants, both legal and illegal, manage to get on the electoral rolls, often assisted by political parties trying to expand their support base. From 1986 to 1989, the number of new voters in Sabah increased more than 25 percent, many of whom appear to be illegal immigrants. Michael Vatikiotis, "Floating Voters," *FEER* (18 June 1992), p. 30.

23. Vatikiotis, "Disarray in the Ranks," p. 26. For example, during the Usukan by-election in Sabah on 11 May 1991, all parties reputedly used money to influence voters. Suhaini Aznam, "Double Blow: Sabah Party Loses By-Election and a Leader," *FEER* (23 May 1991), pp. 11–12.

24. Gillis, "Malaysia: Public Policies and Tropical Forest," p. 123. For historical background on forestry management in Sabah, see A. J. Fyfe, "Forestry in Sabah," *Malayan Forester* 27 (1964), pp. 82–95. For a description of timber extraction methods in East Malaysia

in the first decade after World War II, see G. S. Brown, "Timber Extraction Methods in N. Borneo," *Malayan Forester* 18 (July 1955), pp. 121–132; and Kadir Mohd Nastan, "A Note on Logging Methods Used By a Large Timber Company on the East Coast of Sabah," *Malayan Forester* 29, no. 4 (1966), pp. 303–306. For a broader study of development on the island of Borneo, see Mark Cleary and Peter Eaton, *Borneo: Change and Development* (Singapore: Oxford University Press, 1992).

25. See table 12.

26. Repetto, *The Forest for the Trees?* p. 56; and Gillis, "Malaysia: Public Policies," p. 141.

27. For historical background on Sarawak's timber industry, see B. E. Smythies, "History of Forestry in Sarawak," *Malayan Forester* 25–26 (1962–63), pp. 232–253. A general discussion of Malaysia's forests is provided by S. Robert Aiken and Colin H. Leigh, *Vanishing Rain Forests: The Ecological Transition in Malaysia* (Oxford: Clarendon Press, 1992).

28. Colchester, *Pirates*, p. 34.

29. Malaysian Timber Council, Statistics for 1994, Forested Area by Region, http://www.mtc.com.my/. According to the Malaysian Timber Council, in 1994 dipterocarp forests covered 4.01 million hectares of Sabah and mangrove forests covered 0.34 million hectares (for a total of 4.35 million hectares). Malaysian Timber Council, Statistics for 1994, Distribution and Extent of Forest Types, http://www.mtc.com.my/.

30. Sabah Forestry Department, *Forestry in Sabah* (Sandakan: Sabah Forestry Department, 1989), pp. 51, 53–54, 58. This chapter relies mostly on government or corporate data. Unlike in Indonesia and the Philippines, there are few NGOs to provide alternative estimates. As would be expected with government and business statistics, these figures tend to represent the most optimistic scenario.

31. Malaysian Timber Council, Statistics for 1994, Permanent Forest Estate by Region, http://www.mtc.com.my/.

32. Rahim Sulaiman, "Forest Plantation in Sabah—Development Issues" *Berita Hutan* (September 1993), p. 14.

33. Brookfield, Potter, and Byron, *In Place of the Forest*, p. 98.

34. According to the Malaysian Timber Council, in 1994 dipterocarp forests covered 7.3 million hectares of Sarawak, swamp forests covered 1.2 million hectares, and mangrove forests covered 0.1 million hectares (for a total of 8.6 million hectares). Malaysian Timber Council, Statistics for 1994, Distribution and Extent of Forest Types, http://www.mtc.com.my/.

35. In 1991, Sarawak increased its permanent forest estate from 4.5 million hectares to 6 million hectares. Noorzita Samad, "European Parliament to Review Timber Ban," *New Straits Times* (14 May 1992), p. 16.

36. Sarawak Forest Department, *Forestry in Sarawak, Malaysia* (Kuching: Sarawak Forest Department, 1993), pp. 4, 10.

37. Hong, *Natives of Sarawak,* pp. 128–129, cited in Brookfield, Potter, and Byron, *In Place of the Forest*, p. 101; and Means, *Malaysian Politics*, p. 196.

38. Interviews, WWF Malaysia, Petaling Jaya, 10 March 1994.

39. Repetto, *The Forest for the Trees?*, p. 54.

40. James Clad, "Boom and Bust Leave Sabah's Vault Empty," *FEER* (6 February 1986), p. 64. More recently, Sabah's economy has fared poorly. In 1992–93, GDP grew by only 3 percent, compared with a 9 percent Malaysian average. Michael Vatikiotis, "Slap on the Wrist," *FEER* (27 January 1994), p. 14.

41. Sarawak's GDP growth slipped from over 8 percent at the start of the 1990s to 5 percent in 1992 and 3.7 percent in 1993. Doug Tsuruoka, "Awakening Giant," *FEER* (21 July 1994), p. 68.

42. "Logging in Sabah Reduced Substantially, Chief Minister," *Asian Timber* (January 1993), p. 4.

43. The minister's figures are based on data from the Sabah Forestry Department and assume production from the permanent forest reserves, stateland forests, and primary forests. "Figures on Logging Provided by Sabah Forest Dept: Lim," *Borneo Post* (28 February 1993).

44. See tables 12 and 14.

45. Sarawak Forest Department, *Forestry in Sarawak*, p. 37.

46. See Fred Pearce, "Are Sarawak's Forests Sustainable?" *New Scientist* (26 November 1994), pp. 30–31. The Sarawak government estimates that annual sustainable yield from the permanent forest estate is 11.78 million cubic meters. See Malaysian Timber Council, Library, Forestry in Sarawak, Malaysia, Forest Harvesting, http://www.mtc.com.my/.

47. Stan Sesser, "A Reporter at Large: Logging the Rain Forest," *New Yorker* (27 May 1991), p. 56.

48. James Clad, "Slow the Hill Rises," *FEER* (30 May 1985), p. 36.

49. Some Ibans do receive a small portion of timber profits. The anthropologist Vinson H. Sutlive reported that when a timber company logged communal forests, money was paid out to the district leader, the longhouse headman, and the Ibans living in the longhouse. He found that for every U.S.$10, U.S.$6 went to the district head, U.S.$2 to the longhouse leader, and the rest was divided among the longhouse residents. Sutlive's work is discussed in Peter Searle, *Politics in Sarawak 1970–76: The Iban Perspective* (Singapore: Oxford University Press, 1983), p. 110.

50. Means, *Malaysian Politics*, p. 42. For background on the Sabah Foundation (Yayasan Sabah), see Yayasan Sabah, *Yayasan Sabah: 1966–1991* (Kota Kinabalu: Yayasan Sabah, 1992). For more details on Mustapha's early years in power, see Milne and Ratnam, *Malaysia—New States in a New Nation.*

51. Means, *Malaysian Politics*, p. 42.

52. Ibid.

53. Both quotes are from ibid., p. 154.

54. Ibid., p. 155.

55. Both quotes are from Gillis, "Malaysia: Public Policies," p. 123.

56. Yayasan Sabah, *Yayasan Sabah and Innoprise Corporation Sdn Bhd* (Kota Kinabalu: Yayasan Sabah, 1993), p. 1.

57. Sabah Forestry Department, *Forestry in Sabah*, p. 85.

58. Raphael Pura, "Timber Companies Blossom on Malaysian Stock Market," *AWSJ* (30 November 1993), p. 12.

59. From March 1994 to December 1994, the chief minister of Sabah was Tan Sri Sakaran Dandai. He was the leader of the Sabah wing of UMNO, a key party in the BN coalition which is affiliated with the federal government. For background on the BN coalition and the lead up to the February 1994 election, see "Pairin: I'm Not Ashamed," *Sabah Times* (3 February 1994), p. 1; "Why We Quit the PBS," *Sabah Times* (4 February 1994), p. 1; Haryati A. Karim, "Tun M Snubs Pairin," *Sabah Times* (6 February 1994), p. 1; "Kadazans Splitting PBS," *Sabah Times* (6 February 1994), p. 1; "Pairin Gives Up on the Chinese," *Sabah Times* (7 February 1994), p. 1; "It's BN vs PBS," *Sabah Times* (8 February 1994), p. 1; "Be Bold, Yong Tells Chinese," *Sabah Times* (9 February 1994), p. 1; "BN Fulfils Pledge," *Sabah Times* (13 February 1994), p. 1; "Delivered RM 2 Mil for 30 Schools," *Daily Express* (13 February 1994), p. 1; "Tun M: Vote PBS-Plus," *Borneo Mail* (14 February 1994), p. 1; "Chinese Say No to PBS," *Sabah Times* (14 February 1994), p. 1; and "RM1.3 Billion Scandal," *Sabah Times* (15 February 1994), p. 1. On 1 January 1995, Sakaran Dandai became the eighth governor of Sabah. From late December 1994 to May 1996, Datuk Salleh Said Keruak of UMNO was chief minister of Sabah. The current chief minister is Datuk Yong Teck Lee, leader of the Sabah Progressive Party (SAPP), the most important Chinese political party in the ruling BN coalition government.

60. For background on Innoprise, see Innoprise, *Innoprise Corporation Sdn Bhd: 1991* (Kota Kinabalu: Innoprise, 1992); and Yayasan Sabah, *Yayasan Sabah*.

61. Interview, senior executive, Yayasan Sabah (Sabah Foundation), Kota Kinabalu, 14 February 1994.

62. Statement by Datuk Haji Mohd Noor Mansoor, "Yayasan Isn't Tax Exempt, Says Mansoor," *Sabah Times* (12 July 1990).

63. A statement by Lim Guan Sing, "Allegations Substantiated," *Sabah Times* (11 July 1990), p. 2.

64. Colchester, *Pirates*, p. 35. For a summary of Sarawak politics from 1983 to 1987, see Means, *Malaysian Politics*, pp. 165–172. Since 1966 there have been four forestry ministers: Hj Abdul Taib Mahmud (1966–67); Datuk Tajang Laing (1967–70); Chief Minister Datuk Abdul Rahman Yaakub (1970–81); Datuk Haji Noor Tahir (1981–85); and again, Chief Minister Taib (1985–present).

65. Colchester, *Pirates*, p. 36.

66. Raphael Pura and Stephen Duthie, "How Ekran Bhd. Outfoxed Rival For Power Deal," *AWSJ* (2 February 1994), p. 12.

67. The BN coalition government, led by Chief Minister Taib, has ruled Sarawak since 1981. The BN easily won the election in September 1996 (gaining 57 of the 62 seats in the state assembly). For background on the election, see S. Jayasankaran, "Stand and Deliver: Sarawak chief has forged an unbeatable coalition," *FEER* (12 September 1996), pp. 22–24. For a progovernment account of Taib's reign, see James Ritchie, *A Political Saga: Sarawak 1981–1993* (Singapore: Summer Times, 1993).

68. Zainon Ahmad, "Timber Freeze Sparks 'War,'" *New Straits Times* (10 April 1987), in Yu Loon Ching, *Sarawak: The Plot That Failed 10 March 87–17 April 87* (a collection of newspaper articles) (Singapore: Summer Times, 1987), p. 66.

69. "More of Timber Licences 'Kept' in Rahman's Circle Exposed," *People's Mirror* (13 April 1987), in Ching, *Sarawak*, p. 69.

70. For a list of political connections to timber companies, see Institut Analisa Sosial (Malaysia), *Logging Against the Natives of Sarawak* (Selangor, Malaysia: INSAN [Institut Analisa Sosial], 1989), pp. 73–74.

71. Nick Seaward, "At Loggerheads with Power," *FEER* (2 June 1987), p. 32.

72. See Suhaini Aznam, "Wood for the Trees," *FEER* (5 December 1991), pp. 55–57.

73. Quoted in "International Experts Say Sarawak Natives Badly Affected By Logging," *Utusan Konsumer* (March 1988), in World Rainforest Movement and Sahabat Alam Malaysia, *The Battle For Sarawak's Forests*, second edition (Penang, Malaysia: World Rainforest Movement and Sahabat Alam Malaysia, 1990), p. 54.

74. Quoted in Robin Hanbury-Tenison, president of Survival International, "No Surrender in Sarawak," *New Scientist* (1 December 1990), p. 29.

75. "International Experts," *Utusan Konsumer*, in World Rainforest Movement and Sahabat Alam Malaysia, *The Battle for Sarawak's Forests*, p. 54.

76. Tsuruoka, "Awakening Giant," p. 70. According to the *Star*, Foo Chow Chinese control 90 percent of Sarawak's timber industry. "The Pioneers of Timber Industry," *Star* (19 September 1991), p. 11.

77. A Rimbunan Hijau subsidiary owns 40 percent of Limbang Trading Company Sdn Bhd and holds a majority of Sarawak Plywood Sdn Bhd. Raphael Pura, "Timber Baron Emerges From the Woods," *AWSJ* (15 February 1994), p. 4.

78. Summarized in Pura, "Timber Baron Emerges from the Woods," p. 1.

79. Raphael Pura, "Deal Moves Berjaya into Timber," *AWSJ* (7 December 1993), pp. 1, 4; Raphael Pura, "In Sarawak, a Clash Over Land and Power," *AWSJ* (7 February 1990), p. 1; and Pura, "Timber Baron Emerges from the Woods," pp. 1, 4.

80. Pura, "Timber Baron Emerges from the Woods," p. 4.

81. Quoted in Raphael Pura, "Ekran Is Tapped to Construct Malaysian Dam," *AWSJ* (31 January 1994), p. 4. Pura provides details on the Bakun Dam, ibid., pp. 1, 4.

82. Pura and Duthie, "How Ekran Bhd. Outfoxed Rival for Power Deal."

83. Pura, "Ekran Is Tapped to Construct Malaysian Dam," p. 4. Two other major timber operators in Sarawak are Hiew Teck Seng and Wong Tuong Kwang. Wong's son, Wong Kie Yik, is a federal senator. Pura, "In Sarawak, a Clash Over Land and Power."

84. S. Jayasankaran, "Onward March," *FEER* (24 November 1994), p. 140.

85. Interview, foreign correspondent, Kuala Lumpur, 10 March 1994.

86. Quoted in Toh Lye Huat, "Plan to Counter Anti-Tropical Timber Campaign," *New Straits Times* (11 March 1992), p. 10. This campaign has further clouded the line between propaganda and reality. It has also increased the difficulty of conducting primary research in Malaysia. For further details on the campaign, see "Govt to Counter Foreign 'Green' Smear Campaigns," *Straits Times* (11 March 1992), p. 15; and "Help Sought to Monitor Group," *New Straits Times* (11 March 1992), p. 10.

87. For an excellent set of articles on the links between poorly designed public policies and tropical deforestation, see Gillis and Repetto, eds., *Public Policies*.

88. I. Rajeswary, "Profits vs. Preservation," in *Dwindling Forests: Diminishing Returns* (New York: UNDP [United Nations Development Programme], 1991), p. 15.

89. The federal government also has some indirect influence through its control of areas like the national budget and manpower. Interviews, Universiti Pertanian Malaysia (UPM), Faculty of Forestry, Malaysia, 8 March 1994.

90. Michael Vatikiotis, "Clearcut Mandate," *FEER* (28 October 1993), p. 54. In 1995 the State Natural Resources and Environment Board of Sarawak announced that loggers operating concessions larger than 500 hectares had six months to prepare an environmental impact assessment. It is, however, too early to evaluate the impact of this new policy.

91. Sarawak Forest Department, *Forestry in Sarawak*, pp. 7, 13.

92. Gillis, "Malaysia: Public Policies," pp. 149–153. For background on forest legislation and policy in Sarawak, see Malaysian Forester, "The Forest Resource Base, Policy and Legislation of Sarawak," *Malaysian Forester* 42, no. 4 (1979), pp. 311–327.

93. "Timber Exporters Must Register With STIDC," *Borneo Post* (1 January 1993).

94. Gillis, "Malaysia: Public Policies," pp. 127–128.

95. Interview, Sabah Forestry Department (Jabatan Perhutanan Sabah), Kota Kinabalu Branch, 16 February 1994. For background on the basic goals and policies of the Sabah Forestry Department, see Sabah Forestry Department, *Goals* (Sandakan: Sabah State Government, undated); and Malaysian Forester, "The Forest Resource Base, Policy and Legislation of Sabah," *Malaysian Forester* 42, no. 4 (1979), pp. 286–310.

96. Rush, *The Last Tree*, p. 42.

97. Domingo N. P. Chai and Yahya Awang, "Current Forest Resource Scenario in Sabah," in Ti Teow Chuan, ed., *Opportunities and Incentives for Wood Processing in Sabah*. Proceedings of a seminar organized by Timber Association of Sabah held at Kota Kinabalu, 22–23 August 1989. (Kota Kinabalu: Timber Association of Sabah, 1989), p. 25.

98. Sabah Forestry Department, *Forestry in Sabah*, pp. 63–64.

99. According to a spokesman, since 1993 Innoprise has improved timber management. While still in the early stages, this involves two key changes: leaving some areas undisturbed and planting more indigenous trees. Japan has shown no interest in supporting these efforts. Interview, senior manager, Innoprise Corporation, Kota Kinabalu, 9 February 1994.

100. For details, see Salahudin Yaacob, Isabelle Louis, Geoffrey Davison, Mohd Nizam Basiron, and Sabri Zain (Malaysian FSC Consultative Study Working Group), *Forest Stewardship Council (FSC) Malaysian Consultative Study* (Selangor Malaysia: WWF Malaysia, August 1993), pp. 20–21.

101. Kan Yaw Chong, "Logging and Forest Conservation," *Sabah Times* (22 April 1990).

102. For a description of Sarawak's timber harvesting guidelines, see Sarawak Forest Department, *Forestry in Sarawak*, pp. 18–27.

103. Interview, senior researcher, Forest Department, Kuching, 21 February 1994.

104. "Military to Curb Illegal Logging in Sabah," *Borneo Post* (12 February 1993).

105. For Sarawak, see Brookfield, Potter, and Byron, *In Place of the Forest*, p. 102.

106. Kan Yaw Chong, "Logging and Forest Conservation." Even the Sabah Forestry Department estimated that over 40 percent of a concession was sometimes destroyed after logging. Summarized in Nectoux and Kuroda, *Timber from the South Seas*, p. 20.

107. N. Mark Collins, Jeffrey Sayer, T.C. (Timothy Charles) Whitmore, eds., *The Conservation Atlas of Tropical Forests* (Asia and the Pacific) (New York: Simon and Schuster, 1991), p. 201; and Sabah Forestry Department, *Forestry in Sabah*, p. 46.

108. "Heavier Penalties for Forest Criminals: Pairin," *Borneo Post* (25 October 1993).

109. Summarized in "Loggers' Lament," *Asiaweek* (28 April 1993), p. 50.

110. Joniston Bangkuai, "Illegal Export of Timber Exposed," *New Straits Times* (23 April 1992), p. 1. It is difficult to document the path of illegal logs. Small signs do emerge. During one of my interviews in Sabah, a Japanese corporate executive telephoned and inquired into the possibility of a sawmill doing minor alterations to some "foreign" logs before exporting this timber to Japan. The Sabah official refused to disclose the source of the logs, although they hinted it was Indonesia. Confidential interview, Kota Kinabalu, February 1994.

111. In June 1993 royalties on key tree species in Sarawak increased by 50 percent. James Wong, "New Rates for Timber Royalties," *Borneo Post* (8 June 1993).

112. Murtedza Mohamed and Ti Teow Chuan, "Effects of Deforestation: With Special Reference to East Malaysia," *Borneo Review* 2, no. 2 (December 1991), p. 127.

113. See Gillis, "Malaysia: Public Policies," pp. 139–143. While Sabah's timber charges have generated substantial state revenue, ad valorem royalties on logs and export taxes on sawn timber have encouraged loggers to mine concessions and disregard damage to residual stands. Ibid., p. 130. In Sarawak, timber royalties are volume-based (which are reduced for lower grade species), and export taxes are value-based. While Sarawak has captured remarkably little timber rent, lower forest fees—especially ones differentiated by species—have provided fewer incentives to practice high-grade mining. For this reason, loggers apparently damage less residual stocks in Sarawak than in Sabah. Ibid., pp. 131, 149–151.

114. Sabah timber exporters—including the Sabah Foundation—have reportedly underdeclared the value of log exports by as much as 40 percent. Openg Onn, "Sabah Losing Millions in Timber Scam," *New Straits Times* (15 May 1993), p. 6; "Putting Sabah's Logging Back on the Track," *Borneo Post* (1 February 1993); and "Forestry Dept Seizes Undervalued Sawn Timber," *Borneo Post* (19 August 1993).

115. Openg Onn, "Sabah Losing Millions in Timber Scam."

116. Doug Tsuruoka, "Cutting Down to Size," *FEER* (4 July 1991), p. 45.

117. Quoted in Hurst, *Rainforest Politics*, p. 109.

118. Tsuruoka, "Cutting Down to Size," p. 46.

119. Interview, foreign correspondent, Kuala Lumpur, 9 March 1994.

120. Sarawak Study Group, "Logging in Sarawak: The Belaga Experience," in Institut Analisa Sosial, *Logging Against the Natives of Sarawak*, p. 5.

121. Hurst, *Rainforest Politics*, p. 103.

122. Sarawak Study Group, "Logging in Sarawak," p. 3.

123. Concessionaires receive either a fixed sum or a percentage of the profits from the contractor—generally between 5–10 percent of the value. Hurst notes that "this may seem a low return but revenues build up and involve the concessionaires in almost no financial

risk." Besides, "the concession holder frequently does nothing." Hurst, *Rainforest Politics*, p. 105.

124. Rowley, "Logged Out."

125. The use of nominees makes it difficult to determine who controls timber companies. For a discussion of this problem in Sabah, see Tsuruoka, "Cutting Down to Size," pp. 44–45.

126. K. S. Jomo, "Logging, Politics, Business and the Indigenous People of Sarawak," paper presented at the 5th Annual Conference of Northeast Regional Consortium for Southeast Asian Studies, University of British Columbia, 16–18 October 1992, p. 6. For a description of the harsh conditions for native loggers, see Jeyakumar Devaraj, "Logging Accidents in Sarawak," in Institut Analisa Sosial, *Logging Against the Natives of Sarawak*.

127. The director general of the Forest Research Institute of Malaysia argues: "What happens is that at each stage the individual tries to maximise profit[s]. The responsibility and accountability is fragmented and this does not lead to good forestry practices." Quoted in Azam Aris, "State Govts Urged to Change Timber Concession Policies," *Business Times* (10 February 1993).

128. "Don't Give Timber Concessions to Middlemen, State Told Again," *Borneo Post* (20 September 1993).

129. Azam Aris, "Overhaul Timber Concession System," *Business Times* (1 February 1993).

130. Gillis, "Malaysia: Public Policies," p. 127.

131. To undermine the PBS, the federal government charged Chief Minister Pairin and his brother Jeffrey Kitingan with corruption. For details, see Michael Vatikiotis, "Glacial Justice," *FEER* (27 May 1993), p. 27. In early 1994, Pairin was found guilty. His fine, however, was low enough that he still qualified for office. Although this verdict eroded some of his legitimacy and authority, he still managed to win the ensuing election.

132. Interview, foreign correspondent, Kuala Lumpur, 10 March 1994.

133. Repetto, *The Forest for the Trees?*, p. 54; and Kenji Takeuchi, "Market Prospects for Tropical Hardwoods from Southeast Asia," in James S. Bethel, *World Trade in Forest Products* (Seattle: University of Washington Press, 1983), p. 437.

134. The federal Malaysian Timber Industry Board issues export licenses in Sabah. However in Sarawak, the state government issues these licenses. Interview, Malaysian Timber Industry Board, Ministry of Primary Industries, Kuala Lumpur, 9 March 1994. Although the Malaysian constitution clearly gives the federal government control over exports and imports, Sabah argued that the log export ban was unconstitutional—that precedents had been set after Sabah joined the federation for state control of timber exports. Interview, senior official, Ministry of Primary Industries, Kuala Lumpur, 8 March 1994.

135. Prime Minister Mahathir was also angry that Sabah's log export charges to places like Japan, Taiwan, and South Korea were the same as to Peninsular Malaysia. At the time, mainland processors, facing a serious shortage of logs, wanted Sabah to decrease export charges to the Peninsular. Confidential interview, Sabah Industry Representative, Kota Kinabalu, February 1994; and see Michael Vatikiotis, "Local Hero: Drive to Topple Sabah Leader Stalls," *FEER* (27 May 1993), pp. 26–27.

136. JATAN, "Asia-Pacific Forests," November 1993, presented at the World Rainforest Movement Meeting, New Delhi, India, April 1994, p. 2.

137. P. K. Katharason, "Logs Meant for Japan Stuck in Kota Kinabalu," *Star* (9 May 1993), p. 7; and "Tokyo Protests to KL Over Sabah's Ban on Log Exports," *Straits Times* (8 May 1993), p. 22.

138. Interview, Timber Association of Sabah (TAS), Kota Kinabalu, 8 February 1994; and "Log Ban to Remain—CM," *Sabah Times* (21 May 1993), p. 1.

139. Michael Vatikiotis, "Tables Turned: Sabah Timber-Export Ban Riles Kuala Lumpur," *FEER* (3 June 1993), pp. 66–67; and *Asian Timber* (June 1993), p. 8. Although the federal government has the constitutional power to control exports, the Sabah Forestry Department simply refused to assess royalties on log exports, in effect creating a log export ban. Fadzil Ghazali, "Sabah Timber Firms Get Go-ahead on Exports," *Business Times* (19 May 1993).

140. Joehann Angkie, "Japanese Sceptical on Sabah," *Daily Express*, 17 November 1993, pp. 1–2.

141. Official, TAS, Kota Kinabalu, 8 February 1994.

142. Ibid.

143. John Lim, "Temporary Log Export Ban in Sabah: No Pain, No Gain," *Asian Timber* (December 1992), p. 3.

144. Interviews, TAS, Kota Kinabalu, 8 February 1994; Innoprise Corporation, Kota Kinabalu, 9 February 1994; Institute for Development Studies, Kota Kinabalu, 12 February 1994; and Ministry of Tourism and Environmental Development, Kota Kinabalu, 15 February 1994. In 1994, there were 226 sawmills and 65 plywood and veneer mills. Malaysian Timber Council, Statistics for 1994, "Number of Sawmills and Plywood/Veneer Mills," http://www.mtc.com.my/.

145. See table 12.

146. "Log Ban to Remain—CM."

147. The SSIA denies these charges. Interview, SSIA, Kota Kinabalu, 16 February 1994. To stabilize log prices, in mid-1994 the government was contemplating setting a minimum and maximum price on logs.

148. Senior researcher, Institute for Development Studies, Kota Kinabalu, 12 February 1994.

149. Interview, Ministry of Tourism and Environmental Development, Kota Kinabalu, 15 February 1994.

150. Interview, Sabah timber executive, Kota Kinabalu, 9 February 1994. Although Sarawak log exporters made substantial profits, the rapid rise in prices hurt local processors as log prices climbed much faster than processed wood prices.

151. "S'wak Aggressive in Going Downstream," *Borneo Post* (16 September 1993).

152. "Harwood Takes Charges from February 1," *Sarawak Tribune* (26 January 1994), p. 1.

153. Sarawak Forest Department, *Forestry in Sarawak*, p. 33; "Enough Supply of Logs, Says STA [Sarawak Timber Association] Chairman," *Peoples Mirror* (9 February 1993); and James Wong, "Cheaper Logs for Local Processing," *Borneo Post* (9 February 1993).

154. Interview, STIDC, Kuching, 17 February 1994. In 1993 the government planned to set aside 6.0 million cubic meters of logs for local plywood plants and sawmills. "6 Mil cu m Of Logs Reserved For Local Industry," *Peoples Mirror* (17 January 1993).

155. Sarawak Forest Department, *Forestry in Sarawak*, p. 33.

156. Tan Chin Siang, "Taib: Sarawak Will Adopt Flexible Timber Trade Policy," *New Straits Times* (19 October 1993), p. 10.

157. Interview, senior official, Forest Department, Kuching, 17 February 1994.

158. Interview, STIDC, Kuching, 17 February 1994.

159. Malaysian Timber Council, Statistics for 1994, "Number of Sawmills and Plywood/ Veneer Mills," http://www.mtc.com.my/.

160. Malaysian Timber Council, Statistics for 1994, "Production of Plywood," http:// www.mtc.com.my/.

161. "Sarawak Plywood Mills Raise Wholesale Prices But Expect Log Cost To Ease This Year," *Asian Timber* (March 1993), p. 6.

162. Colchester, *Pirates*, p. 35.

163. Summarized in Martha Belcher and Angela Gennino, eds., *Southeast Asia Rainforests: A Resource Guide and Directory* (San Francisco: Rainforest Action Network, 1993), p. 27.

164. Tsuruoka, "Cutting Down to Size," p. 46.

165. Quoted in "The Private Sector and Reafforestation," *Star* (21 September 1991), pp. 8–9.

166. Interview, TAS, Kota Kinabalu, 8 February 1994. TAS is a private organization. It works to protect its members from detrimental government policies. For example, TAS advises and negotiates with the state government on licensing and royalty fees. It is the main organization for log producers (in the past, exporters).

167. Interview, Institute for Development Studies, Kota Kinabalu, 12 February 1994. For background on Sabah's forest plantations, see "Four Fast Growing Species in Sabah Forest Plantations," *Star* (17 September 1991), pp. 8–9.

168. See Sarawak Forest Department, *Forestry in Sarawak*, passim.

169. Interview, senior researcher, Forest Department, Kuching, 21 February 1994; Interview, senior official, Forest Department, Kuching, 17 February 1994; "Reforestation Does Not Cover Logged Areas," *Borneo Post* (20 November 1993); and "Reforestation Only in Deforested Permanent Estates," *Peoples Mirror* (20 November 1993).

170. Quoted in Vatikiotis, "Clearcut Mandate," p. 55. For background on the federal initiatives to combat illegal logging, see Abu Yamin Salam, "Army Can Nab Illegal Loggers," *New Straits Times* (25 April 1993), p. 2; "Copters to Combat Illegal Logging," *Star* (25 April 1993), p. 3; and "New Law to Allow Troops to Nab Illegal Loggers," *Straits Times* (25 April 1993), p. 14.

171. "Sabah Forestry Law Adequate, says AG," *Business Times* (5 February 1993); and "Forestry Dept Gets Tough on Illegal Loggers," *Sabah Times* (10 March 1993).

172. Tan Chin Siang, "Curbing Illegal Log Exports," *New Straits Times* (17 November 1993), p. 1; and "New Mandatory Jail Term For Illegal Exporters of Logs," *Peoples Mirror* (16 November 1993).

173. "Military to Curb Illegal Logging in Sabah," *Borneo Post* (12 February 1993).

174. "Stop Accusing S'wak's Forest Management Immediately," *Borneo Post* (16 September 1993); and "Log Smugglers Warned of Stern Action," *Peoples Mirror* (16 September 1993).

175. "Training for Sarawak Forestry Officers to Curb Illegal Logging," *New Straits Times* (23 April 1993), p. 7.

176. Bob Kedeni, "Move to Curb Log Smuggling," *Sarawak Tribune* (21 July 1993); and Magdelene Rogers, "Checking Stations to Curb Log Smuggling," *Borneo Post* (21 July 1993).

177. "Sarawak Sets Up an Anti-Smuggling Team," *New Straits Times* (6 February 1993).

178. "Ban on Moving Logs at Night to Be Enforced Soon," *Borneo Post* (1 February 1994), p. 2.

179. Quoted in Seman Endawie, "Cash-for-Logs Scheme Soon," *Sarawak Tribune* (2 February 1993). The Sarawak Forest Department also claims that efforts to capture illegal loggers are frustrated by local residents who work for loggers and refuse to provide information on illegal activities. "Locals Collude With Illegal Loggers," *Borneo Post* (10 June 1994); and "Soon Kai Warns Accomplices," *Peoples Mirror* (14 June 1993). The village singled out by the Forest Department in the above articles denied these charges. "We Have Nothing To Do With Illegal Logging," *Borneo Post* (23 June 1993).

180. Tsuruoka, "Cutting Down to Size," p. 44.

181. This quote is a summary of Munang's comments by Doug Tsuruoka, "Tree Cover: Malaysian State May Hire Inchcape Unit to Track Timber," *FEER* (20 January 1994), p. 54. This article describes Inchcape's proposal.

182. Quoted in Pura, "Timber Baron Emerges from the Woods," p. 4.

183. Ibid.

184. Quoted in Vatikiotis, "Clearcut Mandate," p. 54.

185. Interviews, TAS, Kota Kinabalu, 8 February 1994; Institute for Development Studies, Kota Kinabalu, 12 February 1994; and Ministry of Tourism and Environmental Development, Kota Kinabalu, 15 February 1994.

186. Interview, Institute for Development Studies, Kota Kinabalu, 12 February 1994.

187. Interview, senior JICA official, Sabah Reafforestation Technical Development and Training Project, Kinarut, Sabah, 14 February 1994.

188. Interview, Consulate of Japan, Kota Kinabalu, 9 February 1994; interview, senior manager, SAFODA, Kota Kinabalu, 12 February 1994; and interviews, senior officials, Sabah Re-afforestation Technical Development and Training Project, from JICA and SAFODA, Kinarut, Sabah, 14 February 1994. For background, see "Japan Helping in Development of the Forest Plantations," *Star* (20 September 1991), pp. 8–9; and JICA, and SAFODA, *Official Opening of the SAFODA-JICA Reafforestation Technical Development and Training Center* (Kota Kinabalu, Sabah: JICA-SAFODA, 1989).

189. Interview, senior manager, SAFODA, Kota Kinabalu, 12 February 1994; and interviews, senior officials, Sabah Reafforestation Technical Development and Training Project, from JICA and SAFODA, Kinarut, Sabah, 14 February 1994.

190. Interview, senior manager, SAFODA, Kota Kinabalu, 12 February 1994.

191. Interview, SAFODA official, Sabah Reafforestation Technical Development and Training Project, Kinarut, Sabah, 14 February 1994.

192. Plantations in Sabah are classified as agricultural enterprises and are exempt from the log export ban. Interview, Institute for Development Studies, Kota Kinabalu, 12 February 1994; and interview, senior manager, SAFODA, 12 February 1994.

193. This evaluation of the JICA-SAFODA project is not a criticism of individual researchers. I was impressed by the competence and enthusiasm of JICA-SAFODA staff in Sabah, and within their mandate, these scientists made notable strides. But these were narrow, technical solutions with little impact on the sweeping environmental and management problems facing Sabah foresters.

194. Interview, senior researcher, Forest Department, Kuching, 21 February 1994.

195. Interview, senior JICA official, Effective Wood Utilization Research Project and Timber Research and Training Center, Kuching, 21 February 1994; also see JICA and Timber Research and Technical Training Center, Sarawak Forest Department, "The Effective Wood Utilization Research Project in Sarawak, from April 1993 to March 1998," JICA and the Sarawak Forest Department, July 1993.

196. Interview, foreign correspondent, Kuala Lumpur, 7 March 1994; and interviews, WWF Malaysia, Petaling Jaya, 10 March 1994.

197. Interviews, TAS, Kota Kinabalu, 8 February 1994; Institute for Development Studies, Kota Kinabalu, 12 February 1994; and Ministry of Tourism and Environmental Development, Kota Kinabalu, 15 February 1994.

198. From the data bank of the Department of Industrial Development and Research, Sabah, Malaysia, supplied February 1994. Small foreign investments only require state approval while large ones necessitate federal permission. Of the 11 Japanese projects in Sabah, 7 were large enough to require federal endorsement.

199. Angkie, "Japanese Sceptical on Sabah"; and Joehann Angkie, "Come, Talk To Us: TAS," *Daily Express* (19 November 1993), p. 1. Before 1994, the political struggle between Prime Minister Mahathir and Chief Minister Pairin also contributed to the reluctance of investors. See "No Trade Zone Under PBS: KL," *Daily Express* (15 February 1994).

200. Interview, Sabah timber executive, Kota Kinabalu, 9 February 1994.

201. The foundation's only remaining joint venture is Sabah Softwoods, an agroforest plantation with the British company, North Borneo Timber (which holds a 40 percent share). The foundation offered to buy these shares but North Borneo Timber refused. Interview, senior executive, Yayasan Sabah [Sabah Foundation], Kota Kinabalu, 14 February 1994. For background on Sabah Softwoods, see Raymund G. S. Tan, "Tree Plantation—The Sabah Softwoods Sdn Bhd Experience," in Ti Teow Chuan, ed., *Opportunities and Incentives*, pp. 37–50.

202. Yoichi Kuroda, "Historical Overview of the Timber Trade and Forestry Development in East and Tropical Asia and the Pacific Nations," paper presented at the International Workshop for Forest and Environmental Preservation in Asia-Pacific, Seoul, South Korea, February 1994, p. 3.

203. Interview, senior official, Sarawak Timber Association (STA), Kuching, 20 February 1994; (STA represents nearly 500 private logging and timber processing companies in Sarawak. Sarawak Timber Association Brochure, Kuching, undated); and interview, senior official, Forest Department, Kuching, 17 February 1994.

204. James Ritchie, "Sarawak to Cut Log Production Within Two Years," *New Straits Times* (30 March 1992), p. 3.

205. Taiwan is the most important investor in East Malaysian wood manufacturing. Interviews, Department of Industrial Development and Research, Kota Kinabalu, 16 February 1994; and STIDC, Kuching, 17 February 1994.

206. Japanese funds and equipment helped companies log Sarawak's hill forests during the 1980s. Kuroda, "Historical Overview," p. 2. In 1987 Sarawak politician Datuk Leo Moggie claimed that "the marketing of Sarawak timber is still very much controlled by the Japanese trading houses as Sarawak timber companies are largely dependent on these trading houses for their intricate line of credit." Quoted in Nigel Dudley with Sue Stolton, *The East Asian Timber Trade and Its Environmental Implications* (Surrey, England: WWF, UK, 1994), p. 9, first quoted in Hong, *Natives of Sarawak*. For a discussion of the links between sogo shosha and unsustainable logging in Malaysia, see Jomo, "Malaysian Forests, Japanese Wood."

207. Interview, WWF Malaysia, Kota Kinabalu, 15 February 1994.

208. Interviews, senior manager, Innoprise Corporation, Kota Kinabalu, 9 February 1994; and Sabah Forestry Department (Jabatan Perhutanan Sabah), Kota Kinabalu Branch, 16 February 1994.

209. Interviews, Institute for Development Studies, Kota Kinabalu, 12 February 1994; and senior executive, Yayasan Sabah [Sabah Foundation], Kota Kinabalu, 14 February 1994. Utility companies fund tropical forest plantations and rehabilitation to "off-set" carbon dioxide emissions (utility companies discharge carbon dioxide while forests absorb it). This will presumably improve a corporation's image and perhaps reduce future "carbon-taxes." For details on the American and Dutch projects, see Michael Vatikiotis, "For Profit's Sake," *FEER* (14 April 1994), p. 68; "A Better Way to Cut Trees," *Asiaweek* (28 April 1993), p. 50; and M. Hamzah, "Down the Beautiful Green Danum," *Sabah Times* (2 February 1994), p. 4.

210. Interview, Sabah Forestry Department (Jabatan Perhutanan Sabah), Kota Kinabalu Branch, 16 February 1994.

211. Interview, senior manager, SAFODA, Kota Kinabalu, 12 February 1994.

212. To offset some of these concerns, in mid-1994 the Sabah government started drafting comprehensive investment guidelines. Interview, Institute for Development Studies, Kota Kinabalu, 12 February 1994.

213. Interview, Institute for Development Studies, Kota Kinabalu, 12 February 1994. Some Sabah students have gone to Japan to train with high-tech forestry equipment. Quite naturally, these students become more comfortable with Japanese machines, and are more likely to purchase Japanese equipment in the future. Interview, TAS, Kota Kinabalu, 8 February 1994.

214. Interview, senior Sabah timber executive, Kota Kinabalu, 9 February 1994.

215. Aden Nagrace Timor, "S'wak's First MDF Plant to Start Construction April," *Borneo Post* (20 February 1994), p.6; interview, STIDC, Kuching, 17 February 1994; and *Asian Timber* (June 1994), p. 7.

216. Interviews, senior official, Forest Department, Kuching, 17 February 1994; and senior executive, STA, Kuching, 20 February 1994.

217. See Yusuf Hadi and Abas Said, "Planting Indigenous Tree Species to Rehabilitate Degraded Forest Lands: The Bintulu Project," in Ahmad Said Sajap et al., eds., *Indigenous*

Species for Forest Plantations, proceedings of a national seminar, Faculty of Forestry, Universiti Pertanian Malaysia, Serdang, Malaysia, 23–24 April 1992, pp. 36–44.

218. Confidential interview, University of Tokyo, Tokyo, 17 May 1994.

219. Major Japanese log buyers in Sabah included Mitsui, Itochu, Nissho Iwai, Sumitomo, and Mitsubishi. Interview, SSIA, Kota Kinabalu, 16 February 1994.

220. Calculated from tables 6 and 12.

221. See table 7. Also see Sarawak Timber Industry Development Corporation (Perbadanan Kemajuan Perusahaan Kayu Sarawak) (STIDC), *Statistics of Timber and Timber Products. Sarawak 1993* (Kuching: STIDC, 1993), p. 3.

222. Raphael Pura and Steven Jones, "Sabah Log-Shipping Cartel Defeats Rivals," *AWSJ* (14 March 1989). Also see table 12.

223. Over these sixteen years, Japan imported 108.18 million cubic meters of logs from Sabah (calculated from Table 7). Sabah produced 176.26 million cubic meters and exported 155.20 million cubic meters (calculated from table 12).

224. Calculated from tables 7 and 12.

225. These data were supplied by the SSIA, February 1994.

226. In 1995 China was the main market for Sabah plywood, accounting for 42.3 percent of total exports (Japan imported 22.3 percent). Japan was the major market for sawn timber, accounting for 23.7 percent of total exports, followed by Thailand (19.0 percent) and South Korea (18.8 percent). Japan was the largest market for Sabah veneer, accounting for 47.1 percent of total veneer exports. Calculated from Malaysian Timber Council, Statistics for 1995, http://www.mtc.com.my/.

227. The 1987 and 1992 figures were supplied by the Malaysian Timber Industry Board, Kuala Lumpur, 9 March 1994 (based on data from the Statistics Department of Sabah). The 1995 figure is calculated from data from the Malaysian Timber Council, Statistics for 1995, http://www.mtc.com.my/ (conversion rate, 1.8 for sawn timber, 1.9 for veneer, and 2.3 for plywood).

228. Sarawak Timber Industry Development Corporation, *Statistics of Timber and Timber Products. Sarawak 1993*, p. 3. Also see "Loggers' Lament," p. 49.

229. See table 7.

230. Over these seven years, Japan imported 39.6 million cubic meters of logs from Sarawak (calculated from table 7). Sarawak produced 124.1 million cubic meters over this period (calculated from table 14).

231. Calculated from tables 7 and 14.

232. In 1992 log exports provided the key source of forest revenue, earning M$3.1 billion, compared to M$385 million for sawn timber, and M$255 million for veneer and plywood. Sarawak Forest Department, *Forestry in Sarawak*, p. 34.

233. Statistics for 1987 and 1992 were supplied by the Malaysian Timber Industry Board, Kuala Lumpur, 9 March 1994 (based on data from the Statistics Department of Sarawak). Also see Sarawak Timber Industry Development Corporation, *Statistics of Timber and Timber Products. Sarawak 1993*, p. 3. The 1995 figure is calculated from Malaysian Timber Council data, Statistics for 1995, http://www.mtc.com.my/. In 1995, Japan accounted for 36.7

percent of Sarawak's plywood exports, 15.2 percent of veneer exports, and 5.1 percent of sawn timber exports. In that year Japan was the main importer of Sarawak plywood, China was the largest importer of veneer (30.7 percent), and Thailand was the biggest importer of sawn timber (25.9 percent). Calculated from Malaysian Timber Council, Statistics for 1995, http://www.mtc.com.my/.

234. At an ITTC meeting in May 1993, Chief Minister Taib called for unimpeded market access to allow Sarawak to reduce timber production yet still maintain sufficient funds for sustainable management. "Taib Calls For Unimpeded Markets," *Sarawak Tribune* (13 May 1993).

235. Halinah Todd, "Japan Rubbishes Malaysian Timber," *Utusan Konsumer* (May 1989), in World Rainforest Movement and Sahabat Alam Malaysia, *The Battle for Sarawak's Forests*, p. 502.

236. Quoted in "Loggers Turn To Copters As Prices Rise," *Borneo Post* (19 November 1993).

237. For a discussion of the tense relations between Kuala Lumpur and Sabah, see Audrey R. Kahin, "Crisis on the Periphery: The Rift Between Kuala Lumpur and Sabah," *Pacific Affairs* 65 (spring 1992), pp. 30–49.

Chapter 5: Japan, Patron-Client Politics, and the Collapse of the Philippine Timber Industry

1. For a discussion of the links between logging and deforestation in the Philippines, see Kummer, *Deforestation in the Postwar Philippines*, especially, pp. 62–63, 69, and 95–100. Also see Hiroyasu Oka, "Process of Deforestation in the Philippines," in *The Current State of Japanese Forestry (VII): Its Problems and Future* (Tokyo: Japanese Forest Economic Society, 1991), pp. 93–98.

2. "Manila Fears It Cannot Protect Rich Subic Forest," *New Straits Times* (26 April 1992), p. 14.

3. Poffenberger and Stone, "Hidden Faces in the Forest," p. 204.

4. Percy E. Sajise et al., State of the Nation Reports. *Saving the Present for the Future: The State of the Environment* (Manila: Center for Integrative and Development Studies and University of the Philippines Press, 1992), p. 14; and P. Garrity, David M. Kummer, and Ernesto S. Guiang, "The Philippines," in *Sustainable Agriculture and the Environment in the Humid Tropics*, Committee on Sustainable Agriculture and the Environment in the Humid Tropics, National Research Council (Washington, D.C.: National Academy Press, 1993), p. 550.

5. The Philippines has one of the world's highest rates of soil erosion. Studies for the Philippine government estimate that soil erosion—which reduces agricultural productivity and potential hydroelectric power, and disrupts irrigation and fisheries—costs the Philippines over half a billion U.S. dollars every year. Frances F. Korten, "Questioning the Call for Environmental Loans: A Critical Examination of Forestry Lending in the Philippines," *World Development* 22, no. 7 (1994), p. 972. For more details on the environmental, economic, and social costs of deforestation in the Philippines, see Hurst, *Rainforest Politics*, pp. 165–171.

6. Benedict Kerkvliet documents the decline of traditional patron-client relations in Central Luzon in the 1950s. Benedict J. Kerkvliet, *The Huk Rebellion: A Study of Peasant Revolt in the Philippines* (Berkeley: University of California Press, 1977). For a description of changes

to traditional patron-client relations in other local areas, see the collection of essays in Benedict J. Kerkvliet and Resil B. Mojares, eds., *From Marcos to Aquino: Local Perspectives On Political Transition in the Philippines* (Quezon City: Ateneo de Manila University Press, 1991), especially Alfred W. McCoy, "The Restoration of Planter Power in La Carlota City," pp. 105–142; Cristina Blanc-Szanton, "Change and Politics in a Western Visayan Municipality," pp. 82–104; Fernando N. Zialcita, "Perspectives on Legitimacy in Ilocos Norte," pp. 266–285; James F. Eder, "Political Transition in a Palawan Farming Community," pp. 143–165; and Resil B. Mojares, "Political Change in a Rural District in Cebu Province," pp. 82–104.

7. For a discussion of traditional and modern patron-client networks in the Philippines, see K. G. Machado, "Continuity and Change in Philippine Factionalism," in Frank P. Belloni and Dennis C. Beller, eds., *Faction Politics: Political Parties and Factionalism In Comparative Perspective* (Santa Barbara, CA: ABC-Clio, 1978), pp. 193–217; Kit G. Machado, "From Traditional Faction to Machine: Changing Patterns of Political Leadership and Organization in Rural Philippines," *Journal of Asian Studies* 33, no. 4 (August 1974), pp. 523–547; Thomas C. Nowak and Kay A. Snyder, "Clientelist Politics in the Philippines: Integration or Instability?" *American Political Science Review* 68 (1974), pp. 1147–1170; and Thomas C. Nowak and Kay A. Snyder, "Urbanization and Clientelist Systems in the Philippines," *Philippine Journal of Public Administration* 14–15 (July 1970), pp. 259–275. For a critique of patron-client analysis in the context of the Philippines, see Willem Wolters, *Politics, Patronage, and Class Conflict in Central Luzon* (The Hague: Institute of Social Studies, 1983).

8. David G. Timberman, *A Changeless Land: Continuity and Change in Philippine Politics* (Armonk, NY: M. E. Sharpe, 1991), p. 17.

9. Bryan Johnson, *The Four Days of Courage* (New York: Free Press, 1987), p. 27, cited in Timberman, *A Changeless Land*, p. 16.

10. Eisenstadt and Roniger, *Patrons, Clients, and Friends*, p. 122.

11. Timberman, *A Changeless Land*, p. 17.

12. The impact of patron-client links on Filipino political and social interaction varies depending on the region, historical period, ethnic group and issue. For timber management, patron-client ties are critical. Of course, other factors—both in tandem with patron-clientelism and separately—can also have decisive effects on political and social action. For example, vertical clientelist ties do not eliminate struggles between classes. Kerkvliet persuasively argues: "The question is neither one of class awareness versus patron-client ties (as some scholars have suggested) nor one of whether people act according to class interests or according to vertical linkages. Both occur . . . often for the same individuals." Benedict J. Kerkvliet, *Everyday Politics in the Philippines: Class and Status Relations in a Central Luzon Village* (Berkeley: University of California Press, 1990), p. 244.

13. Eisenstadt and Roniger, *Patrons, Clients, and Friends*, p. 128. For background on the Philippine bureaucracy, see Raul P. De Guzman, Alex B. Brillantes, Jr., and Arturo G. Pacho, "The Bureaucracy," in Raul P. De Guzman and Mila A. Reforma, eds., *Government and Politics of the Philippines* (Singapore: Oxford University Press, 1988), pp. 180–206.

14. Hutchcroft, "Oligarchs and Cronies in the Philippine State," p. 422.

15. Eisenstadt and Roniger, *Patrons, Clients, and Friends*, p. 128.

16. Wurfel, *Filipino Politics*, p. 327.

17. Eisenstadt and Roniger, *Patrons, Clients, and Friends*, p. 129.

18. Wurfel, *Filipino Politics*, p. 96.

19. Jose V. Abueva, "Philippine Ideologies and National Development," in De Guzman and Reforma, eds., *Government and Politics*, p. 52.

20. Ibid.

21. Wurfel, *Filipino Politics*, p. 329 (quote), and p. 100 for the data. As traditional patron-client relations evolved in the 1950s and 1960s, it was increasingly common for voters to accept money from several candidates or accept money from one candidate and vote for another. This further increased election expenses. See ibid., pp. 99–100.

22. For Ilocanos, Marcos was their *apo*, or supreme patron. According to McDougald, "all his trusted generals in the military, and many of his trusted advisers, were Ilocano." Charles C. McDougald, *The Marcos File: Was He a Philippine Hero or Corrupt Tyrant?* (San Francisco: San Francisco Publishers, 1987), p. 114.

23. Wurfel, *Filipino Politics*, pp. 152–153. There are five levels of local government: regions; provinces; cities; municipalities; and barangays. In 1986, there were 42 thousand barangays. For background, see Raul P. De Guzman, Mila A. Reforma, and Elena M. Panganiban, "Local Government," in Guzman and Reforma, eds., *Government and Politics*.

24. "Japanese Envoy and Manila Legal Chief in Row Over 'Bribes' to Marcos," *Straits Times* (14 December 1991), p. 16.

25. Wurfel, *Filipino Politics*, p. 237. For a detailed description of the ties between Marcos, his family, and his followers, and the incredible extravagance and waste, see Ricardo Manapat, *Some Are Smarter Than Others: The History of Marcos' Crony Capitalism* (New York: Aletheia Publications, 1991), especially chapter 3.

26. Belinda A. Aquino, *Politics of Plunder: The Philippines Under Marcos* (Quezon City, Philippines: Great Books Trading and U.P. College of Public Administration, 1987), p. 14.

27. Manapat, *Some Are Smarter Than Others*, see chapter 4.

28. Wurfel, *Filipino Politics*, p. 137.

29. Kummer, *Deforestation in the Postwar Philippines*, p. 71.

30. Alex B. Brillantes, Jr., "The Executive," in De Guzman and Reforma, eds., *Government and Politics*, p. 125. Through loyal clients and prudent appointments, Marcos also kept firm control over the judiciary. See Froilan M. Bacungan and Alfredo Tadiar, "The Judiciary," in De Guzman and Reforma, eds., *Government and Politics*, pp. 164–179.

31. Wurfel, *Filipino Politics*, p. 144.

32. Ibid., pp. 150–151.

33. Eisenstadt and Roniger, *Patrons, Clients, and Friends*, p. 130. For background on the legislature and bureaucracy, see De Guzman, Brillantes, Jr., and Pacho, "The Bureaucracy," pp. 180–206; and Aurora C. Catilo and Proserpina D. Tapales, "The Legislature," in De Guzman and Reforma, eds., *Government and Politics*, pp. 132–163.

34. Marcos required bureaucrats to file letters of resignation, leaving everyone vulnerable to being suddenly dismissed. Brillantes, Jr., "The Executive," p. 125.

35. Of course, not all bureaucrats were absorbed by patron-client networks. Some technocrats had clear policy goals or had a combination of policy and particularistic objectives.

36. Wurfel, *Filipino Politics*, p. 257.

37. Ibid., p. 131.

38. Imelda Marcos had her own followers and in many ways had a confrontational relationship with her husband. Yet her actions still undermined President Marcos's legitimacy.

39. Hutchcroft, "Oligarchs and Cronies," pp. 445–446. Martial law was ostensibly lifted in 1981 but Marcos still maintained the same level of control. Brillantes, Jr., "The Executive," p. 126.

40. Wurfel, *Filipino Politics*, p. 274. Unlike in most of the country, the people of Ilocos Norte backed Marcos to the bitter end. To Ilocanos, he was an effective patron and therefore a legitimate ruler. See Zialcita, "Perspectives on Legitimacy in Ilocos Norte," pp. 266–285.

41. Timberman, *A Changeless Land*, p. 3; Wurfel, *Filipino Politics*, p. 326; and Hutchcroft, "Oligarchs and Cronies," pp. 447–448.

42. Wurfel, *Filipino Politics*, p. 324. Clark D. Neher and Ross Marlay argue that "President Aquino hardly made a dent in the personalistic, patrimonial system that was antithetical to democracy." Clark D. Neher and Ross Marlay, *Democracy and Development in Southeast Asia: The Winds of Change* (Boulder, CO: Westview, 1995), p. 57.

43. See Bobby Capco, "Ramos: Anti-Graft Drive Real, Plunderers to Hang," *Philippine Star* (22 January 1994), p. 1.

44. Hutchcroft, "Oligarchs and Cronies," p. 447. Post-Marcos Philippines confirms the persistence and resilience of patron-client networks. It also supports the picture of the Philippines as a clientelist state rather than a neopatrimonial one which emphasizes *one* dominant patron.

45. Kummer, *Deforestation in the Postwar Philippines*, p. 71. Kummer borrows the term "institutionalized looting" from Warden Bello, "From Dictatorship to Elite Populism: The United States and the Philippines Crisis," in Morris H. Motley, ed., *Crisis and Confrontation: Ronald Reagan's Foreign Policy* (Totowa, N.J.: Rowman and Littlefield, 1988). For a succinct description of personal and family ties among Philippine politicians, including President Ramos, see Rigoberto Tiglao, "All in the Family," *FEER* (27 April 1995), pp. 21–22. For details on members of the House of Representatives, see Eric Gutierrez, *The Ties that Bind: A Guide to Family, Business and Other Interests in the Ninth House of Representatives* (Manila: Philippine Center for Investigative Journalism, 1994).

46. Rush, *The Last Tree*, p. 33.

47. Timberman, *A Changeless Land*, p. 14. Filipino cynicism is fortified by the memory of Marcos who coated most of his actions in a constitutional veneer.

48. Ibid., p. 25.

49. Ibid., p. 22.

50. Carl H. Landé, *Leaders, Factions, and Parties: The Structure of Philippine Politics* (New Haven: Yale University Southeast Asia Studies Program, 1965), p. 80, quoted in Timberman, *A Changeless Land*, p. 22.

51. Rush, *The Last Tree*, p. 34.

52. In 1985, a Presidential Task Force claimed that three timber companies owned by Enrile—Dolores Timber, San Jose Corporation, and JJ Tirador Lumber Corporation (Cresta

Monte)—and his shipping company, Cresta Monte Shipping, were involved in log smuggling. Vitug, *Power from the Forest*, p. 29. Also see Marites Dañguilan Vitug, "Is There a Logger in the House?" in Eric Gamalinda and Sheila Coronel, eds., *Saving the Earth: The Philippine Experience*, 3rd edition (Manila: Philippine Center for Investigative Journalism, 1993), p. 68; and Criselda Yabes, "Boon or Ban?" in Gamalinda and Coronel, eds., *Saving the Earth*, p. 28. The Philippine Veterans Investment and Development Corporation (Phividec)—through its subsidiary, the Construction and Development Corporation (Phicondec)—was also involved in destructive logging and smuggling. See Vitug, *Power from the Forest*, p. 31; for Phividec's logging activities, see Ibid., pp. 30–32.

53. Lim's timber empire was impressive. He effectively controlled about 600 thousand hectares of logging concessions. Vitug, *Power from the Forest*, p. 16. Disini, who married Imelda Marcos's cousin, controlled almost 200 thousand hectares of timber in northern Luzon. James K. Boyce, *The Philippines: The Political Economy of Growth and Impoverishment in the Marcos Era* (London: MacMillan, 1993), p. 233. Vitug provides extensive details on the links between Marcos, his clients, and timber operators. I will not reiterate her work. See Vitug, *Power from the Forest*, especially, pp. 16–24, and 44. In chapter 5 (pp. 85–101), Vitug documents the extensive past and present links—both clear and tenuous—between Congress members and the timber industry.

54. Quoted in James Clad and Marites D. Vitug, "Words, Words, Everywhere and Not a Thing Is Done," *FEER* (24 November 1988), p. 52.

55. See Vitug, "Is There a Logger in the House?" pp. 62–68. In 1993, nine Congress members had significant past or present links to the timber industry. Vitug, *Power from the Forest*, p. 92.

56. Robin Broad and John Cavanagh, "Marcos's Ghost," *Amicus Journal* 11, no. 4 (fall 1989), p. 26.

57. Rush, *The Last Tree*, p. 43; Horacio Severino, "The Challenge Ahead," in Gamalinda and Coronel, eds., *Saving the Earth*, p. 9; Broad and Cavanagh, "Marcos's Ghost," p. 20; and Robin Broad with John Cavanagh, *Plundering Paradise: The Struggle for the Environment in the Philippines* (Berkeley: University of California Press, 1993), pp. 39–55. Besides Alvarez, other concession holders in Palawan in 1988 included "the wife of the provincial governor, a former governor, a member of the provincial board and former town mayor, and other members of influential families, including Alvarez's." Rush, *The Last Tree*, p. 43.

58. Broad and Cavanagh, "Marcos's Ghost," p. 20.

59. Former DENR Secretary Fulgencio Factoran stated: "The political pressure I experienced was not from a higher-up asking me to do something against my will. President Cory never intervened. It was the two houses of Congress." Quoted in Vitug, *Power from the Forest*, p. 50. Aquino once inquired about the suspension of the timber concession operated by Greenbelt Wood Products (linked to Fidel Ramos) but, according to Factoran, "she did not make me change anything." Ibid., p. 51.

60. Vitug, "Is There a Logger in the House?" pp. 60–61. Interwood has also been connected to processing under-sized logs, and inadequate reforestation.

61. Quoted in Ibid., p. 61.

62. Severino, "The Challenge Ahead," p. 10.

63. Ooi Jin-Bee, *Depletion of Forest Resources in the Philippines* (Singapore: ASEAN Economic Research Unit, Institute of Southeast Asian Studies, 1987), p. 14.

64. See table 15.

65. Johnson, "Fire in the Mother Lung," p. 34.

66. Philippine Department of Environment and Natural Resources, Forest Management Bureau, Republic of the Philippines, *1992 Philippine Forestry Statistics* (Quezon City: Republic of the Philippines, annual publication, 1993), p. xi. Also interview, College of Forestry, University of the Philippines at Los Banos, 1 February 1994; and Poffenberger and Stone, "Hidden Faces in the Forest," p. 204. There may in fact be less than 700 thousand hectares of primary dipterocarp forests. See Garrity, Kummer, and Guiang, "The Philippines," in *Sustainable Agriculture and the Environment in the Humid Tropics*, p. 592.

67. Summarized in Alan Robles, "An Ecological Crisis," in Gamalinda and Coronel, eds., *Saving the Earth*, p. 15.

68. Philippine Department of Environment and Natural Resources, *1992 Philippine Forestry Statistics*, p. xi. Rapid policy changes, coupled with a plethora of legislative proposals since 1986, make it difficult to unravel environmental and timber policies in the Philippines. This problem is aggravated by ambitious government officials and overly zealous reporters and NGO activists who distort statistics. Many articles are inconsistent, ambiguous, vague, and based on rumor and accusation rather than concrete evidence. As a result, there is substantial confusion—both inside and outside the Philippines—over current forestry data and policies. Numerous authors note this frustrating problem. For example, see Callister, *Illegal Tropical Timber Trade*, pp. 59–60.

69. Belcher and Gennino, eds. *Southeast Asia Rainforests*, p. 36.

70. Vitug, *Power from the Forest*, p. 40.

71. Korten, "Questioning the Call for Environmental Loans," p. 973.

72. See Hurst, *Rainforest Politics*, p. 188; "Philippines," (based on the work of Cesar Nuevo), in Blockhus, Dillenbeck, Sayer, and Wegge, eds., "Conserving Biological Diversity in Managed Tropical Forests," p. 69; Boyce, *The Philippines*, p. 234; and Eufresina L. Boado, "Incentive Policies and Forest Use in the Philippines," in Gillis and Repetto, eds., *Public Policies*, pp. 169–170.

73. Vitug, *Power from the Forest*, p. 14; Belcher and Gennino, eds., *Southeast Asia Rainforests*, p. 35; and Nectoux and Kuroda, *Timber from the South Seas*, p. 62.

74. Vitug, *Power from the Forest*, p. 15. For details, see ibid., pp. 13–24.

75. Nectoux and Kuroda, *Timber from the South Seas*, p. 68.

76. Vitug, *Power from the Forest*, p. 14.

77. Robles, "An Ecological Crisis," p. 18.

78. Quoted in Vitug, *Power from the Forest*, p. 28.

79. Summarized in Hurst, *Rainforest Politics*, p. 164. In the Marcos era, the Bureau of Forest Development had a reputation as the most "corrupt" government agency. Sajise et al., State of the Nation Reports. *Saving the Present for the Future*, p. 19.

80. Boyce, *The Philippines*, p. 226; and Boado, "Incentive Policies," p. 177.

81. Vitug, *Power from the Forest*, p. 36. Vitug argues that Cortes ruled the Bureau of Forest Development like a "godfather." "The powers of Cortes were enormous. He could suspend

licenses of timber concessions. He recommended export quotas of logging companies. At his disposal was 50 percent of the Ministry's budget. . . . He could assign his personnel to premier positions in Manila and take them out of the hinterlands. He dangled foreign trips and honoraria." Ibid., p. 34.

82. Vitug, *Power from the Forest*, pp. 59–60. The 1995 figure is based on DENR "List of Active Timber Licensing Agreements (as of 1 February 1995)," summarized in Human Rights Watch/Asia, *The Philippines: Human Rights and Forest Management in the 1990s* (New York: Human Rights Watch, April 1996), p. 17.

83. See tables 15 and 16.

84. "RP Losing Race to Save Forests," *Manila Times* (31 January 1994), p. A6.

85. Philippine Department of Environment and Natural Resources, *State of the Philippine Environment and Natural Resources*, Executive Summary Press Release, received by the author, February 1994, p. 9.

86. Human Rights Watch/Asia, *The Philippines: Human Rights and Forest Management in the 1990s*, p. 17. The figure on the number of industrial forest management agreements is from Priscila R. Arias, "P4.7 B for Forests," *Manila Bulletin* (13 January 1994), p. 7.

87. Garrity, Kummer, and Guiang, "The Philippines," p. 608.

88. Canceling concession licenses does not automatically improve timber management. It is also crucial for the state to protect abandoned concessions. A recent study found that many canceled concessions in the Philippines were destroyed by small-scale illegal loggers and slash-and-burn farmers. For a summary of the study, see Rudy A. Fernandez, "Total Log Ban Cannot Stop Forest Denudation," *Philippine Star* (10 January 1994), pp. 1, 5.

89. Interview, College of Forestry, University of the Philippines at Los Banos, 1 February 1994; interview, program director, DENR, Quezon City, 3 February 1994; and Belcher and Gennino, eds., *Southeast Asia Rainforests*, p. 36. In some cases—such as in Quezon—the military simply extracts logs. See Rita Villadiego, "Last Days of the Sierra Madre," in Gamalinda and Coronel, eds., *Saving the Earth*, pp. 41–47.

90. Interview, Program Director, DENR, Quezon City, 3 February 1994. For an account of the links between illegal logging and human rights abuse in the Philippines, see Human Rights Watch/Asia, *The Philippines: Human Rights and Forest Management in the 1990s*.

91. Yabes, "Boon or Ban?" p. 28. For more examples of government and military involvement in illegal logging, see Callister, *Illegal Tropical Timber Trade*, pp. 62–64.

92. Summarized in Boyce, *The Philippines*, p. 234. Also see Rhona Mahony, "Debt-for-Nature Swaps: Who Really Benefits?" *Ecologist* 22 (May/June 1992), p. 101.

93. Summarized in Callister, *Illegal Tropical Timber Trade*, p. 58.

94. Summarized in Dudley with Stolton, *The East Asian Timber Trade and Its Environmental Implications*, p. 29.

95. Summarized in "RP Losing Race to Save Forests."

96. See Vitug, *Power from the Forest*, chapter 6, pp. 103–123.

97. Ibid., p. 121. As with any complex organization, the military has both positive and negative effects on timber management. For example, while some wings of the military facilitate illegal logging, others patrol the forests and the coastline to prevent illegal logging and

smuggling. Military reserves and trainees are also replanting degraded forest areas. Aris R. Ilagan, "AFP's Environment Role," *Manila Bulletin* (20 December 1993), pp. 1, 6.

98. Vitug, *Power from the Forest*, p. 118.

99. Quoted in "PNP to Go After Loggers in Basilan," *Manila Times* (31 January 1994).

100. Quoted in Red Batario, "The Pillage of Isabela," in Gamalinda and Coronel, eds., *Saving the Earth*, pp. 37–38. For a description of links between loggers and local politicians in Isabela, see ibid., pp. 37–40.

101. Debora MacKenzie, "Uphill Battle to Save Filipino Trees," *New Scientist* (30 June 1988), p. 43.

102. Rey Arquiza, "PACC Forms Task Force to Go After Illegal Loggers," *Philippine Star* (2 January 1994), pp. 1, 5.

103. For more details, see Callister, *Illegal Tropical Timber Trade*, pp. 66–67.

104. Vitug, *Power from the Forest*, pp. 48–49. According to one report, in 1993 alone, there were around 1,800 corruption cases filed against DENR officials. "RP Losing Race to Save Forests."

105. "PNP to Go After Loggers in Basilan."

106. Quoted in Alan Robles, "Logging and Political Power," in Gamalinda and Coronel, eds., *Saving the Earth*, p. 22.

107. Batario, "The Pillage of Isabela," p. 35. Batario, a member of this undercover team, claims that loggers harassed and tried to bribe the team. After menacing threats, the team leader, Francis Altarejos, sought refuge in the United States in 1990. Ibid.

108. Ibid., p. 36.

109. Vitug, *Power from the Forest*, pp. 117–118.

110. "RP Losing Race to Save Forests."

111. According to these charges, Alcala appointed his daughter, a son-in-law, and a brother-in-law to DENR positions. Bobby Timonera, "Alcala, DENR Exec Face Graft Charges," *Philippine Inquirer* (23 October 1993), pp. 1, 11.

112. "DENR Men Seek Ouster of Alcala," *Manila Bulletin* (5 February 1994), p. 12.

113. Vitug, *Power from the Forest*, p. 67.

114. The 10 thousand hectare primary forest at the former American naval base in Subic Bay, Luzon, has been one of the best protected areas in the Philippines. But since the withdrawal of U.S. forces, it is unclear whether the Philippine state can keep illegal loggers out of this forest. "Manila Fears It Cannot Protect Rich Subic Forest."

115. Interview, Consultant to DENR and World Bank, Quezon City, 3 February 1994.

116. Robles, "Logging and Political Power," p. 24.

117. Yabes, "Boon or Ban?" p. 29.

118. Quoted in Joy Hofer, "Up in Arms in Bukidnon," in Gamalinda and Coronel, eds., *Saving the Earth*, p. 34.

119. Interview, Consultant to DENR and World Bank, Quezon City, 3 February 1994. In Isabela, to increase profits and evade forest royalties, "loggers use fake . . . invoices." Batario, "The Pillage of Isabela," p. 37.

120. This is a serious problem in Isabela. Batario, "The Pillage of Isabela," pp. 36–37. In most cases, the NPA does not directly participate in illegal logging, but some units do protect or tax illegal operations. See Vitug, *Power from the Forest*, p. 134.

121. Summarized in Boyce, *The Philippines*, p. 234.

122. Myers, *The Primary Source*, p. 109.

123. Nectoux and Kuroda, *Timber from the South Seas*, p. 72.

124. Telephone interview, Center for Investigative Journalism, Manila, 31 January 1994; and interview, College of Forestry, University of the Philippines at Los Banos, 1 February 1994.

125. Interview, program director, DENR, Quezon City, 3 February 1994.

126. Telephone interviews, Center for Investigative Journalism, Manila, 31 January 1994.

127. Nectoux and Kuroda, *Timber from the South Seas*, pp. 68–69.

128. Boado, "Incentive Policies," p. 184.

129. Quoted in Broad with Cavanagh, *Plundering Paradise*, p. 46.

130. Nectoux and Kuroda, *Timber from the South Seas*, p. 72.

131. Summarized in Rigoberto D. Tiglao, "Forest Fires," *FEER* (23 March 1989), p. 13.

132. Philippine Department of Environment and Natural Resources, *State of the Philippine Environment and Natural Resources*, p. 6.

133. Rigoberto Tiglao, "Crusader or Crook?" *FEER* (12 August 1993), p. 15.

134. Hurst, *Rainforest Politics*, p. 175; and Vitug, *Power from the Forest*, p. 35.

135. Belcher and Gennino, eds., *Southeast Asia Rainforests*, p. 37.

136. Plywood and veneer mills were particularly inefficient. Boado, "Incentive Policies," p. 195.

137. Repetto, *The Forest for the Trees?*, p. 64.

138. FAO data, in Nectoux and Kuroda, *Timber from the South Seas*, p. 115.

139. Calculated from ITTO, *Annual Review 1995*, p. 51. The ITTO forecast even lower sawnwood, plywood, and veneer production in 1995. See ibid. For background on the Philippine plywood industry, see Cheng-Tian Kuo, *Global Competitiveness and Industrial Growth in Taiwan and the Philippines* (Pittsburgh: University of Pittsburgh Press, 1995), pp. 128–164.

140. Quoted in Vitug, *Power from the Forest*, p. 189.

141. Ibid.

142. Philippine German Forest Resources Inventory Project, *Survey of Government Reforestation Projects* (Quezon City: Forest Management Bureau, Department of Environment and Natural Resources, 1988), summarized in Korten, "Questioning the Call for Environmental Loans," p. 974.

143. Dionisio S. Tolentino, Jr., Philippine National Forest Program Steering Committee Chairman, presented, "The National Forestation Program: A Review of Lessons and Experiences and Formulation of Action Plans," PENRO/CENRO Convention, Quezon City, 26 November 1992 (revised to include data as of December 1992), p. 1.

144. Philippine Department of Environment and Natural Resources, *1992 Philippine Forestry Statistics*, table 1.07, p. 26.

145. Quoted in Vitug, *Power from the Forest*, p. 61.

146. Interviews, Department of Forest Resources, University of the Philippines at Los Banos, 2 February 1994; program director, DENR, Quezon City, 3 February 1994; and DENR National Forestation Development Office, Quezon City, 3 February 1994.

147. Priscila R. Arias, "DENR Officials Suspended," *Manila Bulletin* (21 January 1994), pp. 1, 8.

148. Vitug, *Power from the Forest*, pp. 60–61.

149. For details on the new policy guidelines, see Tolentino, "The National Forestation Program," pp. 7–12.

150. Rosario N. Banzon, "Loan II for the Forestry Sector," *NFP Bulletin: The Official Newsletter of the National Program Coordinating Office* 3, no. 2 (November 1992), p. 7. The ADB's other major reforestation initiative, the First Forestry Sector Program Loan, was policy based, dispersing funds when the government met certain policy conditions. Interview, senior officer, ADB, Manila, 4 February 1994.

151. Besides improving community reforestation and protection for primary forests, DENR is also working on a new forestry code, better NGO participation, incentives for private forest managers, implementing the Master Plan For Forestry Development, improving watershed management, increasing interagency coordination, and enhancing information flows and forestry education. See Ito N. Banzon, "What Loan II Holds in Store," *NFP Bulletin: The Official Newsletter of the National Program Coordinating Office* 3, no. 2 (November 1992), p. 11; and Philippine Department of Environment and Natural Resources, National Forestation Office, *A Primer on the Community-Based Forest Management Project* (Quezon City: DENR, undated). For details on the Master Plan For Forestry Development, see Philippine Department of Environment and Natural Resources, Asian Development Bank and Finnish International Development Agency, *Caring for the Forest to Safeguard the Future: Master Plan For Forestry Development* (Pasay City: RIVELISA Publishing, August 1992).

152. Boado, "Incentive Policies," p. 174.

153. Wurfel, *Filipino Politics*, p. 200; also see Edberto M. Villegas, *Japanese Economic Presence in Southeast Asia* (Manila: IBON Philippines, Databank and Research Center, 1993), p. 59. For a critical study of Japan's economic impact in the Philippines, see Renato Constantino, *The Second Invasion: Japan in the Philippines* (Quezon City: Karrel, 1989). For a critique of Japan's corporate environmental practices in the Philippines, see Masaki Yokoyama, "Not in Our Backyard: Exporting Pollution to the Philippines," *AMPO: Japan-Asia Quarterly Review* 23, no. 3 (1992), pp. 24–27.

154. Villegas, *Japanese Economic Presence*, pp. 61–62.

155. Reginald Chua, "Philippine Uncertainties Keep Tokyo Investors on the Sidelines," *Straits Times* (18 October 1992), p. 5.

156. Meriam O. Dacara, "Hiked Japanese Aid to Manila Seen," *Times Journal* (17 December 1993), p. 1.

157. R. Ludwig, "Cable Crane Yarding, An Economical and Ecologically Suitable System for Commercial Timber Harvesting in Logged-Over Rainforests of the Philippines," Philippine-German Integrated Rainforest Management Project, PN 88.2047.4-01.100, Technical Report no. 2, 1992, p. 1; Eduardo Tadem, "Conflict Over Land-based Natural Resources in the ASEAN Countries," in Lim Teck Ghee and Mark J. Valencia, eds., *Conflict over Natural Resources in South-East Asia and the Pacific* (Singapore: United Nations University Press, 1990), p. 15; and Gillis, "The Logging Industry in Tropical Asia," p. 179.

158. Nectoux and Kuroda, *Timber from the South Seas*, pp. 62, 79, 86. Also see chapters three and four.

159. M. Suzuki, "Notes for Tropical Rainforest Log Export System Report," Tokyo, 1986, unpublished, quoted in Nectoux and Kuroda, *Timber from the South Seas*, p. 68.

160. Nectoux and Kuroda, *Timber from the South Seas*, p. 86.

161. For example, see the history of Cellophil (1972–86), a company that was part owned by Mitsubishi Rayon (6 percent), Daicel (3 percent) and Marcos's client Herminio Disini. Ibid., pp. 84–85.

162. Ibid., p. 86.

163. As well, starting in 1966, Philippine mangroves—especially from Mindanao and Palawan—were chipped and exported to Japan. Ibid., p. 80.

164. Calculated from tables 6 and 15

165. Ibid.

166. Calculated from table 6.

167. Calculated from tables 6 and 15.

168. Interview, professor, University of the Philippines at Los Banos, 1 February 1994. From 1970 to 1990, seventeen Filipino logging companies invested U.S.$279.5 million in Indonesia. For a description of Philippine investments in Indonesia's timber industry, see Vitug, *Power from the Forest*, pp. 26–28.

169. Calculated from tables 7 and 15.

170. Calculated from tables 6, 7, and 15. During these ten years, total Philippine log production was 102.6 million cubic meters (calculated from table 15).

171. See table 7.

172. Hurst, *Rainforest Politics*, p. 191.

173. See table 1.

174. Japanese Ministry of Foreign Affairs, *Japan's ODA: Annual Report 1995*, pp. 6, 102.

175. Calculated from ibid.

176. JICA, *For Our Green Earth: Outline of JICA's Cooperation in Forestry* (Tokyo: JICA, Forestry and Fisheries Development Cooperation Department, July 1993), pp. 21–26.

177. Interview, coordinator of JICA Indonesia, Jakarta, 1 March 1994. For a list of current JICA technical cooperation projects, see http://www.ific.or.jp/E-jica/.

178. Korten, "Questioning the Call for Environmental Loans," p. 973. The ENR-SECAL program has six main objectives: "a) design an integrated Protected Areas System; b) provide program support for management of ten priority protected areas; c) improve the monitoring of logging operations and enforcement of forestry laws and regulations through the provision of equipment, training and technical assistance to DENR offices . . . ; and d) develop the capacity of LGUs [local government units] and line agencies to generate community-based resource management and livelihood projects in watershed areas. . . ." Philippine Department of Environment and Natural Resources, "Highlights of the ENR-SECAL Program," *DENR Policy Bulletin* (February 1993), p. 9.

179. Frances F. Korten, "Environmental Loans: More Harm Than Good?" paper presented at the Fifth Annual Conference of the Northwest Consortium for Southeast Asian Studies, Vancouver, British Columbia, October 1992, p. 8. (A revised version of this paper was published as Korten, "Questioning the Call for Environmental Loans," pp. 971–981.)

180. Interview, senior officer, ADB, Manila, 4 February 1994. As noted earlier, building on lessons learned from this project, the ADB provided another U.S.$100 million for the Second Forestry Sector Program Loan.

181. Korten, "Questioning the Call for Environmental Loans," p. 974.

182. Ibid., p. 975.

183. Interview, College of Forestry, University of the Philippines at Los Banos, 1 February 1994.

184. Contractors mostly planted a single species—gmelina arborea. This reduced the environmental benefits of many plantations and made them more susceptible to disease and pests. Korten, "Questioning the Call for Environmental Loans," p. 976.

185. Interview, College of Forestry, University of the Philippines at Los Banos, 1 February 1994; and Sajise et al., State of the Nation Reports. *Saving the Present for the Future*, p. 19. The "disappearance" of funds is not unique to the Forestry Sector Program Loan. As noted earlier, reforestation money and contracts have become a key tool of state forestry patrons.

186. Interview, Department of Forest Resources, University of the Philippines at Los Banos, 2 February 1994.

187. Korten, "Environmental Loans," p. 24.

188. Korten, "Questioning the Call for Environmental Loans," footnote 9, p. 980.

189. In May 1993, the Philippine debt was U.S.$34.3 billion. Philippine Department of Environment and Natural Resources, *State of the Philippine Environment and Natural Resources* (Quezon City: Republic of the Philippines, received by author February 1994), p. 2.

190. Korten, "Environmental Loans," p. 30. Korten provides a persuasive critique of environmental loans.

191. For an interesting discussion of the links between international funders and reforms to the content of Philippine forest policies, see Michael Ross, "Conditionality and Logging Reform in the Tropics," in Robert O. Keohane and Marc A. Levy, *Institutions for Environmental Aid: Pitfalls and Promise* (Cambridge, MA: MIT Press, 1996), pp. 167–197, especially pp. 180–184. Michael Ross argues that Philippine reformers, with support from international funders, have been remarkably successful in restructuring logging policies since the late 1980s. As he notes, however, "the projects actually financed by the loans have had a mixed record. . . ." Ibid., p. 184. As this chapter documents, in terms of results, the policy reforms

are not yet a success. The Philippines is still struggling to prevent illegal logging, protect the remaining primary forests, monitor legal logging operations, collect timber royalties and taxes, revitalize the commercial timber industry, and effectively reforest degraded areas.

Chapter 6: Conclusion

1. Of course, the specific nature of patron-client ties differs across and within these heterogeneous states. There are, however, consistent similarities and a general pattern of interaction—what I call "modern" patron-client relations.

2. Southeast Asian governments often blur the distinction between regeneration of natural forests and development of fast-growing single-species plantations. Both are often called reforestation.

3. This section provides a snapshot of the domestic political economies of timber in Southeast Asia. For further evidence, see chapters 3, 4, and 5.

4. Prior to the late 1960s, Indonesia had little logging infrastructure. Risky investments enabled Japanese firms to secure access to Indonesia's vast primary forests. See chapter 3.

5. JATAN, *Tropical Forest Destruction and Japan's Timber Trade*, summary of the revised version of *Timber from the South Seas* (in Japanese) (WWF Report, 28 February 1994), p. 1.

6. Interviews, senior officials, Green Environmental R & D Division, Sumitomo Forestry Company, Ltd., Tokyo, 20 April 1994.

7. Other Northern MNCs have also avoided timber investments, and domestic corporations now control most of the timber operations in the Philippines, East Malaysia, and Indonesia. Gillis, "The Logging Industry in Tropical Asia," p. 179.

8. Interview, Executive Director, JPMA, Tokyo, 8 April 1994. There is of course some Japanese foreign direct investment in tropical timber operations, although considering total Japanese investment, this is quite small. For a list of some tropical timber investments by Itochu, Marubeni, Mitsubishi, Mitsui, and Nissho Iwai, see Dauvergne, *Major Asian Tropical Timber Traders*, pp. 3–5.

9. Quoted in Kathryn Graven, "Japan's Timber Consumption Draws Fire," *AWSJ* (8 February 1990).

10. In 1990, 76 percent of tropical logs were turned into plywood, 23 percent were sawn, and about 1 percent were chipped. Data from the JPMA, in Jaakko Poyry Oy, *Tropical Deforestation*, Annex V, p. v/35.

11. For background on the structural and financial role of sogo shosha, see chapter 1.

12. Correspondence, ITTO official, Yokohama, Japan, October 1995.

13. Interview, World Bank, Washington, DC, 20 September 1995.

14. This is also generally true for other multinational log traders.

15. Calculated from tables 5 and 7.

16. Japan has also increased imports from Africa. In 1990, Japan imported 126 thousand cubic meters of tropical logs from Africa; in 1995, Japan imported 531 thousand cubic metres. See table 5.

17. Calculated from tables 5 and 7.

18. In 1993, more than forty Japanese mills manufactured softwood or mixed (softwood and hardwood) plywood, accounting for 14.6 percent of total production. "Wholly or Partly Softwood Plywood is 15% of Total Plywood Production Last Year," *Japan Lumber Reports* (published by *Japan Forest Products Journal*), no. 198 (9 September 1994), p. 1.

19. Malaysian investors—especially from Sarawak—are also critical forces driving unsustainable logging in PNG and the Solomon Islands. See Dauvergne, *Major Asian Tropical Timber Traders*, pp. 32–34, and 36.

20. Calculated from data from the Malaysian Timber Council, Statistics for 1995, http://www.mtc.com.my/.

21. Calculated from table 14.

22. Calculated from table 5; ITTO, *Annual Review 1995*, p. 51; and *Forestry Review Update*, June 1996, an internal Solomon Islands government study, supplied confidentially by a senior Solomon Islands government official during a research trip by the author to the Solomon Islands, 4–14 July 1996.

23. Calculated from table 5.

24. ITTO, *Annual Review 1993–1994*, p. 57; and ITTO, *Annual Review 1995*, p. 51.

25. See table 5 and *Forestry Review Update*, June 1996.

26. The latest forest survey was finished in 1992. At this time, annual sustainable production was estimated at 325 thousand cubic meters. With heavy logging over the last three years, experts calculate that annual sustainable yield has fallen to 275 thousand cubic meters. Nicola Baird, "In a Jungle of Vested Interests," *Financial Times* (15 January 1996), p. 23. Also see *Forestry Review Update*, June 1996.

27. *Forestry Review Update*, June 1996.

28. "UNTAC Accuses Mitsui of Violating Ban on Log Exports from Cambodia," *Japan Times* (18 February 1993), p. 2.

29. Quoted in Bernard Maladina, "Japanese Group Inspects Timber Operations by Japanese Companies," *Times of Papua New Guinea* (27 June 1991), p. 3.

30. Calculated from table 4, Urano, "Commercial Exploitation," p. 71. Data are from the JLIA. For more details, see chapter 3.

31. Calculated from table 8.

32. See chapter 3, section on Apkindo and Nippindo.

33. Malaysia, however, has been increasing its share of Japan's plywood market in the last few years. See table 1.

34. Calculated from tables 1 and 5 (conversion rate is 2.3).

35. Japanese plywood processors import 92 percent of their log supply. JPMA, *Plywood Industry in Japan* (Tokyo: JPMA, April 1994), p. 5.

36. The 1994 figure is calculated from tables 3 and 4.

37. This points to a neglected area of research: the impact of environmental change and political responses in the South on economic and social change in the North. This suggests

a mutual interdependence and vulnerability of South-North resource extraction and consumption. Some authors have started to explore these issues. For an analysis of the social consequences of international timber markets on Japan, see Patricia M. Marchak, "Global Markets in Forest Products," in Peter N. Nemetz, ed., *Emerging Issues in Forest Policy* (Vancouver: University of British Columbia Press, 1992), pp. 339–369.

38. See Dauvergne, *Major Asian Tropical Timber Traders*, pp. 15–16.

39. Although import charges increase consumer prices, which presumably reduces total consumption, these charges do not lower consumption in a way that promotes sustainable management. Instead, they contribute to even greater South-North inequity, undermine Southern processors, and encourage Southern leaders to ban log exports and subsidize domestic processors.

40. See chapter 3 for further details.

41. In 1990, tropical timber producers issued a joint call on the North to adjust timber prices "so that the costs of forest management and reforestation can be considered." Quoted in Third World Network, "South-North Development Monitor," 2591 (24 April 1991), in World Rainforest Movement, *The Endangered Rainforests and the Fight for Survival*, volume 1 (Penang, Malaysia: World Rainforest Movement, 1992), p. 521. But many Southeast Asian leaders are nervous that temperate wood will substitute for more expensive tropical timber. For this reason, most Southeast Asian leaders insist that temperate and boreal timber also internalize environmental and social costs. Interviews, the Philippines, Sabah, Sarawak, Indonesia, and Peninsular Malaysia, January to March 1994.

42. Summarized in Arden-Clarke, "South-North Terms of Trade," p. 127.

43. One study of the Japanese timber market concludes: "our discussions with Japanese wood importers and users suggest that for most uses where tropical hardwood is preferred, temperate conifer products could perform as well or almost so. An overriding advantage of tropical plywood has been its lower price." Sedjo, Wiseman, Brooks, and Lyon, *Changing Timber Supply and the Japanese Market*, p. 20.

44. In volume terms, kon-pane (plywood over 12 mm thick) accounts for two-thirds of Japanese plywood production. Despite its name, however, only about half of this kon-pane is used to mold concrete. See Jaakko Poyry Oy, *Tropical Deforestation*, Annex V, pp. v/40–v/43.

45. Presumably, if consumer prices for products like kon-pane reflected environmental and social costs then Japanese builders would either find cheaper substitutes or change their construction techniques. According to Japanese industry sources in 1994, Japanese builders now use more coated kon-pane, which can be reused three to ten times. But this is still an incredibly wasteful use of tropical timber.

46. Summarized in Boyce, *The Philippines*, pp. 227–228.

47. Japanese Forestry Agency, *Forestry White Paper: Fiscal Year 1992, Summary* (Tokyo: Government of Japan, 1993), p. 2.

48. Calculated from tables 8 and 10.

49. Interview, senior official, ENR-SECAL Program, Department of Environment and Natural Resources, Quezon City, 3 February 1994. This presents a practical logjam for reformers. It is unreasonable to expect tropical timber exporters to strengthen state controls and implement sustainable policies without adequate funds. Yet it is equally unreasonable for

consumers to pay higher prices only to bolster wealthy elites and fuel patron-client networks. The world community will need innovative bilateral and multilateral mechanisms to tackle this problem.

50. Calculated from tables 7 and 15.

51. Calculated from tables 15 and 16.

52. Chapter 5 provides further evidence of the residual impact of ecological shadows.

53. Japanese Ministry of Foreign Affairs, "The Concept of Economic Cooperation—Why Do We Carry Out Official Development Assistance?" cited in Constantino, *The Second Invasion*, p. 71.

54. See chapters 3, 4, and 5.

55. At present, the EXIM Bank of Japan is not financing any logging projects in the Philippines, Malaysia, or Indonesia, although unlike the World Bank, the EXIM Bank is prepared to provide loans to tropical loggers. Interview, senior official, Environment Section, EXIM Bank of Japan, Tokyo, 11 April 1994.

56. For example, Japanese ODA funds were apparently channeled to Ramon Mitra's 1992 Philippine presidential campaign. Takashi Sadahiro, "ODA Allegedly Used in Manila Election," *Daily Yomiuri* (16 May 1994), p. 1. For details on the general problems with Japanese ODA, see chapter 1.

57. According to forest managers in Indonesia and Malaysia, environmental aid has had little impact on timber management. Based on more than fifty interviews in Sabah, Sarawak, Kuala Lumpur, and Indonesia, from late January to late March 1994.

58. See chapter 5.

59. There are no plans to increase the scope of reforestation or conservation in Southeast Asia. Interviews at Mitsubishi, Sumitomo Forestry, Marubeni, Nissho Iwai, Itochu, and Keidanren, Tokyo, April to July 1994.

60. Of course, some corporate officials are concerned, keen, and want to make a difference. Interview, professor, University of Tokyo, 17 May 1994.

61. Based on interviews at Mitsubishi Corporation, Sumitomo Forestry, Keidanren, Itochu & Company Ltd., Marubeni Corporation, and Nissho Iwai Corporation, April–June 1994, Tokyo, Japan.

62. For details, see chapter 1.

63. See table 4.

64. See table 2.

65. See table 4.

66. In Dauvergne, "A Model of Sustainable International Trade in Tropical Timber," I propose a set of interconnected trade conditions that, in theory, would promote sustainable tropical timber management. I then outline some practical options to push trade toward these optimal conditions. It would, however, still be necessary to implement reforms to increase Southern state capacity to manage forest resources.

Glossary

ADB Asian Development Bank

Apkindo Asosiasi Panel Kayu Indonesia (Indonesian Wood Panel Association)

ASEAN Association of Southeast Asian Nations

AWSJ *Asian Wall Street Journal*

Bappenas Badan Perencanaan Pembangunan Nasional (Indonesian National Development Planning Agency)

Barangays The smallest unit of local government in the Philippines

Berjaya Bersatu Rakyat Jelata Sabah (Sabah United People's Party)

BFD Philippine Bureau of Forest Development

Bhd Berhad (limited)

BN Barisan Nasional (National Front, a coalition of Malaysian political parties)

Bulog Badan Urusan Logistik (Indonesian National Logistics Board)

Bumiputera, bumiputra Indigenous person in Malaysia

CIFOR Center for International Forestry Research, in Bogor Indonesia

DAC OECD Development Assistance Committee

Datuk Malaysian title (below Tan Sri)

Datuk Amar Sarawak title

Datuk Patinggi Sarawak title

Datuk Seri Malaysian title

DENR Philippine Department of Environment and Natural Resources

DPR Dewan Perwakilan Rakyat (Indonesian House of Representatives; parliament)

EIA Environmental impact assessment

ENR-SECAL World Bank and OECF Environment and Natural Resources Sector Adjustment Loan for the Philippines

EPA Japanese Economic Planning Agency

EXIM Bank Export-Import Bank of Japan

FAO Food and Agriculture Organization

FEER *Far Eastern Economic Review*

FY Fiscal year

GATT General Agreement on Tariffs and Trade

GDP Gross domestic product

GNP Gross national product

ICETT International Center for Environmental Technology Transfer (located in Japan)

IISD International Institute for Sustainable Development (located in Canada)

INSAN Institut Analisa Sosial (Malaysia)

INTEP International Environmental Planning Agency, University of Tokyo

ITCI International Timber Corporation of Indonesia

ITTC International Tropical Timber Council

ITTO International Tropical Timber Organization

JANNI Japan NGO Network on Indonesia

JAS Japan Agricultural Standard

JICA Japan International Cooperation Agency

JLIA Japan Lumber Importers' Association

JPMA Japan Plywood Manufacturers' Association

Keidanren Japanese Federation of Economic Organizations

Kon-pane Disposable Japanese construction panels for molding concrete

MDF Medium-density fiberboard

MITI Japanese Ministry of International Trade and Industry

MNCs Multinational corporations

MPR Majelis Perwakilan Rakyat (Indonesian People's Consultative Assembly)

NFP Philippine National Forestation Program

NGO Nongovernmental organization

Nippindo A branch of Apkindo designed to import and market plywood in Japan

NPA Philippine communist New People's Army

ODA Official Development Assistance

OECD Organization for Economic Cooperation and Development

OECF Japanese Overseas Economic Cooperation Fund

PBB Parti Pesaka Bumiputera Bersatu, formerly Parti Bumiputra Bersatu (United Bumiputera Pesaka Party, the most powerful member in the current Sarawak Barisan Nasional coalition government)

PBDS Parti Bangsa Dayak Sarawak (Sarawak Dayak People's Party)

PBS Parti Bersatu Sabah (United Sabah Party)

PNG Papua New Guinea

Pribumi Indigenous Indonesian

P.T. Perusahaan Terbatas (limited liability company)

Repelita Rencana Pembangunan Lima Tahun (Indonesian five-year development plan)

RETROF Japanese Research Association for Reforestation of Tropical Forest

RITE Japanese Research Institute of Innovative Technology for the Earth

SAFODA Sabah Forestry Development Authority

SAPP Sabah Progressive Party

Sdn Bhd Sendirian Berhad (proprietary limited)

SKEPHI Sekretariat Kerjasama Pelestarian Hutan Indonesia (Indonesian NGO Network for Forest Conservation)

SNAP Sarawak National Party

Sogo shosha Japanese general trading company

SSIA Sabah Sawmilling Industries Association

STA Sarawak Timber Association

STIDC Sarawak Timber Industry Development Corporation

Tan Sri Malaysian title (below Tun)

TAS Timber Association of Sabah

TLA Philippine timber license agreement

TPI Tebang Pilih Indonesia (Indonesian selective cutting system)

TPTI Tebang Pilih Tanam Indonesia (Indonesian selective cutting and replanting system)

Tun Highest honorary Malaysian title

UMNO United Malays National Organization

UNCED United Nations Conference on Environment and Development

USAID United States Agency for International Development

USNO United Sabah National Organization

WALHI Wahana Lingkungan Hidup Indonesia (Indonesian NGO Forum for the Environment)

WWF World Wide Fund for Nature / World Wildlife Fund

Yayasan Sabah Sabah Foundation

YLBHI Yayasan Lembaga Bantuan Hukum Indonesia (Indonesian Legal Aid Foundation)

Bibliography

Abueva, Jose V. "Philippine Ideologies and National Development," in De Guzman and Reforma, eds., *Government and Politics*.

Adams, Patricia. *Odious Debts: Loose Lending, Corruption, and the Third World's Environmental Legacy*. Toronto: Earthscan Canada, 1991.

Adams, William M. *Green Development: Environment and Sustainability in the Third World*. London: Routledge, 1990.

Ahmad Said Sajap et al., eds., *Indigenous Species for Forest Plantations*. Proceedings of a national seminar, Faculty of Forestry, Universiti Pertanian Malaysia. Serdang, Malaysia, 23–24 April 1992.

Aiken, S. Robert, and Colin H. Leigh. *Vanishing Rain Forests: The Ecological Transition in Malaysia*. Oxford: Clarendon Press, 1992.

AMPO: Japan-Asia Quarterly Review 12. Special Issue on "Japanese Transnational Enterprises in Indonesia," no. 4 (1980), pp. 3–54.

Anderson, Benedict. "Old State, New Society: Indonesia's New Order in Comparative Historical Perspective." *Journal of Asian Studies* 42, no. 3 (May 1983), pp. 477–496.

Anderson, Benedict, and Audrey Kahin, eds. *Interpreting Indonesian Politics: Thirteen Contributions to the Debate*. Interim Reports Series, publication no. 62. Ithaca, NY: Cornell University, 1982.

Aquino, Belinda A. *Politics of Plunder: The Philippines Under Marcos*. Manila: Great Books Trading and U.P. College of Public Administration, 1987.

Arden-Clarke, Charles. "An Action Agenda for Trade Policy Reform to Support Sustainable Development: A United Nations Conference on Environment and Development Follow-up," in Zaelke, Orbuch, and Housman, eds., *Trade and the Environment*.

Arden-Clarke, Charles. "South-North Terms of Trade: Environmental Protection and Sustainable Development." *International Environmental Affairs* 4, no. 2 (spring 1992), pp. 122–139.

Bacungan, Froilan M., and Alfredo Tadiar. "The Judiciary," in De Guzman and Reforma, eds., *Government and Politics*.

Bagchi, Amiya Kumar. "The GATT Final Act—A Declaration of Rights of TNCs." *Third World Resurgence*, no. 46 (June 1994), pp. 26–29.

Banzon, Ito N. "What Loan II Holds in Store." *NFP Bulletin: The Official Newsletter of the National Program Coordinating Office* 3, no. 2 (November 1992), p. 11.

Banzon, Rosario N. "Loan II for the Forestry Sector." *NFP Bulletin: The Official Newsletter of the National Program Coordinating Office* 3, no. 2 (November 1992).

Barber, Charles Victor. "The State, the Environment, and Development: The Genesis and Transformation of Social Forestry Policy in New Order Indonesia." Doctoral dissertation. Berkeley: University of California, 1989.

Barber, Charles Victor, Nels C. Johnson, and Emmy Hafild. *Breaking the Logjam: Obstacles to Forest Policy Reform in Indonesia and the United States*. Washington, DC: World Resources Institute, March 1994.

Barbier, Edward B., Joanne C. Burgess, Joshua Bishop, and Bruce Aylard. *The Economics of the Tropical Timber Trade*. London: Earthscan, 1994.

Barbier, Edward B., Joanne C. Burgess, and Anil Markandya. "The Economics of Tropical Deforestation." *Ambio* 20, no. 2 (April 1991), pp. 55–58.

Barbier, Edward B., Joanne Burgess, Timothy M. Swanson, and David W. Pearce. "The Economic Linkages Between the International Trade in Tropical Timber and the Sustainable Management of Tropical Forests." *Final Report*. ITTO Activity (PCM [XI] / 4), 19 March 1993.

Batario, Red. "The Pillage of Isabela," in Gamalinda and Coronel, eds., *Saving the Earth*.

Belcher, Martha, and Angela Gennino, eds. *Southeast Asia Rainforests: A Resource Guide and Directory.* San Francisco: Rainforest Action Network, 1993.

Belloni, Frank P., and Dennis C. Beller, eds. *Faction Politics: Political Parties and Factionalism in Comparative Perspective*. Santa Barbara, CA: ABC-Clio, 1978.

Benda, Harry J. "Democracy in Indonesia," in Anderson and Kahin, eds., *Interpreting Indonesian Politics*.

Bethel, James S., ed. *World Trade in Forest Products*. Seattle: University of Washington Press, 1983.

Blaikie, Piers. *The Political Economy of Soil Erosion in Developing Countries*. London: Longman, 1985.

Blanc-Szanton, Cristina. "Change and Politics in a Western Visayan Municipality," in Kerkvliet and Mojares, eds., *From Marcos to Aquino*, pp. 82–104.

Blockhus, Jill M., Mark R. Dillenbeck, Jeffrey A. Sayer, and Per Wegge, eds. "Conserving Biological Diversity in Managed Tropical Forests." Proceedings of a workshop held at the IUCN General Assembly, Perth, Australia, 1990. Gland, Switzerland: World Conservation Union (IUCN) / ITTO, 1992.

Boado, Eufresina L. "Incentive Policies and Forest Use in the Philippines," in Gillis and Repetto, eds., *Public Policies*.

Boyce, James K. *The Philippines: The Political Economy of Growth and Impoverishment in the Marcos Era*. London: MacMillan, 1993.

Braga, Carlos Alberto Primo. "Tropical Forests and Trade Policy: The Cases of Indonesia and Brazil," in Low, ed., *International Trade*.

Brillantes, Alex B., Jr. "The Executive," in De Guzman and Reforma, eds., *Government and Politics*.

Broad, Robin, and John Cavanagh. "Marcos's Ghost." *Amicus Journal* 11, no. 1 (fall 1989), pp. 18–29.

Broad, Robin, with John Cavanagh. *Plundering Paradise: The Struggle for the Environment in the Philippines*. Berkeley: University of California Press, 1993.

Brookfield, Harold, and Yvonne Byron. "Deforestation and Timber Extraction in Borneo and Malay Peninsula." *Global Environmental Change* 1, no. 1 (December 1990), pp. 42–56.

Brookfield, Harold, and Yvonne Byron, eds. *South-East Asia's Environmental Future: The Search for Sustainability*. Tokyo: United Nations University Press/Oxford University Press, 1993.

Brookfield, Harold, Lesley Potter, and Yvonne Byron. *In Place of the Forest: Environmental and Socio-economic Transformation in Borneo and the Eastern Malay Peninsula*. Tokyo: United Nations University Press, 1995.

Brooks, William L., and Robert M. Orr, Jr. "Japan's Foreign Economic Assistance." *Asian Survey* 25, no. 3 (March 1985), pp. 322–340.

Brown, G. S. "Timber Extraction Methods in N. Borneo." *Malayan Forester* 18 (July 1955), pp. 121–132.

Bryant, Raymond L. "Political Ecology: An Emerging Research Agenda in Third-World Studies." *Political Geography* 11 (January 1992), pp. 12–36.

Budiman, Arief. "Human Rights, Foreign Aid and People to People Cooperation," in JANNI, *Reshaping "Development,"* pp. 24–31.

Callister, Debra J. *Illegal Tropical Timber Trade: Asia Pacific*. Cambridge: Traffic International, 1992.

Catilo, Aurora C., and Proserpina D. Tapales. "The Legislature," in De Guzman and Reforma, eds., *Government and Politics*.

Chai, Domingo N. P., and Yahya Awang. "Current Forest Resource Scenario in Sabah," in Ti Teow Chuan, ed., *Opportunities and Incentives*.

Chalmers, Douglas A. "Corporatism and Comparative Politics," in Wiarda, ed., *New Directions*, revised edition.

Charnovitz, Steve. "Improving Environmental and Trade Governance." *International Environmental Affairs* 7, no. 1 (winter 1995), pp. 59–91.

Cheng, Peter P. "Political Clientelism in Japan: The Case of 'S.'" *Asian Survey* 28, no. 4 (1988), pp. 471–483.

Chichilnisky, Graciela. "North-South Trade and the Global Environment." *American Economic Review* 84, no. 4 (September 1994), pp. 851–874.

Chin, John M. *The Sarawak Chinese*. Kuala Lumpur: Oxford University Press, 1981.

Choong, Elvin T., Rubini Atmawidjaja, and Suminar S. Achmadi. "The Forest Products Industry in Southeast Asia: An Emphasis on Indonesia." *Forest Products Journal* 43, no. 5 (May 1993), pp. 44–52.

Choucri, Nazli. "Multinational Corporations and the Global Environment," in Choucri, ed., *Global Accord*.

Choucri, Nazli, ed. *Global Accord: Environmental Challenges and International Responses*. Cambridge, MA: MIT Press, 1993.

Clapham, Christopher. "Clientelism and the State," in Clapham, ed., *Private Patronage.*

Clapham, Christopher, ed. *Private Patronage and Public Power: Political Clientelism in the Modern State.* London: Frances Pinter, 1982.

Cleary, Mark and Peter Eaton. *Borneo: Change and Development.* Singapore: Oxford University Press, 1992.

Colchester, Marcus. "The International Tropical Timber Organization: Kill or Cure for the Rainforests?" *Ecologist* 20 (September / October 1990), pp. 166–173.

Colchester, Marcus. *Pirates, Squatters and Poachers: The Political Ecology of Dispossession of the Native People of Sarawak.* London: Survival International, INSAN (Institut Analisa Sosial, Malaysia), 1989.

Collins, N. Mark, Jeffrey Sayer, T. C. (Timothy Charles) Whitmore, eds. *The Conservation Atlas of Tropical Forests.* (Asia and the Pacific). New York: Simon and Schuster, 1991.

Conroy, Czech, and Miles Litvinoff, eds. *The Greening of Aid: Sustainable Livelihoods in Practice.* London: Earthscan, 1988.

Constantino, Renato. *The Second Invasion: Japan in the Philippines.* Quezon City: Karrel, 1989.

Cramb, Rob. A. "Shifting Cultivation and Resource Degradation in Sarawak: Perceptions and Policies." *Review of Indonesian and Malaysian Affairs* 22, no. 1 (winter 1988), pp. 115–149.

Crouch, Harold. *The Army and Politics in Indonesia.* Revised ed. Ithaca, NY: Cornell University Press, 1988.

Crouch, Harold. "Generals and Business in Indonesia." *Pacific Affairs* 48, no. 4 (winter 1975–76), pp. 519–540.

Crouch, Harold. "Patrimonialism and Military Rule in Indonesia." *World Politics* 31, no. 4 (July 1979), pp. 571–587.

Darusman, Dudung. "The Economic Rent of Tropical Forest Utilization in Indonesia." A Paper Presented at the National Seminar on the Economic Aspect of the Forestry Business in Indonesia, the Association of Forest Concessionaires, and the Ministry of Forestry. Jakarta, 6–7 October 1992.

Dauvergne, Peter. "Japanese Trade and Deforestation in Southeast Asia," in De Koninck and Veilleux, dirs. [eds.], *L'Asie du Sud-Est face à la mondialisation.*

Dauvergne, Peter. *Major Asian Tropical Timber Traders and Overseas Corporate Investors: Current Trends.* Ottawa: Government of Canada, Department of Foreign Affairs and International Trade, November 1995.

Dauvergne, Peter. "A Model of Sustainable International Trade in Tropical Timber." Forthcoming in *International Environmental Affairs* 9, no. 1 (winter 1997).

Dauvergne, Peter. "The Politics of Deforestation in Indonesia." *Pacific Affairs* 66, no. 4 (winter 1993–94), pp. 497–518.

De Guzman, Raul P., Alex B. Brillantes, Jr., and Arturo G. Pacho. "The Bureaucracy," in Guzman and Reforma, eds., *Government and Politics.*

De Guzman, Raul P., and Mila A., Reforma, eds. *Government and Politics of the Philippines.* Singapore: Oxford University Press, 1988.

De Guzman, Raul P., Mila A., Reforma, and Elena M. Panganiban. "Local Government," in Guzman and Reforma, eds., *Government and Politics.*

De Koninck, Rodolphe and Christine Veilleux, dirs. [eds.] *L' Asie du Sud-Est face à la mondialisation: les nouveaux champs d'analyse / Southeast Asia and Globalization: New Domains of Analysis*. Québec: GÉRAC [Research and Study Group on Contemporary Southeast Asia], Université Laval, 1996.

Dean, Judith. "Trade and the Environment: A Survey of the Literature," in Low, ed., *International Trade*.

Denslow, Julie Sloan, and Christine Padoch, eds. *People of the Tropical Rain Forest*. Berkeley: University of California Press, 1988.

Devaraj Jeyakumar. "Logging Accidents in Sarawak," in Institut Analisa Sosial (Malaysia), *Logging Against the Natives of Sarawak*, pp. 31–56.

Dobson, Wendy. *Japan in East Asia: Trading and Investment Strategies*. Singapore: Institute of Southeast Asian Studies, 1993.

Doran, Christine, ed. *Indonesian Politics: A Reader*. North Queensland: James Cook University, 1987.

Dove, Michael R. "Marketing the Rainforest: 'Green' Panacea or Red Herring?" *Asia-Pacific Issues. Analysis from the East-West Center*, no. 13 (May 1994), pp. 1–8.

Down to Earth. *Pulping the Rainforest: The Rise of Indonesia's Paper and Pulp Industry.* Down to Earth, the International Campaign for Ecological Justice in Indonesia, Special Report No. 1, July 1991.

Dudley, Nigel, Jean Paul Jeanrenaud, and Francis Sullivan. *Bad Harvest? The Timber Trade and the Degradation of the World's Forests*. London: Earthscan, 1995.

Dudley, Nigel, with Sue Stolton. *The East Asian Timber Trade and Its Environmental Implications*. Surrey, England: WWF UK, 1994.

Durbin, Andrea C. "The North-South Divide." *Environment* 37 (September 1995), pp. 16–20 (continued on p. 35).

Ecologist. "Mainstream Solutions." *Ecologist* 22, no. 4 (July / August 1992), pp. 165–194.

Economic and Social Commission for Asia and the Pacific. *Transnational Corporations and the Tropical Hardwood Industry of Indonesia*. United Nations, Joint CTC / ESCAP Unit on Transnational Corporations. Working Paper No. 16. Bangkok, 1981.

Eder, James F. "Political Transition in a Palawan Farming Community," in Kerkvliet and Mojares, eds., *From Marcos to Aquino*.

Edie, Carlene J. *Democracy by Default: Dependency and Clientelism in Jamaica*. London: Lynne Rienner, 1991.

Eglin, Richard. "GATT and Environment." *Ecodecision*, no. 8 (March 1993), pp. 34–36.

Eisenstadt, Shmuel N., and René Lemarchand. "Introduction," in Eisenstadt and Lemarchand, eds., *Political Clientelism*.

Eisenstadt, Shmuel N., and René Lemarchand, eds. *Political Clientelism, Patronage and Development*. London: Sage, 1981.

Eisenstadt, Shmuel N., and Luis Roniger. *Patrons, Clients, and Friends: Interpersonal Relations and the Structure of Trust in Society.* Cambridge: Cambridge University Press, 1984.

Eisenstadt, Shmuel N., and Luis Roniger. "The Study of Patron-Client Relations and Recent Developments in Sociological Theory," in Eisenstadt and Lemarchand, eds., *Political Clientelism*.

Eli, Max. Translation by Michael Capone, Tristam Carrington-Windo, and Charles Foot. *Japan Inc.: Global Strategies of Japanese Trading Corporations*. London: McGraw-Hill, 1990.

Elliot, Chris. *Tropical Forest Conservation*. Gland, Switzerland: WWF International, 1991.

Emmerson, Donald K. "The Bureaucracy in Political Context: Weakness in Strength," in Jackson and Pye, eds., *Political Power*.

Emmerson, Donald K. "Indonesia in 1990: A Foreshadow Play." *Asian Survey* 31, no. 2 (February 1991), pp. 179–187.

Emmerson, Donald K. *Indonesia's Elite: Political Culture and Cultural Politics*. Ithaca, NY: Cornell University Press, 1976.

Emmerson, Donald K. "Understanding the New Order: Bureaucratic Pluralism in Indonesia." *Asian Survey* 23, no. 11 (November 1983), pp. 1220–1241.

Esty, Daniel C. "Beyond Rio: Trade and the Environment." *Environmental Law* 23, no. 2, (1993), pp. 387–396.

EXIM Bank of Japan. *The Export-Import Bank of Japan: Annual Report 1993*. Tokyo: EXIM Bank of Japan, 1993.

EXIM Bank of Japan. *Guide to the Export-Import Bank of Japan*. Tokyo: EXIM Bank of Japan, February 1994.

Feith, Herbert. "Political Control, Class Formation and Legitimacy in Suharto's Indonesia," in Doran, ed., *Indonesian Politics*.

Food and Agriculture Organization of the United Nations (FAO). *FAO Yearbook: Forest Products*. Rome: FAO, various years.

Food and Agriculture Organization of the United Nations. *Yearbook of Forest Products*. Rome: FAO, various years.

Forestry Review Update, June 1996, an internal Solomon Islands government study, supplied confidentially by a senior Solomon Islands government official during a research trip by the author to the Solomon Islands, 4–14 July 1996.

Forrest, Richard. "Japanese Aid and the Environment." *Ecologist* 21 (January/February 1991), pp. 24–32.

Forrest, Richard. *Japanese Economic Assistance and the Environment: The Need for Reform*. Washington, DC: National Wildlife Federation, 1989.

Forrest, Richard, and Yuta Harago. *Japan's Official Development Assistance (ODA) and Tropical Forests*. Gland, Switzerland: WWF International, 1990.

Fortes, Miguel D. "Mangroves and Seagrass Beds in East Asia: Habitats Under Stress." *Ambio* 17, no. 3 (1988), pp. 207–213.

Fox, Jonathan. "The Difficult Transition from Clientelism to Citizenship: Lessons from Mexico." *World Politics* 46, no. 2 (January 1994), pp. 151–184.

Fujisaki, Shigeaki. "Environmental Issues in Developing Countries and the Role of ODA." *Japan Review of International Affairs* 70, no. 1 (winter 1993), pp. 68–83.

Fyfe, A. J. "Forestry in Sabah." *Malayan Forester* 27 (1964), pp. 82–95.

Gale, Bruce. "Politics at the Periphery: A Study of the 1981 and 1982 Election Campaigns in Sabah," in Gale, ed., *Readings in Malaysian Politics*.

Gale, Bruce. *Politics and Public Enterprise in Malaysia*. Singapore: Eastern Universities Press, 1981.

Gale, Bruce, ed. *Readings in Malaysian Politics*. Selangor, Malaysia: Pelanduk Publications, 1986.

Gamalinda, Eric, and Sheila Coronel, eds. *Saving the Earth: The Philippine Experience*, 3rd edition. Manila: Philippine Center for Investigative Journalism, 1993.

Garrity, P., David M. Kummer, and Ernesto S. Guiang. "The Philippines," in *Sustainable Agriculture and the Environment in the Humid Tropics*. Committee on Sustainable Agriculture and the Environment in the Humid Tropics, National Research Council. Washington, DC: National Academy Press, 1993, pp. 549–623.

Gay, Robert. "Community Organization and Clientelist Politics in Contemporary Brazil: A Case Study from Suburban Rio de Janeiro." *International Journal of Urban and Regional Research* 14 (December 1990), pp. 648–666.

George, Susan. *The Debt Boomerang: How Third World Debt Harms Us All*. London: Pluto Press, 1992.

Gillis, Malcolm. "Indonesia: Public Policies, Resource Management, and the Tropical Forest," in Gillis and Repetto, eds., *Public Policies*.

Gillis, Malcolm. "The Logging Industry in Tropical Asia," in Denslow and Padoch, eds., *People of the Tropical Rain Forest*.

Gillis, Malcolm, "Malaysia: Public Policies and Tropical Forest," in Gillis and Repetto, eds., *Public Policies*.

Gillis, Malcolm. "Multinational Enterprises and Environmental and Resource Management Issues in the Indonesian Tropical Forest Sector," in Pearson, ed., *Multinational Corporations*.

Gillis, Malcolm, and Robert Repetto, eds. *Public Policies and the Misuse of Forest Resources*. Cambridge: Cambridge University Press, 1988.

Girling, John L. S. *The Bureaucratic Polity in Modernizing Societies*. Occasional Paper No. 64. Singapore: Institute of Southeast Asian Studies, 1981.

Glassburner, Bruce. "Indonesia's New Economic Policy and Its Sociopolitical Implications," in Jackson and Pye, eds., *Political Power*.

Go, Gien Tjwan. "The Chinese in Indonesia, Past and Present," in Doran, ed., *Indonesian Politics*.

Gutierrez, Eric. *The Ties that Bind: A Guide to Family, Business and Other Interests in the Ninth House of Representatives*. Manila: Philippine Center for Investigative Journalism, 1994.

Hall, Anthony. "Patron-Client Relations: Concepts and Terms," in Schmidt et al., eds., *Friends, Followers and Factions*.

Hardjono, Joan, ed. *Indonesia, Resources, Ecology, and Environment*. Singapore: Oxford University Press, 1991.

Hasan, Mohamad Bob. Keynote Address. "Prospects for Plywood into the 21st Century." *Proceedings of the World Conference on Tropical Plywood*. Jakarta: ITTO, December 1991.

Hayter, Teresa. *Exploited Earth: Britain's Aid and the Environment*. London: Earthscan, 1989.

Head, Ivan L. *On a Hinge of History: The Mutual Vulnerability of South and North*. Toronto: University of Toronto Press, 1991.

Herbig, Paul. *Marketing Japanese Style*. Westport, Connecticut: Quorum Books, 1995.

Higuchi, Yasuko, and Norio Umahashi. "The Campaign Against 3rd World Forest Resources Exploitation by Japan," in Sahabat Alam Malaysia, ed., *Forest Resources Crisis*.

Hill, Hal, ed. *Indonesia's New Order: The Dynamics of Socio-economic Transformation*. St Leonards, Australia: Allen and Unwin, 1994.

Hofer, Joy. "Up in Arms in Bukidnon," in Gamalinda and Coronel, ed., *Saving the Earth*.

Hong, Evelyne. *Natives of Sarawak: Survival in Borneo's Vanishing Forest*. Pulau Pinang, Malaysia: Institut Masyarakat, 1987.

Hudson, Stewart. "Trade, Environment and the Pursuit of Sustainable Development," in Low, ed., *International Trade*.

Hueting, Roefie, Peter Bosch, and Bart de Boer. *Methodology for the Calculation of Sustainable National Income*. Gland, Switzerland: WWF International, 1992.

Human Rights Watch/Asia. *The Philippines: Human Rights and Forest Management in the 1990s*. New York: Human Rights Watch, April 1996.

Hurst, Philip. *Rainforest Politics: Ecological Destruction in South-East Asia*. London: Zed Books, 1990.

Hutchcroft, Paul D. "Oligarchs and Cronies in the Philippine State: The Politics of Patrimonial Plunder." *World Politics* 43, no. 3 (April 1991), pp. 414–450.

ICETT (International Center for Environmental Technology Transfer). Yokkaichi, Japan: International Center for Environmental Technology Transfer, June 1993.

Imura, Hidefumi. "Japan's Environmental Balancing Act: Accomodating Sustained Development." *Asian Survey* 34, no. 4 (April 1994), pp. 355–368.

Indonesian Department of Information. *Indonesia 1990: An Official Handbook*. Jakarta: Department of Information, Republic of Indonesia, 1990.

Indonesian Ministry of Forestry. "Daftar Proyek Bantuan Luar Negeri (On-going Projects), Departemen Kehutanan (Tahun Anggaran 1993/1994), and the Evaluation of CGIF Questionnaire Proyek of On-Going Forestry Foreign Cooperation Project as of October 1993." Supplied by an official at the Indonesian Ministry of Forestry. Jakarta, 1 March 1994.

Indonesian Ministry of Forestry. *Indonesia and the Management of Its Forests*. Jakarta: Republic of Indonesia, 1992.

Indonesian Ministry of Forestry. *The Indonesian Tropical Rain Forest Conservation Areas*. Jakarta: Republic of Indonesia, 1990.

Indonesian Ministry of Forestry. *The Timber Industry in Indonesia*. Jakarta: Republic of Indonesia, 1992.

Indonesian Ministry of Forestry, directorate-general of Reforestation and Land Rehabilitation. *The Development of Industrial Forest Plantation (HTI)*. Jakarta: Republic of Indonesia, 1993.

Indonesian Ministry of Forestry and FAO. *Indonesian Tropical Forestry Action Programme: Executive Summary.* Jakarta: Republic of Indonesia and the United Nations, 1991.

Innoprise. *Innoprise Corporation Sdn Bhd: 1991*. Kota Kinabalu: Innoprise, 1992.

Inoue, Makoto. "Who's Killing the Rain Forests?" *Japan Views Quarterly* (autumn/winter 1992), pp. 12–13.

Institut Analisa Sosial (Malaysia). *Logging Against the Natives of Sarawak*. Selangor, Malaysia: INSAN (Institut Analisa Sosial), 1989.

International Institute for Sustainable Development (IISD). Main contributors, David Runnalls and Aaron Cosbey. *Trade and Sustainable Development: A Survey of the Issues and a New Research Agenda*. Winnipeg: IISD, 1992.

Inyaku, Tomoya. "A Step Forward? Debt-for-Nature Swaps." *AMPO: Japan-Asia Quarterly Review* 23, no. 3 (1992), pp. 46–49.

Islam, Shafigul, ed. *Yen for Development: Japanese Foreign Aid and the Politics of Burden-Sharing*. New York: Council on Foreign Relations Press, 1991.

ITCI (International Timber Corporation Indonesia). *PT. International Timber Corporation Indonesia*. Jakarta: ITCI, 1992.

Itochu. "Global Environment Problem and Itochu Corporation." Internal document. Tokyo: Department of Global Environment, 30 November 1993.

ITTO (International Tropical Timber Organization). *Annual Review and Assessment of the World Tropical Timber Situation: 1993–1994*. Yokohama: ITTO, 1995.

ITTO. *Annual Review and Assessment of the World Tropical Timber Situation 1995*. Yokohama, Japan: ITTO, 1996.

ITTO. "The Promotion of Sustainable Forest Management: A Case Study in Sarawak, Malaysia." Report submitted to the International Tropical Timber Council (ITTC). ITTC (VIII)/7, 7 May 1990.

Iwao, Ichlishi. "Sogo Shosha: Meeting New Challenges." *Journal of Japanese Trade and Industry* 14, no. 1 (1995), pp. 16–18.

Jaakko Poyry Oy, World Bank Commissioned Study. *Tropical Deforestation in Asia and Market for Wood*. Annex II, Wood Supply from Indonesia. Finland: Jaakko Poyry Oy, 1992.

Jaakko Poyry Oy, World Bank Commissioned Study. *Tropical Deforestation in Asia and Market for Wood*. Annex V, Tropical Wood Markets in Japan. Finland: Jaakko Poyry Oy, 1992.

Jackson, Karl D. "Bureaucratic Polity: A Theoretical Framework for the Analysis of Power and Communications in Indonesia," in Jackson and Pye, eds., *Political Power.*

Jackson, Karl D. "The Political Implications of Structure and Culture in Indonesia," in Jackson and Pye, eds., *Political Power.*

Jackson, Karl D. *Traditional Authority, Islam, and Rebellion: A Study of Indonesian Political Behavior.* Berkeley: University of California Press, 1980.

Jackson, Karl D. "Urbanization and the Rise of Patron-Client Relations: The Changing Quality of Interpersonal Communications in the Neighborhoods of Bandung and the Villages of West Java," in Jackson and Pye, eds., *Political Power.*

Jackson, Karl D., and Lucian W. Pye, eds. *Political Power and Communications in Indonesia.* Berkeley: University of California Press, 1978.

JANNI (Japan NGO Network on Indonesia). *Reshaping "Development": Indonesia-Japan Relation from Grassroots' Perspective* [sic]. Proceedings of the INGI Kanagawa Symposium. Tokyo: Japan NGO Network on Indonesia, 1993.

Japan Building Contractors' Society. "Methods to Reduce the Consumption of Plywood Forms Which Use Tropical Timber." Internal document. Tokyo, Building Contractors' Society, Board of Directors, 19 February 1992.

Japan, Government of. The Basic Environment Law. Law no. 91, 1993. Effective 19 November 1993.

Japan, Government of. "Japan's Paper for Proposed Progress Towards the Year 2000 Target." Presented at the International Tropical Timber Council, November 1991.

Japan, Government of. *National Action Plan for Agenda 21*. Internal document supplied by a MITI official. Tokyo: Government of Japan, January 1994.

Japanese Ministry of Foreign Affairs. *Japan's ODA 1993*. Tokyo: Association for Promotion of International Cooperation, 1994.

Japanese Ministry of Foreign Affairs. *Japan's ODA: Annual Report 1995*. Tokyo: Association for Promotion of International Cooperation, February 1996.

Japan Plywood Manufacturers' Association. *Plywood Industry in Japan*. Tokyo: Japan Plywood Manufacturers' Association, April 1994.

Japanese Forestry Agency. *Forestry White Paper: Fiscal Year 1992, Summary.* Tokyo: Government of Japan, 1993.

JATAN. "Asia-Pacific Forests." November 1993. Presented at the World Rainforest Movement Meeting. New Delhi, India. April 1994.

JATAN. *Tropical Forest Destruction and Japan's Timber Trade*. Summary of the revised version of *Timber from the South Seas* (in Japanese). WWF report. 28 February 1994.

Jawan, Jayum A. *The Ethnic Factor in Modern Politics: The Case of Sarawak, East Malaysia.* Occasional Paper No. 20. University of Hull: Center for Southeast Asian Studies, 1991.

JICA (Japan International Cooperation Agency). *Development Loan and Investment Program.* Tokyo: JICA, 1991.

JICA. *Environment*. Indonesia Office, Jakarta, 1993.

JICA. *For the Future of the Earth*. Tokyo: JICA, 1992.

JICA. *For Our Green Earth: Outline of JICA's Cooperation in Forestry.* Tokyo: JICA, Forestry and Fisheries Development Cooperation Department, July 1993.

JICA. *Support for Japanese Enterprises in Developing Countries: Long-Term, Low-Interest Financing System*. Tokyo, JICA, undated.

JICA, and SAFODA (Sabah Forestry Development Authority). *Official Opening of the SAFODA-JICA Reafforestation Technical Development and Training Center.* Kota Kinabalu, Sabah: JICA-SAFODA, 1989.

JICA, and Timber Research and Technical Training Center, Sarawak Forest Department. "The Effective Wood Utilization Research Project in Sarawak, from April 1993 to March 1988." JICA and the Sarawak Forest Department. July 1993.

Johnson, Peyton. "Fire in the Mother Lung." *CERES FAO* 24, no. 3 (May–June, 1992), pp. 33–37.

Johnson, Nels C., and Bruce Cabarle. *Surviving the Cut: Natural Forest Management in the Humid Tropics.* Washington, DC: World Resources Institute, 1993.

Jomo, K. S. "Logging, Politics, Business and the Indigenous People of Sarawak." Paper presented at the Fifth Annual Conference of Northeast Regional Consortium for Southeast Asian Studies, University of British Columbia, 16–18 October 1992.

Jomo, K. S. "Malaysian Forests, Japanese Wood: Japan's role in Malaysia's deforestation," in Jomo ed., *Japan and Malaysian Development.*

Jomo, K. S., ed. *Japan and Malaysian Development: In the shadow of the rising sun.* London: Routledge, 1994.

Kahin, Audrey R. "Crisis on the Periphery: The Rift Between Kuala Lumpur and Sabah." *Pacific Affairs* 65, no. 1 (spring 1992), pp. 30–49.

Kamieniecki, Sheldon, and Eliz Sanasarian. "Conducting Comparative Research on Environmental Policy." *Natural Resources Journal* 30 (spring 1990), pp. 321–339.

Kanda, Hiroshi. "A Big Lie: Japan's ODA and Environmental Policy." *AMPO: Japan-Asia Quarterly Review* 23, no. 3 (1992), pp. 42–45.

Kane, Hal. "Managing Through Prices, Managing Despite Prices," in Zaelke, Orbuch, and Housman, eds., *Trade and the Environment.*

Kano, Hiroyoshi. "The Structure of Japan-Indonesia Relations and the Relations of NGOs of Both Countries," in JANNI, *Reshaping "Development,"* pp. 5–23.

Kaufman, Robert R. "The Patron-Client Concept and Macro-Politics: Prospects and Problems." *Comparative Studies in Society and History* 16, no. 1 (June 1974), pp. 284–308.

Keidanren (Japanese Federation of Economic Organizations). *Keidanren Global Environment Charter.* Tokyo: Keidanren, April 1991.

Keidanren. "Keidanren Nature Conservation Fund Makes First Pledge to Conservation Projects." Internal document. Tokyo: Keidanren, undated, acquired by the author April 1994.

Keidanren. "Keidanren Policy and Activities for 1994." Internal document. Tentative translation. Tokyo: Keidanren, 4 January 1994.

Keidanren. *Towards Preservation of the Global Environment.* Tentative translation. Tokyo: Keidanren, 27 May 1992.

Keohane, Robert O., and Marc A. Levy. *Institutions for Environmental Aid: Pitfalls and Promise.* Cambridge, MA: MIT Press, 1996.

Kerkvliet, Benedict J. *Everyday Politics in the Philippines: Class and Status Relations in a Central Luzon Village.* Berkeley: University of California Press, 1990.

Kerkvliet, Benedict J. *The Huk Rebellion: A Study of Peasant Revolt in the Philippines.* Berkeley: University of California Press, 1977.

Kerkvliet, Benedict J., and Resil B. Mojares, eds. *From Marcos to Aquino: Local Perspectives on Political Transition in the Philippines*. Quezon City: Ateneo de Manila University Press, 1991.

Khor Kok Peng, Martin. "The Global Environment Crisis: A Third World Perspective." Briefing paper for UNCED, no. 5, 1991.

Khor Kok Peng, Martin. "North-South Relations Revisited in Light of UNCED." Briefing paper for UNCED, no. 8, 1991.

King, Dwight Y. "Indonesia's New Order as a Bureaucratic Polity, a Neopatrimonial Regime or a Bureaucratic-Authoritarian Regime: What Difference Does It Make?" in Anderson and Kahin, eds., *Interpreting Indonesian Politics*, pp. 104–116.

Kingston, Jeff. "Bolstering the New Order: Japan's ODA Relationship with Indonesia," in Koppel and Orr, eds., *Japan's Foreign Aid*.

Kitazawa, Yoko. "Japan-Indonesia Corruption." *AMPO: Japan-Asia Quarterly Review* 8, no. 1 (1976), parts I and II.

Kneen, Brewster. "The Invisible Giant: Cargill and Its Transnational Strategies." *Ecologist* 25, no. 5 (September/October 1995), pp. 195–199.

Koichi, Mera. "Problems in the Aid Program." *Japan Echo* 16, no. 1 (1989), pp. 13–18. An abridged translation of "ODA wa 'senshinkoku kurabu no sankahi' de wa nai." *Economic Today* (summer 1988), pp. 88–97.

Kojima, Kiyoshi, and Terutomo Ozawa. *Japan's General Trading Companies*. Paris: OECD, 1984.

Koppel, Bruce M. and Robert M. Orr, Jr., eds. *Japan's Foreign Aid: Power and Policy in a New Era*. Boulder, CO: Westview Press, 1993.

Korten, Frances F. "Environmental Loans: More Harm Than Good?" Paper presented at the Fifth Annual Conference of the Northwest Consortium for Southeast Asian Studies, Vancouver, British Columbia, October 1992.

Korten, Frances F. "Questioning the Call for Environmental Loans: A Critical Examination of Forestry Lending in the Philippines." *World Development* 22, no. 7 (1994), pp. 971–981.

Krause, Lawrence B., and Sueo Sekiguchi. "Japan in the World Economy," in Hugh Patrick and Henry Rosovsky, eds., *Asia's New Giant: How the Japanese Economy Works*. Washington, DC: Brookings Institution, 1976.

Kummer, David M. *Deforestation in the Postwar Philippines*. Chicago: University of Chicago Press, 1991.

Kuo, Cheng-Tian. *Global Competitiveness and Industrial Growth in Taiwan and the Philippines*. Pittsburgh: University of Pittsburgh Press, 1995.

Kuroda, Yoichi. "Commercial Exploitation of Indonesian Tropical Forests by Japan." A presentation, in JANNI, *Reshaping "Development,"* pp. 43–45.

Kuroda, Yoichi. "Historical Overview of the Timber Trade and Forestry Development in East and Tropical Asia and the Pacific Nations." Paper presented at the International Workshop for Forest and Environmental Preservation in Asia-Pacific, Seoul, South Korea, February 1994.

Kuroda, Yoichi. "The Tropical Forest Crisis and the Future Course of Japanese Society."

Research on Environmental Disruption toward Interdisciplinary Cooperation. Special edition, Global/International Environmental Problems 2, Iwanami Shoten, July 1991.

Landé, Carl H. "The Dyadic Basis of Clientelism," in Schmidt et al., eds., *Friends, Followers and Factions*.

Landé, Carl H. *Leaders, Factions, and Parties: The Structure of Philippine Politics*. New Haven: Yale University Southeast Asia Studies Program, 1965.

Leigh, Michael B. *The Rising Moon: Political Change in Sarawak*. Sydney: Sydney University Press, 1974.

Lemarchand, René. "Political Clientelism and Ethnicity in Tropical Africa: Competing Solidarities in Nation Building." *American Political Science Review* 66, no. 1 (March 1972), pp. 68–90.

Liddle, R. William. *Leadership and Culture in Indonesian Politics*. Sydney: Asian Studies Association of Australia in association with Allen and Unwin, 1996.

Lim, Teck Ghee, and Mark J. Valencia, eds. *Conflict Over Natural Resources in South-East Asia and the Pacific*. Singapore: Oxford University Press, 1990.

Lindsay, Holly. "The Indonesian Export Ban: An Estimation of Foregone Export Earnings." *Bulletin of Indonesian Economic Studies* 25, no. 2 (August 1989), pp. 111–123.

Low, Patrick. "International Trade and the Environment: An Overview," in Low, ed., *International Trade*.

Low, Patrick, ed. *International Trade and the Environment*. Washington, DC: World Bank, 1992.

Ludwig, R. "Cable Crane Yarding, An Economical and Ecologically Suitable System for Commercial Timber Harvesting in Logged-Over Rainforests of the Philippines." Philippine-German Integrated Rainforest Management Project, PN 88.2047.4-01.100, technical report no. 2, 1992.

MacAndrews, Colin. "Politics of the Environment in Indonesia." *Asian Survey* 34, no. 4 (April 1994), pp. 369–380.

MacAndrews, Colin. "The Structure of Government in Indonesia," in MacAndrews, ed. *Central Government*.

MacAndrews, Colin, ed. *Central Government and Local Development in Indonesia*. Singapore: Oxford University Press, 1986.

Machado, Kit G. "Continuity and Change in Philippine Factionalism," in Belloni and Beller, eds., *Faction Politics*.

Machado, Kit G. "From Traditional Faction to Machine: Changing Patterns of Political Leadership and Organization in Rural Philippines." *Journal of Asian Studies* 33, no. 4 (August 1974), pp. 523–547.

MacIntyre, Andrew. *Business and Politics in Indonesia*. Sydney: Allen and Unwin, 1990.

MacKerron, Conrad B. *Business in the Rain Forests: Corporations, Deforestation and Sustainability*. Washington, DC: Investor Responsibility Research Center, 1993.

MacNeill, Jim, Pieter Winsemius, and Taizo Yakushiji. *Beyond Interdependence: The Meshing of the World's Economy and the Earth's Ecology*. New York: Oxford University Press, 1991.

Mahony, Rhona. "Debt-for-Nature Swaps: Who Really Benefits?" *Ecologist* 22 (May/June 1992), pp. 97–103.

Malaysian Forester. "The Forest Resource Base, Policy and Legislation of Sabah." *Malaysian Forester* 42, no. 4 (1979), pp. 286–310.

Malaysian Forester. "The Forest Resource Base, Policy and Legislation of Sarawak." *Malaysian Forester* 42, no. 4 (1979), pp. 311–327.

Manapat, Ricardo. *Some Are Smarter Than Others: The History of Marcos' Crony Capitalism*. New York: Aletheia Publications, 1991.

Manning, Chris. "The Timber Boom with Special Reference to East Kalimantan." *Bulletin of Indonesian Economic Studies* 7, no. 3 (November 1971), pp. 30–60.

Marchak, Patricia M. "Global Markets in Forest Products," in Nemetz, ed., *Emerging Issues*.

Marshall, George. "FAO and Tropical Forestry." *Ecologist* 21 (March/April 1991), pp. 66–72.

Martens, Todd K. "Ending Tropical Deforestation: What Is the Proper Role for the World Bank?" *Harvard Environmental Law Review* 13 (1989), pp. 485–515.

Martz, John D. "Bureaucratic-Authoritarianism, Transitions to Democracy, and the Political-Culture Dimension," in Wiarda, ed., *New Directions*. Revised ed.

Marubeni. *Earth Conscious*. Tokyo: Marubeni, March 1994.

Marubeni. "Friendly to Forests and to Our Mother Planet." Internal document. Tokyo: Marubeni, undated.

Marubeni. "Guidelines on Global Environmental Issues." Internal document. Tokyo: Marubeni, 1991.

Marubeni. *Marubeni Corporation: Annual Report 1993*. Tokyo: Marubeni, 1993.

Mauzy, Diane K., and R. S. (Robert Steven) Milne. *Malaysia: Tradition, Modernity and Islam*. Boulder, CO: Westview Press, 1986.

McCoy, Alfred W. "The Restoration of Planter Power in La Carlota City," in Kerkvliet and Mojares, eds., *From Marcos to Aquino*.

McDougald, Charles C. *The Marcos File: Was He a Philippine Hero or Corrupt Tyrant?* San Francisco: San Francisco Publishers, 1987.

McGuire, G., and Bob Hering. "The Indonesian Army: Harbingers of Progress or Reactionary Predators?" in Doran, ed., *Indonesian Politics*.

McKendrick, David. "Indonesia in 1991, Growth, Privilege and Rules." *Asian Survey* 32, no. 2 (February 1992), pp. 103–110.

McVey, Ruth T. "The Beamtenstaat in Indonesia," in Anderson and Kahin, eds., *Interpreting Indonesian Politics*.

McVey, Ruth T. "The Post-Revolutionary Transformation of the Indonesian Army," Part I. *Indonesia*, no. 11 (April 1971), pp. 131–176.

Means, Gordon P. *Malaysian Politics: The Second Generation*. Singapore: Oxford University Press, 1991.

Medard, Jean-François. "The Underdeveloped State in Tropical Africa: Political Clientelism or Neo-Patrimonialism?" in Clapham, ed., *Private Patronage*.

Migdal, Joel S. "A Model of State-Society Relations," in Wiarda, ed., *New Directions*. Revised ed.

Migdal, Joel S. *Strong Societies and Weak States: State-Society Relations and State Capabilities in the Third World*. Princeton: Princeton University Press, 1988.

Miller, Alan S., and Curtis Moore. *Japan and the Global Environment*. College Park, MD: Center for Global Change, University of Maryland, 1991.

Milne, R. S. (Robert Steven). "Patrons, Clients and Ethnicity: The Case of Sarawak and Sabah in Malaysia." *Asian Survey* 13, no. 10 (October 1973), pp. 891–907.

Milne, R. S. (Robert Steven), and K. J. Ratnam. *Malaysia—New States in a New Nation: Political Development of Sarawak and Sabah*. London: Frank Cass, 1974.

Mirza, Hafiz. "The Past, Present and Future of the *Sogo Shosha*," in Howard Cox, Jeremy Clegg, and Grazia Ietto-Gillies, eds., *The Growth of Global Business*. London and New York: Routledge, 1993.

MITI (Japanese Ministry of International Trade and Industry). "Green Aid Plan." Internal document. Supplied by a MITI official, April 1994.

MITI. "The New Earth 21." Internal document. Supplied by a MITI official, April 1994.

MITI. "Voluntary Plans for the Environment." 12 October 1992. Internal document. Supplied by a MITI official, April 1994.

MITI and the Agency of Industrial Science and Technology. *New Sunshine Program*. Tokyo: New Sunshine Program Promotion Headquarters, 1993.

Mojares, Resil B. "Political Change in a Rural District in Cebu Province," in Kerkvliet and Mojares, eds., *From Marcos to Aquino*.

Moniaga, Sandra. "Status of Forest Resources in Indonesia," in JANNI, *Reshaping "Development,"* pp. 39–42.

Morita Tsuneyuki. "Environmental and Natural Resource Accounting in Japan." CIDIE (Committee on International Development Institutions on the Environment) Workshop on Environmental and Natural Resource Accounting, UNEP (United Nations Environment Programme) Headquarters, Nairobi, 1992.

Mukonoweshuro, Eliphas. "Ethnicity, Class and Clientelism in Sierra Leone Politics: A Methodological Critique." *Plural Societies* 20 (September 1990), pp. 65–91.

Murtedza Mohamed, and Ti Teow Chuan. "Effects of Deforestation: With Special Reference to East Malaysia." *Borneo Review* 2, no. 2 (December 1991), pp. 122–141.

Myers, Norman. *The Primary Source: Tropical Forests and Our Future* (updated for the 1990s). New York: W. W. Norton, 1992.

Nakamura, Yoichi. "The Ecobusiness Logic." *AMPO: Japan-Asia Quarterly Review* 23, no. 3 (1992), pp. 55–57.

Nastan, Kadir Mohd. "A Note on Logging Methods Used by a Large Timber Company on the East Coast of Sabah." *Malayan Forester* 29, no. 4 (1966), pp. 303–306.

Nectoux, François, and Yoichi Kuroda. *Timber from the South Seas: An Analysis of Japan's Tropical Environmental Impact*. Gland, Switzerland: World Wildlife Fund International, 1989.

Neher, Clark D., and Ross Marlay, *Democracy and Development in Southeast Asia: The Winds of Change*. Boulder, CO: Westview, 1995.

Nemetz, Peter N., ed. *Emerging Issues in Forest Policy.* Vancouver: University of British Columbia Press, 1992.

NGONET. Computer database of the Alternative Conference at UNCED, Rio de Janerio, 1992.

Nissho-Iwai. "Environment 21: Nissho-Iwai Corp." Internal document. Tokyo: Environmental 21 Division, Nissho-Iwai, 12 February 1991.

Nowak, Thomas C., and Kay A. Snyder. "Urbanization and Clientelist Systems in the Philippines." *Philippine Journal of Public Administration* 14–15 (July 1970), pp. 259–275.

Nowak, Thomas C., and Kay A. Snyder. "Clientelist Politics in the Philippines: Integration or Instability?" *American Political Science Review* 68 (1974), pp. 1147–1170.

OECF (Japanese Overseas Economic Cooperation Fund). *OECF Annual Report 1993*. Tokyo: OECF, 1993.

OECF. *OECF and the Environment*. Tokyo: OECF, 1993.

OECF. *OECF Environmental Guidelines*. Tokyo: OECF, 1989.

Oi, Jean C. "Communism and Clientelism: Rural Politics in China." *World Politics* 37, no. 2 (January, 1985), pp. 238–266.

Oka, Hiroyasu. "Process of Deforestation in the Philippines," in *The Current State of Japanese Forestry (VII): Its Problems and Future*. Tokyo: Japanese Forest Economic Society, 1991, pp. 93–98.

Ooi, Jin-Bee. *Depletion of Forest Resources in the Philippines*. Singapore: ASEAN Economic Research Unit, Institute of Southeast Asian Studies, 1987.

Orr, Robert M., Jr. *The Emergence of Japan's Foreign Aid Power.* New York: Columbia University Press, 1990.

Orr, Robert M., Jr. "The Rising Sun: Japan's Foreign Aid to ASEAN, the Pacific Basin and the Republic of Korea." *Journal of International Affairs* 41 (1987/88), pp. 39–62.

Orr, Robert M., Jr., and Bruce M. Koppel. "A Donor of Consequence: Japan as a Foreign Aid Power," in Koppel and Orr, eds., *Japan's Foreign Aid*.

Padoch, Christine, and Nancy L. Peluso, eds. *Borneo in Transition: People, Forests, Conservation and Development* (Selangor, Malaysia: Oxford University Press, 1995).

Panglaykim, J. *Indonesia's Economic and Business Relations with ASEAN and Japan*. Jakarta: Center for Strategic and International Studies, 1977.

Pante, Filologo, Jr., and Romeo A. Reyes. "Japanese and U.S. Aid to the Philippines: A Recipient Country Perspective," in Islam, ed., *Yen for Development*.

Papanek, Gustav F., ed. *The Indonesian Economy.* New York: Praeger Publishers, 1980.

Parikh, Jyoti, and Kirit Parikh. "Consumption Patterns: The Driving Force of Environmental Stress." Bombay, Indira Gandhi Institute of Development Research, 1991, in NGONET 0795.

Pearson, Charles S. "The Trade and Environment Nexus: What Is New Since '72?" in Zaelke, Orbuch, and Housman, eds., *Trade and the Environment*.

Pearson, Charles S., ed. *Multinational Corporations, Environment, and the Third World: Business Matters*. Durham, NC: Duke University Press, 1987.

Peluso, Nancy Lee. *The Impact of Social and Environmental Change on Forest Management: A Case Study from West Kalimantan, Indonesia*. Community Forestry Case Study Series, no. 8. United Nations: FAO, 1995.

Peluso, Nancy Lee. "The Political Ecology of Extraction and Extractive Reserves in East Kalimantan, Indonesia," *Development and Change* 23, no. 4 (October 1992), pp. 49–74.

Peluso, Nancy Lee. *Rich Forests, Poor People: Resource Control and Resistance in Java*. Berkeley: University of California Press, 1992.

Peluso, Nancy Lee, Peter Vandergeest, and Lesley Potter. "Social Aspects of Forestry in Southeast Asia: A Review of Postwar Trends in the Scholarly Literature." *Journal of Southeast Asian Studies* 26, no. 1 (March 1995), pp. 196–218.

Philippine Department of Environment and Natural Resources (DENR). "Highlights of the ENR-SECAL Program." *DENR Policy Bulletin* (February 1993), pp. 9–11.

Philippine Department of Environment and Natural Resources. *The Philippine Natural Resources Accounting Project: Executive Summary.* Quezon City: Department of Environment and Natural Resources, 1991.

Philippine Department of Environment and Natural Resources. *State of the Philippine Environment and Natural Resources*. Executive summary press release, received by author February 1994.

Philippine Department of Environment and Natural Resources. *State of the Philippine Environment and Natural Resources*. Quezon City: Republic of the Philippines, received by author February 1994.

Philippine Department of Environment and Natural Resources. Forest Management Bureau. *1992 Philippine Forestry Statistics*. Quezon City: Republic of the Philippines, annual publication, 1993.

Philippine Department of Environment and Natural Resources. National Forestation Office. *A Primer on the Community-Based Forest Management Project*. Quezon City: DENR, undated.

Philippine Department of Environment and Natural Resources, Asian Development Bank, and Finnish International Development Agency. *Caring for the Forest to Safeguard the Future: Master Plan for Forestry Development*. Pasay City: RIVELISA Publishing House, August 1992.

Poffenberger, Mark. "Facilitating Change in Forest Bureaucracies," in Poffenberger, ed., *Keepers of the Forest*.

Poffenberger, Mark, ed. *Keepers of the Forest: Land Management Alternatives in Southeast Asia*. Hartford: Kumarian Press, 1990.

Poffenberger, Mark, and Roger D. Stone. "Hidden Faces in the Forest: A 21st Century Challenge for Tropical Asia." *Sais Review* 16, no. 1 (winter 1996), pp. 203–219.

Poore, Duncan. "The Sustainable Management of Natural Forest: the Issues," in Poore, ed., *No Timber Without Trees*.

Poore, Duncan, ed. *No Timber Without Trees: Sustainability in the Tropical Forest*. A study for ITTO. London: Earthscan, 1989.

Porter, Gareth. "The Environmental Hazards of Asia Pacific Development: The Southeast Asian Rainforests." *Current History* 93, no. 587 (December 1994), pp. 430–434.

Porter, Gareth, and Janet Welsh Brown. *Global Environmental Politics*. Boulder, CO: Westview Press, 1991.

Potter, David. "Assessing Japan's Environmental Aid Policy." *Pacific Affairs* 67, no. 2 (summer 1994), pp. 200–215.

Potter, Lesley. "Environmental and Social Aspects of Timber Exploitation in Kalimantan, 1967–1989," in Hardjono, ed., *Indonesia, Resources, Ecology, and Environment*.

Potter, Lesley. "The Onslaught on the Forests in South-East Asia," in Brookfield and Byron, eds., *South-East Asia's Environmental Future*.

Powell, John Duncan. "Peasant Society and Clientelist Politics." *American Political Science Review* 64 (June 1970), pp. 411–426.

Putra, Heddy Shri Ahimsa. "The Politics of Agrarian Change and Clientelism in Indonesia: Bantaeng, South Sulawesi, 1883 to 1990." Doctoral dissertation. New York: Columbia University, 1993.

Rajeswary, I. "Profits vs. Preservation," in *Dwindling Forests: Diminishing Returns*. New York: UNDP (United Nations Development Programme), 1991.

Rath, Amitav, and Brent Herbert-Copley. *Green Technologies for Development: Transfer, Trade and Cooperation*. Ottawa: International Development Research Center [IDRC], 1993.

Redclift, Michael. *Sustainable Development: Exploring the Contradictions*. London: Methuen, 1987.

Reeve, David. *Golkar of Indonesia: An Alternative to the Party System*. Singapore: Oxford University Press, 1985.

Repetto, Robert. *The Forest for the Trees? Government Policies and the Misuse of Forest Resources*. Washington, DC: World Resources Institute, 1988.

Repetto, Robert. "Overview," in Gillis and Repetto, eds., *Public Policies*.

Repetto, Robert. *Promoting Environmentally Sound Economic Progress: What the North Can Do*. Washington, DC: World Resources Institute, 1990.

RETROF (Research Association For Reforestation of Tropical Forest). "Research Association for Reforestation of Tropical Forest." Internal document. Tokyo: RETROF, October 1991.

Riggs, Fred W. *Thailand: The Modernization of a Bureaucratic Polity*. Honolulu: East-West Center Press, 1966.

Ritchie, James. *A Political Saga: Sarawak 1981–1993*. Singapore: Summer Times, 1993.

RITE (Research Institute of Innovative Technology for the Earth). *RITE*. Tokyo: RITE, March 1992.

Rix, Alan. *Japan's Foreign Aid Challenge: Policy Reform and Aid Leadership*. London: Routledge, 1993.

Rix, Alan. "Managing Japan's Aid: ASEAN," in Koppel and Orr, eds., *Japan's Foreign Aid*, pp. 19–40.

Robison, Richard. *Indonesia: The Rise of Capital*. Sydney and London: Allen and Unwin, 1986.

Robison, Richard. "The middle class and the bourgeoisie in Indonesia," in Robison and Goodman, eds. *The New Rich in Asia*.

Robison, Richard. "Toward a Class Analysis of the Indonesian Military Bureaucratic State." *Indonesia*, no. 25 (April 1978), pp. 17–39.

Robison, Richard, and David S. G. Goodman, eds. *The New Rich in Asia: Mobile phones, McDonald's and middle-class revolution*. Routledge: London and New York, 1996.

Robles, Alan. "An Ecological Crisis," in Gamalinda and Coronel, eds., *Saving the Earth*.

Robles, Alan. "Logging and Political Power," in Gamalinda and Coronel, eds., *Saving the Earth*.

Roniger, Luis. *Hierarchy and Trust in Modern Mexico and Brazil*. New York: Praeger, 1990.

Roniger, Luis, and Ayse Gunes-Ayata, eds. *Democracy, Clientelism and Civil Society*. Boulder, CO: Lynne Rienner, 1994.

Ross, Michael. "Conditionality and Logging Reform in the Tropics," in Keohane and Levy, eds., *Institutions for Environmental Aid*.

Roy, Bunker. "Population or Over-Consumption: Which Is Destroying the World?" India, 1992, in NGONET 1251.

Rush, James. *The Last Tree: Reclaiming the Environment in Tropical Asia*. New York: Asia Society, 1991.

Sabah Forestry Department. *Forestry in Sabah*. Sandakan: Sabah Forestry Department, 1989.

Sabah Forestry Department. *Goals*. Sandakan: Sabah State Government, undated.

Sahabat Alam Malaysia, ed. *Forest Resources Crisis in the Third World*. Proceedings of the conference, "Forest Resources Crisis in the Third World," 6–8 September 1986. Sahabat Alam Malaysia, 1987.

Sajise, Percy E. et al. State of the Nation Reports. *Saving the Present for the Future: The State of the Environment*. Manila: Center for Integrative and Development Studies and University of the Philippines Press, 1992.

Sarawak Forest Department. *Forestry in Sarawak, Malaysia*. Kuching: Sarawak Forest Department, 1993.

Sarawak Study Group. "Logging in Sarawak: The Belaga Experience," in Institut Analisa Sosial (Malaysia), *Logging Against the Natives of Sarawak*, pp. 1–30.

Sarawak Timber Industry Development Corporation (Perbadanan Kemajuan Perusahaan Kayu Sarawak), (STIDC). *Statistics of Timber and Timber Products. Sarawak 1993*. Kuching: STIDC, 1993.

Schmidt, Steffen W., Laura Guasti, Carl H. Landé, and James C. Scott., eds. *Friends, Followers, and Factions: A Reader in Political Clientelism*. Berkeley: University of California Press, 1977.

Schwarz, Adam. *A Nation in Waiting: Indonesia in the 1990s*. St Leonards, NSW, Australia: Allen and Unwin, 1994.

Scott, James C. "Patron-Client Politics and Political Change in Southeast Asia." *American Political Science Review* 66, no. 1 (March 1972), pp. 91–113.

Searle, Peter. *Politics in Sarawak 1970–76: The Iban Perspective*. Singapore: Oxford University Press, 1983.

Sedjo, Roger A., A. Clark Wiseman, David J. Brooks, and Kenneth S. Lyon. *Changing Timber Supply and the Japanese Market*. Discussion paper 94–25. Washington, DC: Resources for the Future, 1994.

Sesser, Stan. "A Reporter at Large: Logging the Rain Forest." *New Yorker* (27 May 1991), pp. 42–67.

Severino, Horacio. "The Challenge Ahead," in Gamalinda and Coronel, eds., *Saving the Earth*.

Shao, Alan T., and Paul Herbig. "The Future of Sogo Shosha in a Global Economy." *International Marketing Review* 10, no. 5 (1993), pp. 37–55.

Sizer, Nigel, and Richard Rice. *Backs to the Wall in Suriname: Forest Policy in a Country in Crisis*. Washington, DC: World Resources Institute, 1995.

SKEPHI (Indonesian NGO Network of Tropical Forest Conservation). *Forest Fire Profile in Indonesia*. Jakarta: SKEPHI, 1992.

SKEPHI. *Forest Management Is Inefficient*. Position paper for the Austria Parliament. Jakarta: SKEPHI, 1993.

SKEPHI. *Forest Problem in Indonesia Issues and Solution*. Jakarta: SKEPHI, 1989.

SKEPHI. *Selling Our Common Heritage: Commercialization of Indonesian Forest*. Jakarta: SKEPHI, 1990.

SKEPHI. *Setiakawan: A Call for International Solidarity on Indonesian Tropical Forest Issues*, nos. 4–5 (January–June 1990); no. 7 (January–June 1992); no. 8 (July–September 1992); no. 10 (January–June 1993); no. 11 (July–September 1993).

SKEPHI. *Setiakawan: A Call for International Solidarity on Indonesian Tropical Forest Issues*. A Special Edition on Japan's Role in the Timber Industry. No. 3, November–December 1989.

Smith, Theodore M. "Corruption, Tradition, and Change." *Indonesia*, no. 11 (April 1971), pp. 25–26.

Smythies, B. E. "History of Forestry in Sarawak." *Malayan Forester* 25–26 (1962 63), pp. 232–253.

Soesastro, Hadi. *Japan's ODA and Indonesia: Resource Security Aid?* Jakarta: Center for Strategic and International Studies, 1991.

Soetrisno, Loekman. "Patron-Client Relationships." *Review Indonesia*, no. 98 (26 February 1994), p. 18.

Starke, Linda. *Signs of Hope: Working Towards Our Common Future*. Oxford: Oxford University Press, 1990.

Stone, Roger D., and Eve Hamilton. *Global Economics and the Environment*. New York: Council on Foreign Relations Press, 1991.

Sulaiman, Rahim. "Forest Plantation in Sabah—Development Issues." *Berita Hutan* (September 1993), pp. 14–17.

Sumitomo Forestry. *Sumitomo Forestry: Annual Report 1993*. Tokyo: Sumitomo Forestry, 1993.

Sumitomo Forestry. "Tropical Rain Forest Regeneration Project Gets Under Way in Indonesia." *Greengraph: Sumitomo Forestry Newsletter* 1 (March 1992), pp. 1–2.

Sumitomo Forestry, Ministry of Forestry (Republic of Indonesia), P.T. Kutai Timber Indonesia, and the University of Tokyo. *Research Report on the Sebulu Experimental Forest: 1992*. July 1993.

Sundhaussen, Ulf. "The Military: Structure, Procedures, and Effects on Indonesian Society," in Jackson and Pye, eds., *Political Power*.

Suryadinata, Leo. *Military Ascendancy and Political Culture: A Study of Indonesia's Golkar*. Athens, OH: Ohio University Center for International Studies, 1989.

Tadem, Eduardo. "Conflict Over Land-based Natural Resources in the ASEAN Countries," in Lim Teck Ghee and Valencia, eds., *Conflict over Natural Resources*.

Takahashi, Akira. "From Reparations to Katagawari: Japan's ODA to the Philippines," in Koppel and Orr, eds., *Japan's Foreign Aid*.

Takeuchi, Kenji. "Market Prospects for Tropical Hardwoods from Southeast Asia," in Bethel, *World Trade in Forest Products*.

Tan, Raymund G. S. "Tree Plantation—The Sabah Softwoods Sdn Bhd Experience," in Ti Teow Chuan, ed., *Opportunities and Incentives*.

Taylor, D. M., D. Hortin, M. J. G. Parnell, and T. K. Marsden. "The Degradation of Rainforests in Sarawak, East Malaysia, and Its Implications for Future Management Policies." *Geoforum* 25, no. 3 (1994), pp. 351–369.

Ti Teow Chuan, ed. *Opportunities and Incentives for Wood Processing in Sabah*. Proceedings of a seminar organized by the Timber Association of Sabah held at Kota Kinabalu, 22–23 August 1989. Kota Kinabalu: Timber Association of Sabah, 1989.

Timberman, David G. *A Changeless Land: Continuity and Change in Philippine Politics*. Armonk, NY: M. E. Sharpe, 1991.

Tolentino, Dionisio S., Jr. Philippine National Forest Program Steering Committee chairman. Presented "The National Forestation Program: A Review of Lessons and Experiences and Formulation of Action Plans." PENRO / CENRO Convention, Quezon City, 26 November 1992 (revised to include data as of December 1992), pp. 1–12.

Trisoglio, Alex, and Kerry ten Tate. "Systemic Integration of the Environment and Trade," *Ecodecision*, no. 8 (March 1993), pp. 23–28.

Tsurumi, Yoshi. "Japanese Investments in Indonesia: Ownership, Technology Transfer, and Political Conflict," in Papanek, ed., *The Indonesian Economy*.

Urano, Mariko. "Commercial Exploitation of Indonesian Tropical Forests by Japan," in JANNI, *Reshaping "Development."*

Utrecht, Ernst. *The Indonesian Army: A Socio-Political Study of an Armed, Privileged Group in the Developing Countries*. Townsville: James Cook University, 1980.

Utrecht, Ernst. "Indonesia's Foreign Private Corporate System, Past and Present," in Doran, ed., *Indonesian Politics*.

Vatikiotis, Michael R. J. *Indonesian Politics Under Suharto: Order, Development and Pressure for Change*. London: Routledge, 1993.

Villadiego, Rita. "Last Days of the Sierra Madre," in Gamalinda and Coronel, eds., *Saving the Earth*.

Villegas, Emberto M. *Japanese Economic Presence in Southeast Asia*. Manila: IBON Philippines, Databank and Research Center, 1993.

Vitug, Marites Dañguilan. "Is There a Logger in the House?" in Gamalinda and Coronel, eds., *Saving the Earth*.

Vitug, Marites Dañguilan. *Power from the Forest: The Politics of Logging*. Manila: Philippine Center for Investigative Journalism, 1993.

WALHI (Indonesian Forum for the Environment) and YLBHI (Indonesian Legal Aid Foundation). *Mistaking Plantations for the Indonesia's Tropical Forest* [sic]. Jakarta: Wahana Lingkungan Hidup Indonesia (WALHI), 1992.

Ward, R. Gerald, and Elizabeth Kingdon, eds. *Land, Custom and Practice in the South Pacific*. Cambridge: Cambridge University Press, 1995.

Waterbury, John. "Clientelism Revisited." *Government and Opposition* 14, no. 2 (1979), pp. 217–228.

Wathen, Tom. "A Guide to Trade and the Environment," in Zaelke, Orbuch, and Housman, eds., *Trade and the Environment*.

Wellner, Pamela. "A Pipeline Killing Field: Exploitation of Burma's Natural Gas." *Ecologist* 24, no. 5 (September/October 1994), pp. 189–193.

Wiarda, Howard J. "Toward the Future: Old and New Directions in Comparative Politics," in Wiarda, eds., *New Directions*. Revised ed.

Wiarda, Howard J., ed. *New Directions in Comparative Politics*. Revised ed. Boulder, CO: Westview Press, 1991.

Wolters, Willem. *Politics, Patronage, and Class Conflict in Central Luzon*. The Hague: Institute of Social Studies, 1983.

Wood, William B. "Tropical Deforestation: Balancing Regional Development Demands and Global Environmental Concerns." *Global Environmental Change* 1, no. 1 (December 1990), pp. 23–41.

Wood, William B. "Two Boom Cities In The Resource Frontier: An Indonesian Case Study." *Asian Geographer* 5, no. 1 (1986), pp. 25–41.

World Commission on Environment and Development. *Our Common Future*. Oxford: Oxford University Press, 1987.

World Rainforest Movement. *The Endangered Rainforests and the Fight for Survival*. Volume 1. Penang, Malaysia: World Rainforest Movement, 1992.

World Rainforest Movement and Sahabat Alam Malaysia. *The Battle for Sarawak's Forests*. 2nd ed. Penang, Malaysia: World Rainforest Movement and Sahabat Alam Malaysia, 1990.

Wurfel, David. *Filipino Politics: Development and Decay.* Quezon City: Ateneo de Manila University Press (also published by Cornell University Press), 1988.

Yaacob, Salahudin, Isabelle Louis, Geoffrey Davison, Mohd Nizam Basiron, and Sabri Zain (Malaysian FSC Consultative Study Working Group). *Forest Stewardship Council (FSC) Malaysian Consultative Study.* Selangor Malaysia: WWF Malaysia, August 1993.

Yabes, Criselda. "Boon or Ban?" in Gamalinda and Coronel, eds., *Saving the Earth.*

Yanagihara, Toru, and Anne Emig. "An Overview of Japan's Foreign Aid," in Islam, ed., *Yen for Development.*

Yayasan Sabah (Sabah Foundation). *Yayasan Sabah: 1966–1991.* Kota Kinabalu: Yayasan Sabah, 1992.

Yayasan Sabah. *Yayasan Sabah and Innoprise Corporation Sdn Bhd.* Kota Kinabalu: Yayasan Sabah, 1993.

Yokoyama, Masaki. "Not in Our Backyard: Exporting Pollution to the Philippines." *AMPO: Japan-Asia Quarterly Review* 23, no. 3 (1992), pp. 24–27.

Yoshino, Michael Y., and Thomas B. Lifson. *The Invisible Link: Japan's* Sogo Shosha *and the Organization of Trade.* Cambridge, MA: MIT Press, 1986.

Young, Alexander K. *The Sogo Shosha: Japan's Multinational Trading Companies.* Boulder, CO: Westview Press, 1979.

Yu Loon Ching. *Sarawak. The Plot That Failed 10 March 87–17 April 87.* Singapore: Summer Times, 1987.

Yusuf Hadi, and Abas Said. "Planting Indigenous Tree Species to Rehabilitate Degraded Forest Lands: The Bintulu Project," in Ahmad Said Sajap et al., eds., *Indigenous Species for Forest Plantations.*

Zaelke, Durwood, Paul Orbuch, and Robert F. Housman, eds. *Trade and the Environment: Law, Economics and Policy.* Washington, DC: Island Press, 1993.

Zerner, Charles. *Legal Options for the Indonesian Forestry Sector.* Jakarta: Ministry of Forestry, Government of Indonesia, and FAO. Indonesia UTF/INS/065/INS, Forestry Field Studies Field Document, no. VI-4, 1990.

Zialcita, Fernando N. "Perspectives on Legitimacy in Ilocos Norte," in Kerkvliet and Mojares, eds., *From Marcos to Aquino.*

Newspapers and Magazines Cited

Aliran

Ambio

Asahi Shimbun

Asian Timber

Asian Wall Street Journal

Asiaweek

Australian

Borneo Post

Business Times

Daily Express

Daily Yomiuri

Economic and Business Review Indonesia

Economist

Far Eastern Economic Review

Financial Times

Fortune

Globe and Mail

Guardian

Indonesian Business Weekly

INTEP Newsletter (International Environmental Planning Center, University of Tokyo)

International Herald Tribune

Jakarta Post

Japan Lumber Reports

Japan Times

Japan Update

Jiji Press Newswire

Manila Bulletin

Manila Times

New Scientist

New Straits Times

New York Times

New York Times International

Peoples Mirror

Philippine Inquirer

Philippine Star

Reuter News Service

Sabah Times

Sarawak Tribune

Star

Straits Times

Times Journal

Times of Papua New Guinea

Tokyo Business Today

Utusan Konsumer

Vancouver Sun

Interviews

From late January 1994 to the end of July 1994, I conducted more than one hundred in-depth, open-ended, confidential interviews—generally between one to three hours—with government officials, business leaders, academics, private consultants (whose firms remain anonymous), and nongovernmental organization representatives in the Philippines, the Malaysian states of Sabah and Sarawak, Peninsular Malaysia (Kuala Lumpur), Indonesia, Singapore, and Japan. I am indebted to numerous individuals at the following organizations.

Indonesia

Apkindo (Indonesian Wood Panel Association), Jakarta

Asian Wetlands Bureau, Bogor

Bappenas (Indonesian National Development Planning Agency), Jakarta

Bogor Agricultural University, Environmental Research Center, Kampus IPB Darmaga, Bogor

Bogor Agricultural University, Faculty of Forestry, Kampus IPB Darmaga, Bogor

Center for Economic and Environmental Studies, Environmental Economics Studies Foundation, Jakarta

Center for International Forestry Research (CIFOR), Bogor

Indonesian Ecolabeling Program, Jakarta

International Tropical Timber Organization (ITTO), Indonesia Office, Jakarta

Japan International Cooperation Agency (JICA), Indonesia Office, Jakarta

Ministry of Forestry, Indonesia, Bureau of International Cooperation and Investment, Jakarta

Ministry of Forestry, Indonesia, Forest Protection and Nature Conservation, Jakarta

Ministry of Forestry, Indonesia, Forest Utilization, Jakarta

Ministry of Forestry, Indonesia, PHPA (Forestry Conservation), Bogor

PELANGI INDONESIA (Policy Research for Sustainable Development), Jakarta

Rimbawan Muda Indonesia (RMI) (Indonesian Institute for Forestry and Environmental Research and Service), Bogor

SKEPHI (NGO Network for Forest Conservation in Indonesia), Jakarta

State Ministry for the Environment, Jakarta

WALHI (Indonesian Forum for the Environment), Jakarta

Japan

Center for Environmental Policy and Advocacy (CEPAT), Tokyo

Environment Agency, Global Environment Department, Tokyo

Environment Agency, Office of Overseas Environmental Cooperation, Tokyo

Export-Import (EXIM) Bank of Japan, Environment Section, Tokyo

Friends of the Earth Japan, Tokyo

International Development Center of Japan, Tokyo

International Tropical Timber Organization (ITTO), Yokohama

Itochu Corporation, Department of Global Environment, Tokyo

Japan Lumber Importers' Association (JLIA), Tokyo

Japan Overseas Forestry Consultants Association (JOFCA), Tokyo

Japan Plywood Inspection Corporation, Tokyo

Japan Plywood Manufacturers' Association (JPMA), Tokyo

Japan Tropical Forest Action Network (JATAN), Tokyo

JICA, Forestry Cooperation Division, Forestry and Fisheries Development Cooperation Department, Tokyo

Keidanren (Japan Federation of Economic Organizations), Global Environment Department, Tokyo

Marubeni, Environmental Protection Department, Tokyo

Ministry of Agriculture, Forestry, and Fisheries, Forestry Agency, International Forestry Cooperation Center, Tokyo

Ministry of International Trade and Industry (MITI), Environmental Policy Division, Industrial Location and Environmental Protection Bureau, Tokyo

MITI, Global Environment Division, Tokyo

Mitsubishi Corporation, Environmental Affairs Department, Tokyo

Nissho Iwai, Environment 21, Tokyo

Overseas Economic Cooperation Fund (OECF), Environment and Social Development Division, Tokyo

Research Association for Reforestation of Tropical Forest (RETROF), Tokyo

Sumitomo Forestry Company Ltd., Green Environmental R & D Division, Tokyo

University of Tokyo, Faculty of Agriculture, Department of Forestry, Tokyo

University of Tokyo, International Environmental Planning Center (INTEP), Tokyo

WWF Japan, Tokyo

Peninsula Malaysia

Asian Wall Street Journal, Kuala Lumpur

Far Eastern Economic Review, Kuala Lumpur

Malaysian Timber Industry Board, Ministry of Primary Industries, Kuala Lumpur

Ministry of Primary Industries, Kuala Lumpur

Universiti Pertanian Malaysia (UPM), Faculty of Forestry, Serdang, Selangor

WWF Malaysia, Petaling Jaya

Philippines

Asian Development Bank, Mandaluyong, Metro Manila

Center For Investigative Journalism, Manila

Department of Environment and Natural Resources (DENR), ENR-SECAL Program (World Bank/DENR), Quezon City

DENR, ENR-SECAL Program (World Bank/DENR), Monitoring and Enforcement Office, Quezon City

DENR, Forest Management Bureau, Forest Economic Division, Quezon City

DENR, National Forestation Development Office, Quezon City

International Rice Research Institute (IRRI), Los Banos, Laguna

Philippine Institute for Development Studies (PIDS), Makati, Metro Manila

Philippine News and Features

University of the Philippines, College of Forestry, Los Banos, Laguna

WWF Philippine Program, San Juan, Metro Manila

Sabah, Malaysia

Consulate of Japan, Kota Kinabalu

Department of Industrial Development and Research (Sabah), Kota Kinabalu

Innoprise Corporation Sdn Bhd, a subsidiary of Yayasan Sabah (Sabah Foundation), Kota Kinabalu

Institute For Development Studies, Institut Kajian Pembangunan (Sabah), Kota Kinabalu

Ministry of Tourism and Environmental Development (Sabah), Kota Kinabalu

Rakyat Berjaya Sdn Bhd, a subsidiary of Innoprise Corporation Sdn Bhd, Kota Kinabalu

Sabah Forestry Department (Jabatan Perhutanan Sabah), Regional Office, Kota Kinabalu

Sabah Forestry Development Authority (SAFODA), Kota Kinabalu

Sabah Melale Wood Industries Sdn Bhd, Kota Kinabalu

Sabah Re-afforestation Technical Development and Training Project, Kinarut

Sabah Sawmilling Industries Association, Kota Kinabalu

Sabah State Library (Perpustakaan Negeri Sabah), Kota Kinabalu

Timber Association of Sabah (TAS), Kota Kinabalu

WWF Malaysia, Sabah Office, Kota Kinabalu

Yayasan Sabah (Sabah Foundation), Kota Kinabalu

Sarawak, Malaysia

JICA's Effective Wood Utilization Research Project, Timber Research and Technical Training Center, Kuching

Sarawak Forest Department (various sections), Kuching

Sarawak Timber Association (Persatuan Kayu Kayan Sarawak), Kuching

Sarawak Timber Industry Development Corporation (Perbadanan Kemajuan Perusahaan Kayu Sarawak), Kuching

Universiti Malaysia Sarawak, Kota Samarahan

Singapore

Institute of Southeast Asian Studies Library

Washington, DC, United States of America

I also conducted research in Washington, DC, in September and again in December 1995. I am grateful for information and advice from individuals from the following organizations: Conservation International; Environment and Energy Studies; Investor Responsibility Research Center; Library of Congress; National Wildlife Federation; Resources for the Future; World Bank (various sections); and the World Resources Institute.

Index